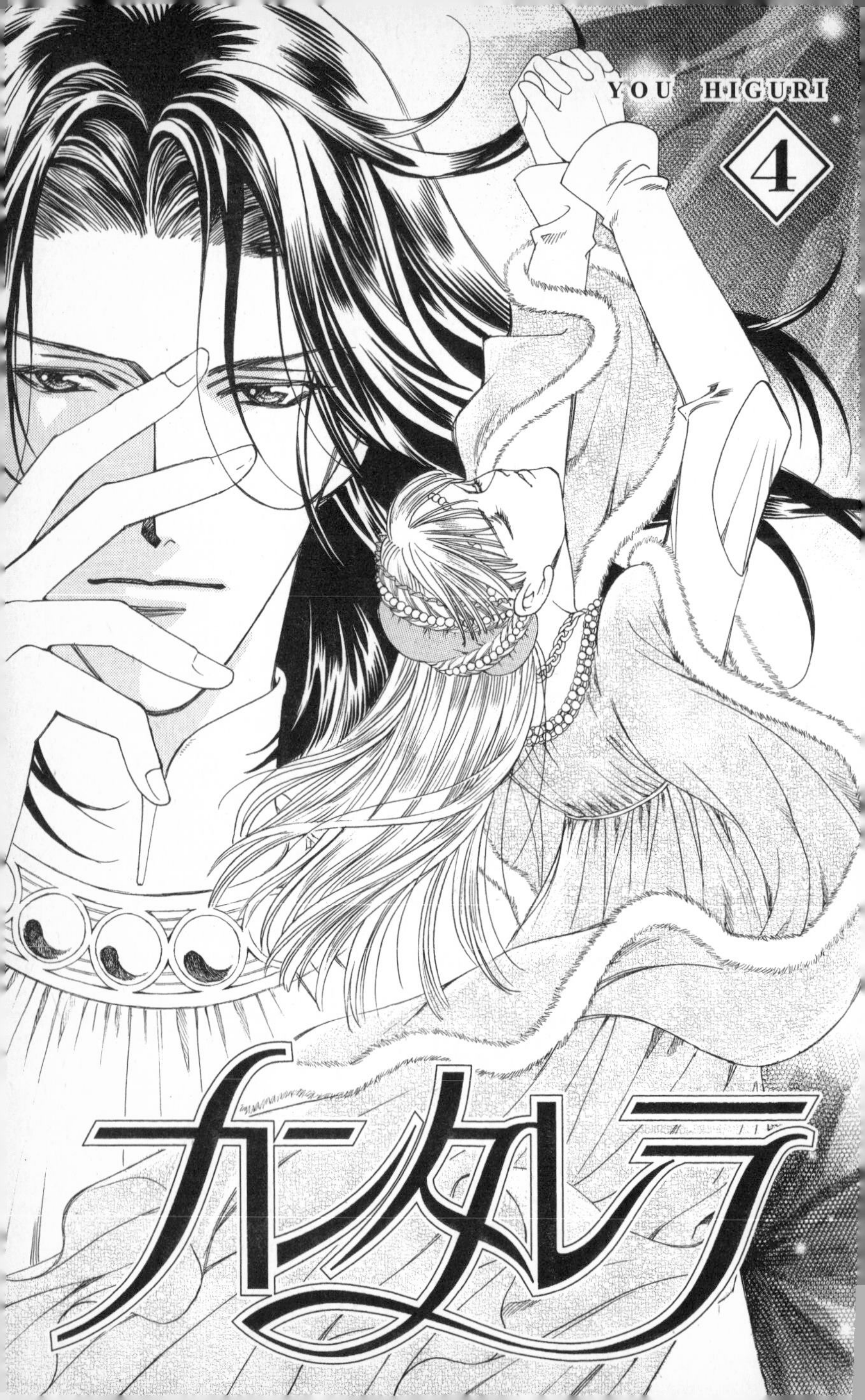
YOU HIGURI
4
カンタレラ

Translation – Chrissy Schilling
Adaptation – Audry Taylor
Production Assistant – Mallory Reaves
Lettering & Design– Fawn Lau
Production Manager – James Dashiell
Editor – Audry Taylor

A Go! Comi manga

Published by Go! Media Entertainment, LLC

Cantarella Volume 4
© YOU HIGURI 2002
Originally published in Japan in 2002 by Akita Publishing Co., Ltd., Tokyo.
English translation rights arranged with Akita Publishing Co., Ltd.
through TOHAN CORPORATION, Tokyo.

English Text © 2006 Go! Media Entertainment, LLC. All rights reserved.

Visit us online at www.gocomi.com
e-mail: info@gocomi.com

ISBN 1-933617-02-0

First printed in July 2006

1   2   3   4   5   6   7   8   9

Manufactured in the United States of America

Cantarella

STORY AND ART BY

YOU HIGURI

VOLUME 4

go!comi

Cantarella 4

TABLE OF CONTENTS

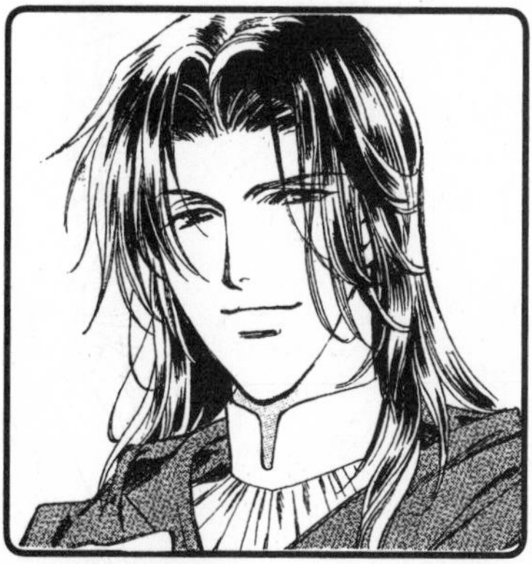

OUR STORY SO FAR AND INTRODUCTION OF CHARACTERS

Enter the forsaken Cesare Borgia, whose soul was sold to the devil by his father, Cardinal Rodrigo, in exchange for the Papal throne. On gaining the office of Cardinal, Cesare plotted to achieve a greater ambition -- uniting all of Italy under one ruler. His schemes were sidetracked when he was kidnapped and tortured by allies of the invading French army. Unable to save his beloved step-mother Vanozza from a cruel death at the hands of marauding soldiers, Cesare withdrew deeper into the darkness haunting his soul; a darkness that now threatens to suck him into the bleakest depths of Hell...

CESARE BORGIA

The hero of our story. His father sold the boy's soul to the devil in exchange for religious power. Now a Cardinal, Cesare will wear the sacred scarlet robe even when his eyes glow golden with wicked intent.

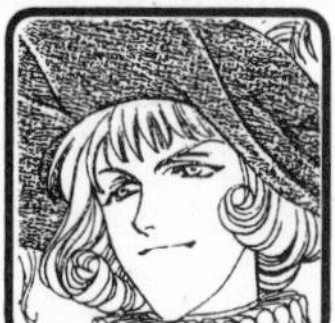

JUAN BORGIA

Unlike his older brother, Juan is favored by his father. Securely ensconced in the Spanish court, Juan leads a decadent, lecherous lifestyle.

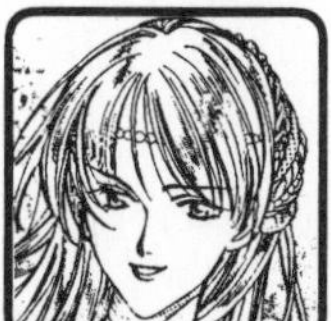

LUCREZIA BORGIA

A sweet girl who adores her older brother Cesare. She was forced to wed the Lord of Pesaro in an arranged marriage, but her heart remains loyal to Cesare.

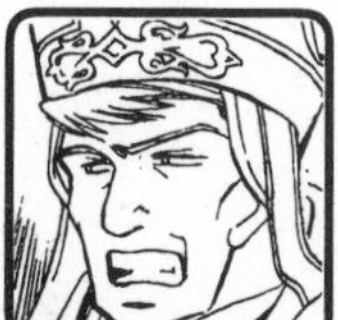

POPE ALEXANDER VI

An ambitious man who sold his own son's soul in exchange for the title of Pope. His birth name was Rodrigo Borgia.

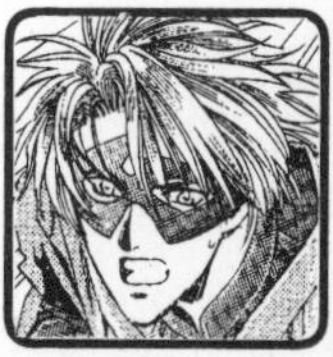

MICHELOTTO (CHIARO)

A legendary assassin. After saving Cesare's life, he now serves him, and goes in public by the false name of Michele da Corella. His true name is Chiaro.

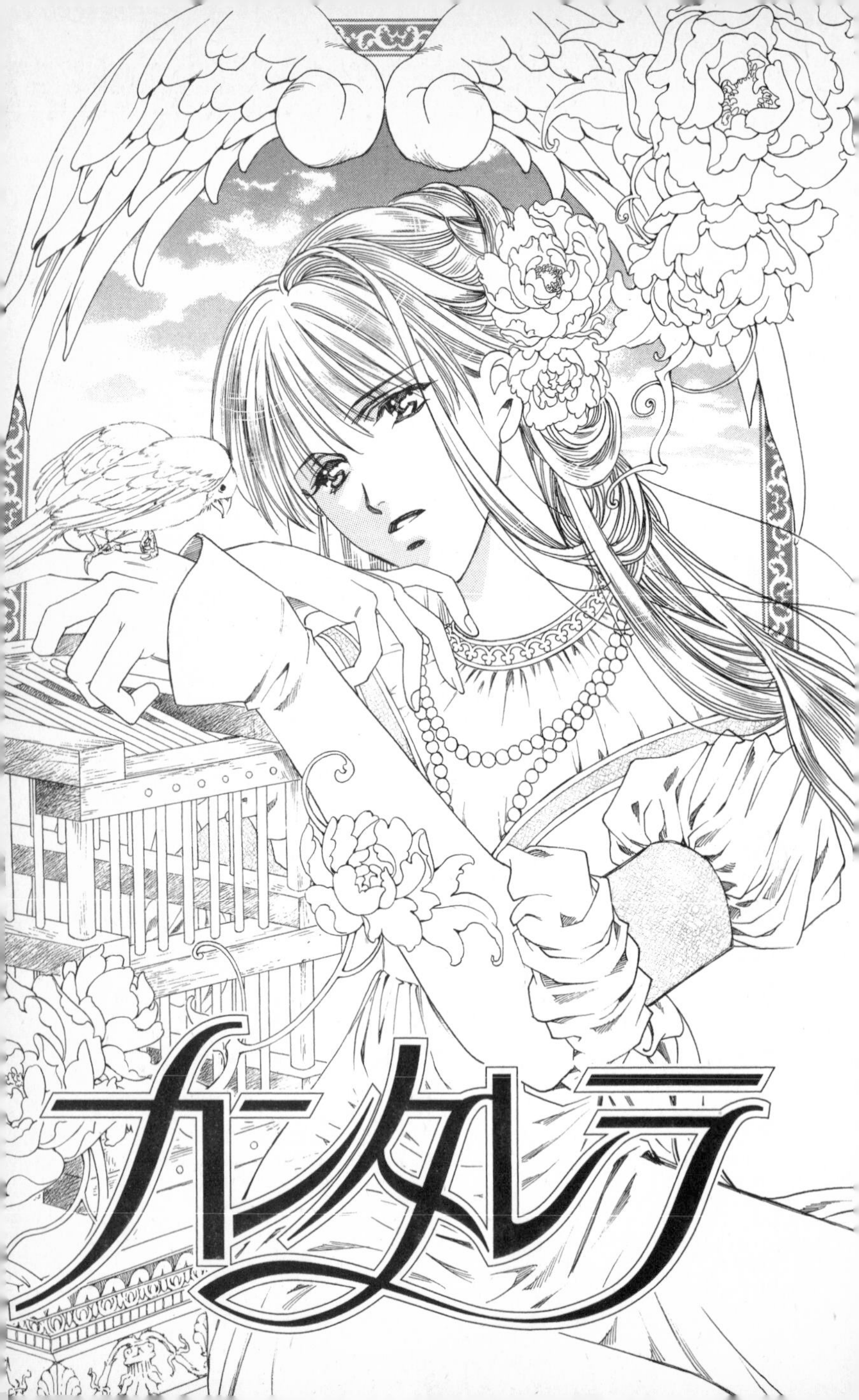
カタレア

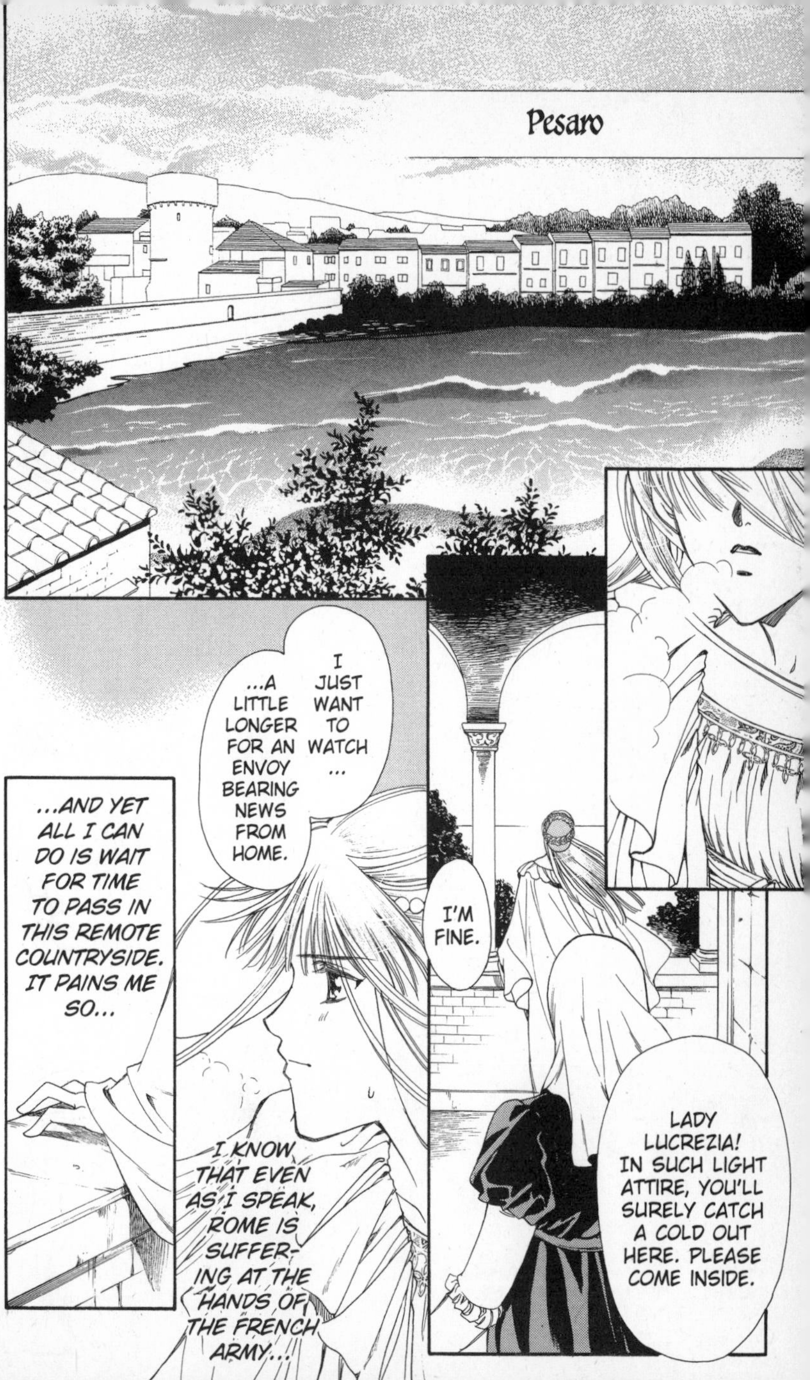
Pesaro
LADY LUCREZIA! IN SUCH LIGHT ATTIRE, YOU'LL SURELY CATCH A COLD OUT HERE. PLEASE COME INSIDE.
I'M FINE.
I JUST WANT TO WATCH ...
...A LITTLE LONGER FOR AN ENVOY BEARING NEWS FROM HOME.
I KNOW THAT EVEN AS I SPEAK, ROME IS SUFFERING AT THE HANDS OF THE FRENCH ARMY...
...AND YET ALL I CAN DO IS WAIT FOR TIME TO PASS IN THIS REMOTE COUNTRYSIDE. IT PAINS ME SO...

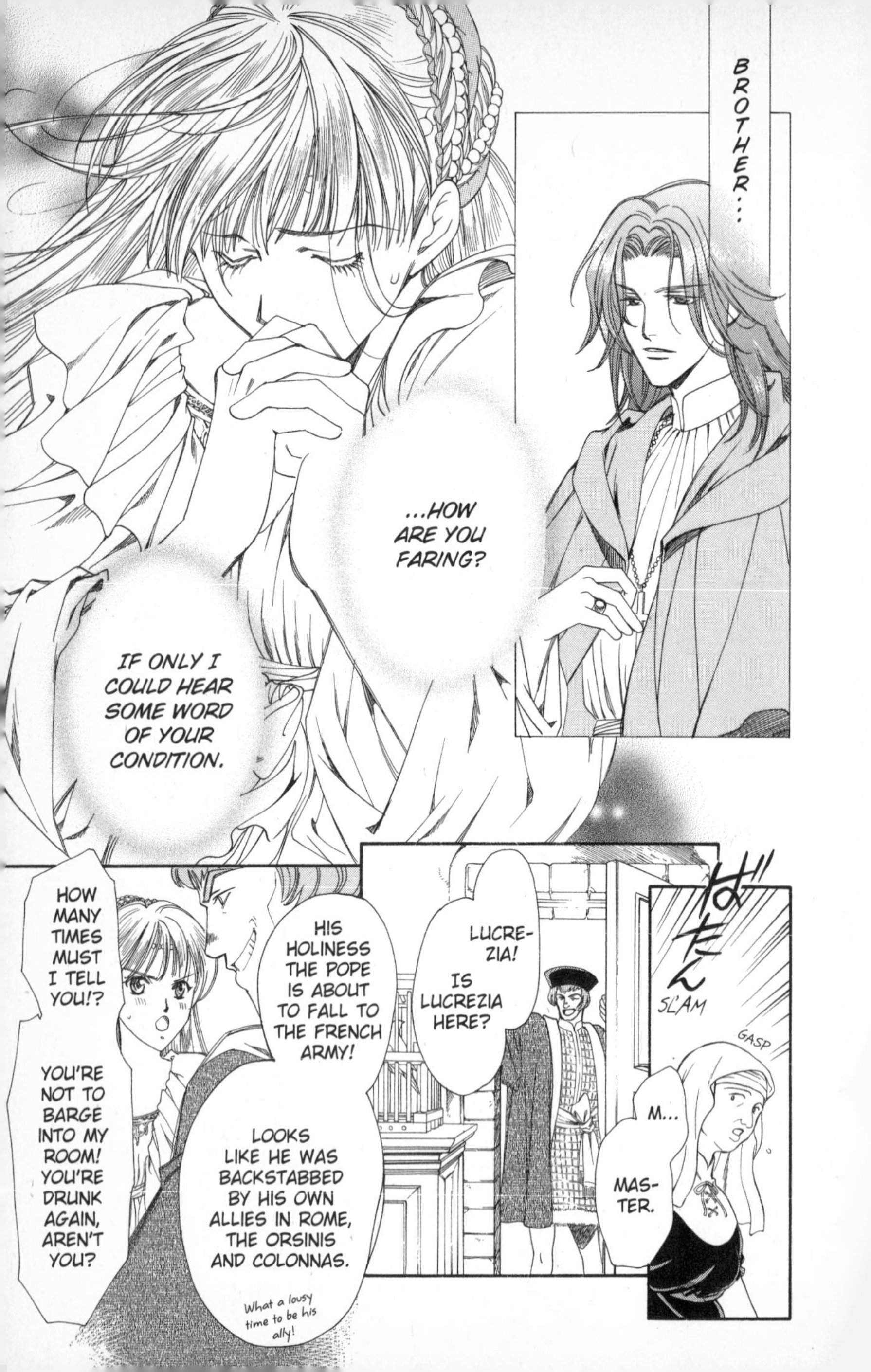
BROTHER...
...HOW ARE YOU FARING?
IF ONLY I COULD HEAR SOME WORD OF YOUR CONDITION.
ばたん
SLAM
GASP
M...
MASTER.
LUCREZIA!
IS LUCREZIA HERE?
HIS HOLINESS THE POPE IS ABOUT TO FALL TO THE FRENCH ARMY!
HOW MANY TIMES MUST I TELL YOU!?
LOOKS LIKE HE WAS BACKSTABBED BY HIS OWN ALLIES IN ROME, THE ORSINIS AND COLONNAS.
What a lousy time to be his ally!
YOU'RE NOT TO BARGE INTO MY ROOM! YOU'RE DRUNK AGAIN, AREN'T YOU?

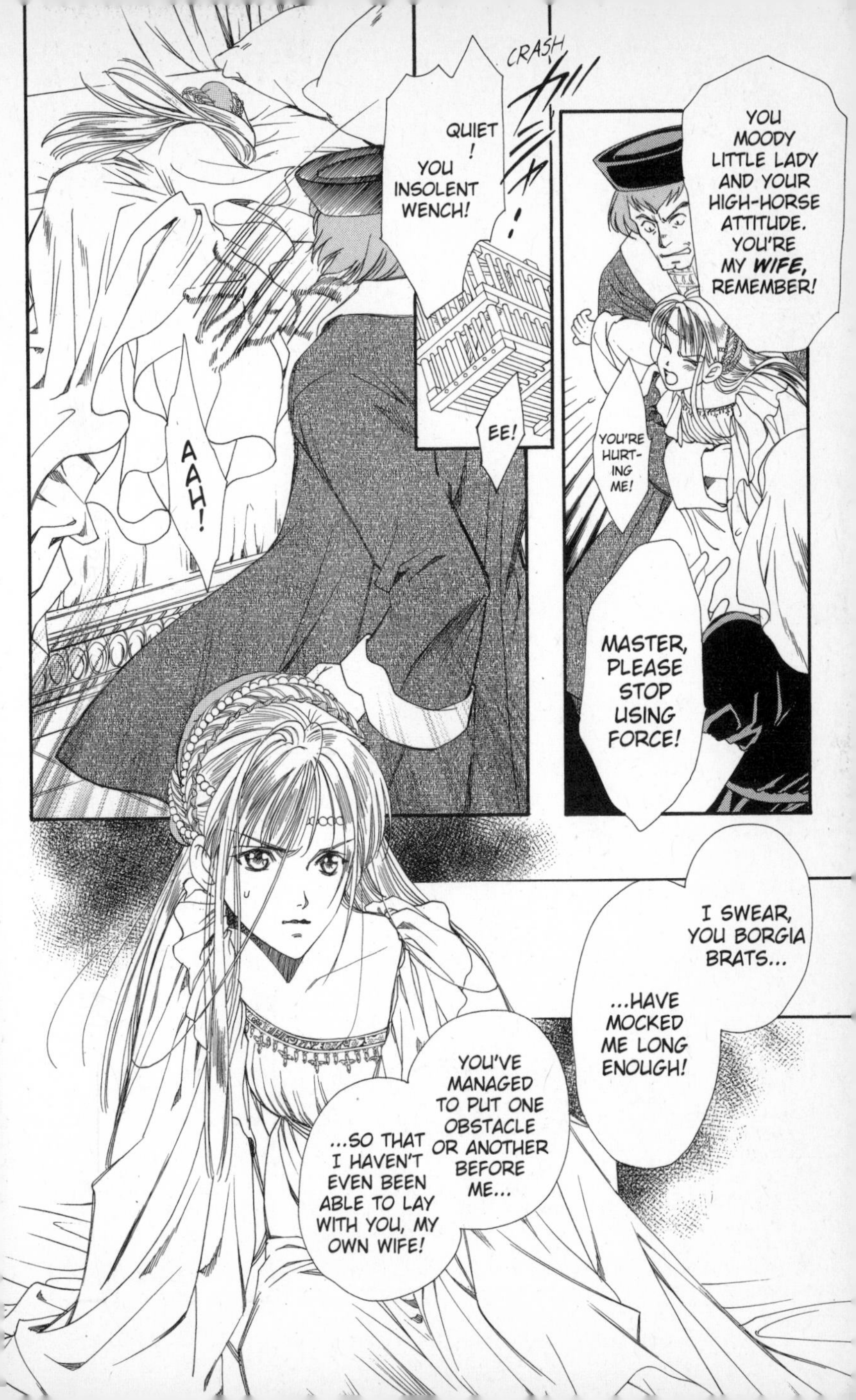
YOU MOODY LITTLE LADY AND YOUR HIGH-HORSE ATTITUDE. YOU'RE MY *WIFE,* REMEMBER!
YOU'RE HURT-ING ME!
MASTER, PLEASE STOP USING FORCE!
CRASH
QUIET! YOU INSOLENT WENCH!
EE!
AAH!
I SWEAR, YOU BORGIA BRATS...
...HAVE MOCKED ME LONG ENOUGH!
YOU'VE MANAGED TO PUT ONE OBSTACLE OR ANOTHER BEFORE ME...
...SO THAT I HAVEN'T EVEN BEEN ABLE TO LAY WITH YOU, MY OWN WIFE!

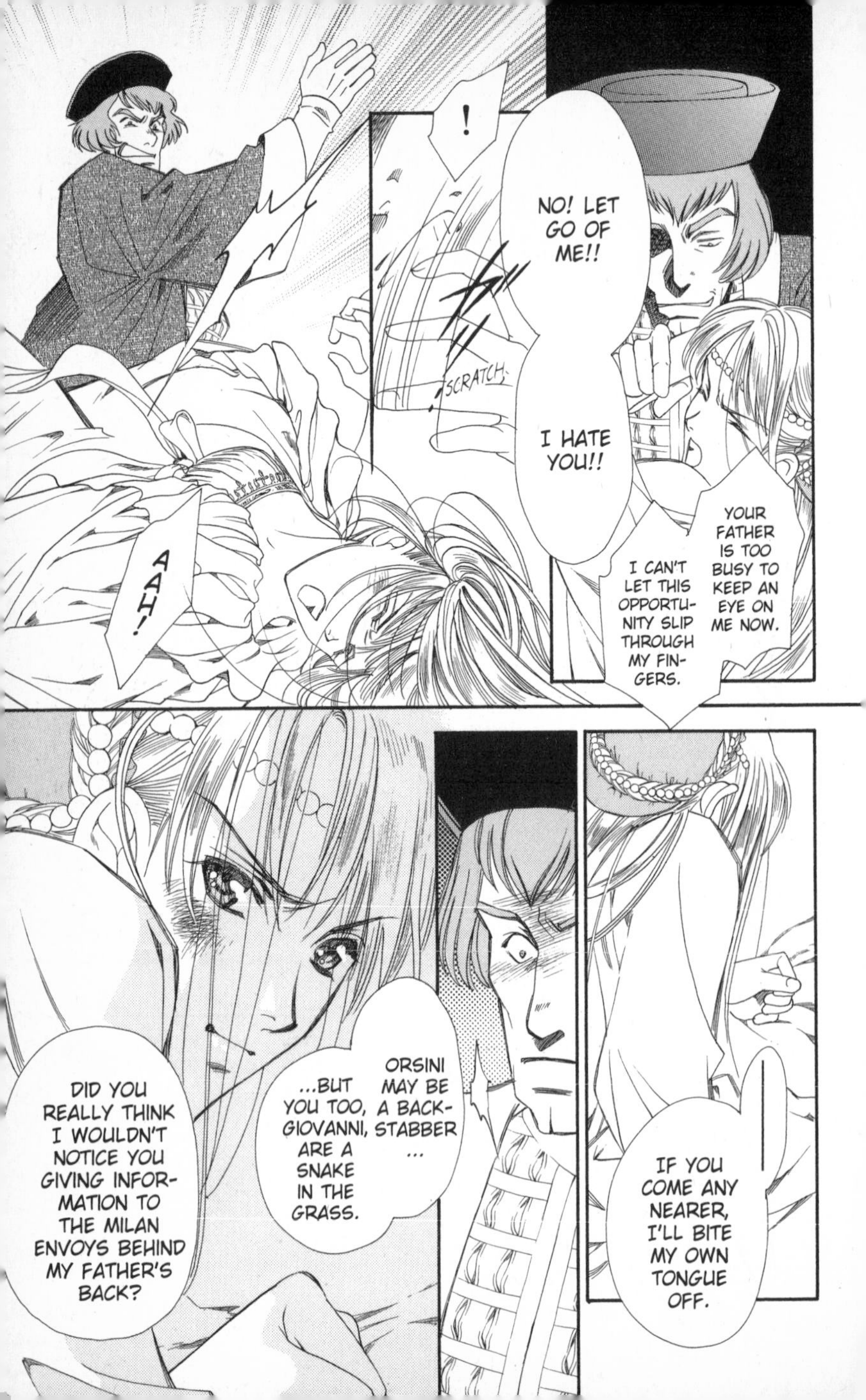
YOUR FATHER IS TOO BUSY TO KEEP AN EYE ON ME NOW.
I CAN'T LET THIS OPPORTUNITY SLIP THROUGH MY FINGERS.
NO! LET GO OF ME!!
I HATE YOU!!
!
SCRATCH
AAH!
IF YOU COME ANY NEARER, I'LL BITE MY OWN TONGUE OFF.
ORSINI MAY BE A BACK-STABBER ...
...BUT YOU TOO, GIOVANNI, ARE A SNAKE IN THE GRASS.
DID YOU REALLY THINK I WOULDN'T NOTICE YOU GIVING INFORMATION TO THE MILAN ENVOYS BEHIND MY FATHER'S BACK?

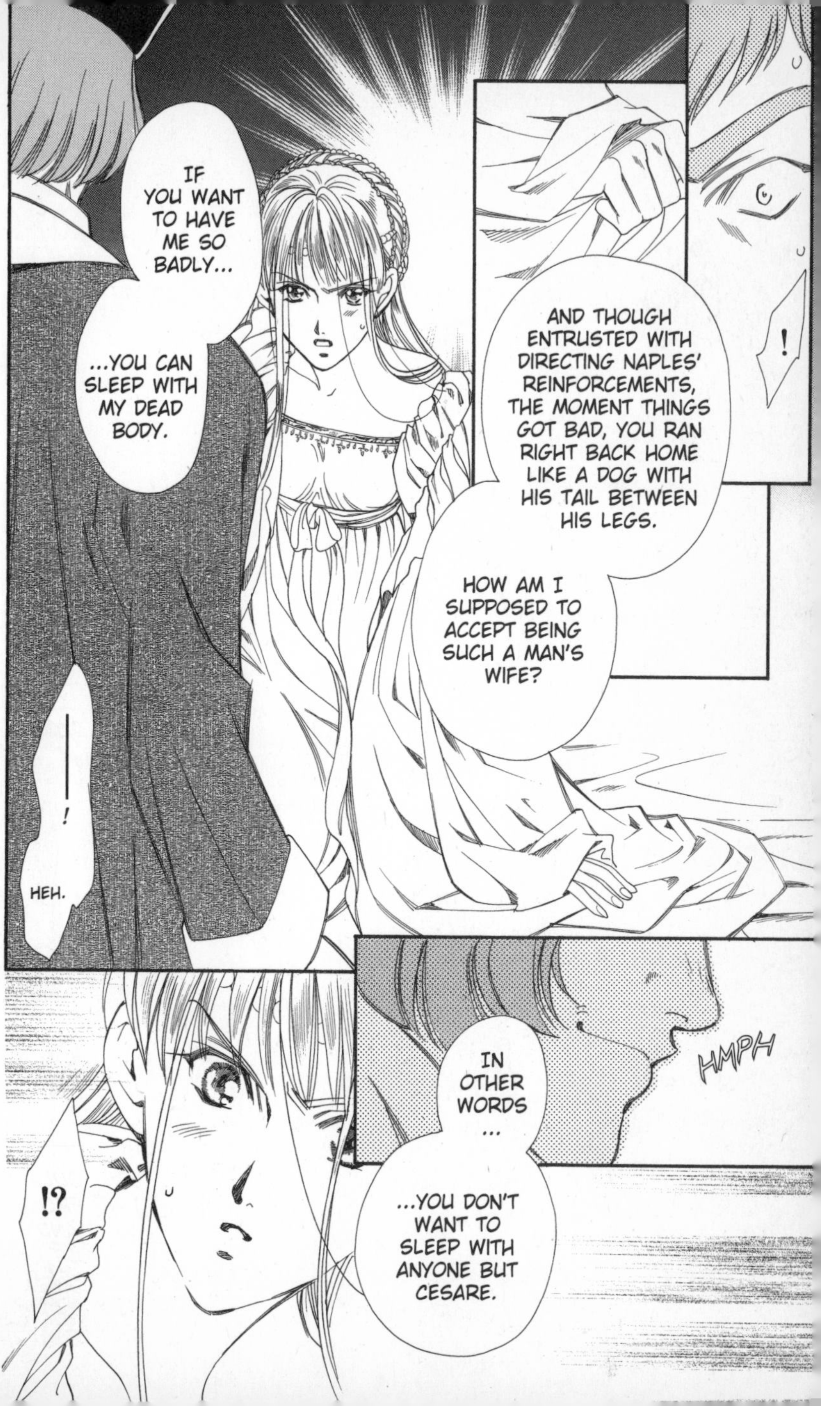
!
AND THOUGH ENTRUSTED WITH DIRECTING NAPLES' REINFORCEMENTS, THE MOMENT THINGS GOT BAD, YOU RAN RIGHT BACK HOME LIKE A DOG WITH HIS TAIL BETWEEN HIS LEGS.
HOW AM I SUPPOSED TO ACCEPT BEING SUCH A MAN'S WIFE?
IF YOU WANT TO HAVE ME SO BADLY...
...YOU CAN SLEEP WITH MY DEAD BODY.
—!
HEH.
HMPH
IN OTHER WORDS ...
...YOU DON'T WANT TO SLEEP WITH ANYONE BUT CESARE.
!?

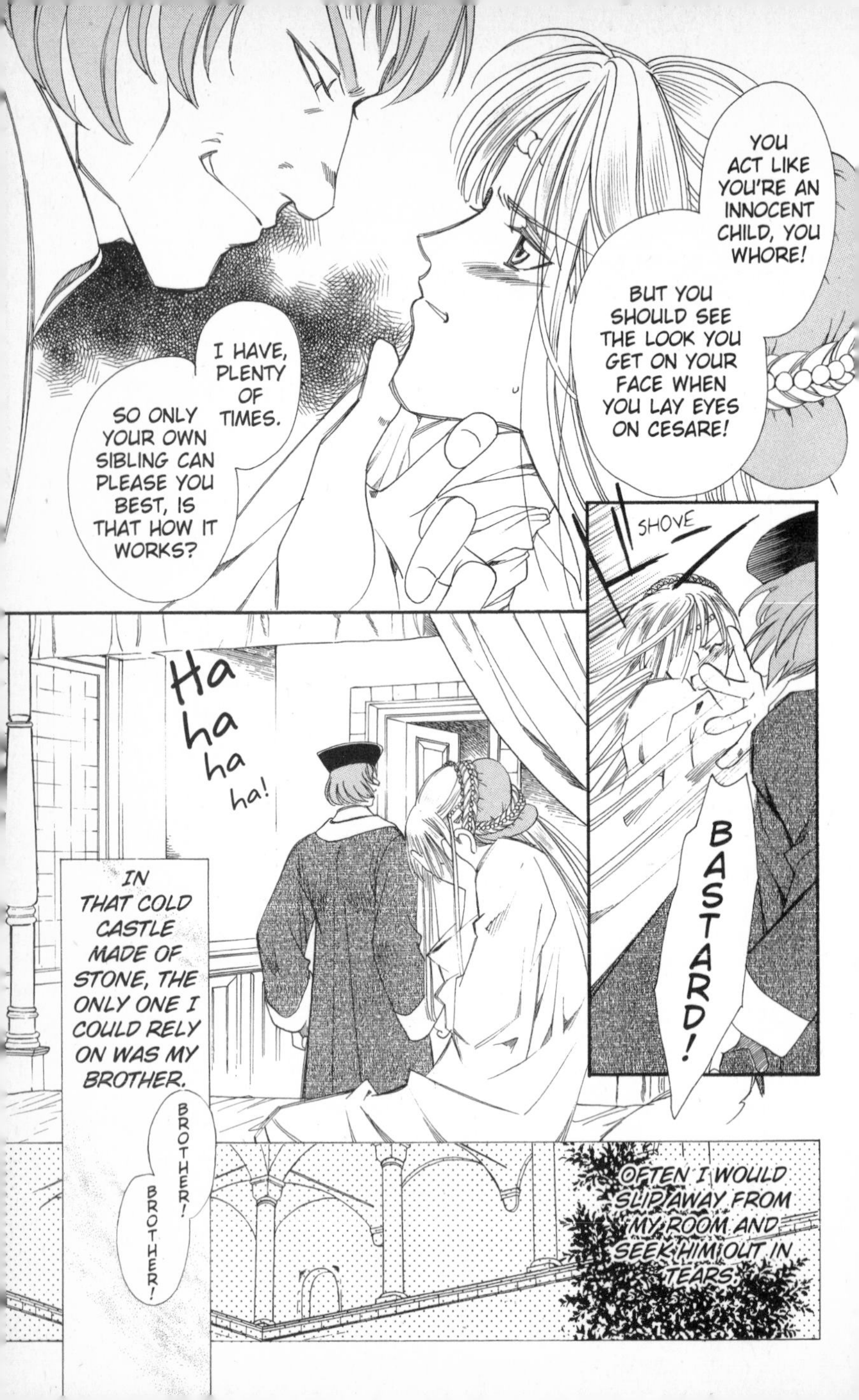
YOU ACT LIKE YOU'RE AN INNOCENT CHILD, YOU WHORE!
BUT YOU SHOULD SEE THE LOOK YOU GET ON YOUR FACE WHEN YOU LAY EYES ON CESARE!
I HAVE, PLENTY OF TIMES.
SO ONLY YOUR OWN SIBLING CAN PLEASE YOU BEST, IS THAT HOW IT WORKS?
SHOVE
BASTARD!
Ha ha ha ha!
IN THAT COLD CASTLE MADE OF STONE, THE ONLY ONE I COULD RELY ON WAS MY BROTHER.
OFTEN I WOULD SLIP AWAY FROM MY ROOM AND SEEK HIM OUT IN TEARS.
BROTHER!
BROTHER!

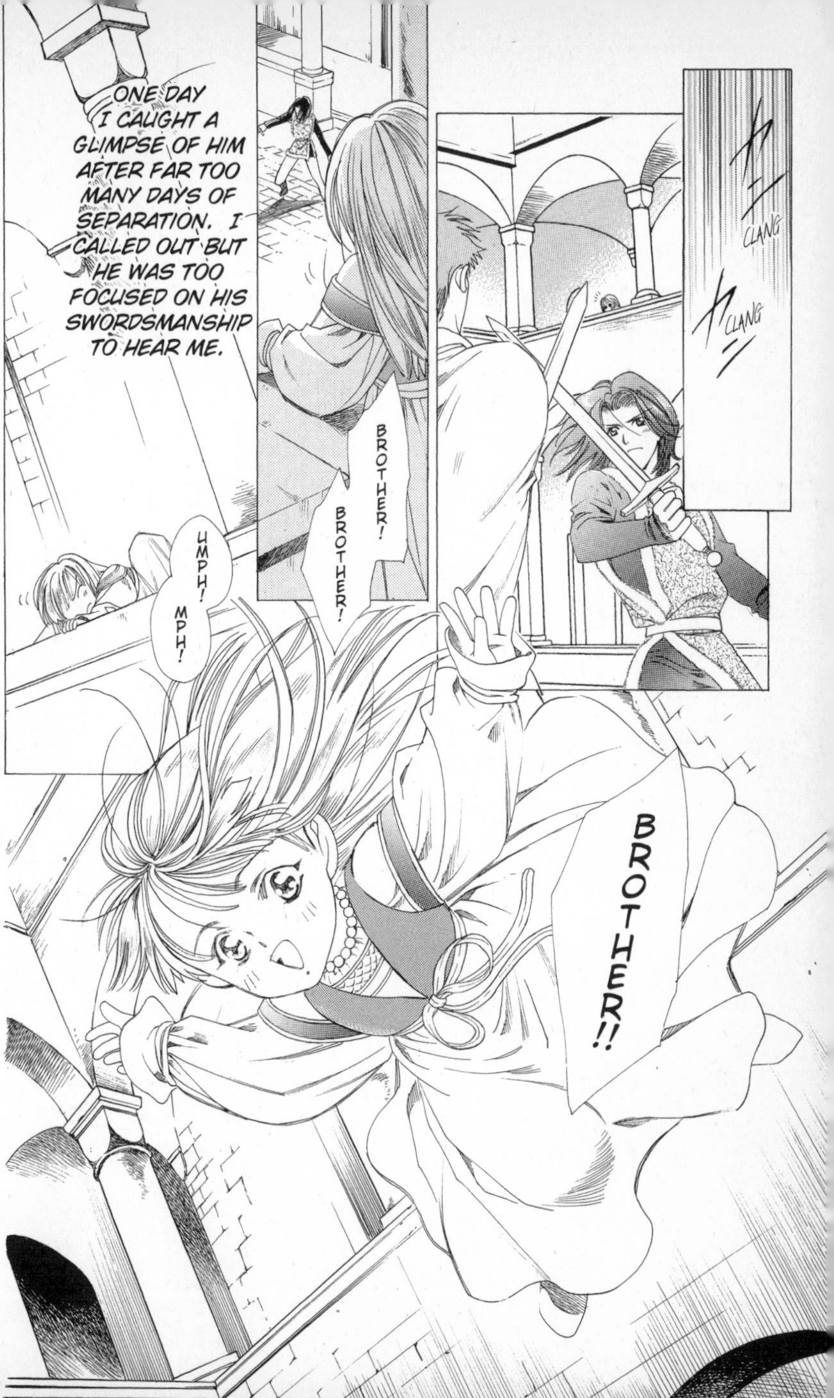

CLANG
CLANG
BROTHER! BROTHER!
ONE DAY I CAUGHT A GLIMPSE OF HIM AFTER FAR TOO MANY DAYS OF SEPARATION. I CALLED OUT BUT HE WAS TOO FOCUSED ON HIS SWORDSMANSHIP TO HEAR ME.
UMPH! MPH!
BROTHER!!

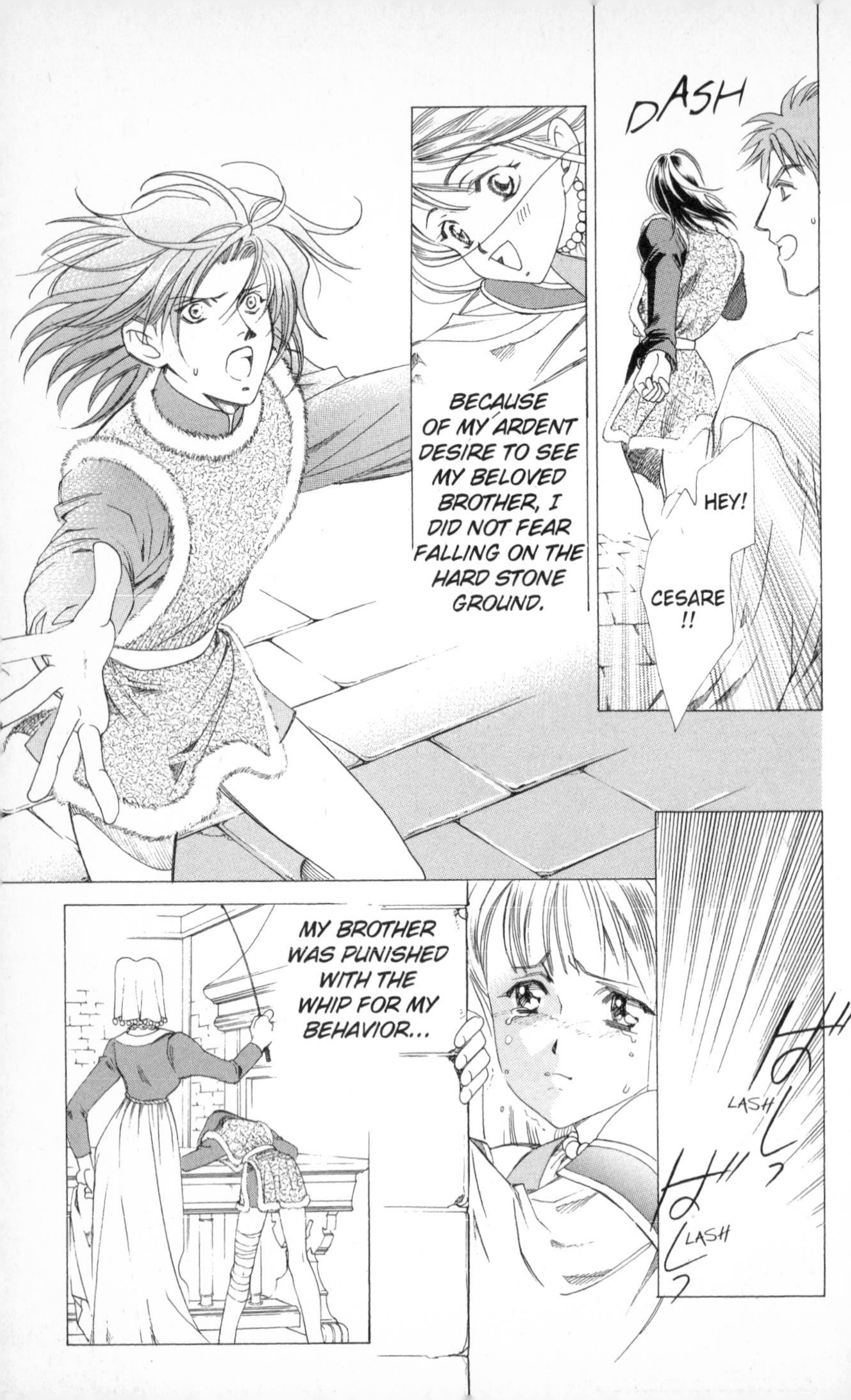
DASH
HEY!
CESARE !!
BECAUSE OF MY ARDENT DESIRE TO SEE MY BELOVED BROTHER, I DID NOT FEAR FALLING ON THE HARD STONE GROUND.
LASH
LASH
MY BROTHER WAS PUNISHED WITH THE WHIP FOR MY BEHAVIOR...

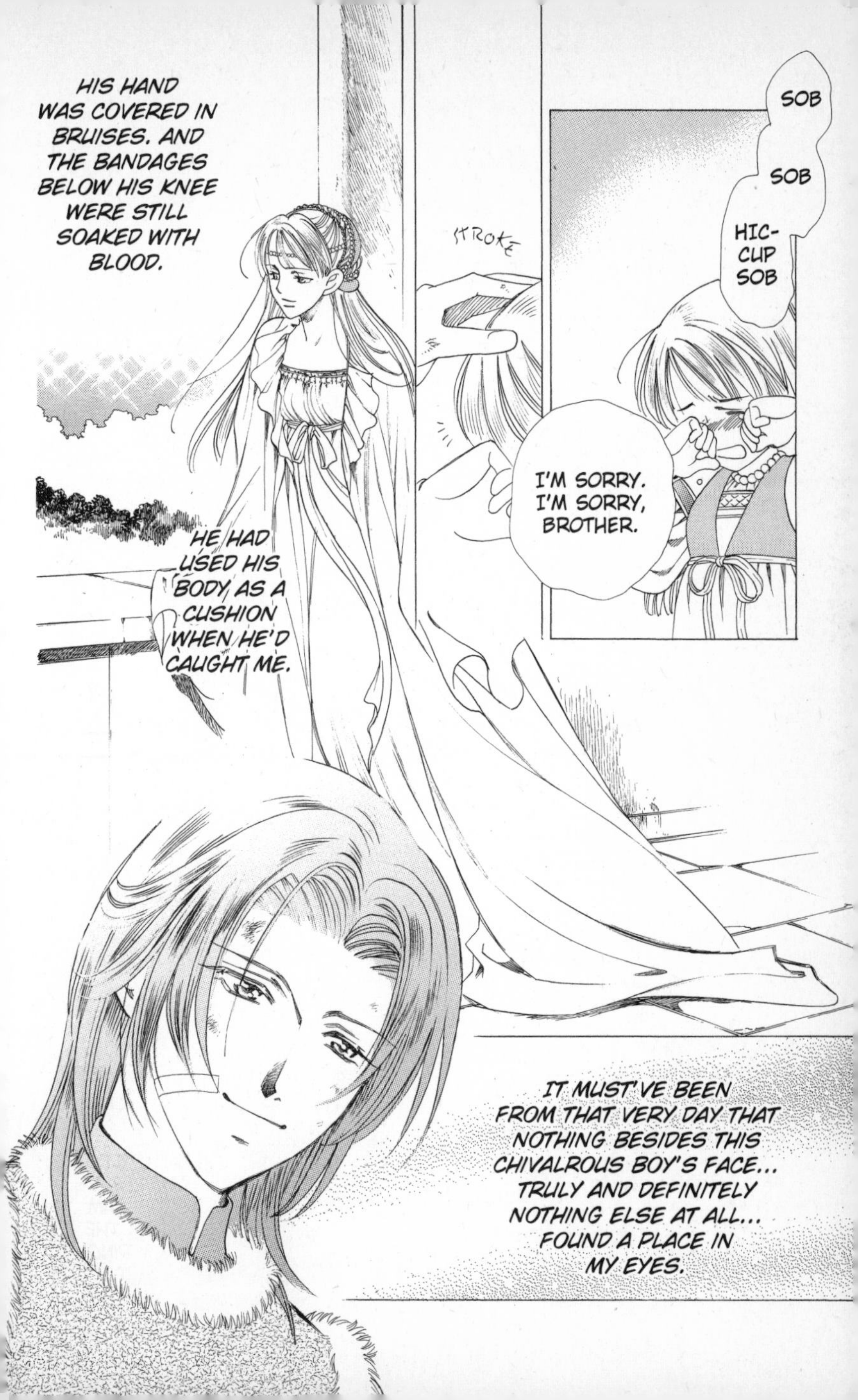
SOB
SOB
HIC-CUP SOB
STROKE
I'M SORRY. I'M SORRY, BROTHER.
HIS HAND WAS COVERED IN BRUISES. AND THE BANDAGES BELOW HIS KNEE WERE STILL SOAKED WITH BLOOD.
HE HAD USED HIS BODY AS A CUSHION WHEN HE'D CAUGHT ME.
IT MUST'VE BEEN FROM THAT VERY DAY THAT NOTHING BESIDES THIS CHIVALROUS BOY'S FACE... TRULY AND DEFINITELY NOTHING ELSE AT ALL... FOUND A PLACE IN MY EYES.

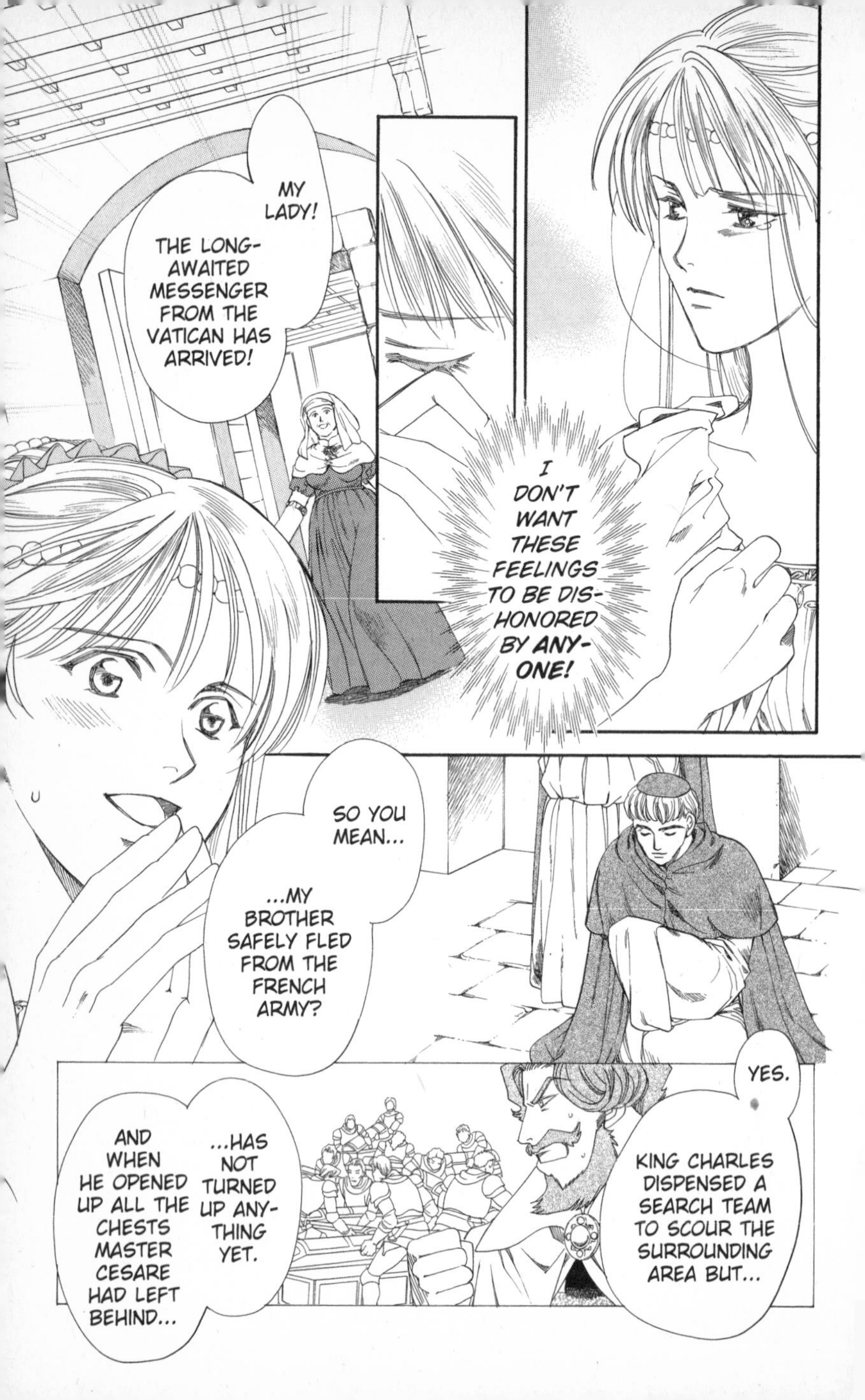
I DON'T WANT THESE FEELINGS TO BE DIS-HONORED BY ANY-ONE!
MY LADY!
THE LONG-AWAITED MESSENGER FROM THE VATICAN HAS ARRIVED!
SO YOU MEAN...
...MY BROTHER SAFELY FLED FROM THE FRENCH ARMY?
YES.
KING CHARLES DISPENSED A SEARCH TEAM TO SCOUR THE SURROUNDING AREA BUT...
...HAS NOT TURNED UP ANY-THING YET.
AND WHEN HE OPENED UP ALL THE CHESTS MASTER CESARE HAD LEFT BEHIND...

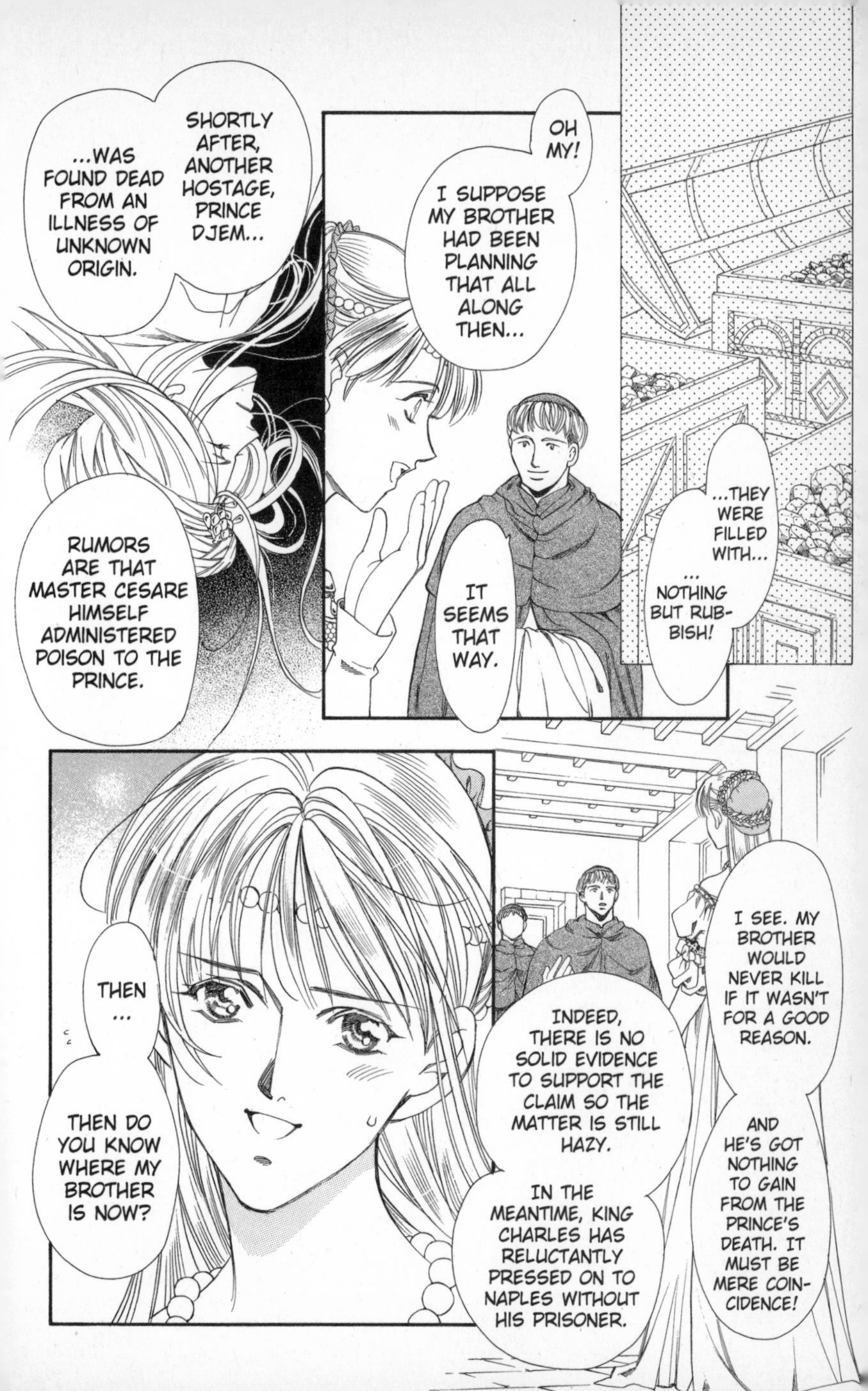
...THEY WERE FILLED WITH...
...NOTHING BUT RUB-BISH!
OH MY!
I SUPPOSE MY BROTHER HAD BEEN PLANNING THAT ALL ALONG THEN...
IT SEEMS THAT WAY.
SHORTLY AFTER, ANOTHER HOSTAGE, PRINCE DJEM...
...WAS FOUND DEAD FROM AN ILLNESS OF UNKNOWN ORIGIN.
RUMORS ARE THAT MASTER CESARE HIMSELF ADMINISTERED POISON TO THE PRINCE.
I SEE. MY BROTHER WOULD NEVER KILL IF IT WASN'T FOR A GOOD REASON.
AND HE'S GOT NOTHING TO GAIN FROM THE PRINCE'S DEATH. IT MUST BE MERE COIN-CIDENCE!
INDEED, THERE IS NO SOLID EVIDENCE TO SUPPORT THE CLAIM SO THE MATTER IS STILL HAZY.
IN THE MEANTIME, KING CHARLES HAS RELUCTANTLY PRESSED ON TO NAPLES WITHOUT HIS PRISONER.
THEN...
THEN DO YOU KNOW WHERE MY BROTHER IS NOW?

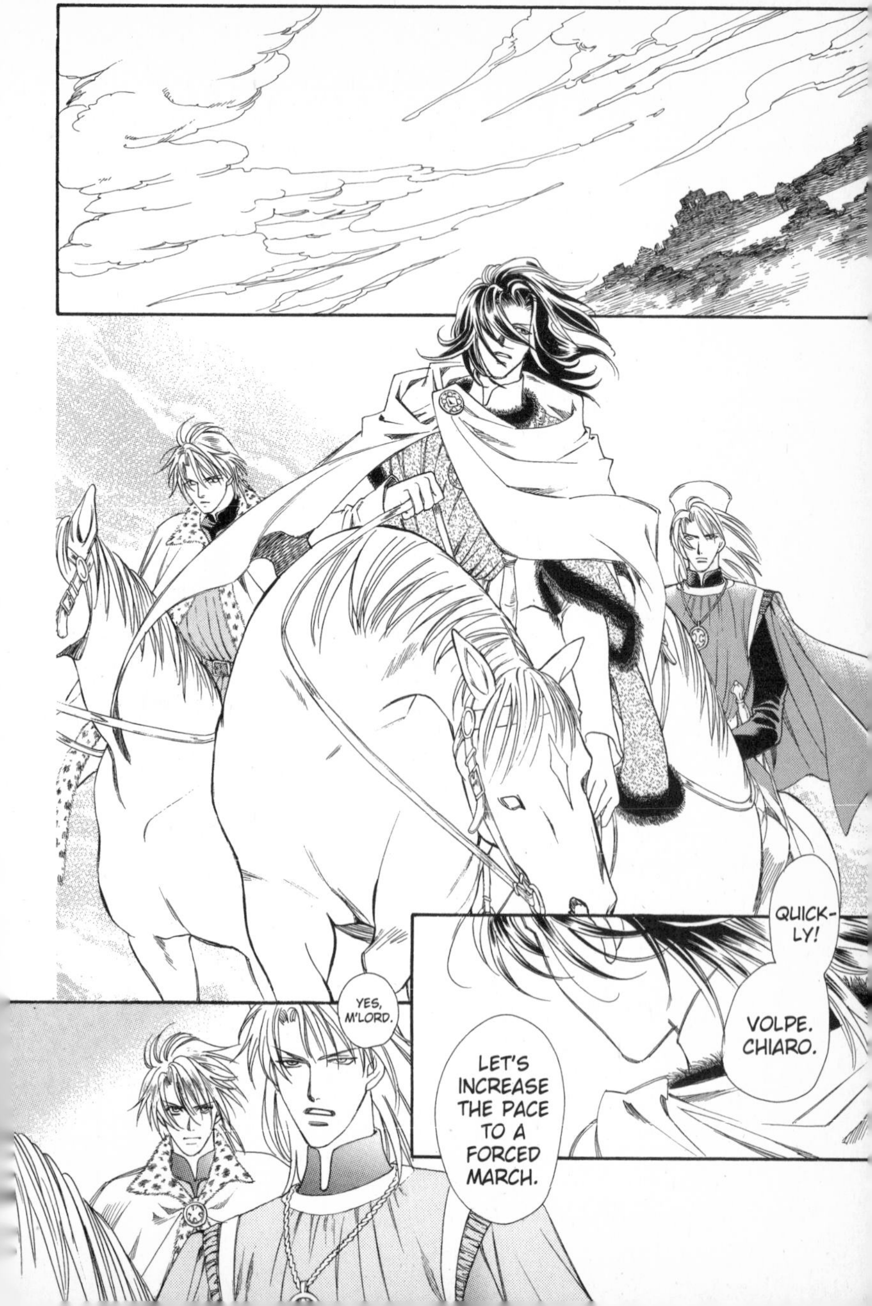
QUICKLY!
VOLPE. CHIARO.
LET'S INCREASE THE PACE TO A FORCED MARCH.
YES, M'LORD.

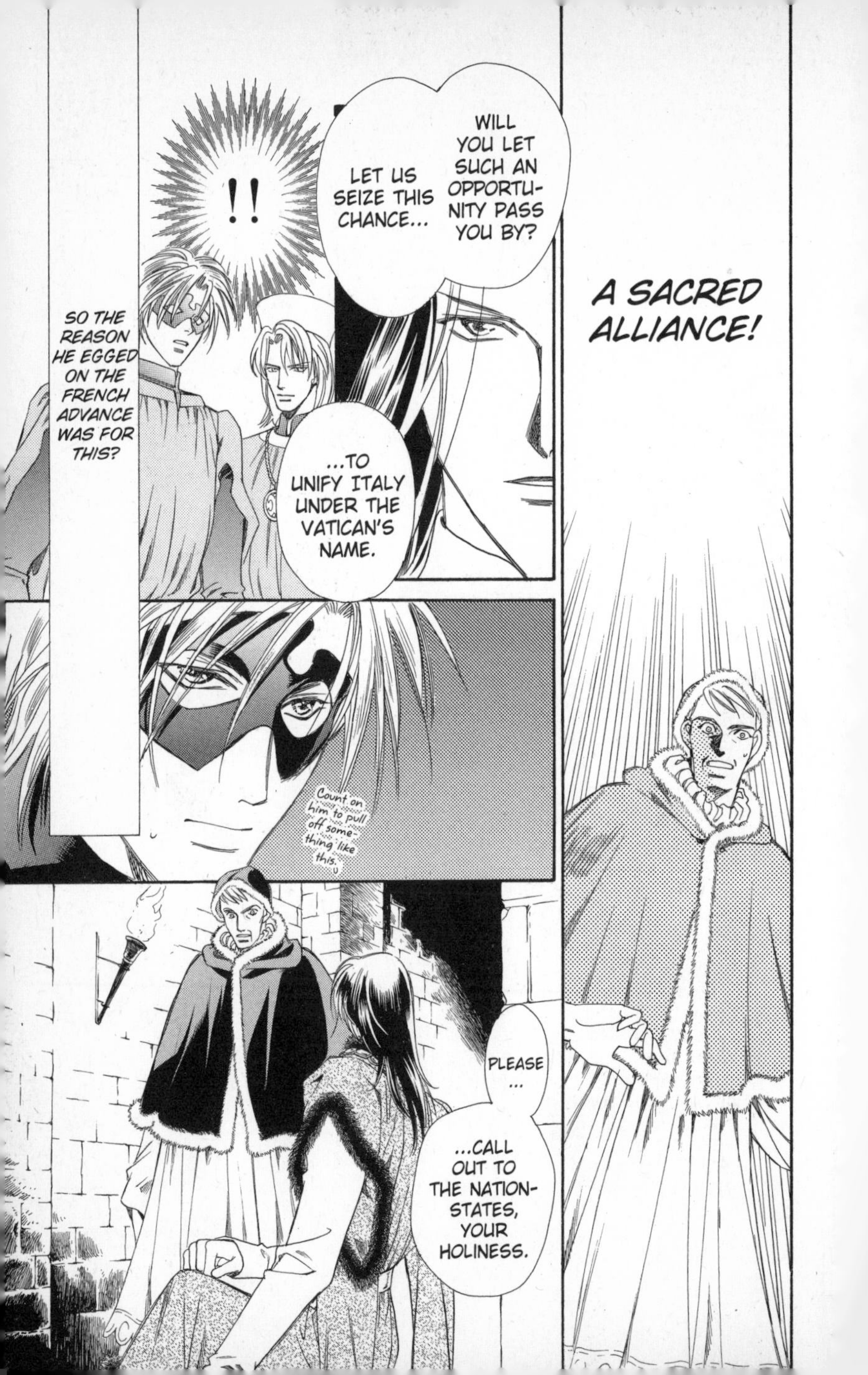
A SACRED ALLIANCE!
WILL YOU LET SUCH AN OPPORTUNITY PASS YOU BY?
LET US SEIZE THIS CHANCE...
!!
...TO UNIFY ITALY UNDER THE VATICAN'S NAME.
SO THE REASON HE EGGED ON THE FRENCH ADVANCE WAS FOR THIS?
Count on him to pull off something like this.
PLEASE...
...CALL OUT TO THE NATION-STATES, YOUR HOLINESS.

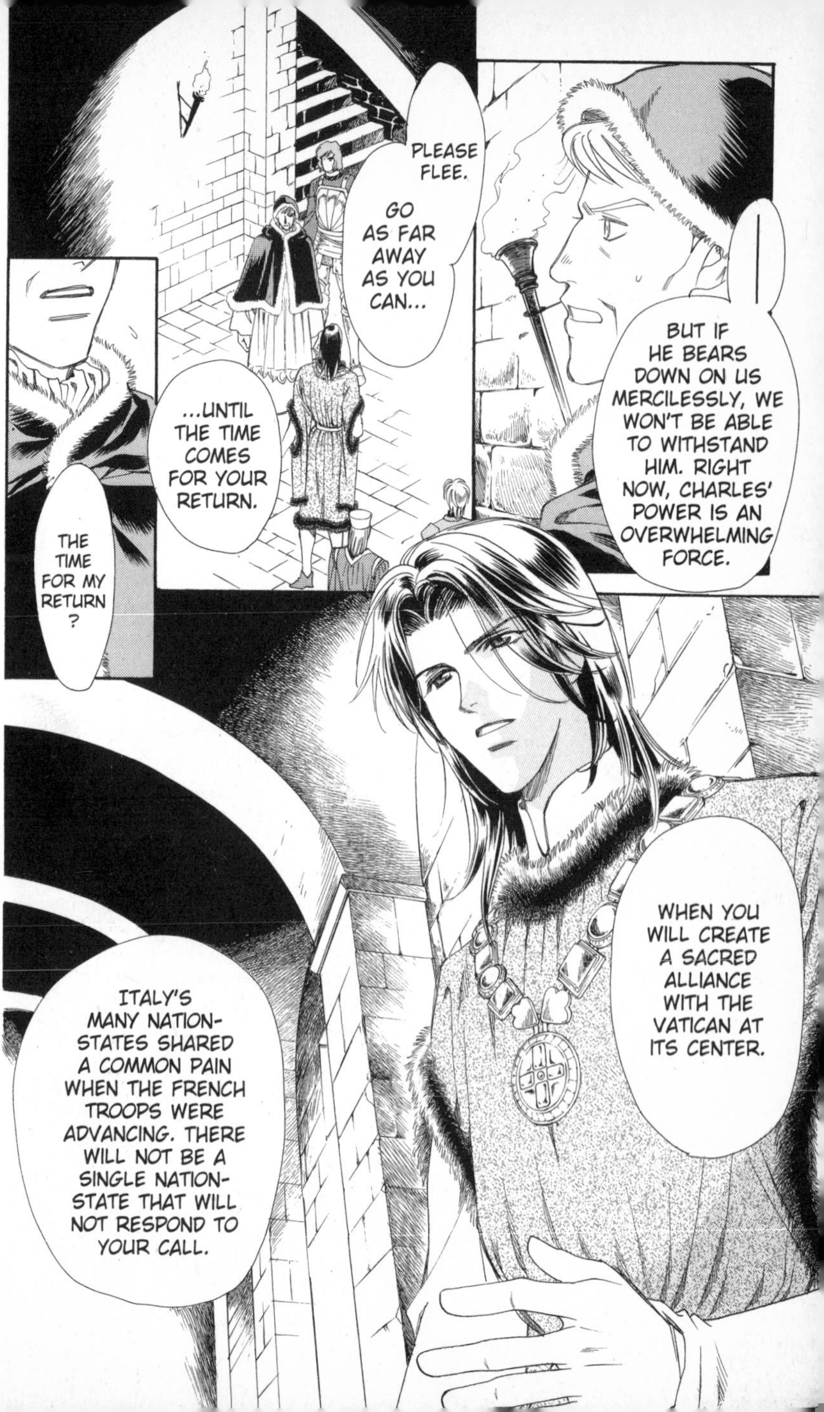
BUT IF HE BEARS DOWN ON US MERCILESSLY, WE WON'T BE ABLE TO WITHSTAND HIM. RIGHT NOW, CHARLES' POWER IS AN OVERWHELMING FORCE.
PLEASE FLEE.
GO AS FAR AWAY AS YOU CAN...
...UNTIL THE TIME COMES FOR YOUR RETURN.
THE TIME FOR MY RETURN?
WHEN YOU WILL CREATE A SACRED ALLIANCE WITH THE VATICAN AT ITS CENTER.
ITALY'S MANY NATION-STATES SHARED A COMMON PAIN WHEN THE FRENCH TROOPS WERE ADVANCING. THERE WILL NOT BE A SINGLE NATION-STATE THAT WILL NOT RESPOND TO YOUR CALL.

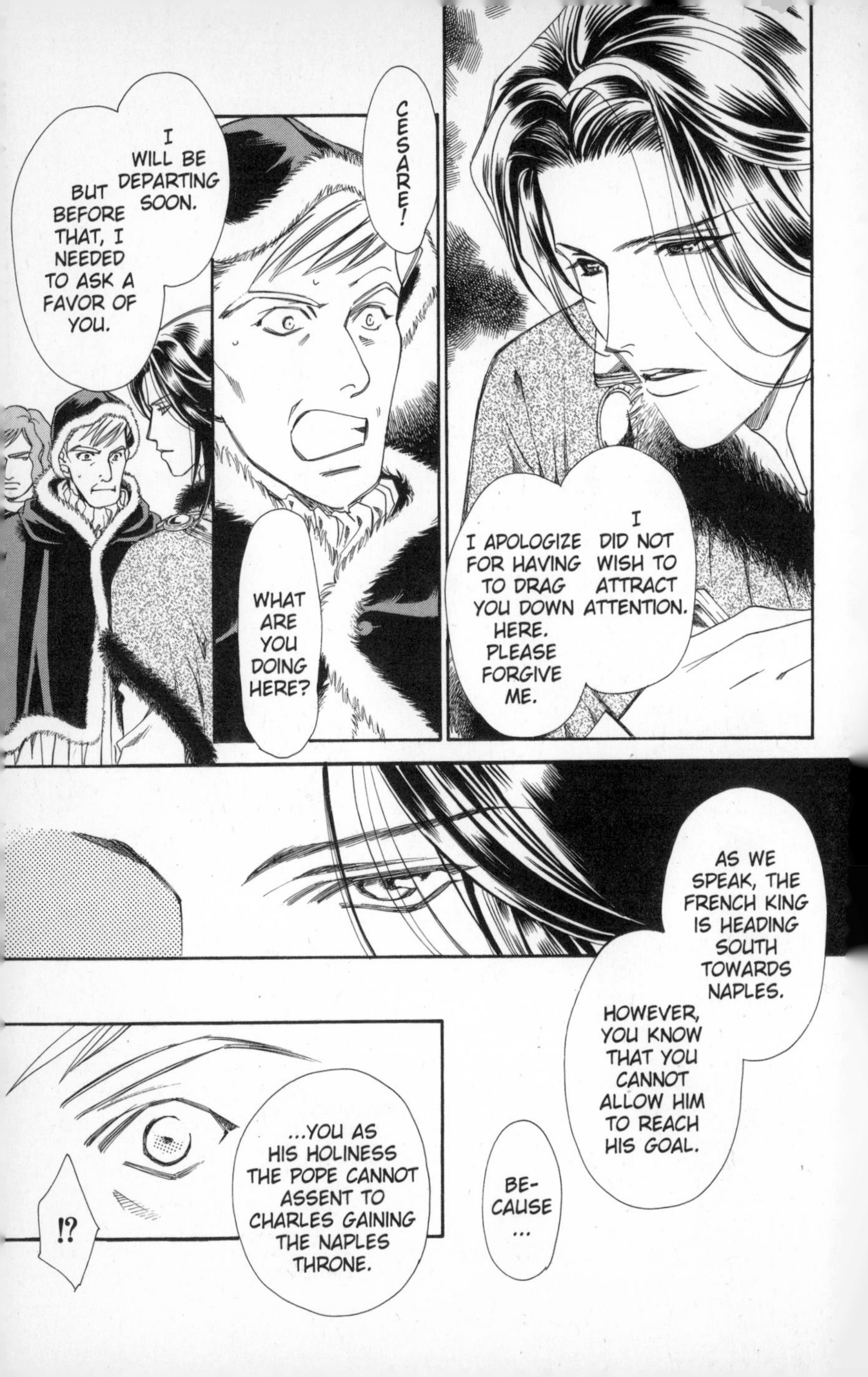
I DID NOT WISH TO ATTRACT ATTENTION.
I APOLOGIZE FOR HAVING TO DRAG YOU DOWN HERE. PLEASE FORGIVE ME.
CESARE!
WHAT ARE YOU DOING HERE?
I WILL BE DEPARTING SOON.
BUT BEFORE THAT, I NEEDED TO ASK A FAVOR OF YOU.
AS WE SPEAK, THE FRENCH KING IS HEADING SOUTH TOWARDS NAPLES.
HOWEVER, YOU KNOW THAT YOU CANNOT ALLOW HIM TO REACH HIS GOAL.
BE-CAUSE ...
...YOU AS HIS HOLINESS THE POPE CANNOT ASSENT TO CHARLES GAINING THE NAPLES THRONE.
!?

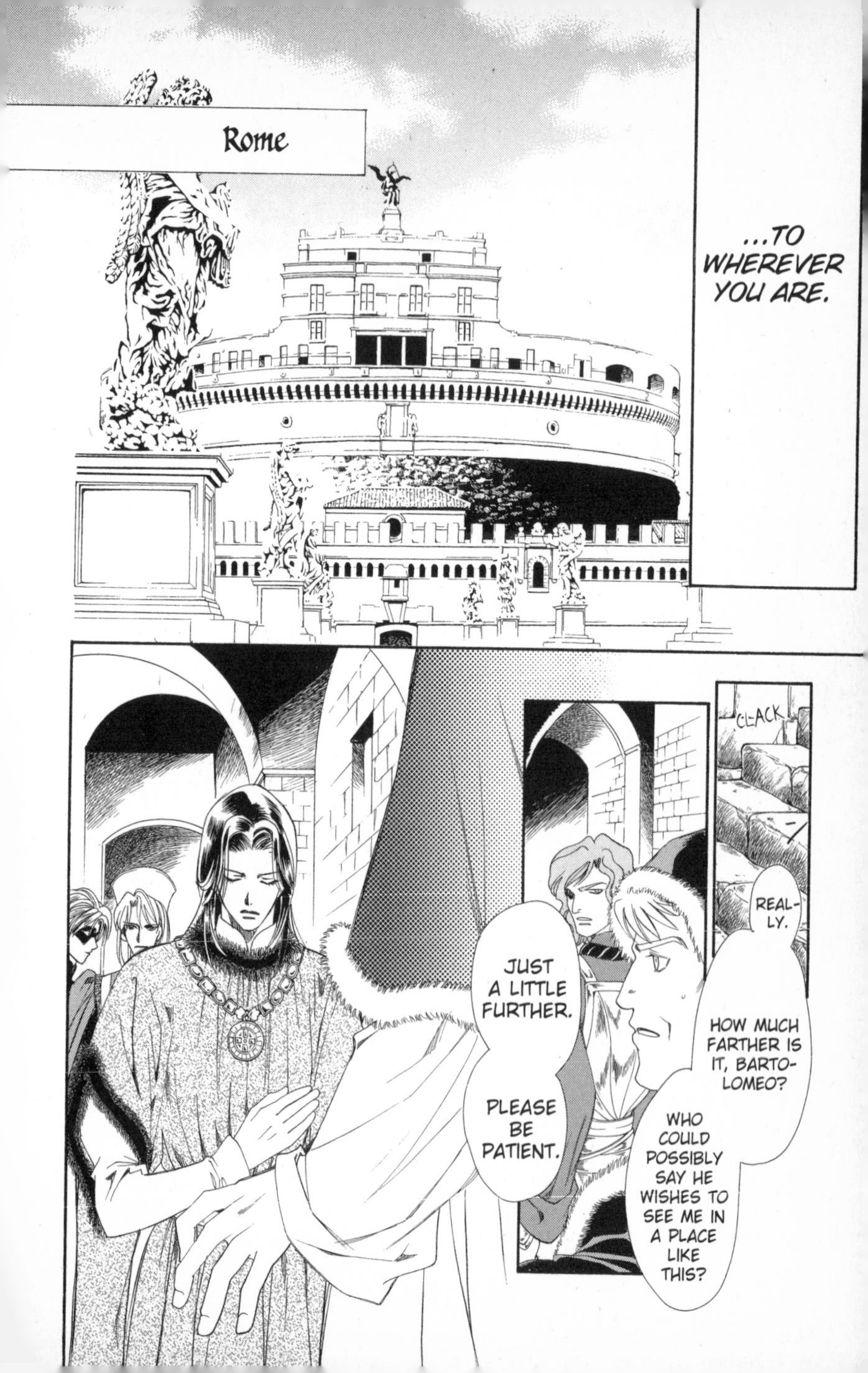
...TO WHEREVER YOU ARE.
Rome
CLACK
REAL-LY.
HOW MUCH FARTHER IS IT, BARTO-LOMEO?
JUST A LITTLE FURTHER.
PLEASE BE PATIENT.
WHO COULD POSSIBLY SAY HE WISHES TO SEE ME IN A PLACE LIKE THIS?

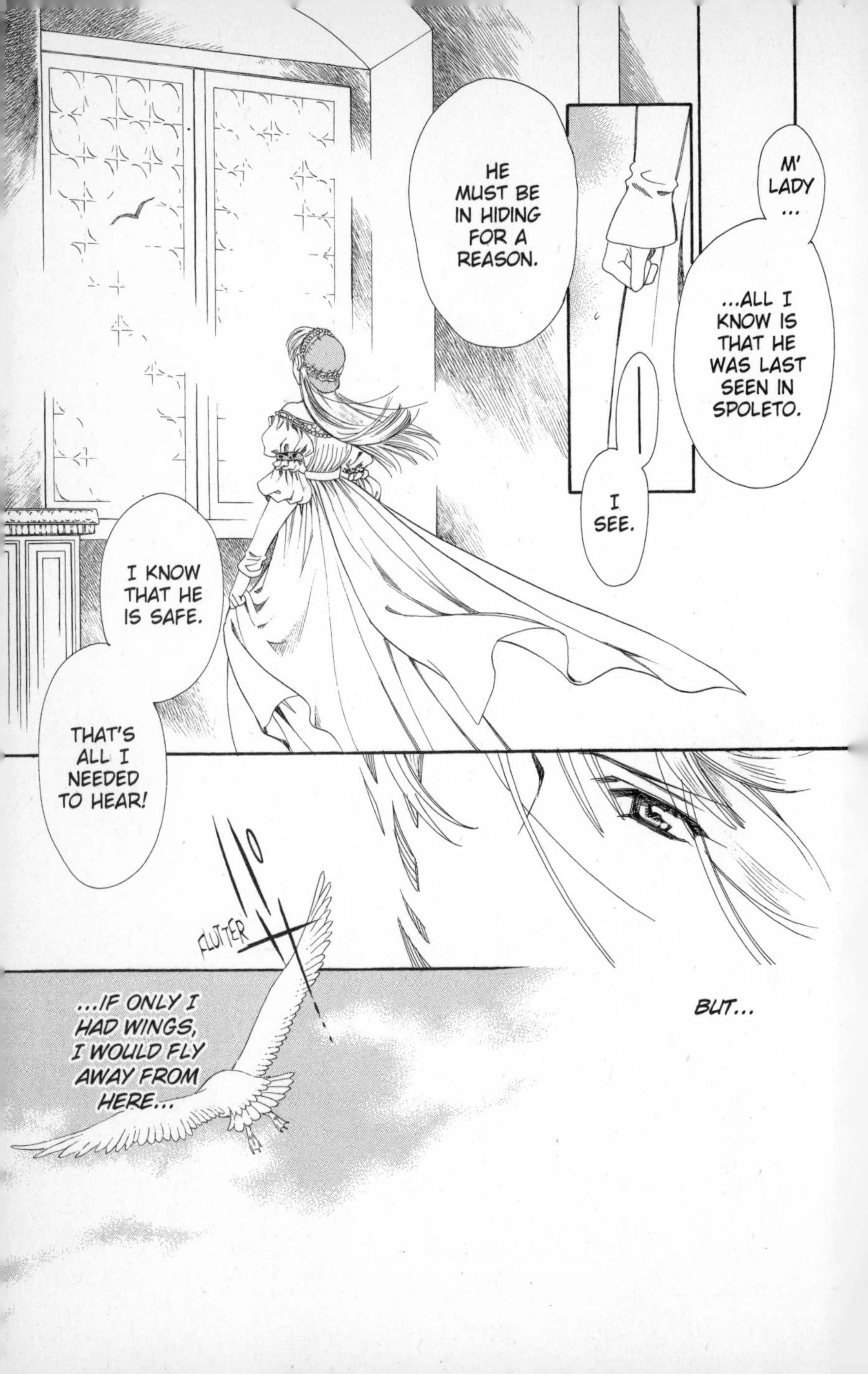
M' LADY ...
...ALL I KNOW IS THAT HE WAS LAST SEEN IN SPOLETO.
I SEE.
HE MUST BE IN HIDING FOR A REASON.
I KNOW THAT HE IS SAFE.
THAT'S ALL I NEEDED TO HEAR!
FLUTTER
BUT...
...IF ONLY I HAD WINGS, I WOULD FLY AWAY FROM HERE...

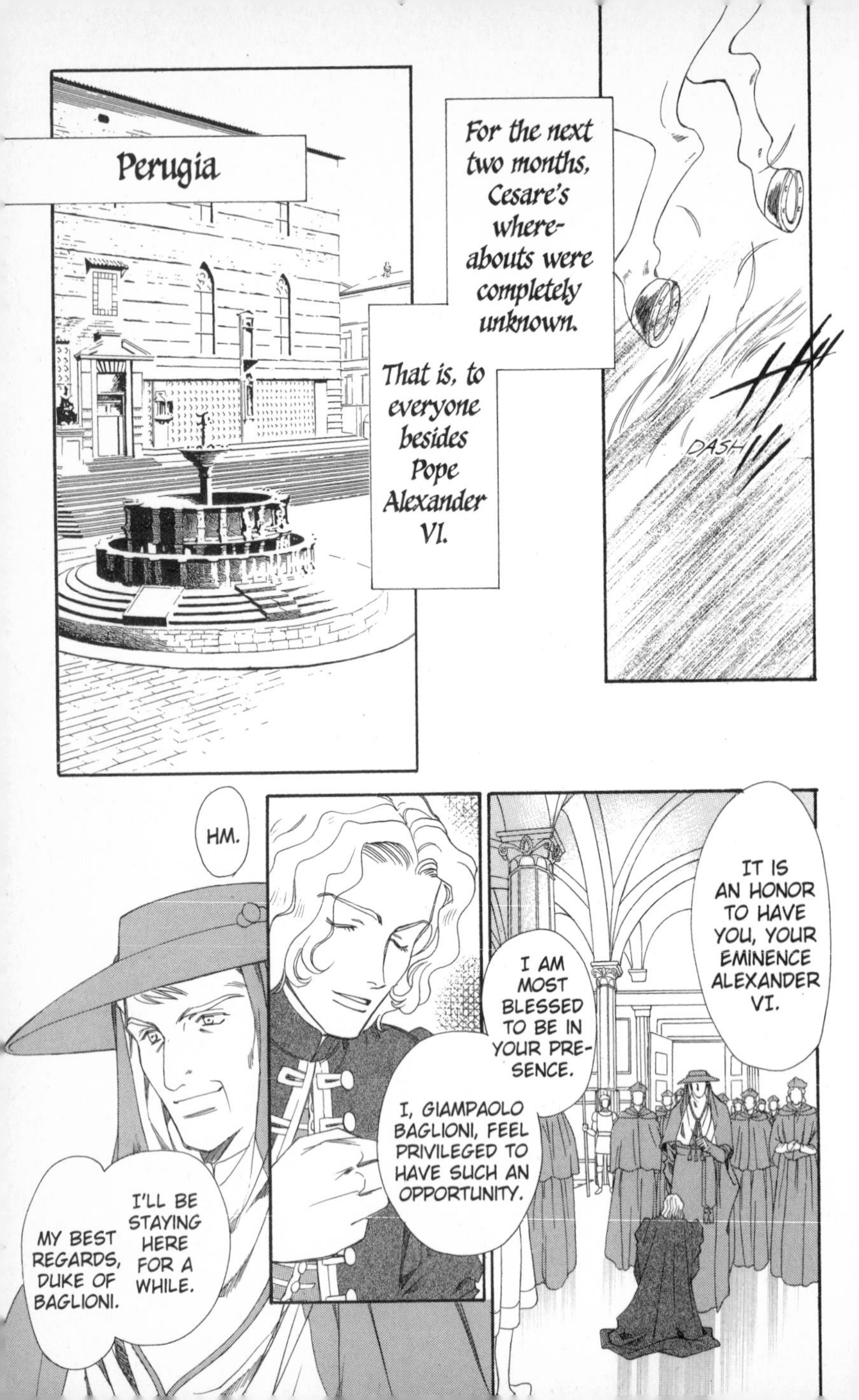
DASH
For the next two months, Cesare's whereabouts were completely unknown.
That is, to everyone besides Pope Alexander VI.
Perugia
IT IS AN HONOR TO HAVE YOU, YOUR EMINENCE ALEXANDER VI.
I AM MOST BLESSED TO BE IN YOUR PRESENCE.
I, GIAMPAOLO BAGLIONI, FEEL PRIVILEGED TO HAVE SUCH AN OPPORTUNITY.
HM.
I'LL BE STAYING HERE FOR A WHILE.
MY BEST REGARDS, DUKE OF BAGLIONI.

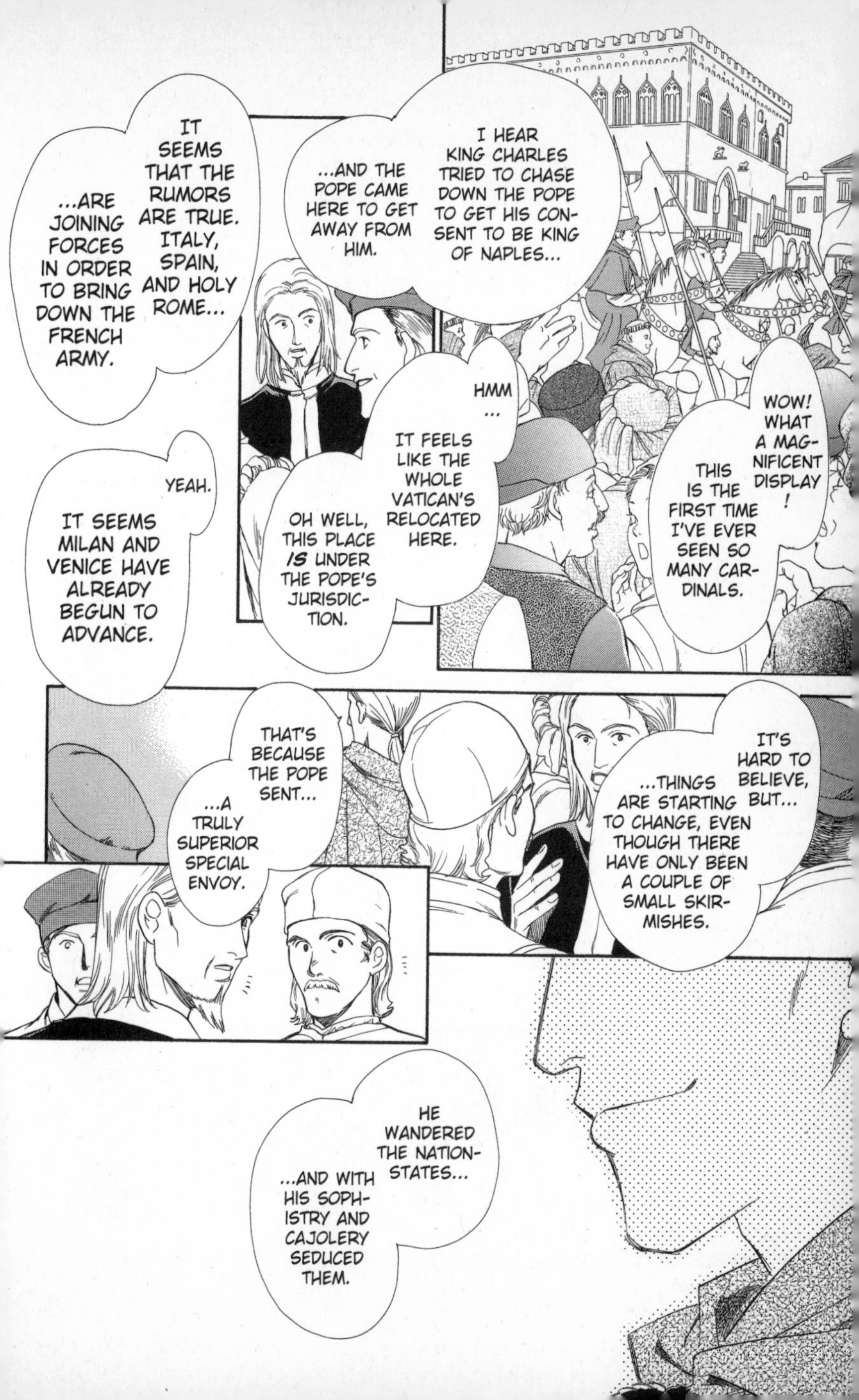
I HEAR KING CHARLES TRIED TO CHASE DOWN THE POPE TO GET HIS CONSENT TO BE KING OF NAPLES...
...AND THE POPE CAME HERE TO GET AWAY FROM HIM.
WOW! WHAT A MAGNIFICENT DISPLAY!
THIS IS THE FIRST TIME I'VE EVER SEEN SO MANY CARDINALS.
HMM...
IT FEELS LIKE THE WHOLE VATICAN'S RELOCATED HERE.
OH WELL, THIS PLACE *IS* UNDER THE POPE'S JURISDICTION.
IT SEEMS THAT THE RUMORS ARE TRUE. ITALY, SPAIN, AND HOLY ROME...
...ARE JOINING FORCES IN ORDER TO BRING DOWN THE FRENCH ARMY.
YEAH.
IT SEEMS MILAN AND VENICE HAVE ALREADY BEGUN TO ADVANCE.
IT'S HARD TO BELIEVE, BUT...
...THINGS ARE STARTING TO CHANGE, EVEN THOUGH THERE HAVE ONLY BEEN A COUPLE OF SMALL SKIRMISHES.
THAT'S BECAUSE THE POPE SENT...
...A TRULY SUPERIOR SPECIAL ENVOY.
HE WANDERED THE NATION-STATES...
...AND WITH HIS SOPHISTRY AND CAJOLERY SEDUCED THEM.

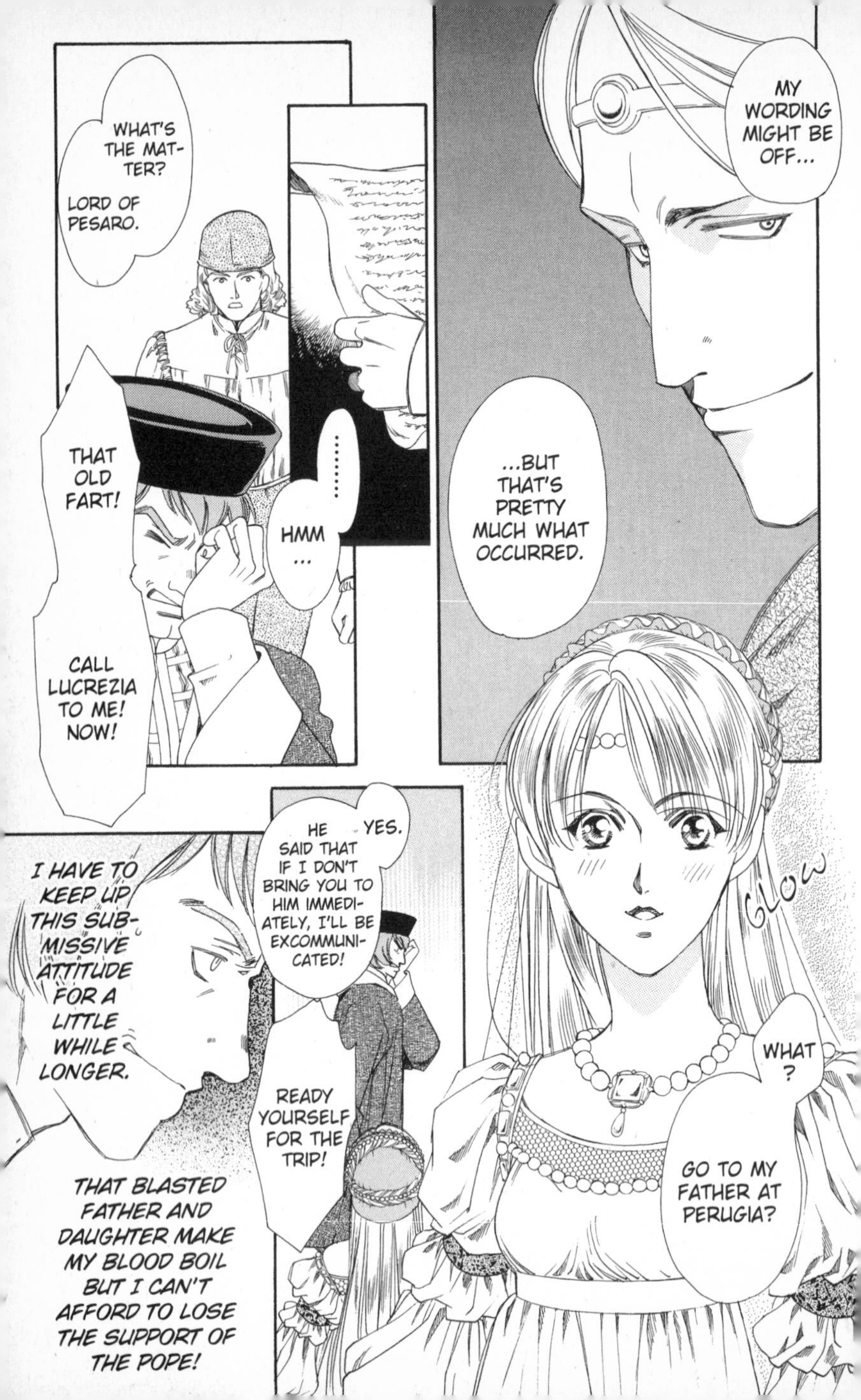
MY WORDING MIGHT BE OFF...
...BUT THAT'S PRETTY MUCH WHAT OCCURRED.
......
HMM ...
WHAT'S THE MAT-TER?
LORD OF PESARO.
THAT OLD FART!
CALL LUCREZIA TO ME! NOW!
GLOW
WHAT?
GO TO MY FATHER AT PERUGIA?
YES.
HE SAID THAT IF I DON'T BRING YOU TO HIM IMMEDI-ATELY, I'LL BE EXCOMMUNI-CATED!
READY YOURSELF FOR THE TRIP!
I HAVE TO KEEP UP THIS SUB-MISSIVE ATTITUDE FOR A LITTLE WHILE LONGER.
THAT BLASTED FATHER AND DAUGHTER MAKE MY BLOOD BOIL BUT I CAN'T AFFORD TO LOSE THE SUPPORT OF THE POPE!

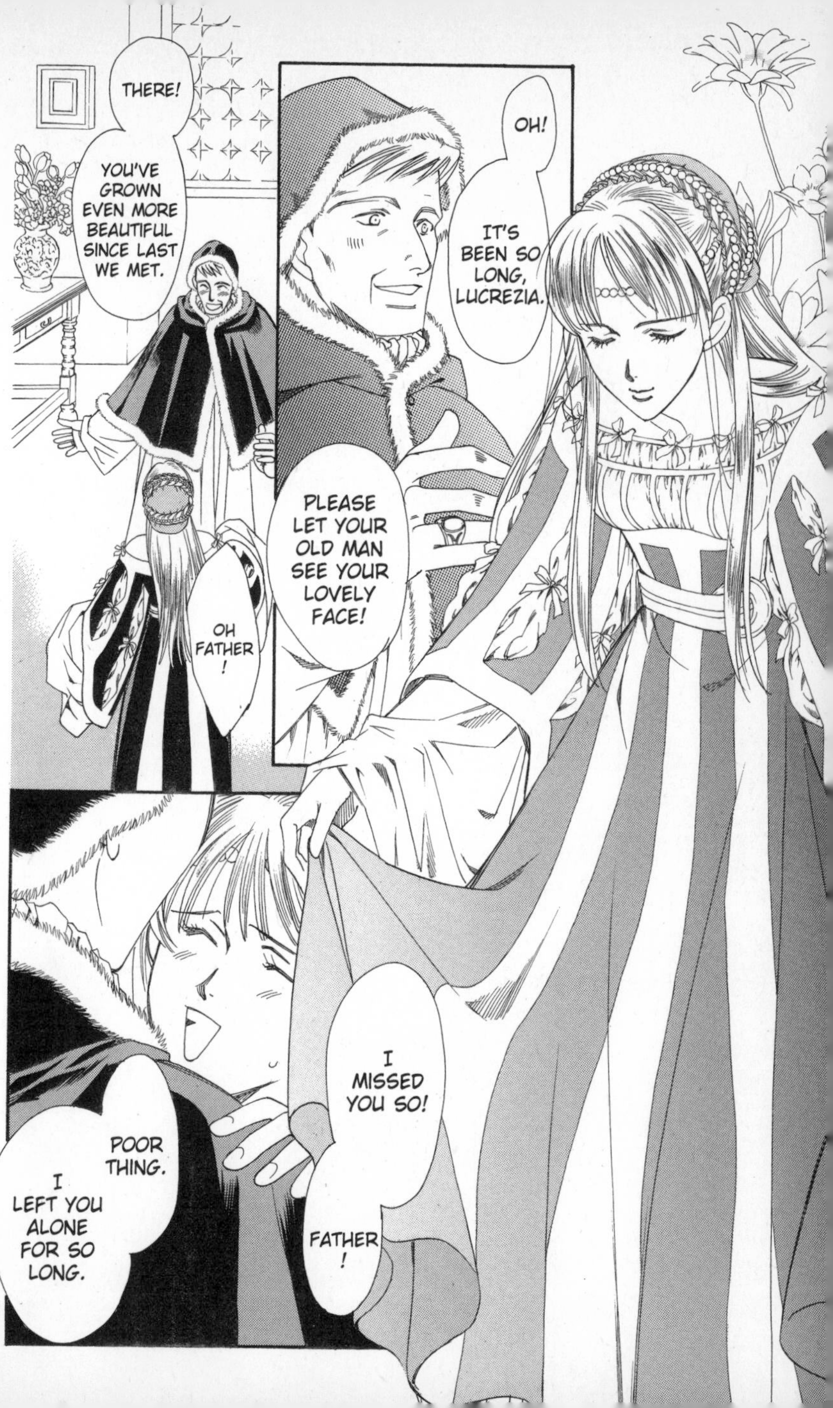
OH!
IT'S BEEN SO LONG, LUCREZIA.
PLEASE LET YOUR OLD MAN SEE YOUR LOVELY FACE!
THERE!
YOU'VE GROWN EVEN MORE BEAUTIFUL SINCE LAST WE MET.
OH FATHER!
I MISSED YOU SO!
FATHER!
POOR THING.
I LEFT YOU ALONE FOR SO LONG.

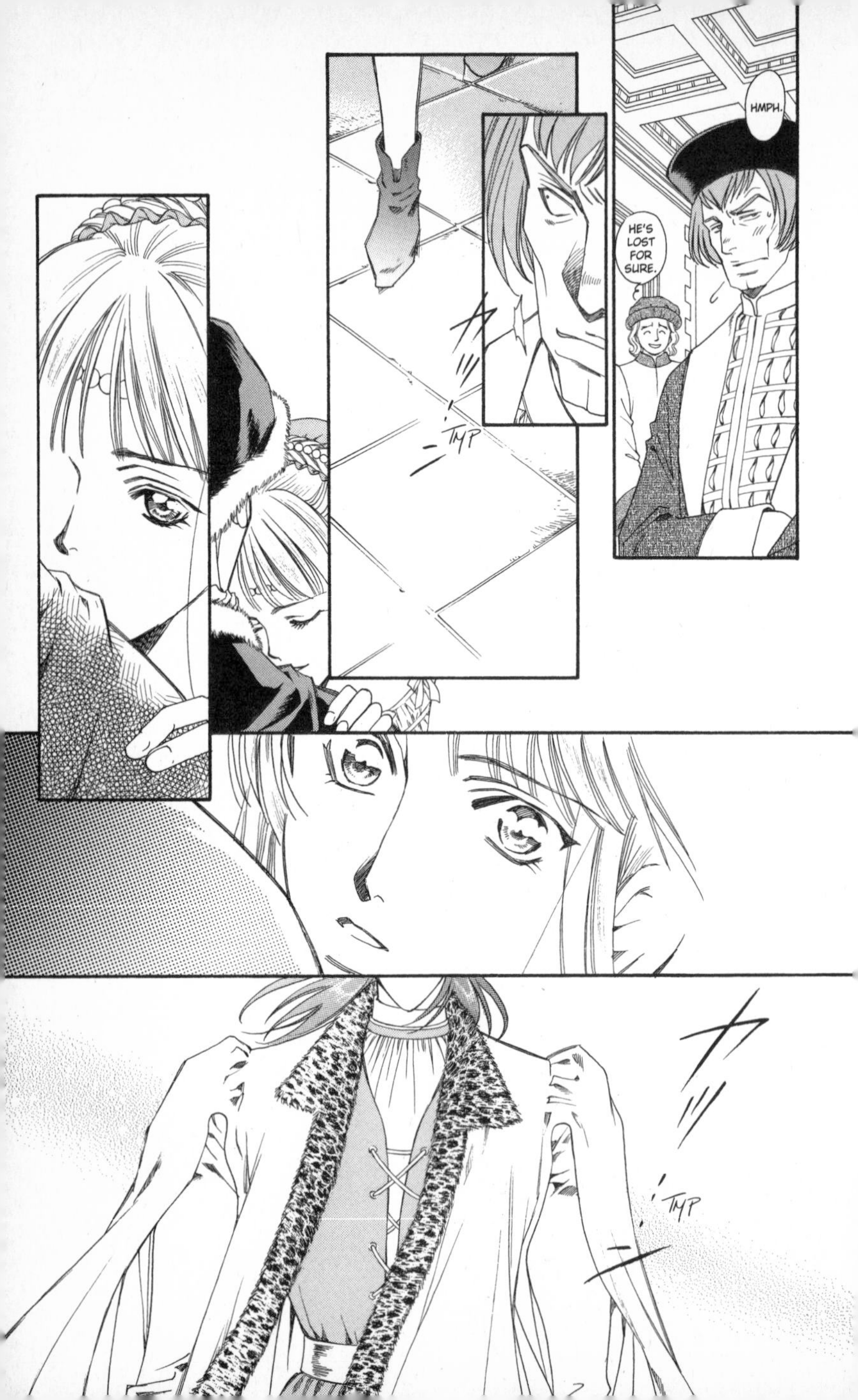
HMPH.
HE'S LOST FOR SURE.
TMP
TMP

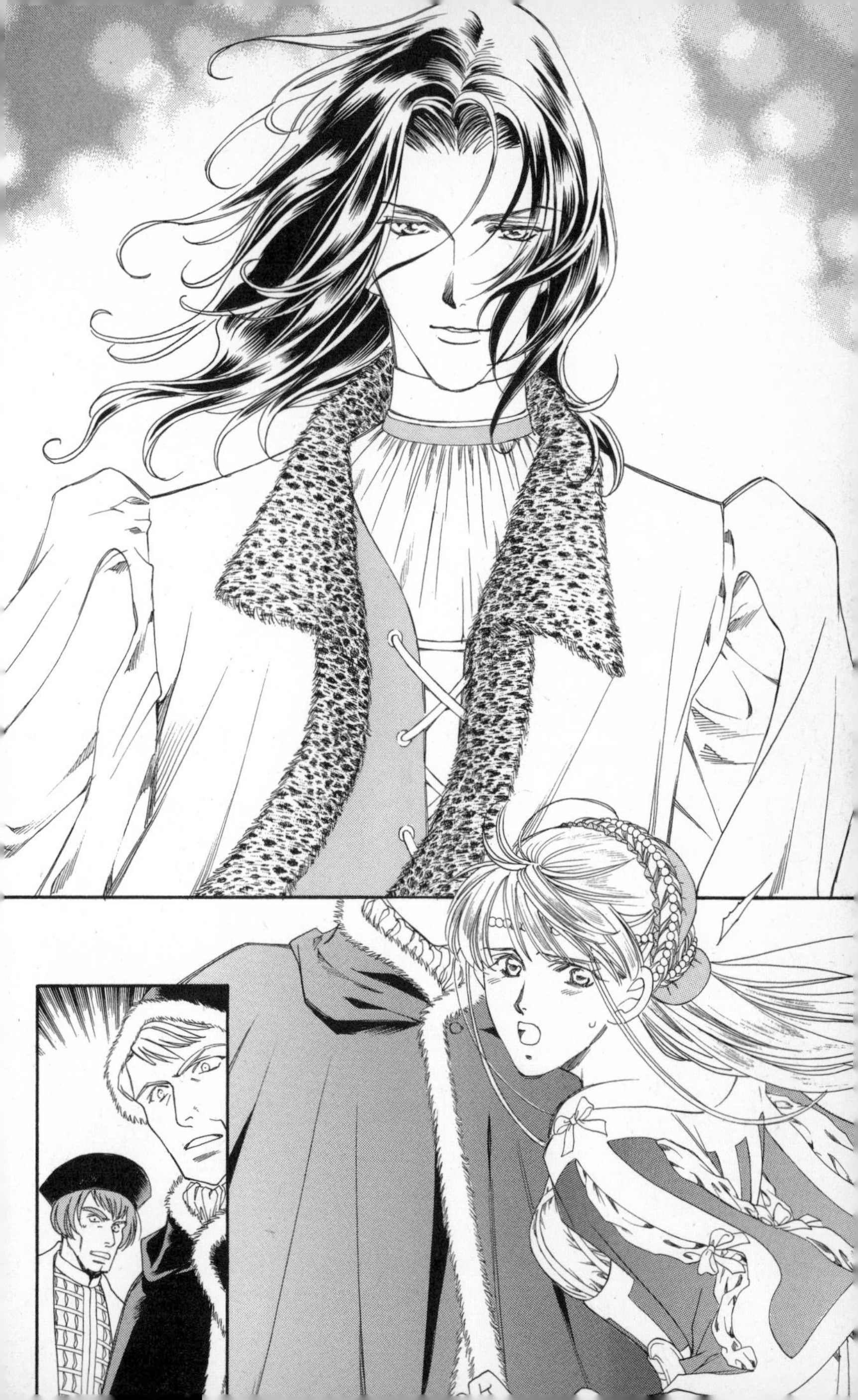

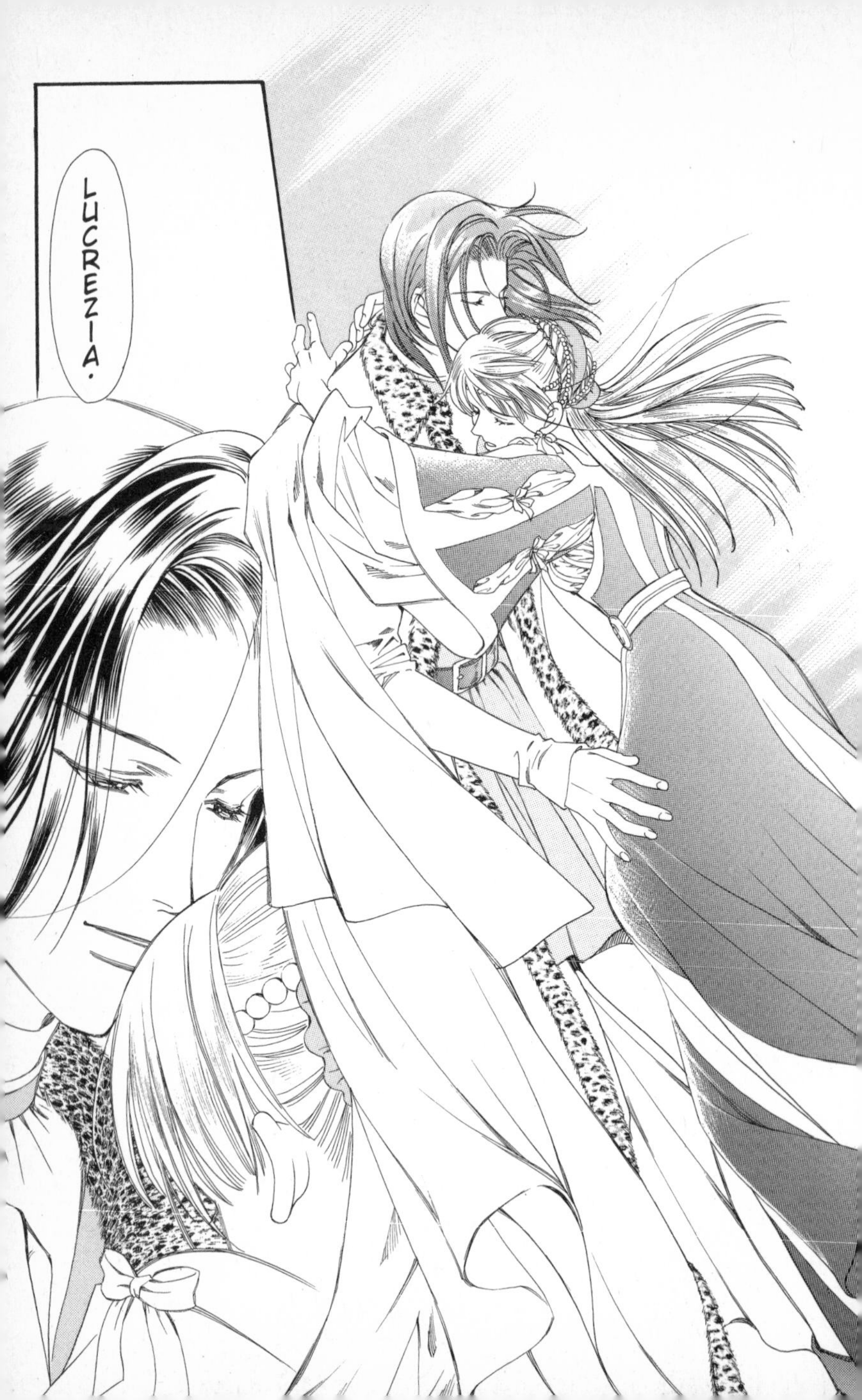
LUCREZIA.

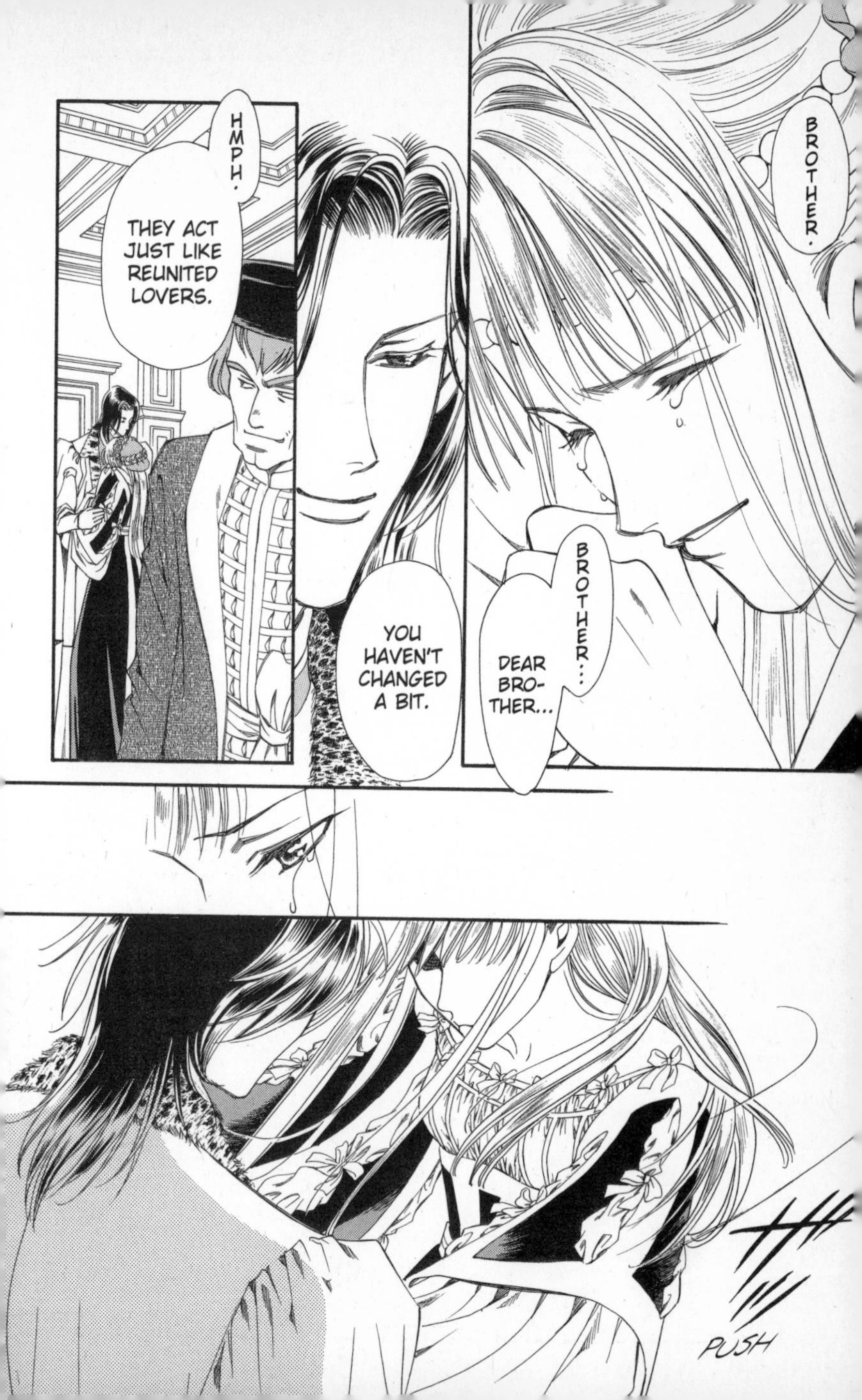
BROTHER.
BROTHER...
DEAR BROTHER...
YOU HAVEN'T CHANGED A BIT.
HMPH.
THEY ACT JUST LIKE REUNITED LOVERS.
PUSH

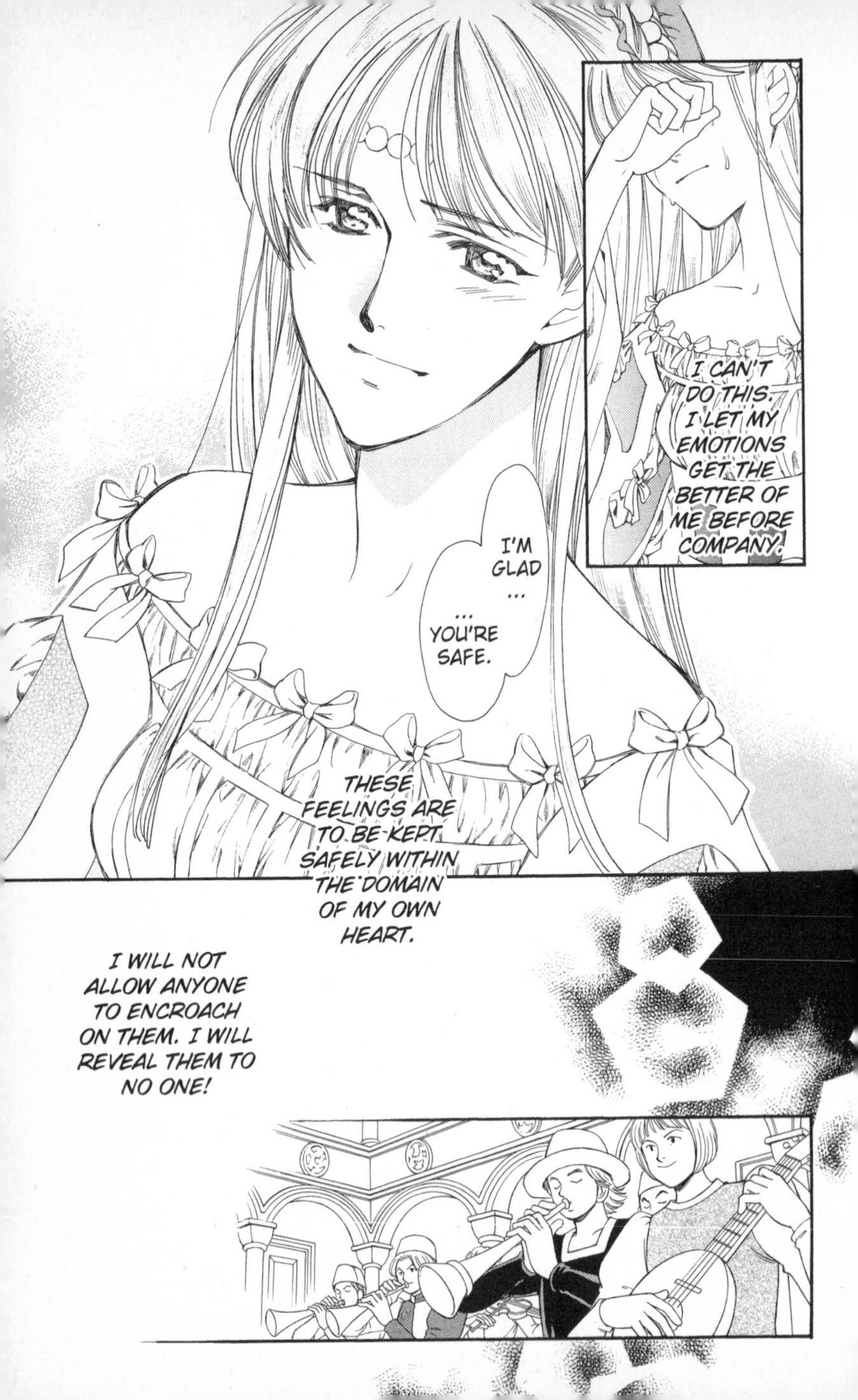
I CAN'T DO THIS. I LET MY EMOTIONS GET THE BETTER OF ME BEFORE COMPANY.
I'M GLAD ... ... YOU'RE SAFE.
THESE FEELINGS ARE TO BE KEPT SAFELY WITHIN THE DOMAIN OF MY OWN HEART.
I WILL NOT ALLOW ANYONE TO ENCROACH ON THEM. I WILL REVEAL THEM TO NO ONE!

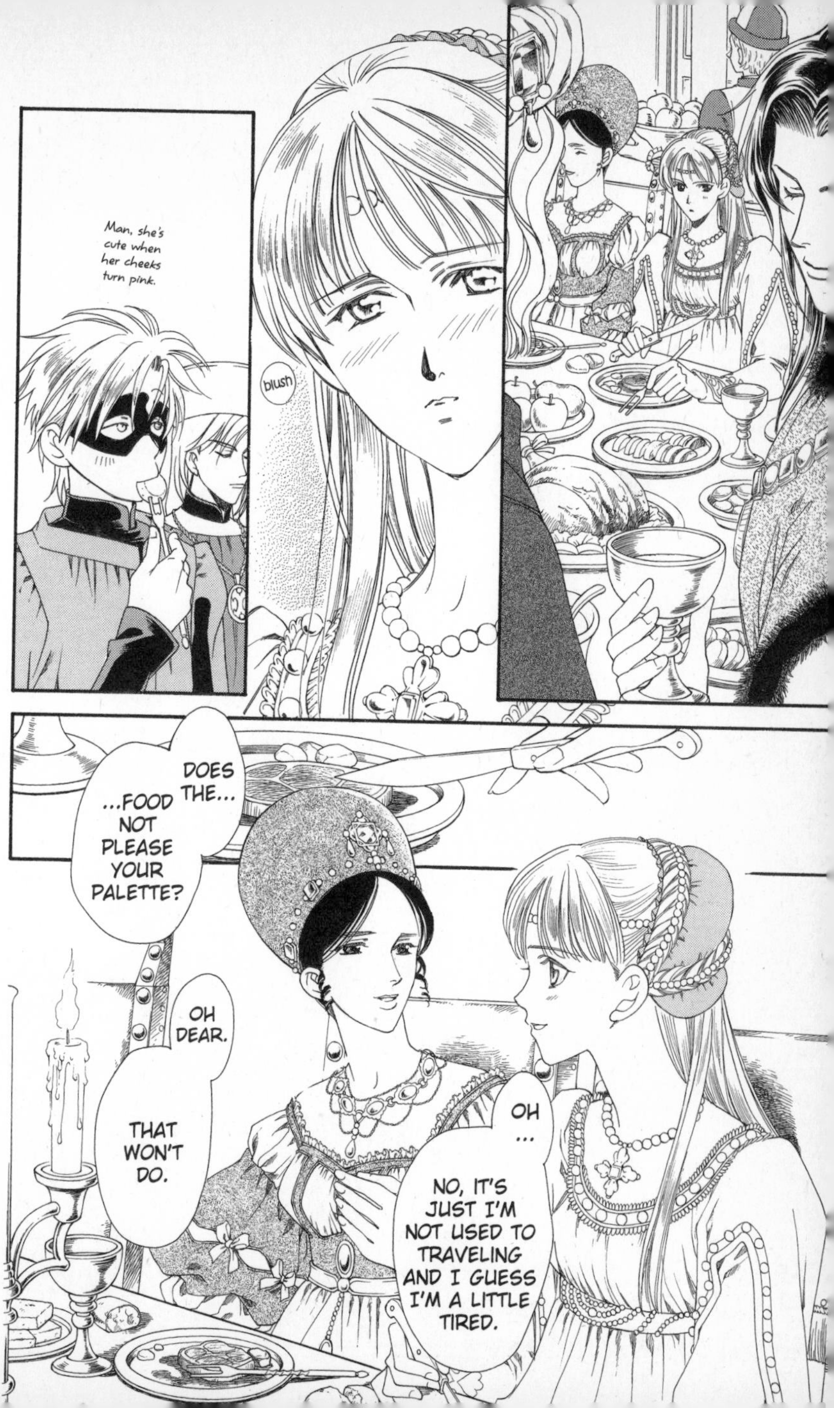
blush
Man, she's cute when her cheeks turn pink.
DOES THE... ...FOOD NOT PLEASE YOUR PALETTE?
OH ...
NO, IT'S JUST I'M NOT USED TO TRAVELING AND I GUESS I'M A LITTLE TIRED.
OH DEAR.
THAT WON'T DO.

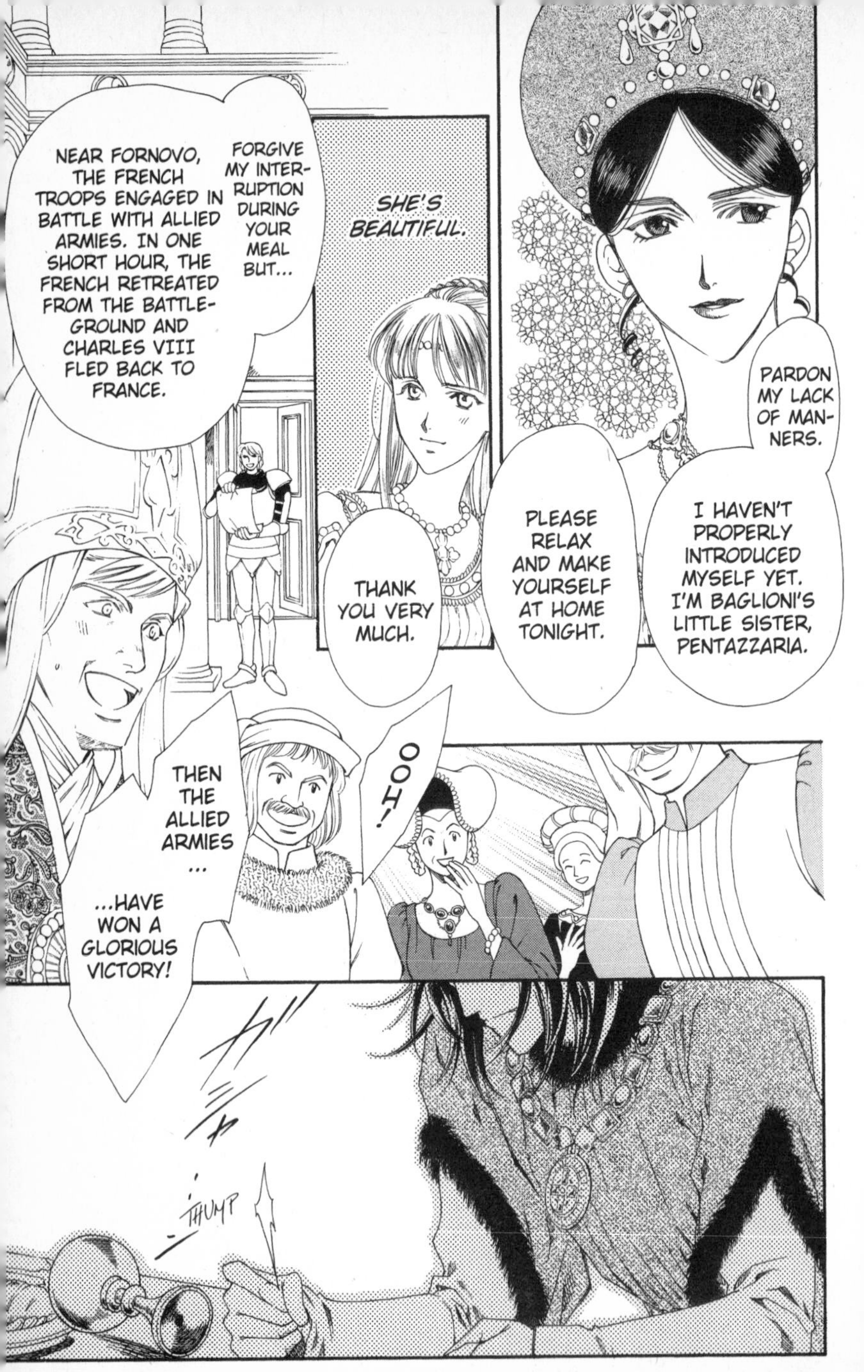
PARDON MY LACK OF MANNERS.
I HAVEN'T PROPERLY INTRODUCED MYSELF YET. I'M BAGLIONI'S LITTLE SISTER, PENTAZZARIA.
PLEASE RELAX AND MAKE YOURSELF AT HOME TONIGHT.
SHE'S BEAUTIFUL.
THANK YOU VERY MUCH.
FORGIVE MY INTERRUPTION DURING YOUR MEAL BUT...
NEAR FORNOVO, THE FRENCH TROOPS ENGAGED IN BATTLE WITH ALLIED ARMIES. IN ONE SHORT HOUR, THE FRENCH RETREATED FROM THE BATTLEGROUND AND CHARLES VIII FLED BACK TO FRANCE.
OOH!
THEN THE ALLIED ARMIES...
...HAVE WON A GLORIOUS VICTORY!
THUMP

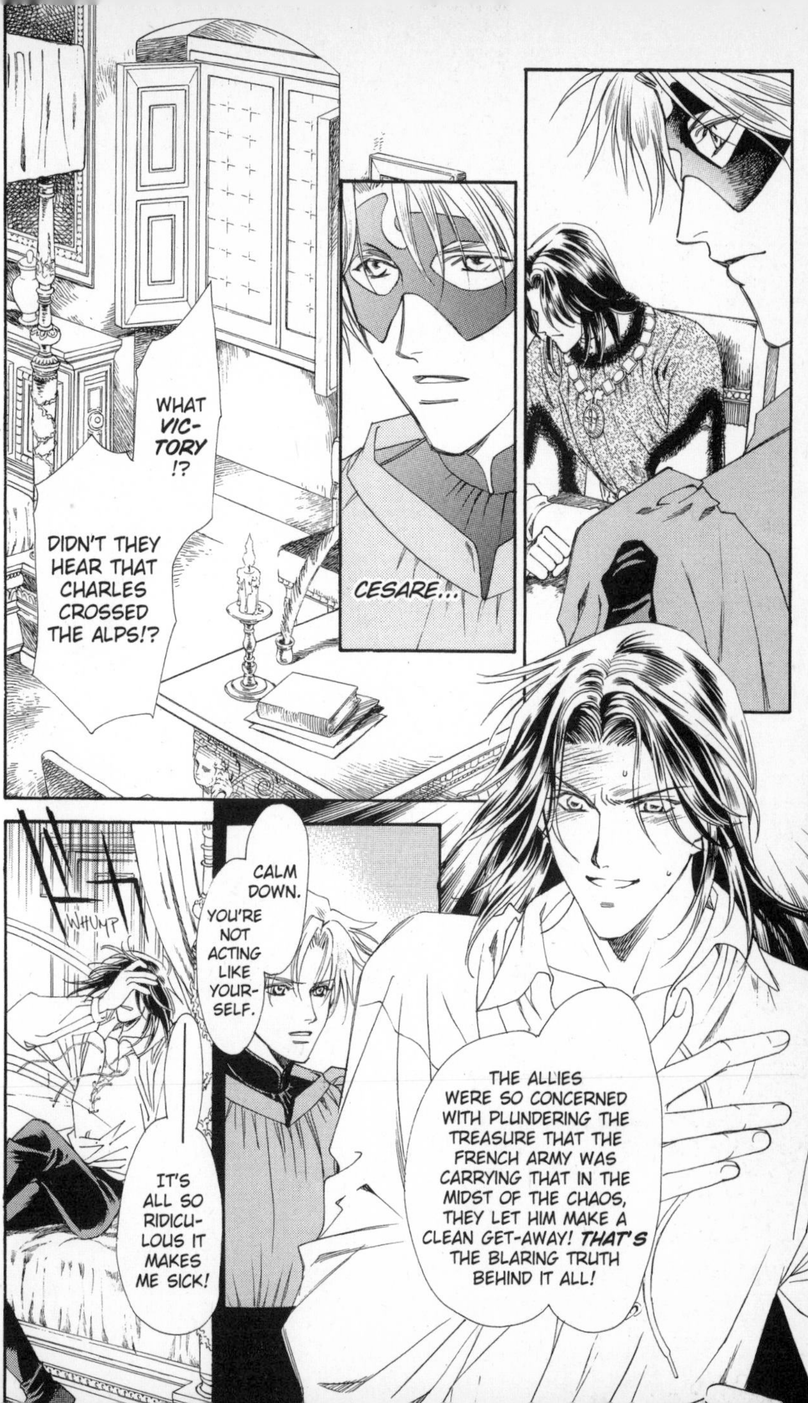
CESARE...
WHAT VICTORY!?
DIDN'T THEY HEAR THAT CHARLES CROSSED THE ALPS!?
THE ALLIES WERE SO CONCERNED WITH PLUNDERING THE TREASURE THAT THE FRENCH ARMY WAS CARRYING THAT IN THE MIDST OF THE CHAOS, THEY LET HIM MAKE A CLEAN GET-AWAY! THAT'S THE BLARING TRUTH BEHIND IT ALL!
CALM DOWN.
YOU'RE NOT ACTING LIKE YOURSELF.
WHUMP
IT'S ALL SO RIDICULOUS IT MAKES ME SICK!

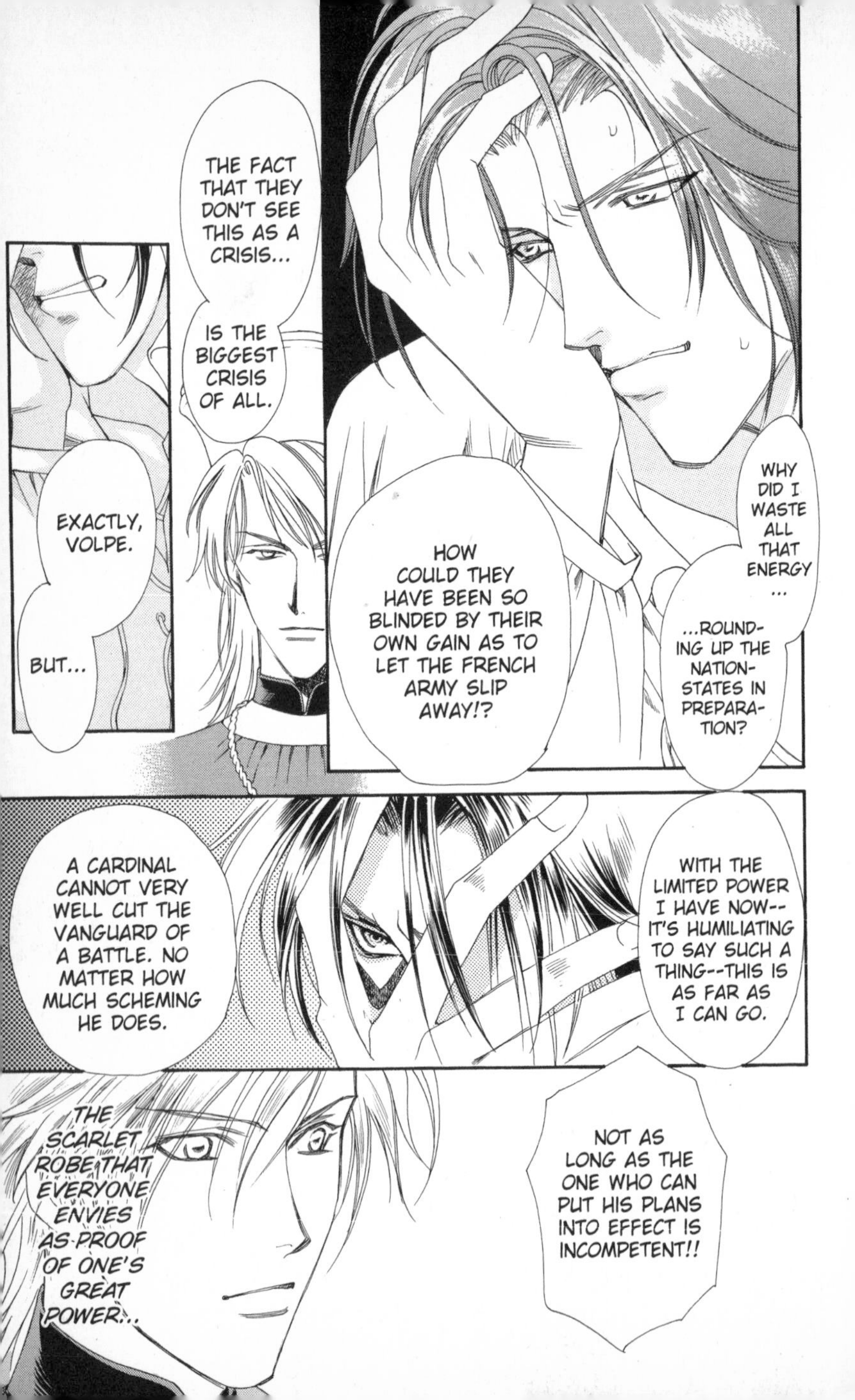
WHY DID I WASTE ALL THAT ENERGY...
...ROUNDING UP THE NATION-STATES IN PREPARATION?
HOW COULD THEY HAVE BEEN SO BLINDED BY THEIR OWN GAIN AS TO LET THE FRENCH ARMY SLIP AWAY!?
THE FACT THAT THEY DON'T SEE THIS AS A CRISIS...
IS THE BIGGEST CRISIS OF ALL.
EXACTLY, VOLPE.
BUT...
WITH THE LIMITED POWER I HAVE NOW--IT'S HUMILIATING TO SAY SUCH A THING--THIS IS AS FAR AS I CAN GO.
A CARDINAL CANNOT VERY WELL CUT THE VANGUARD OF A BATTLE. NO MATTER HOW MUCH SCHEMING HE DOES.
NOT AS LONG AS THE ONE WHO CAN PUT HIS PLANS INTO EFFECT IS INCOMPETENT!!
THE SCARLET ROBE THAT EVERYONE ENVIES AS PROOF OF ONE'S GREAT POWER...

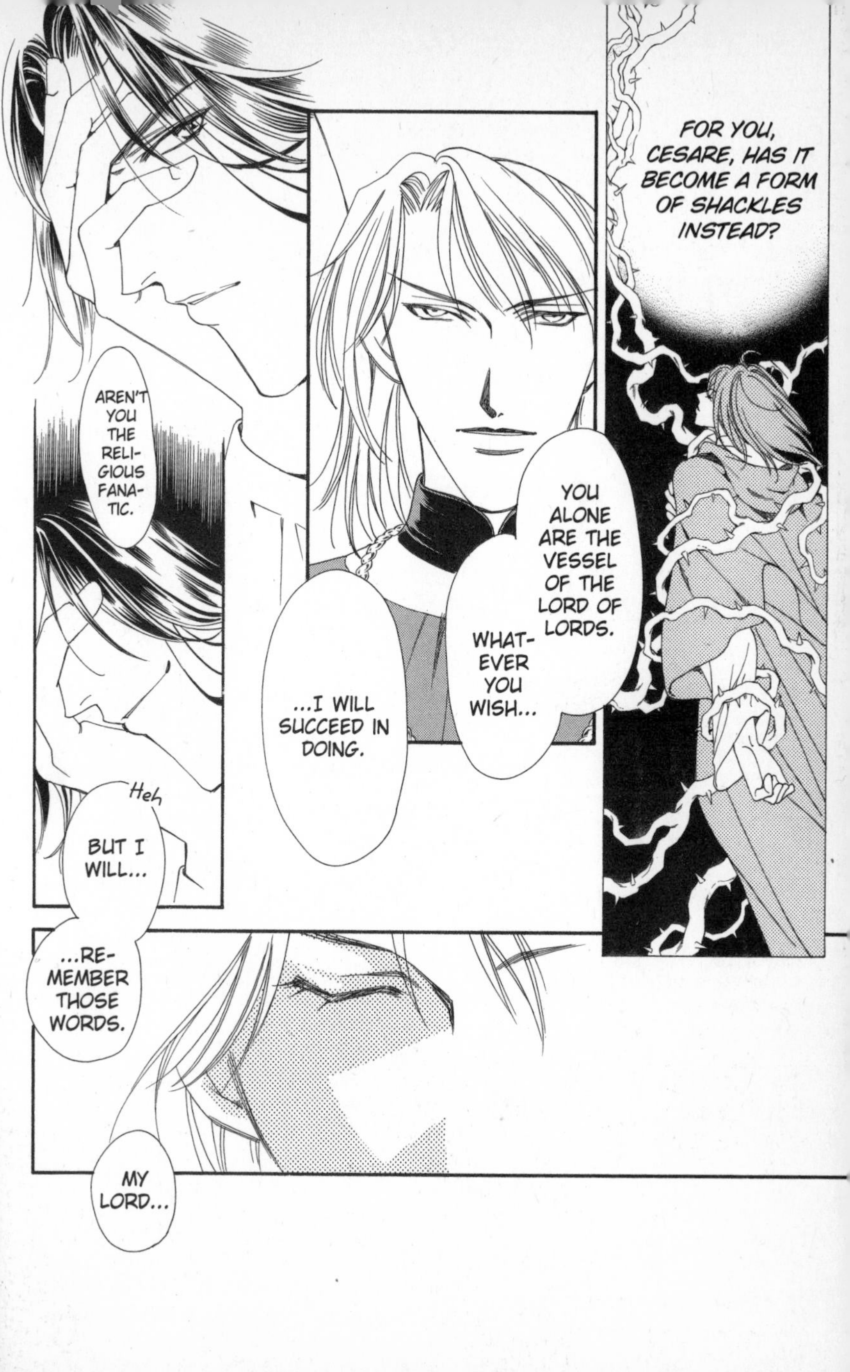
FOR YOU, CESARE, HAS IT BECOME A FORM OF SHACKLES INSTEAD?
YOU ALONE ARE THE VESSEL OF THE LORD OF LORDS.
WHAT-EVER YOU WISH...
...I WILL SUCCEED IN DOING.
AREN'T YOU THE RELI-GIOUS FANA-TIC.
Heh
BUT I WILL...
...RE-MEMBER THOSE WORDS.
MY LORD...

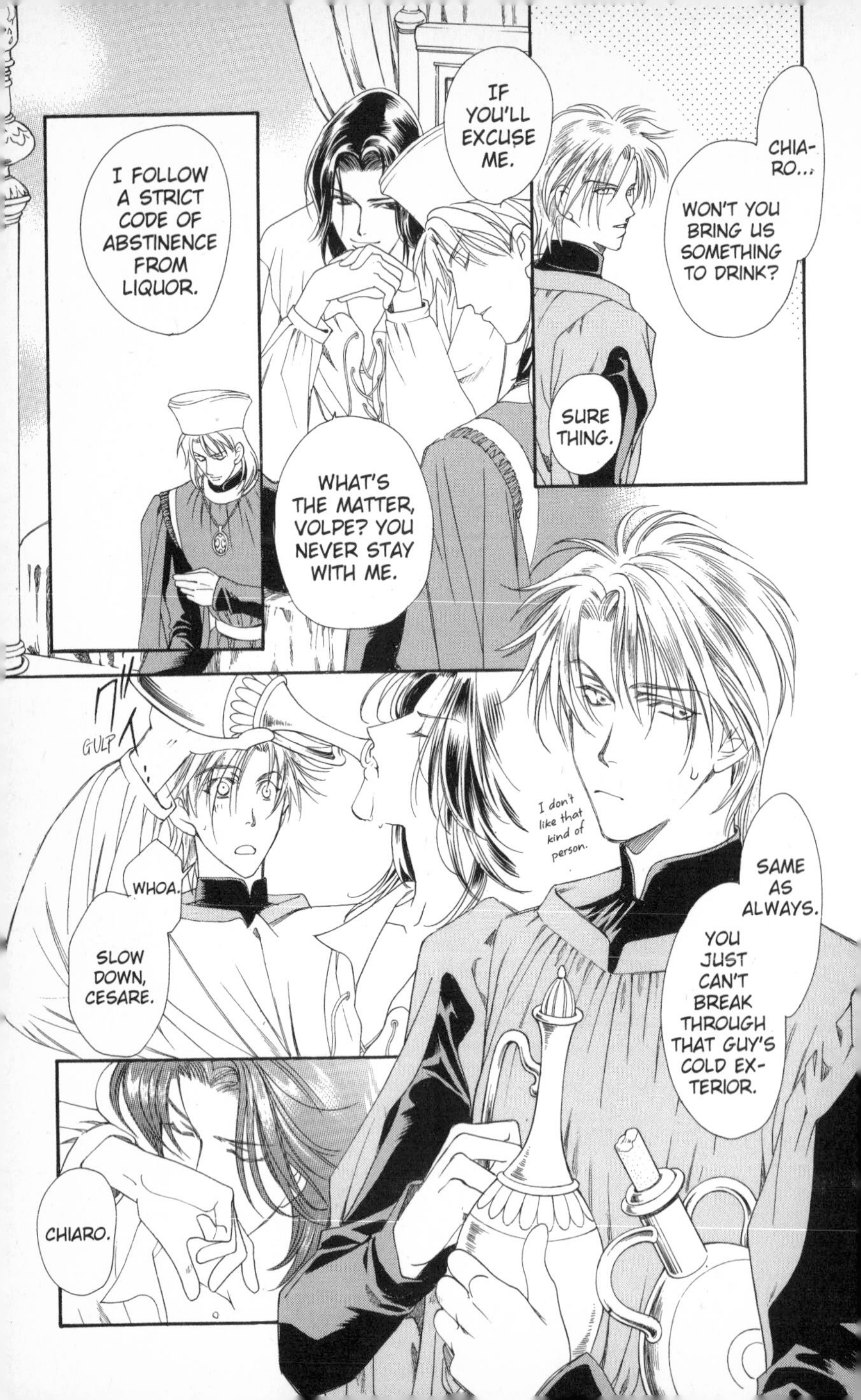
CHIA-RO...
WON'T YOU BRING US SOMETHING TO DRINK?
SURE THING.
IF YOU'LL EXCUSE ME.
WHAT'S THE MATTER, VOLPE? YOU NEVER STAY WITH ME.
I FOLLOW A STRICT CODE OF ABSTINENCE FROM LIQUOR.
I don't like that kind of person.
SAME AS ALWAYS.
YOU JUST CAN'T BREAK THROUGH THAT GUY'S COLD EX-TERIOR.
GULP
WHOA.
SLOW DOWN, CESARE.
CHIARO.

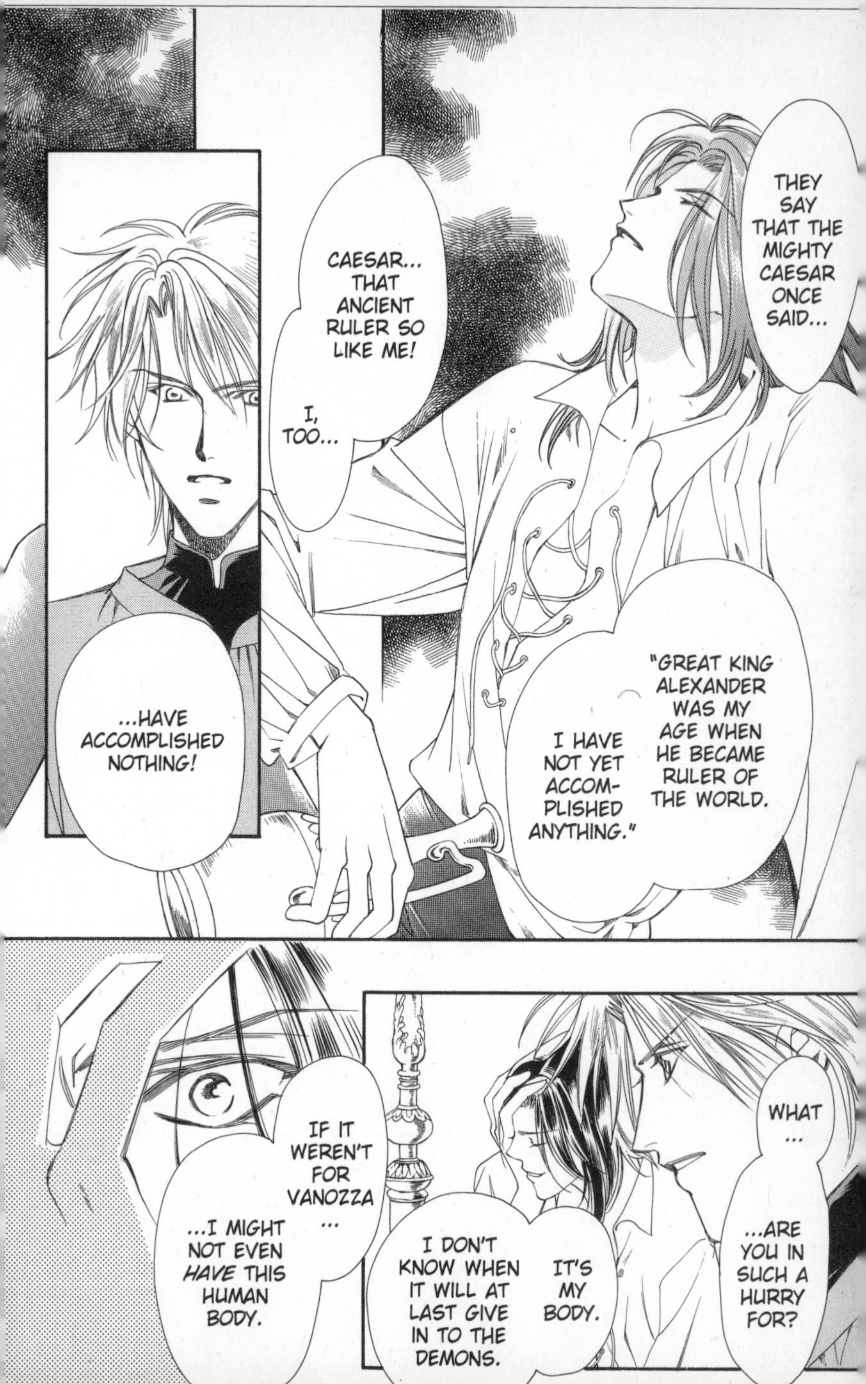
THEY SAY THAT THE MIGHTY CAESAR ONCE SAID...
"GREAT KING ALEXANDER WAS MY AGE WHEN HE BECAME RULER OF THE WORLD.
I HAVE NOT YET ACCOMPLISHED ANYTHING."
CAESAR... THAT ANCIENT RULER SO LIKE ME!
I, TOO...
...HAVE ACCOMPLISHED NOTHING!
WHAT ...
...ARE YOU IN SUCH A HURRY FOR?
IT'S MY BODY.
I DON'T KNOW WHEN IT WILL AT LAST GIVE IN TO THE DEMONS.
IF IT WEREN'T FOR VANOZZA ...
...I MIGHT NOT EVEN *HAVE* THIS HUMAN BODY.

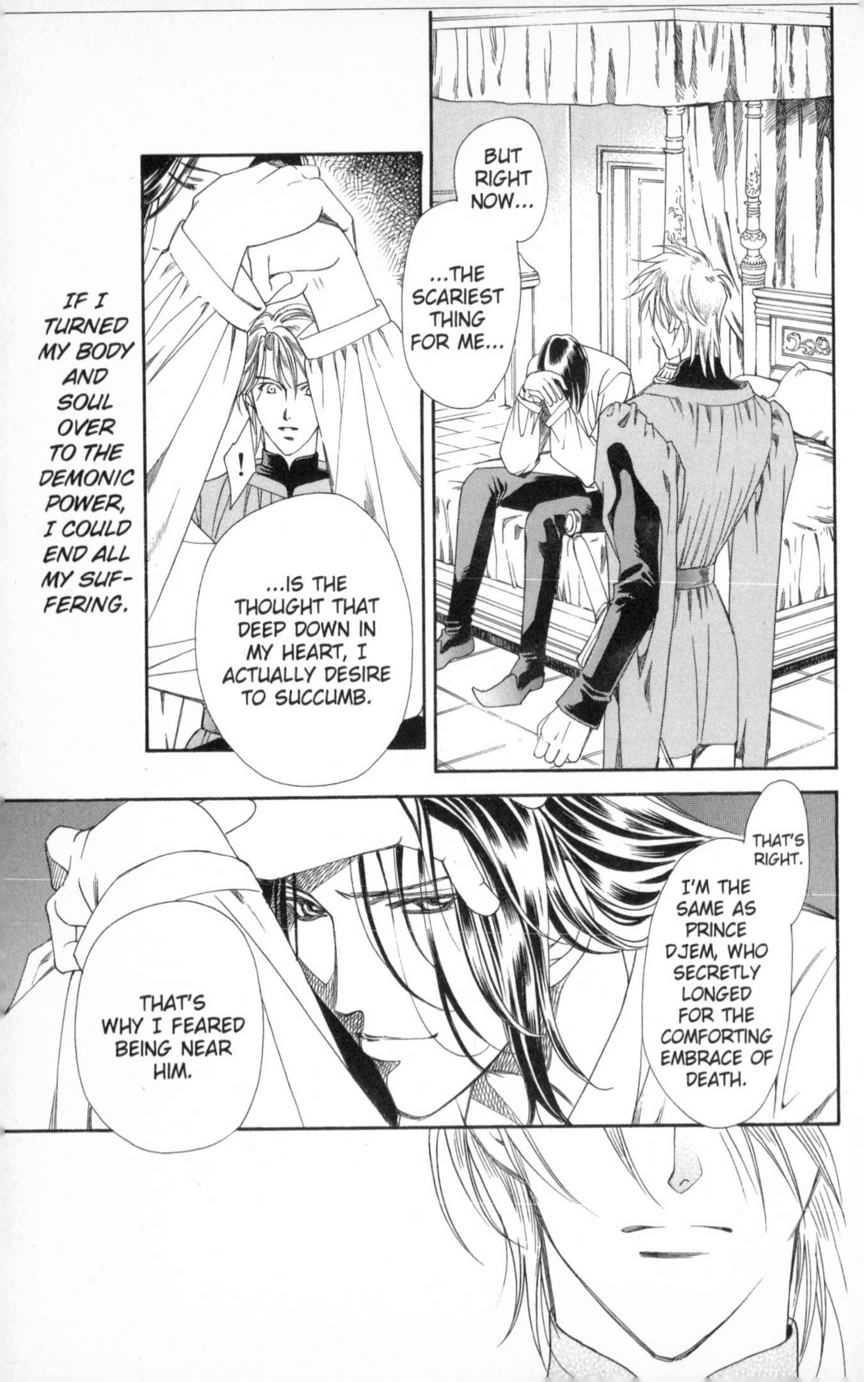
BUT RIGHT NOW...
...THE SCARIEST THING FOR ME...
...IS THE THOUGHT THAT DEEP DOWN IN MY HEART, I ACTUALLY DESIRE TO SUCCUMB.
!
IF I TURNED MY BODY AND SOUL OVER TO THE DEMONIC POWER, I COULD END ALL MY SUF-FERING.
THAT'S RIGHT.
I'M THE SAME AS PRINCE DJEM, WHO SECRETLY LONGED FOR THE COMFORTING EMBRACE OF DEATH.
THAT'S WHY I FEARED BEING NEAR HIM.

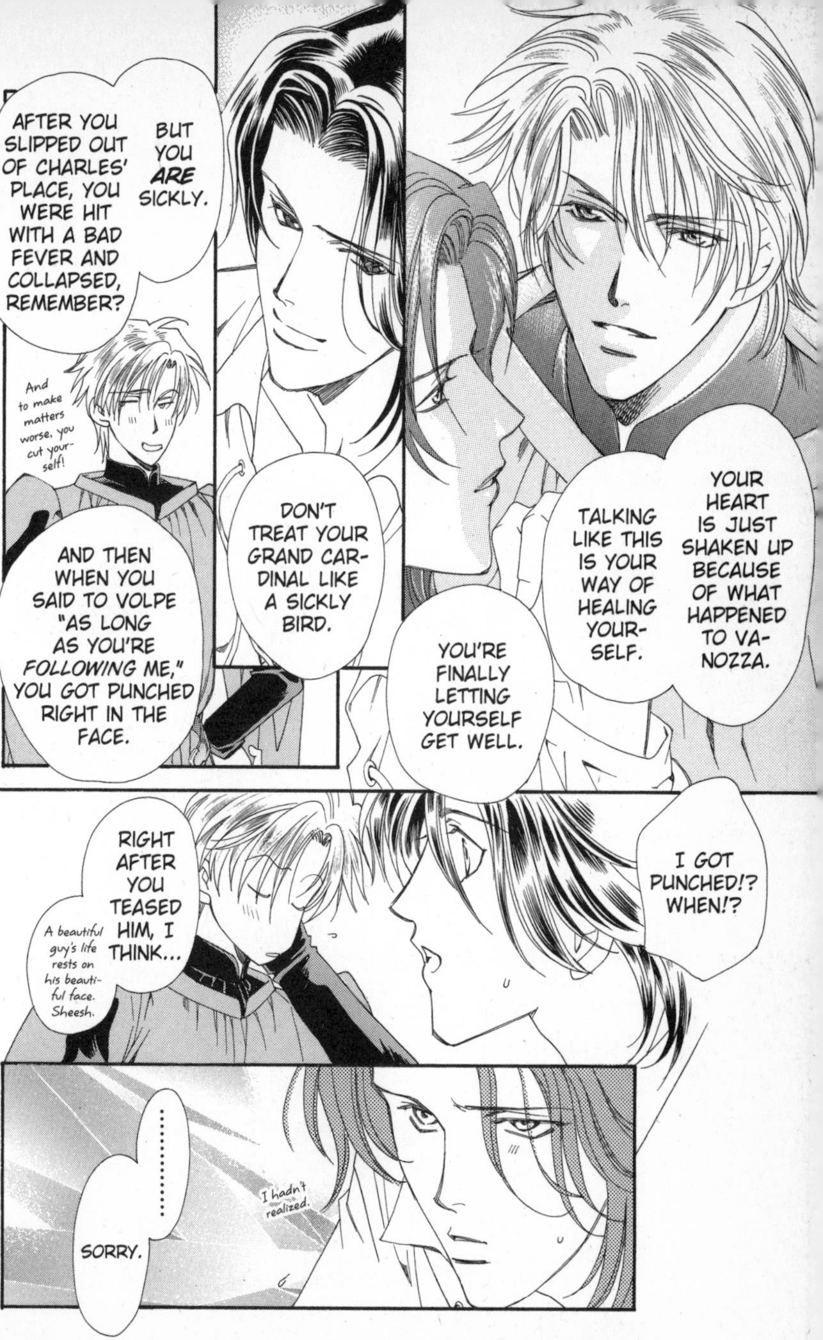

YOUR HEART IS JUST SHAKEN UP BECAUSE OF WHAT HAPPENED TO VA-NOZZA.
TALKING LIKE THIS IS YOUR WAY OF HEALING YOUR-SELF.
YOU'RE FINALLY LETTING YOURSELF GET WELL.
DON'T TREAT YOUR GRAND CAR-DINAL LIKE A SICKLY BIRD.
BUT YOU *ARE* SICKLY.
AFTER YOU SLIPPED OUT OF CHARLES' PLACE, YOU WERE HIT WITH A BAD FEVER AND COLLAPSED, REMEMBER?
And to make matters worse, you cut your-self!
AND THEN WHEN YOU SAID TO VOLPE "AS LONG AS YOU'RE *FOLLOWING ME*," YOU GOT PUNCHED RIGHT IN THE FACE.
I GOT PUNCHED!? WHEN!?
RIGHT AFTER YOU TEASED HIM, I THINK...
A beautiful guy's life rests on his beauti-ful face. Sheesh.
....
I hadn't realized.
SORRY.

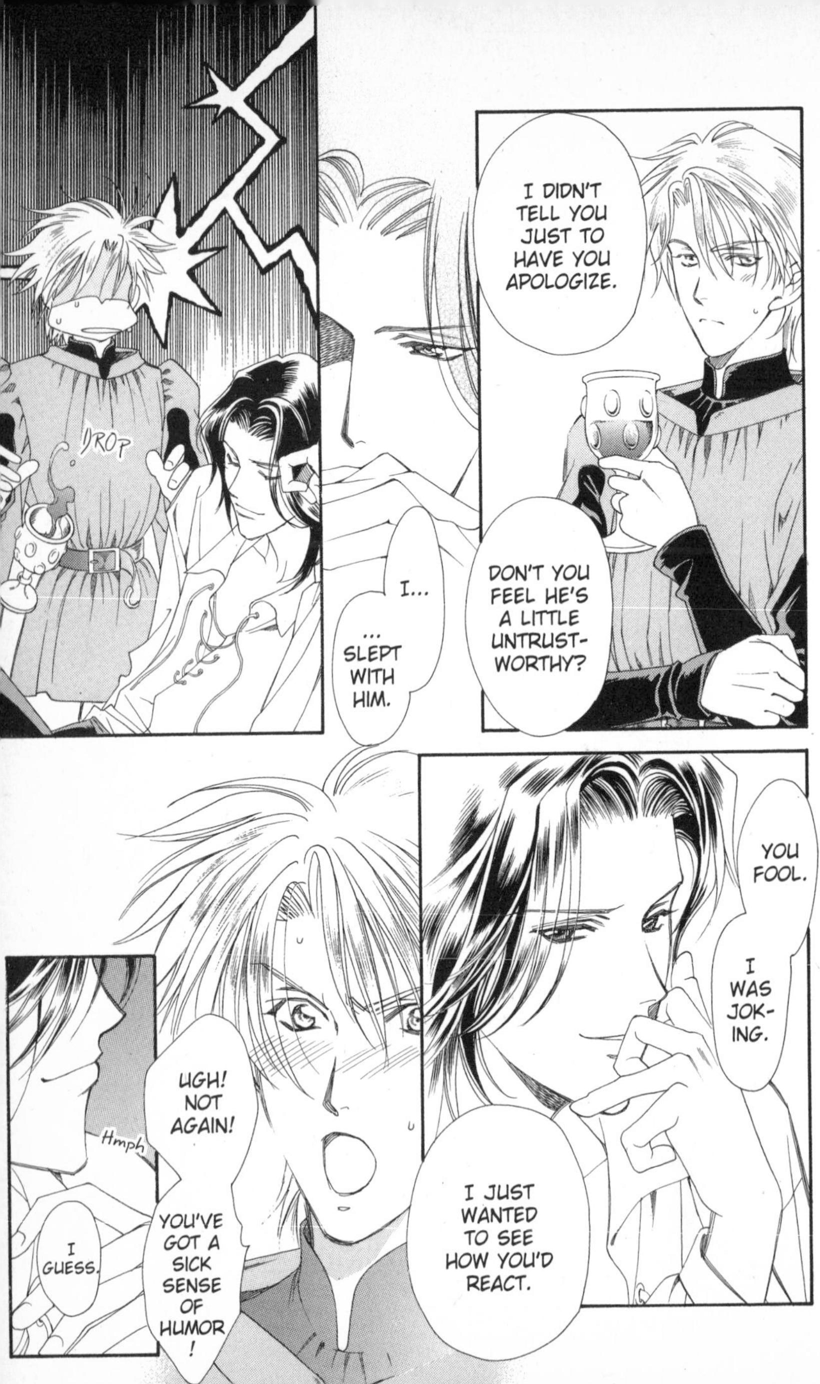
I DIDN'T TELL YOU JUST TO HAVE YOU APOLOGIZE.
DON'T YOU FEEL HE'S A LITTLE UNTRUST-WORTHY?
I...
... SLEPT WITH HIM.
DROP
YOU FOOL.
I WAS JOK-ING.
I JUST WANTED TO SEE HOW YOU'D REACT.
UGH! NOT AGAIN!
YOU'VE GOT A SICK SENSE OF HUMOR!
Hmph
I GUESS.

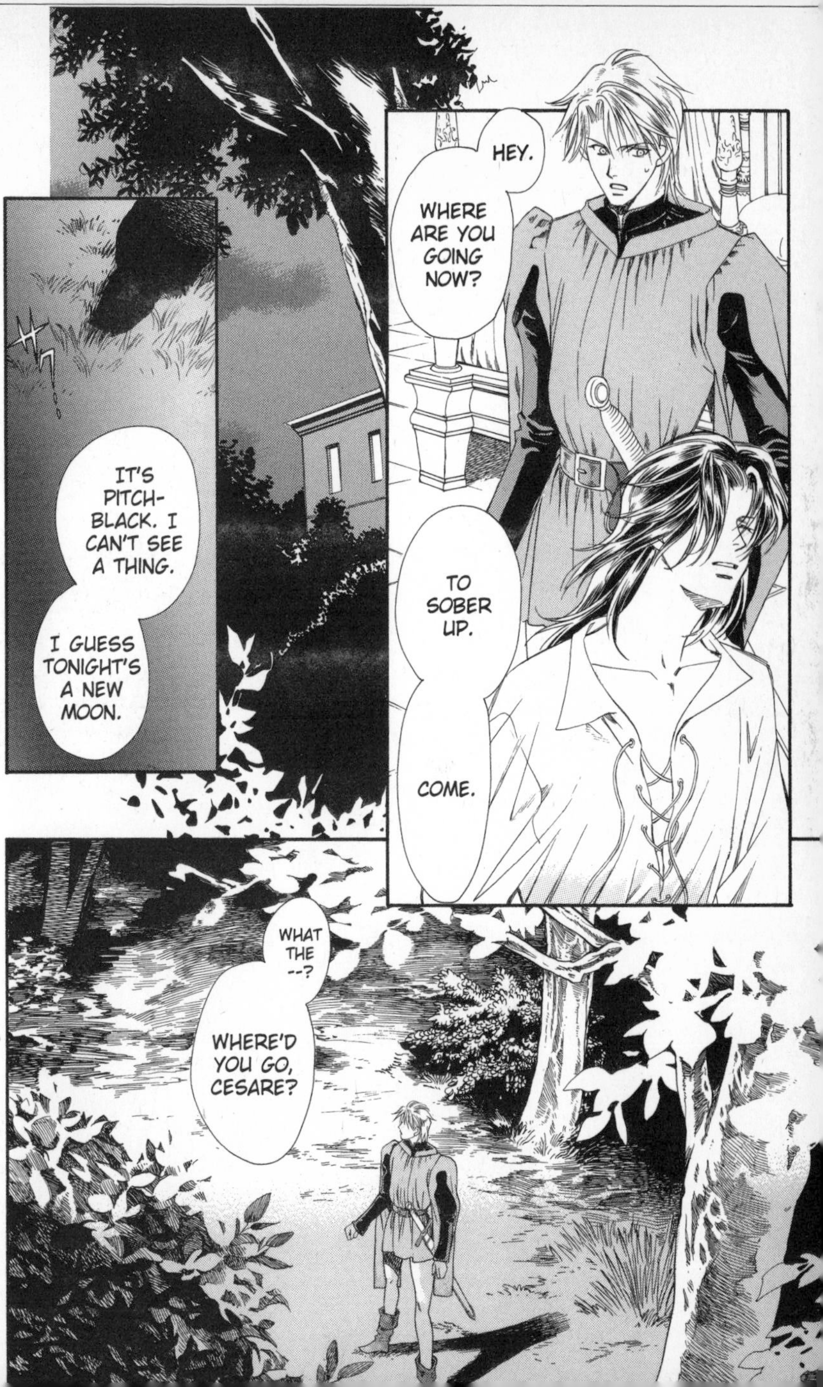
HEY.
WHERE ARE YOU GOING NOW?
TO SOBER UP.
COME.
IT'S PITCH-BLACK. I CAN'T SEE A THING.
I GUESS TONIGHT'S A NEW MOON.
WHAT THE --?
WHERE'D YOU GO, CESARE?

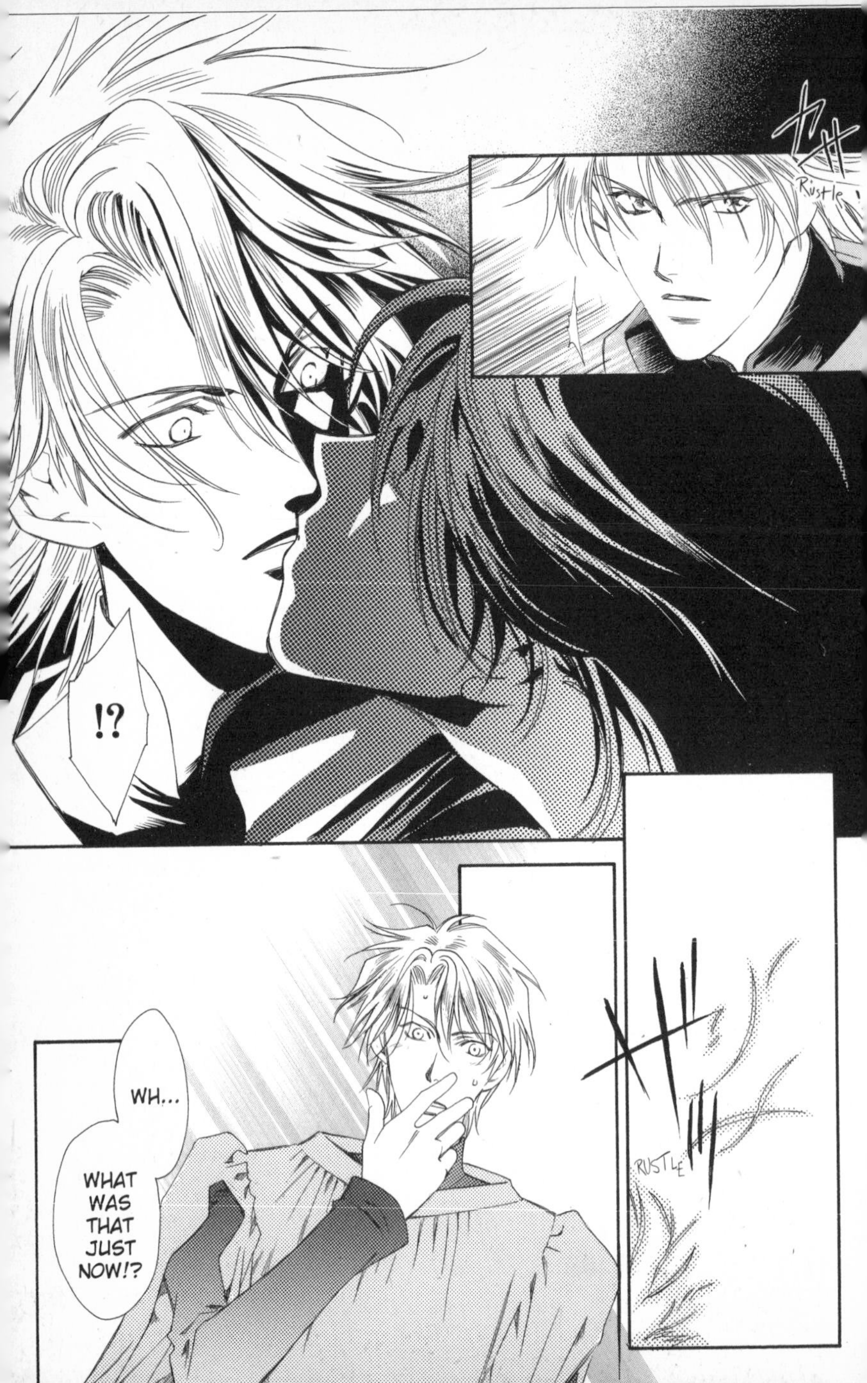
カサ
Rustle!
!?
RUSTLE
WH...
WHAT WAS THAT JUST NOW!?

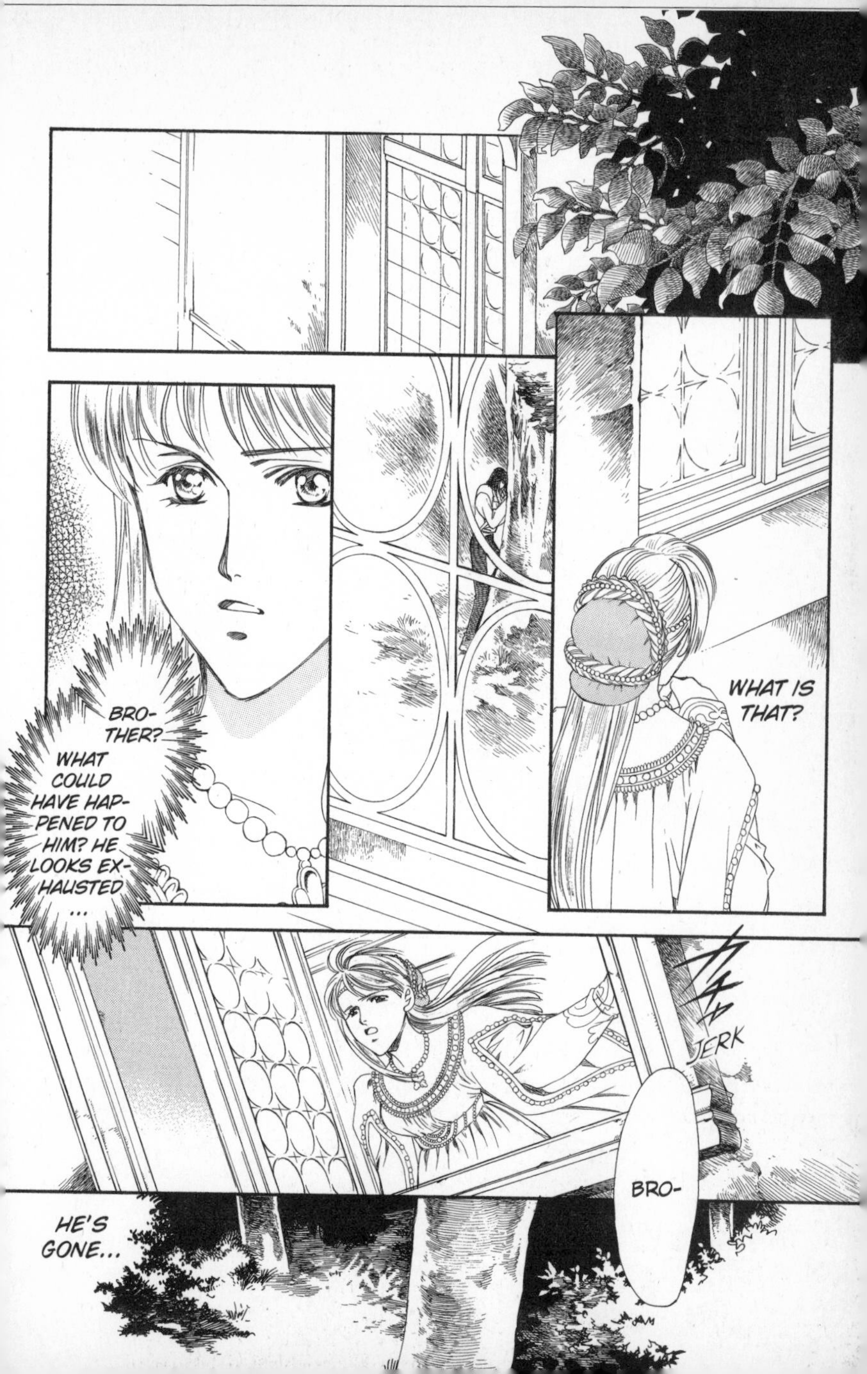
WHAT IS THAT?
BROTHER? WHAT COULD HAVE HAPPENED TO HIM? HE LOOKS EXHAUSTED ...
JERK
BRO-
HE'S GONE...

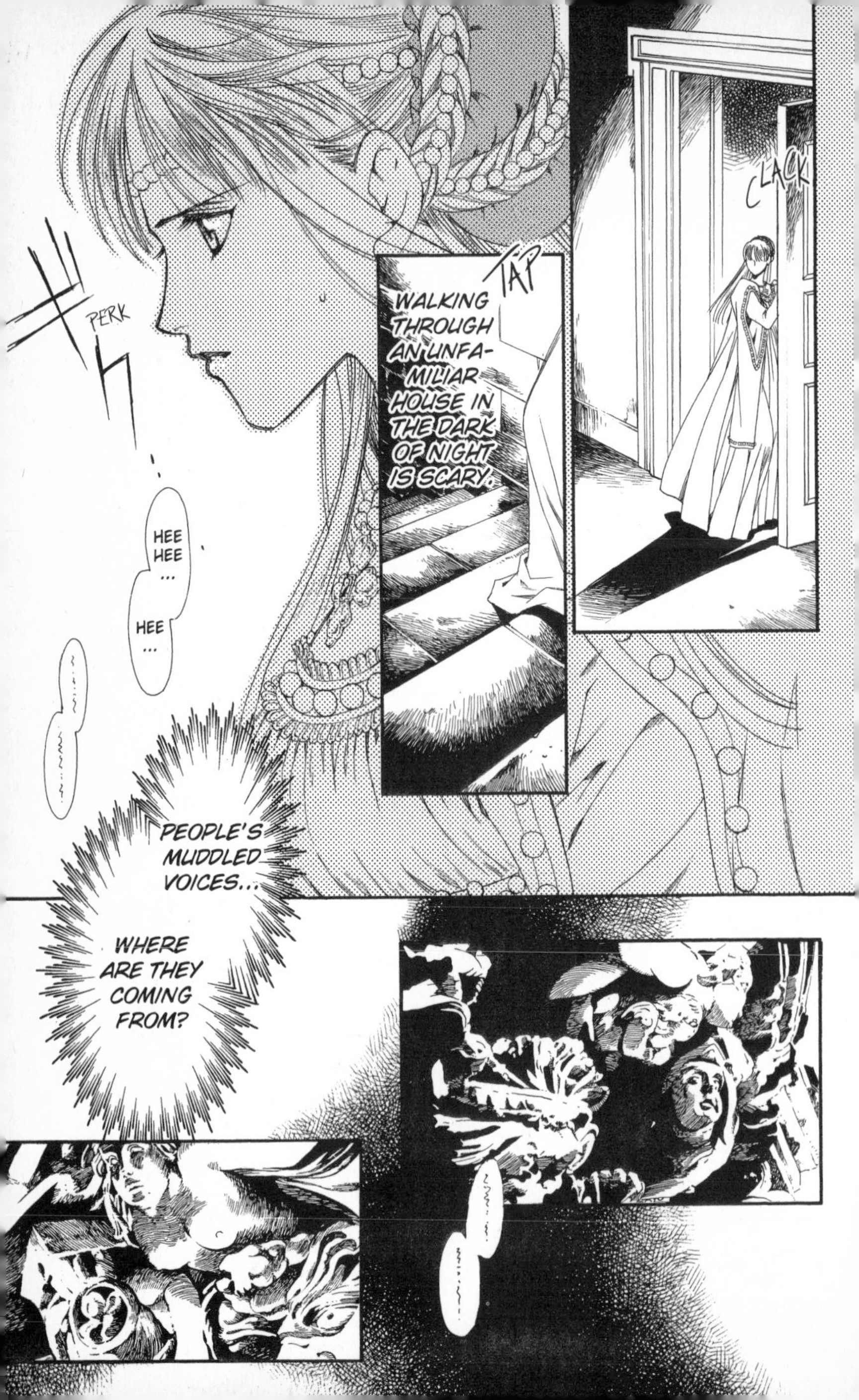
CLACK
TAP
WALKING THROUGH AN UNFAMILIAR HOUSE IN THE DARK OF NIGHT IS SCARY.
PERK
HEE HEE ...
HEE ...
PEOPLE'S MUDDLED VOICES...
WHERE ARE THEY COMING FROM?

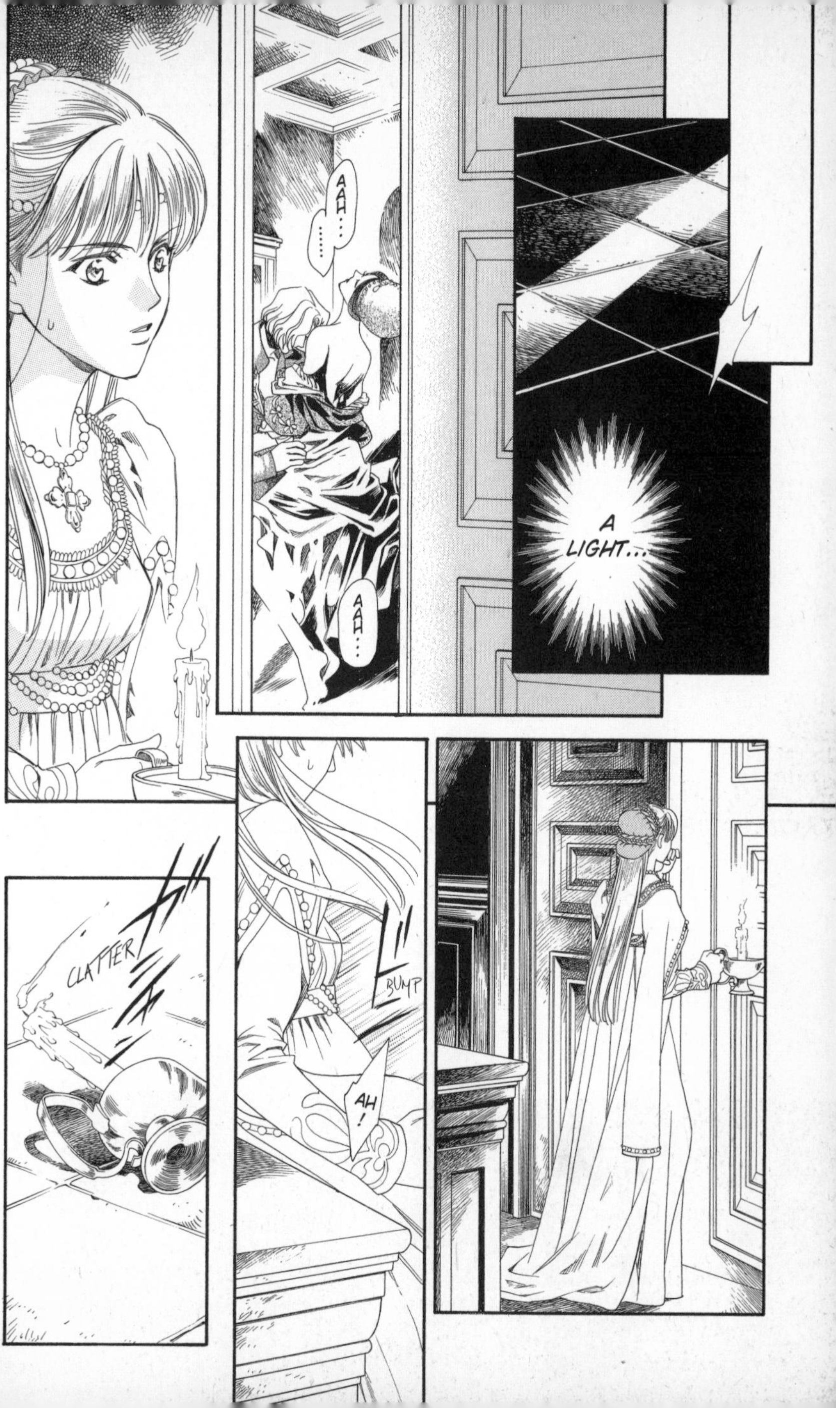
A LIGHT...
AAH... ......
AAH...
BUMP
AH!
CLATTER

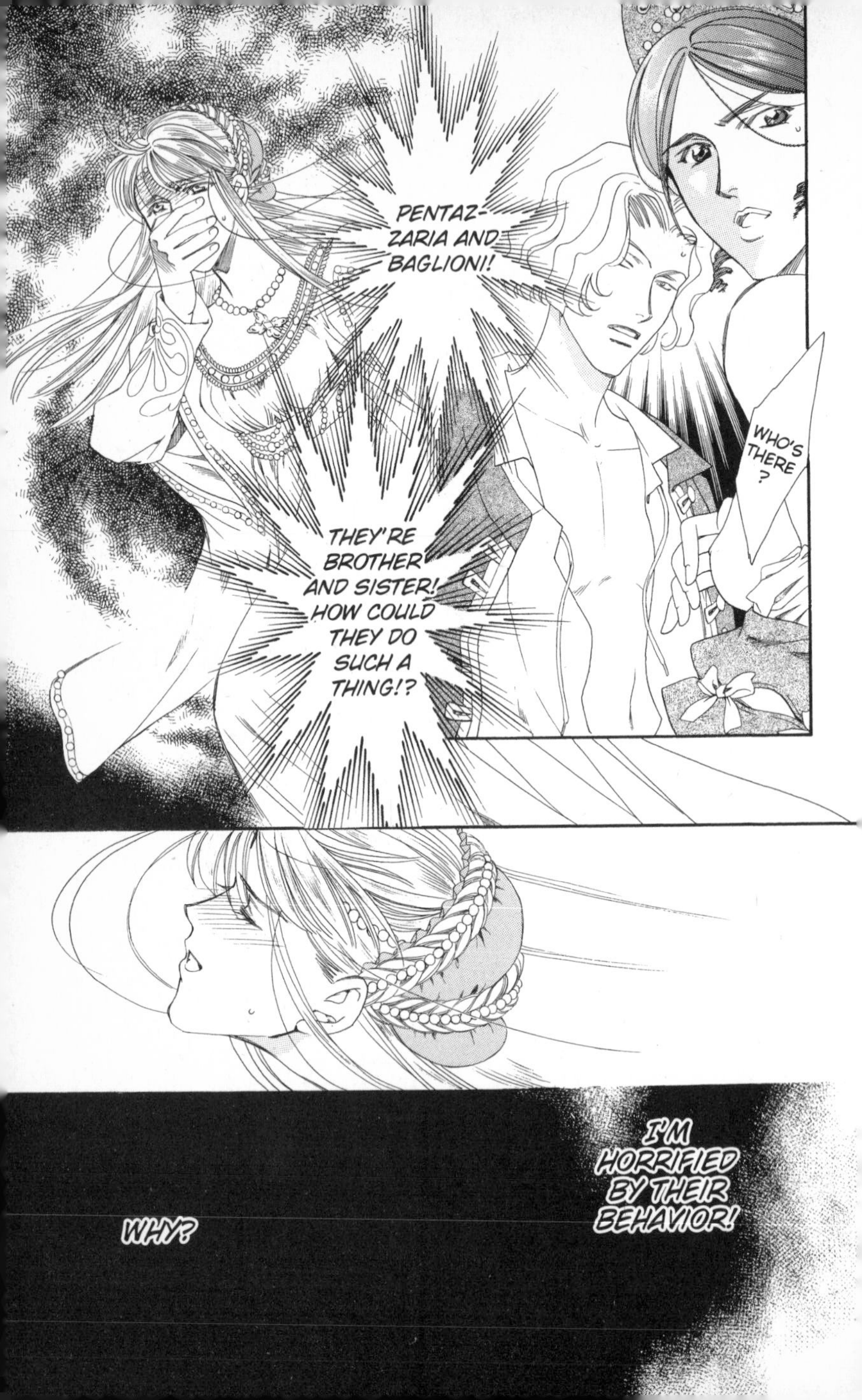
WHO'S THERE?
PENTAZ-ZARIA AND BAGLIONI!
THEY'RE BROTHER AND SISTER! HOW COULD THEY DO SUCH A THING!?
I'M HORRIFIED BY THEIR BEHAVIOR!
WHY?

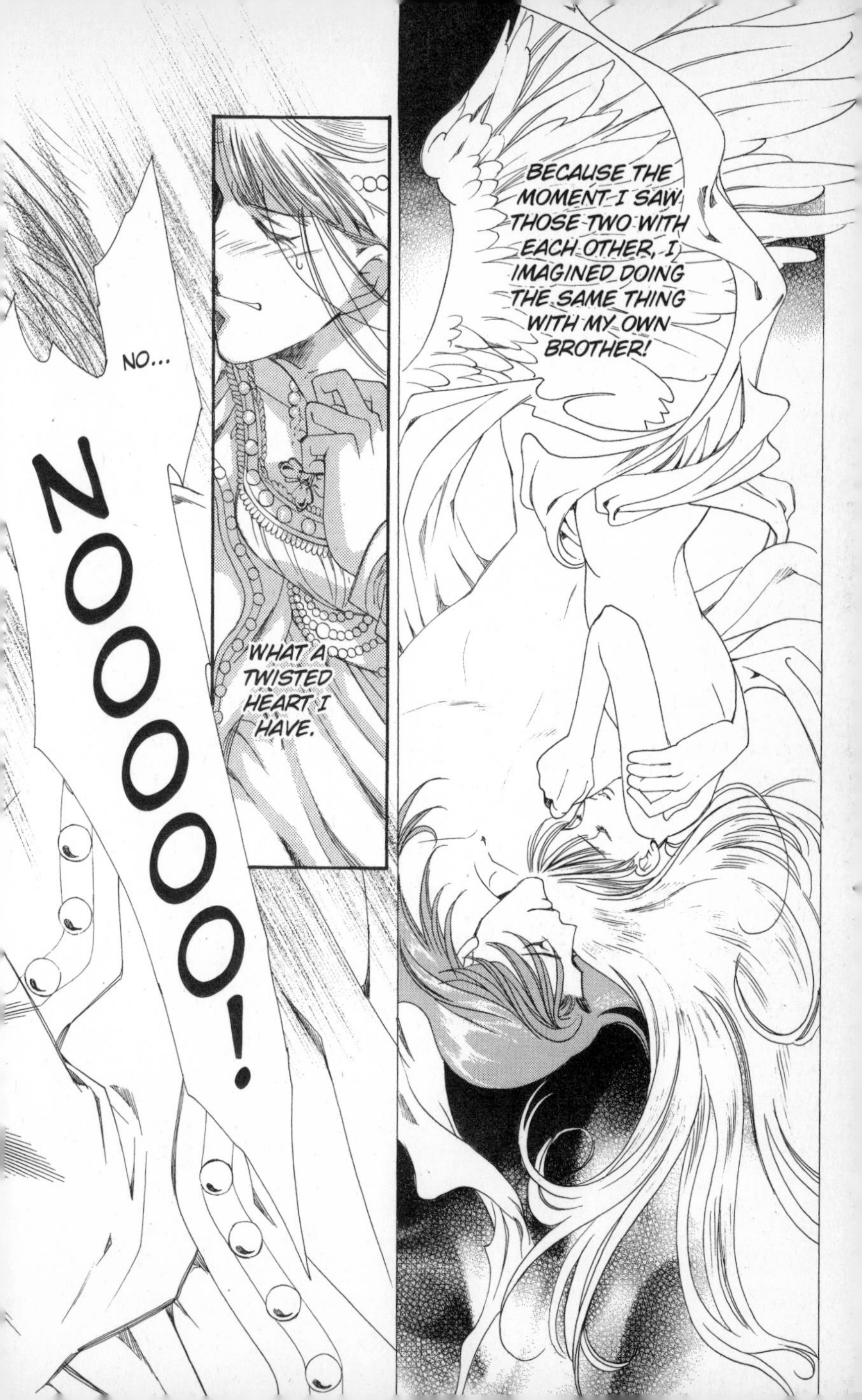
BECAUSE THE MOMENT I SAW THOSE TWO WITH EACH OTHER, I IMAGINED DOING THE SAME THING WITH MY OWN BROTHER!
WHAT A TWISTED HEART I HAVE.
NO...
NOOOOO!

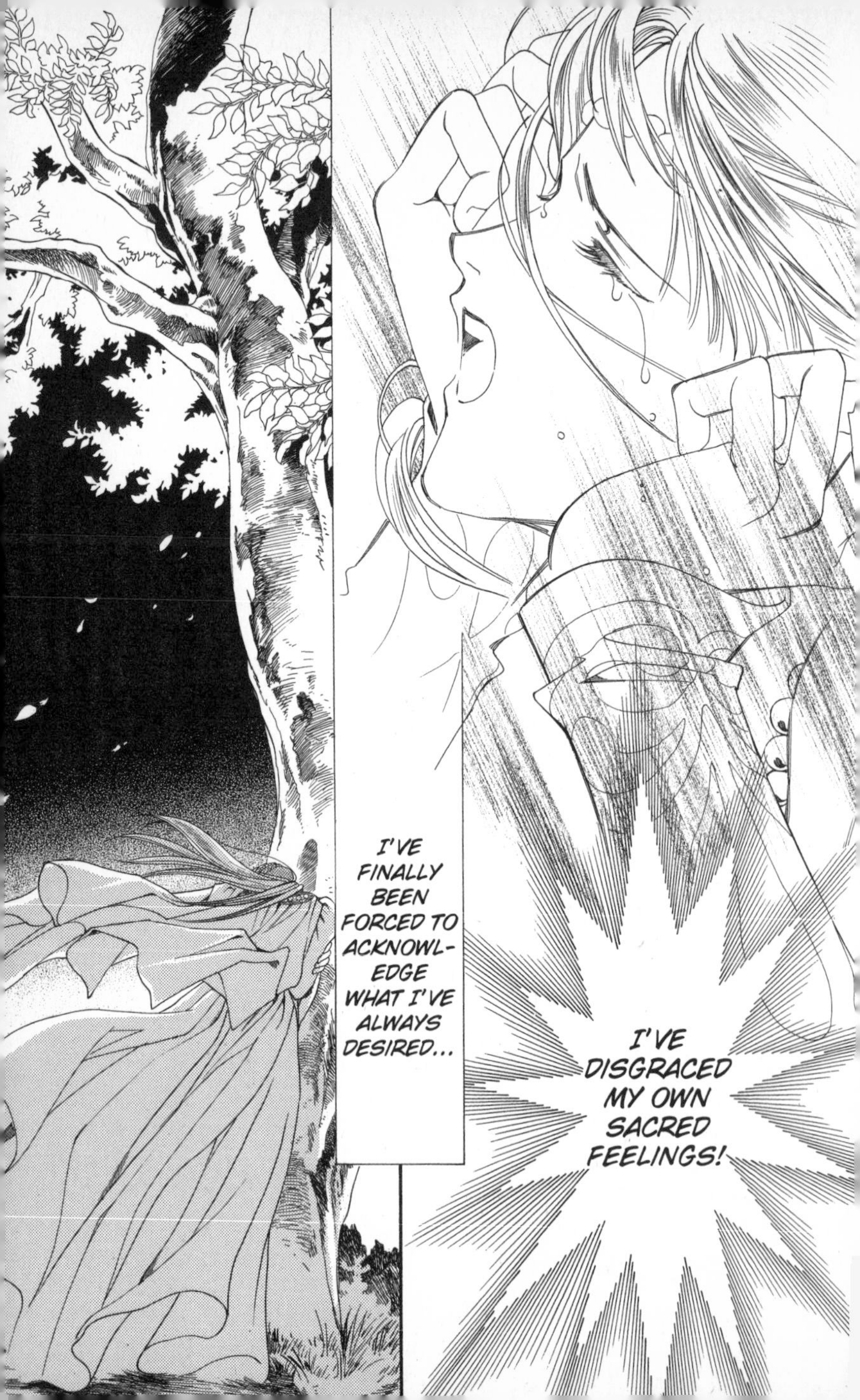
I'VE FINALLY BEEN FORCED TO ACKNOWL-EDGE WHAT I'VE ALWAYS DESIRED...
I'VE DISGRACED MY OWN SACRED FEELINGS!

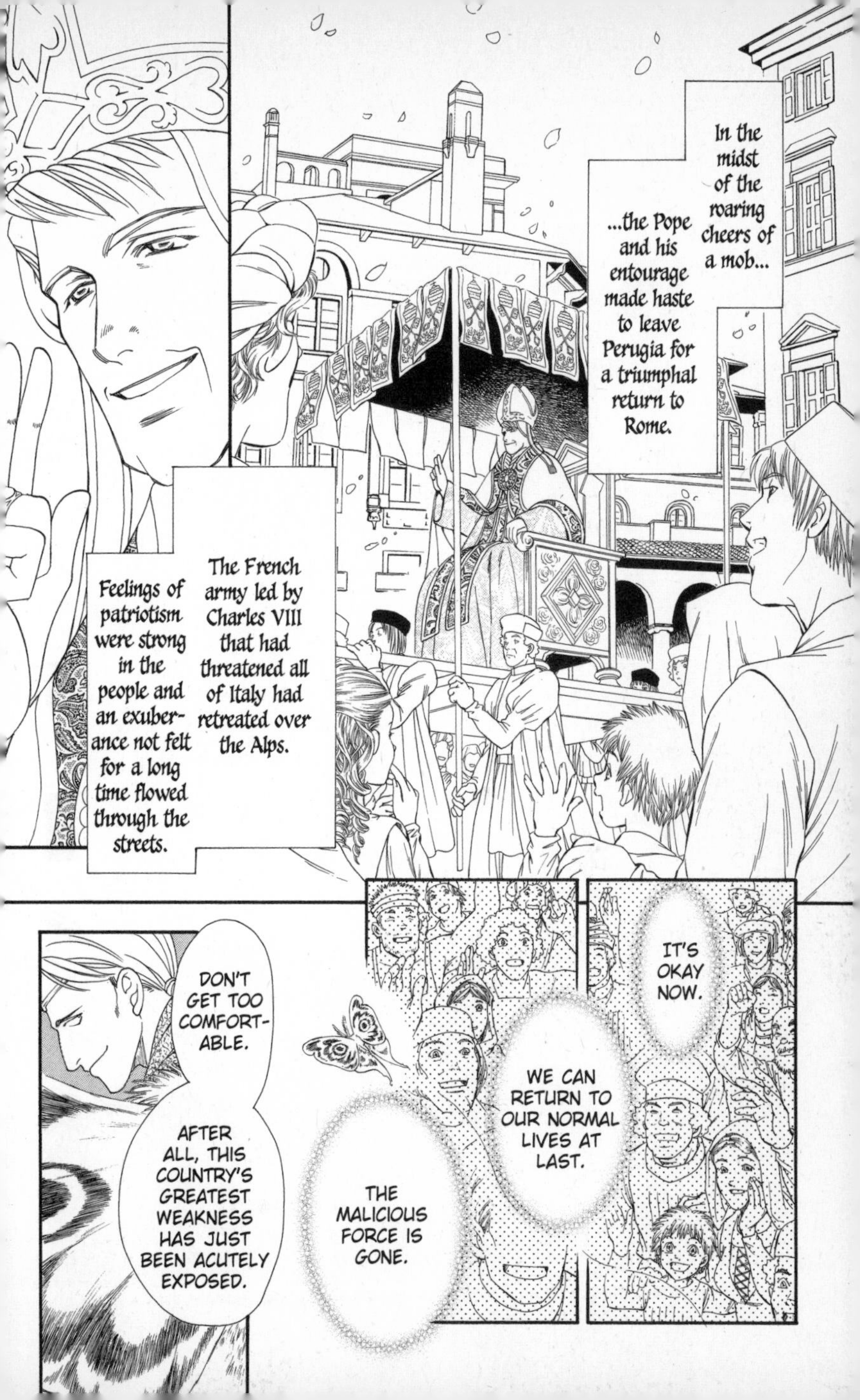
In the midst of the roaring cheers of a mob...
...the Pope and his entourage made haste to leave Perugia for a triumphal return to Rome.
The French army led by Charles VIII that had threatened all of Italy had retreated over the Alps.
Feelings of patriotism were strong in the people and an exuberance not felt for a long time flowed through the streets.
IT'S OKAY NOW.
WE CAN RETURN TO OUR NORMAL LIVES AT LAST.
THE MALICIOUS FORCE IS GONE.
DON'T GET TOO COMFORT-ABLE.
AFTER ALL, THIS COUNTRY'S GREATEST WEAKNESS HAS JUST BEEN ACUTELY EXPOSED.

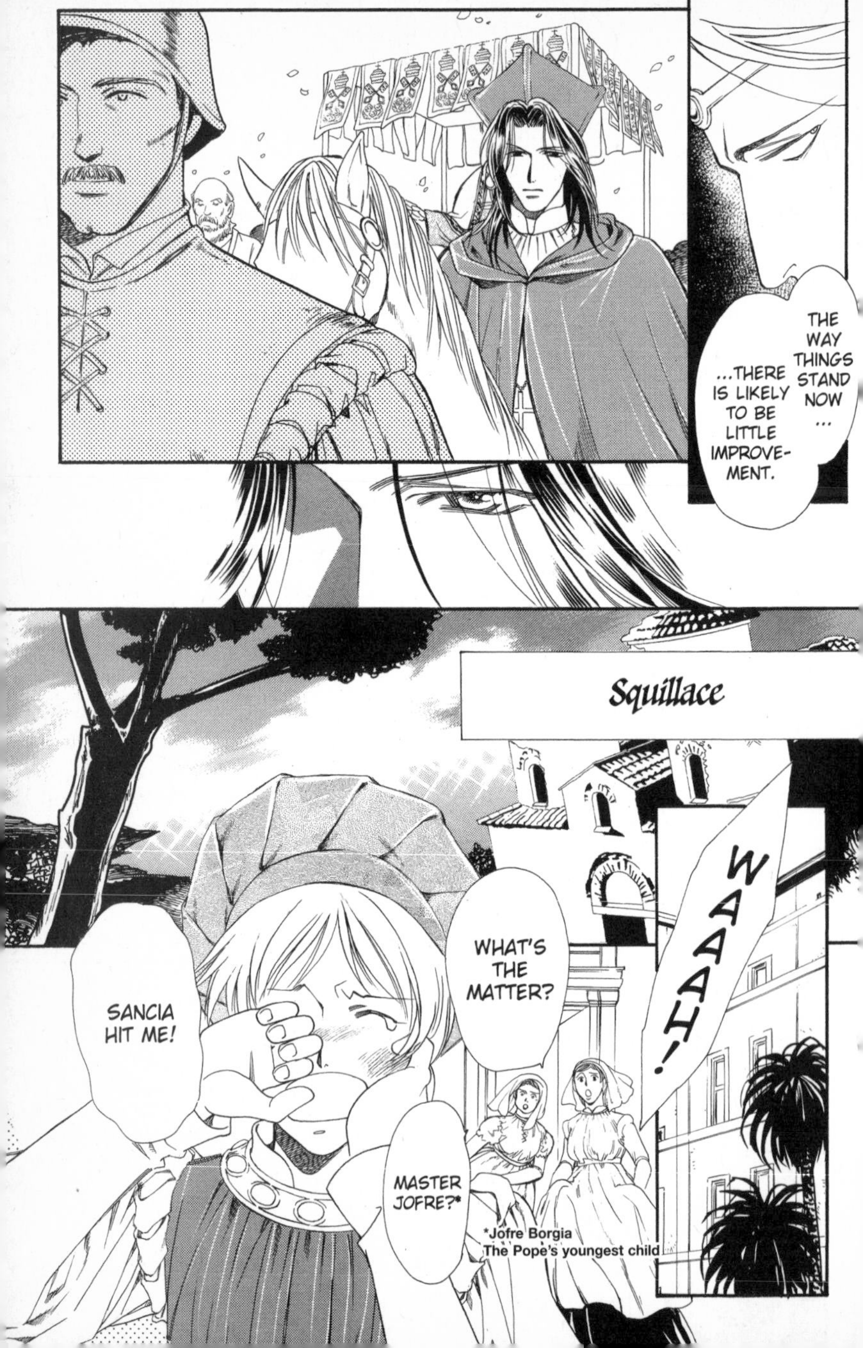
THE WAY THINGS STAND NOW ...
...THERE IS LIKELY TO BE LITTLE IMPROVEMENT.
Squillace
WAAAAH!
WHAT'S THE MATTER?
MASTER JOFRE?*
SANCIA HIT ME!
*Jofre Borgia
The Pope's youngest child

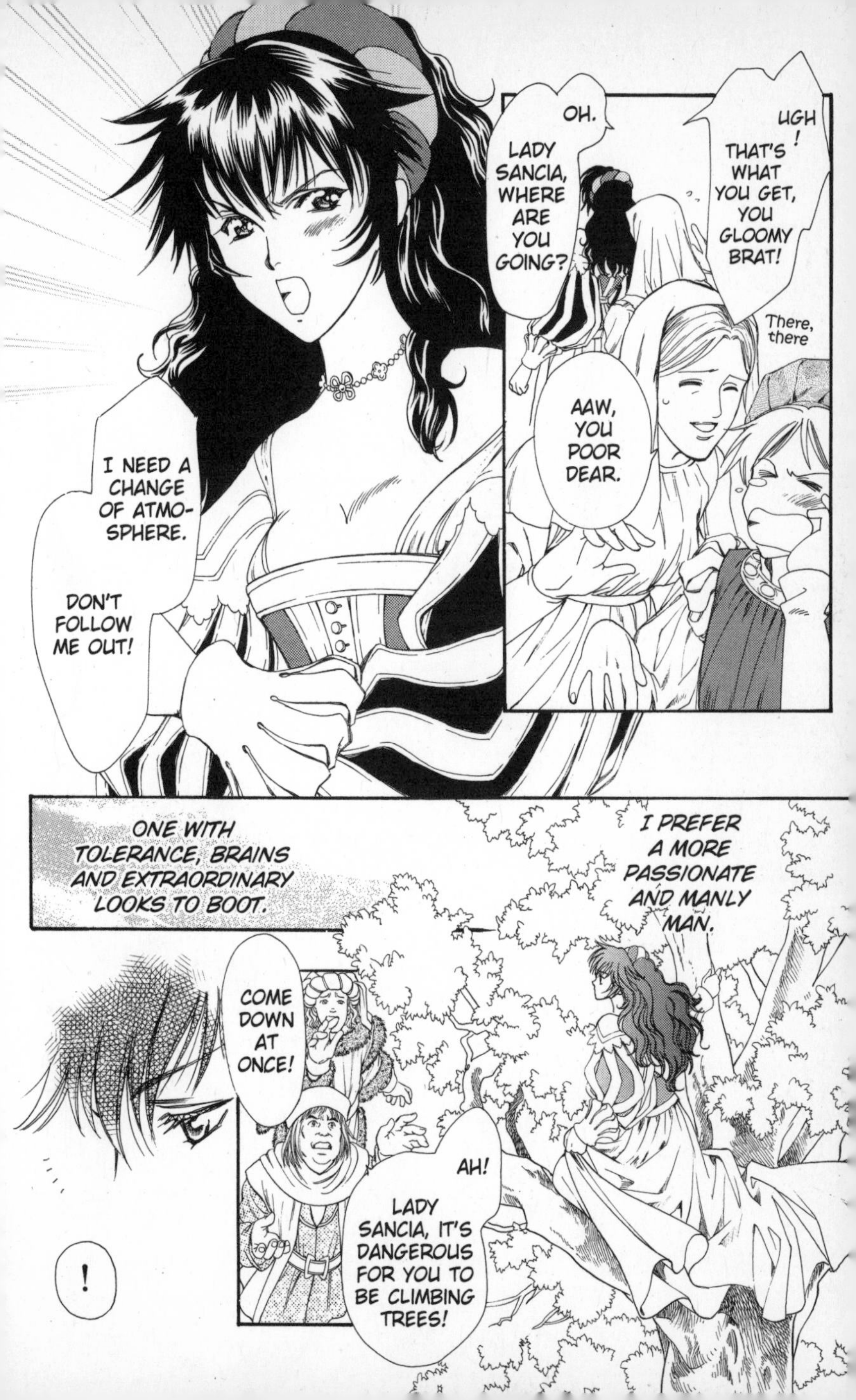

UGH! THAT'S WHAT YOU GET, YOU GLOOMY BRAT!
OH.
LADY SANCIA, WHERE ARE YOU GOING?
There, there
AAW, YOU POOR DEAR.
I NEED A CHANGE OF ATMO-SPHERE.
DON'T FOLLOW ME OUT!
ONE WITH TOLERANCE, BRAINS AND EXTRAORDINARY LOOKS TO BOOT.
I PREFER A MORE PASSIONATE AND MANLY MAN.
COME DOWN AT ONCE!
AH!
LADY SANCIA, IT'S DANGEROUS FOR YOU TO BE CLIMBING TREES!
!

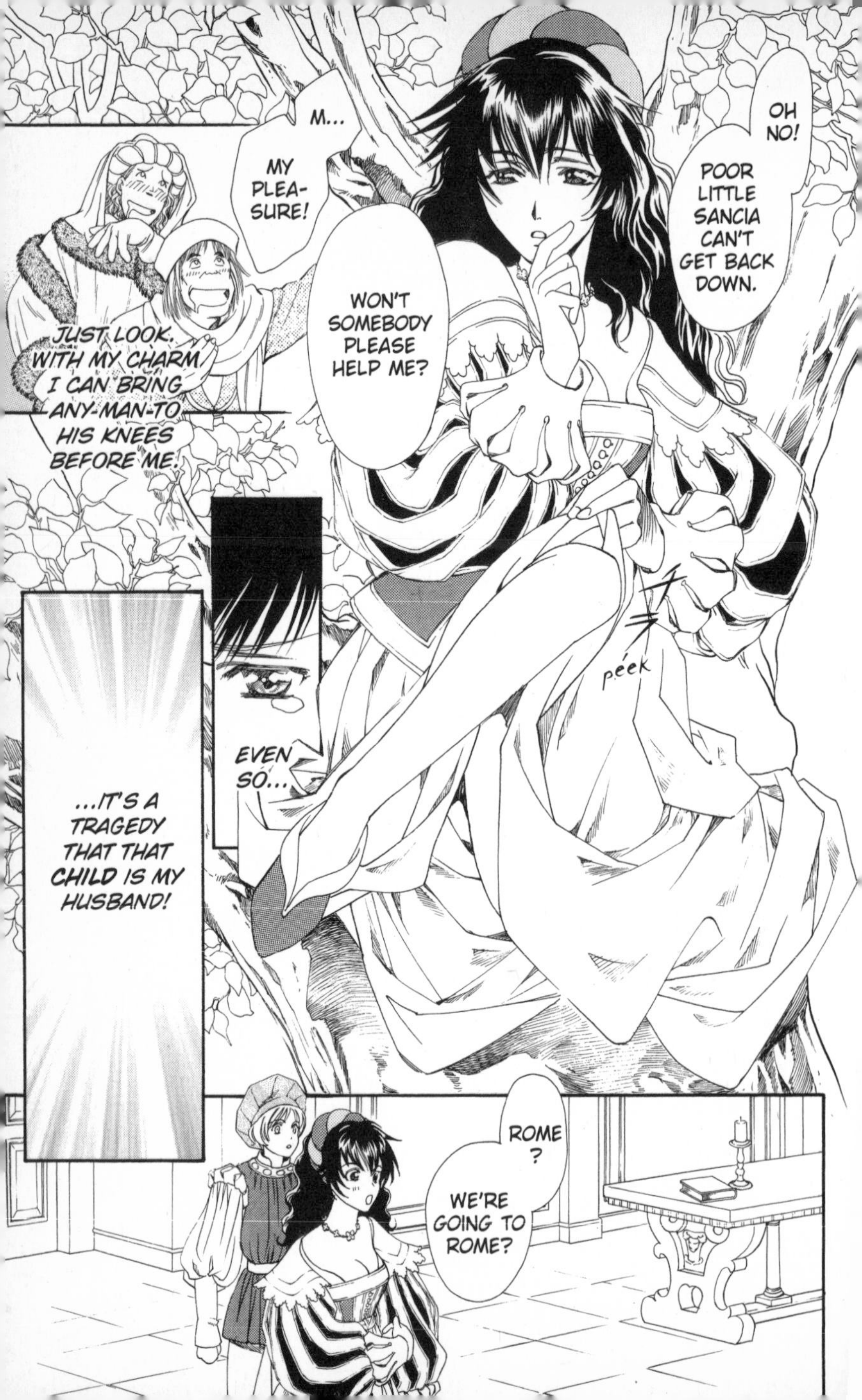
OH NO!
POOR LITTLE SANCIA CAN'T GET BACK DOWN.
WON'T SOMEBODY PLEASE HELP ME?
M...
MY PLEASURE!
JUST LOOK. WITH MY CHARM I CAN BRING ANY MAN TO HIS KNEES BEFORE ME.
peek
EVEN SO...
...IT'S A TRAGEDY THAT THAT CHILD IS MY HUSBAND!
ROME?
WE'RE GOING TO ROME?

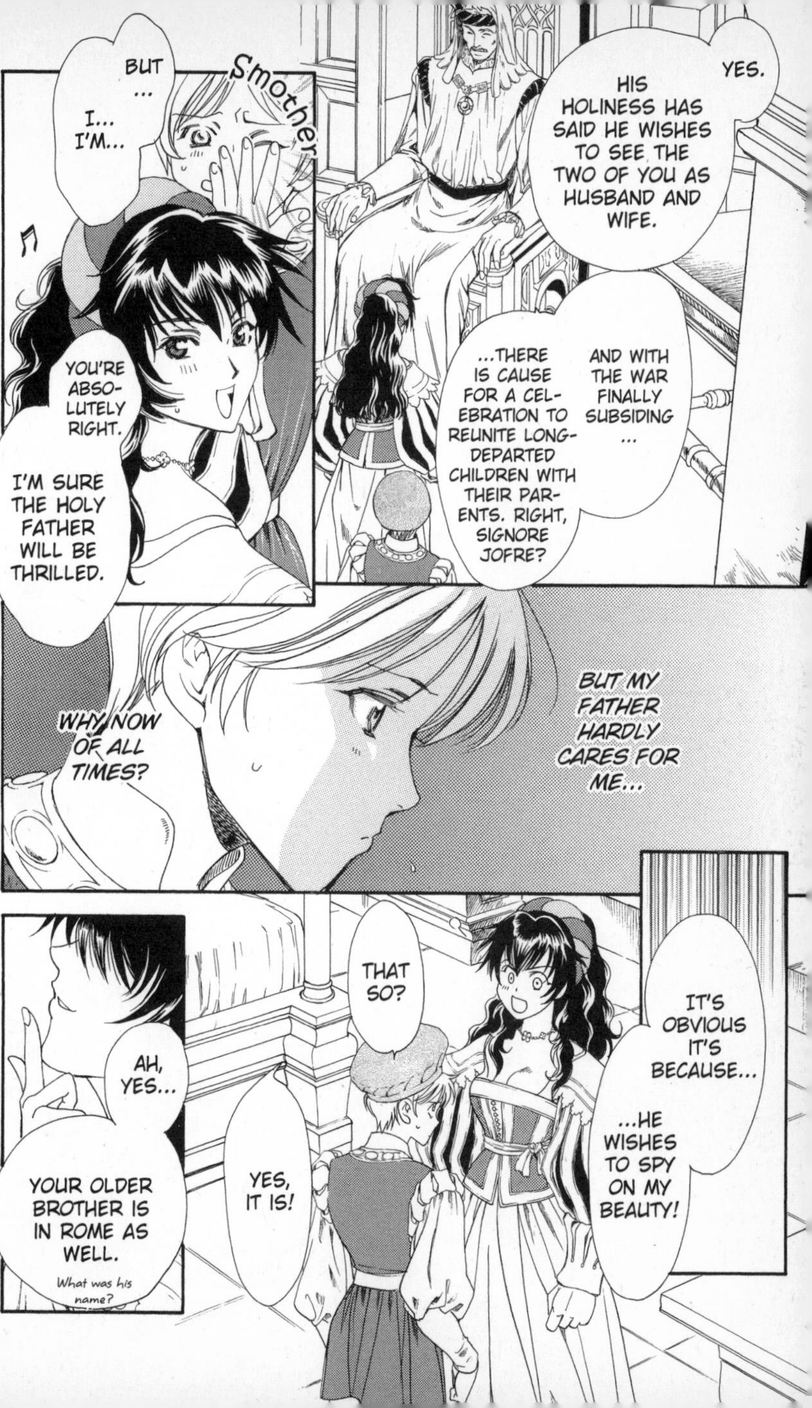
YES.
HIS HOLINESS HAS SAID HE WISHES TO SEE THE TWO OF YOU AS HUSBAND AND WIFE.
AND WITH THE WAR FINALLY SUBSIDING...
...THERE IS CAUSE FOR A CEL-EBRATION TO REUNITE LONG-DEPARTED CHILDREN WITH THEIR PAR-ENTS. RIGHT, SIGNORE JOFRE?
BUT ...
I... I'M...
Smother
YOU'RE ABSO-LUTELY RIGHT.
I'M SURE THE HOLY FATHER WILL BE THRILLED.
BUT MY FATHER HARDLY CARES FOR ME...
WHY NOW OF ALL TIMES?
IT'S OBVIOUS IT'S BECAUSE...
...HE WISHES TO SPY ON MY BEAUTY!
THAT SO?
YES, IT IS!
AH, YES...
YOUR OLDER BROTHER IS IN ROME AS WELL.
What was his name?

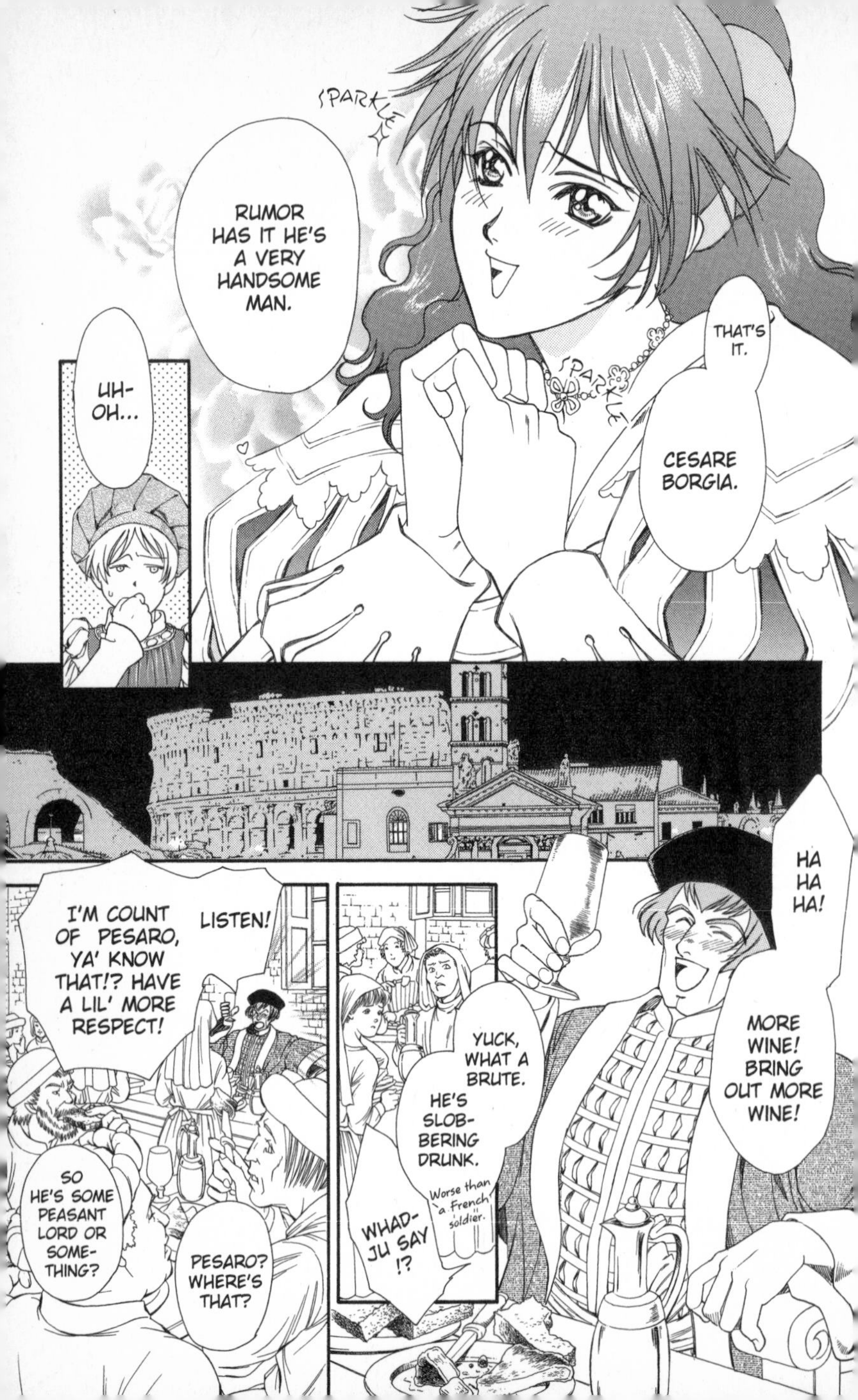
SPARKLE
THAT'S IT.
SPARKLE
CESARE BORGIA.
RUMOR HAS IT HE'S A VERY HANDSOME MAN.
UH-OH...
HA HA HA!
MORE WINE! BRING OUT MORE WINE!
YUCK, WHAT A BRUTE.
HE'S SLOB-BERING DRUNK.
Worse than a French soldier.
WHAD-JU SAY !?
LISTEN!
I'M COUNT OF PESARO, YA' KNOW THAT!? HAVE A LIL' MORE RESPECT!
SO HE'S SOME PEASANT LORD OR SOME-THING?
PESARO? WHERE'S THAT?

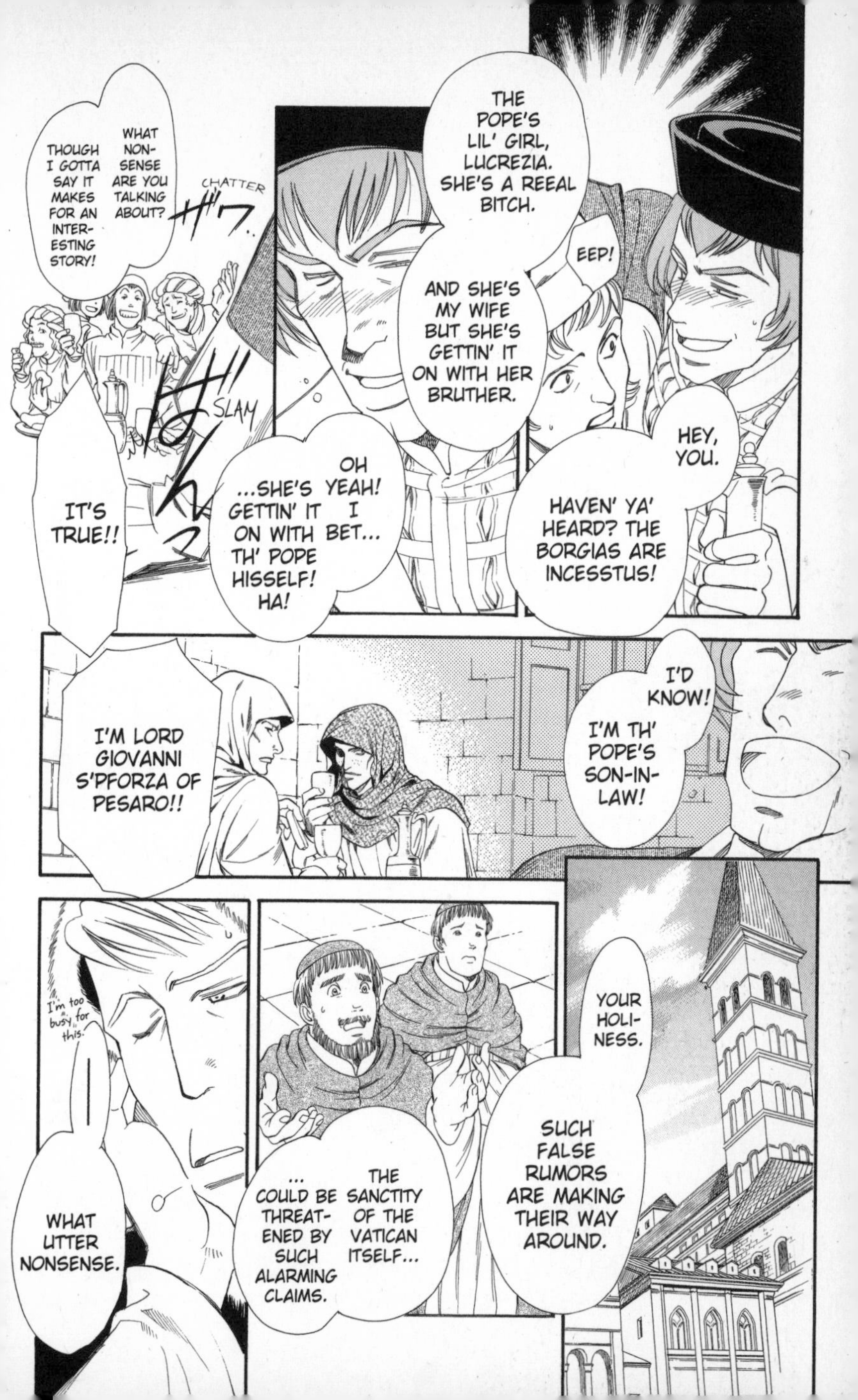
HEY, YOU.
HAVEN' YA' HEARD? THE BORGIAS ARE INCESSTUS!
THE POPE'S LIL' GIRL, LUCREZIA. SHE'S A REEAL BITCH.
EEP!
AND SHE'S MY WIFE BUT SHE'S GETTIN' IT ON WITH HER BRUTHER.
OH YEAH! I BET...
...SHE'S GETTIN' IT ON WITH TH' POPE HISSELF! HA!
WHAT NON-SENSE ARE YOU TALKING ABOUT?
THOUGH I GOTTA SAY IT MAKES FOR AN INTER-ESTING STORY!
CHATTER
SLAM
IT'S TRUE!!
I'D KNOW!
I'M TH' POPE'S SON-IN-LAW!
I'M LORD GIOVANNI S'PFORZA OF PESARO!!
YOUR HOLI-NESS.
SUCH FALSE RUMORS ARE MAKING THEIR WAY AROUND.
THE SANCTITY OF THE VATICAN ITSELF...
...COULD BE THREAT-ENED BY SUCH ALARMING CLAIMS.
I'm too busy for this.
WHAT UTTER NONSENSE.

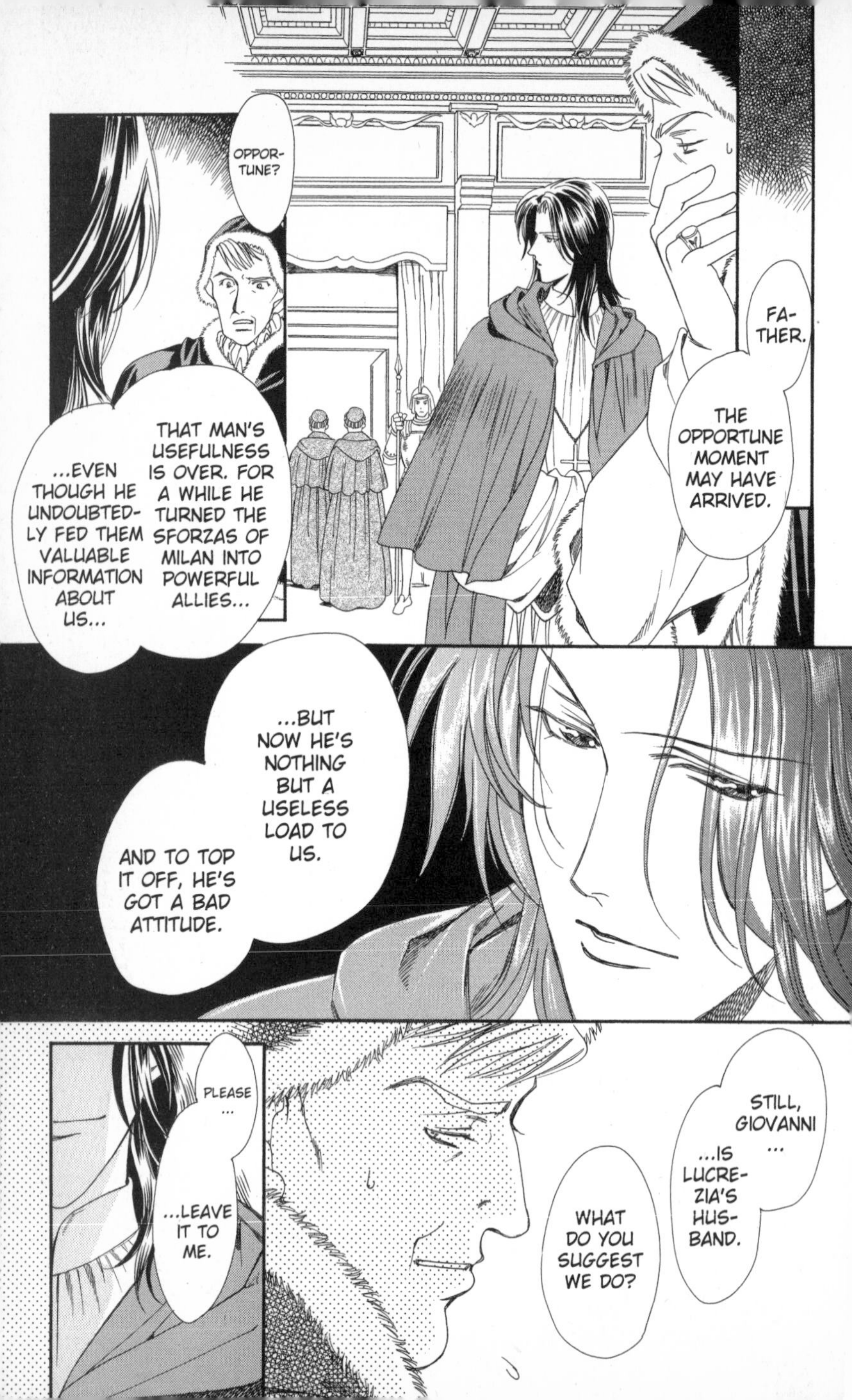
FATHER.
THE OPPORTUNE MOMENT MAY HAVE ARRIVED.
OPPORTUNE?
THAT MAN'S USEFULNESS IS OVER. FOR A WHILE HE TURNED THE SFORZAS OF MILAN INTO POWERFUL ALLIES...
...EVEN THOUGH HE UNDOUBTEDLY FED THEM VALUABLE INFORMATION ABOUT US...
...BUT NOW HE'S NOTHING BUT A USELESS LOAD TO US.
AND TO TOP IT OFF, HE'S GOT A BAD ATTITUDE.
STILL, GIOVANNI...
...IS LUCREZIA'S HUSBAND.
WHAT DO YOU SUGGEST WE DO?
PLEASE...
...LEAVE IT TO ME.

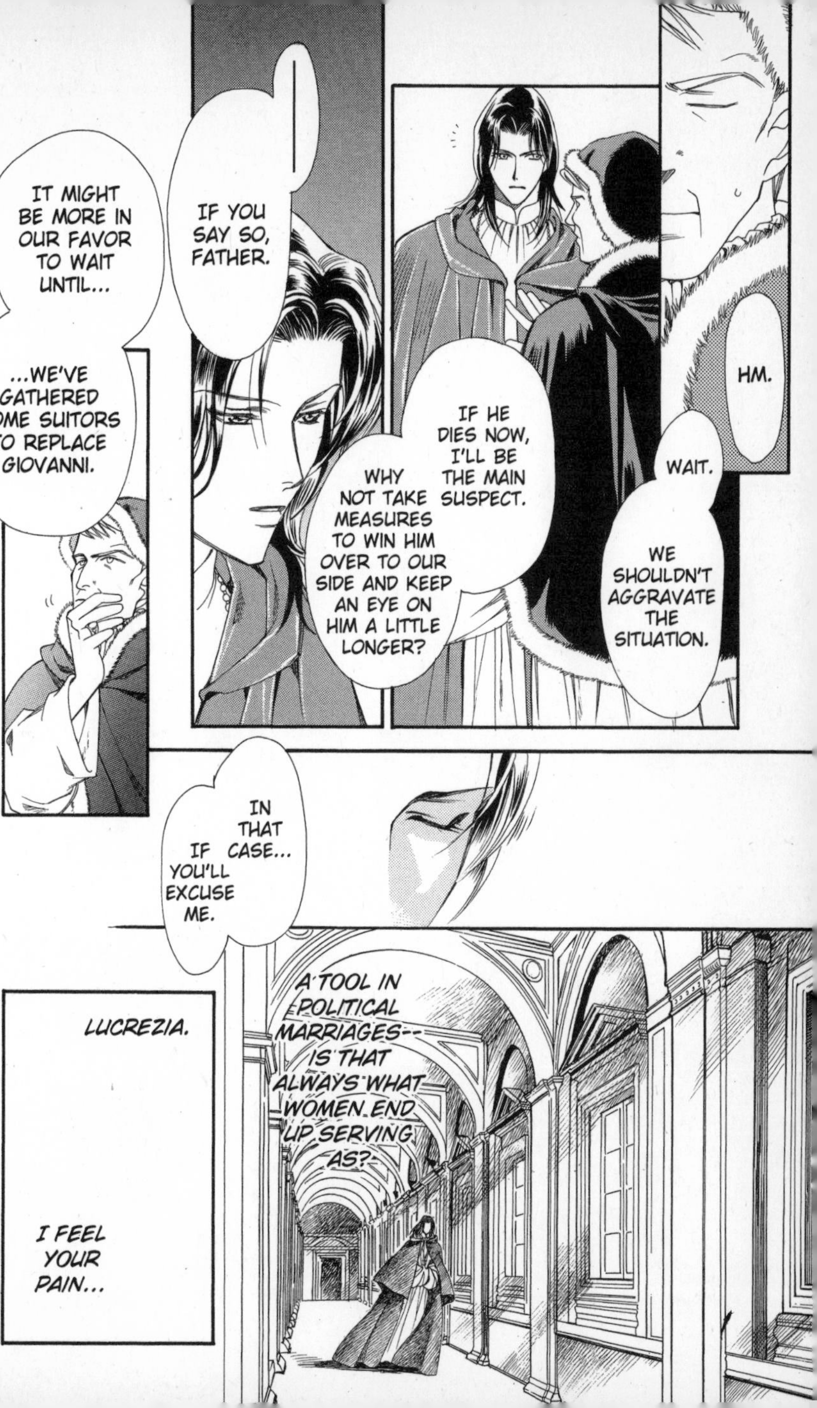
HM.
WAIT.
WE SHOULDN'T AGGRAVATE THE SITUATION.
IF HE DIES NOW, I'LL BE THE MAIN SUSPECT.
WHY NOT TAKE MEASURES TO WIN HIM OVER TO OUR SIDE AND KEEP AN EYE ON HIM A LITTLE LONGER?
IF YOU SAY SO, FATHER.
IT MIGHT BE MORE IN OUR FAVOR TO WAIT UNTIL...
...WE'VE GATHERED SOME SUITORS TO REPLACE GIOVANNI.
IN THAT CASE... IF YOU'LL EXCUSE ME.
A TOOL IN POLITICAL MARRIAGES-- IS THAT ALWAYS WHAT WOMEN END UP SERVING AS?
LUCREZIA.
I FEEL YOUR PAIN...

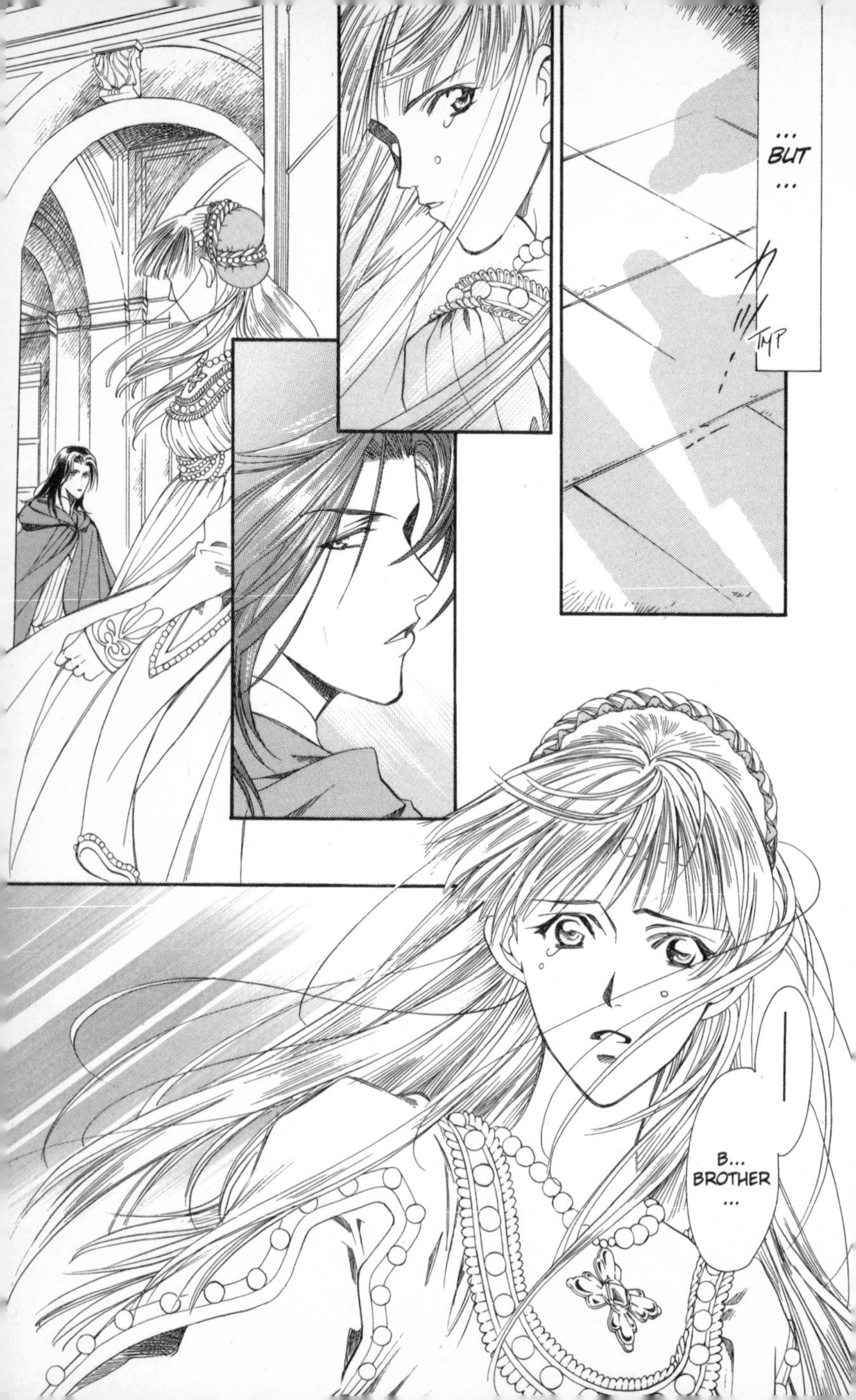
...BUT...
TMP
B... BROTHER...

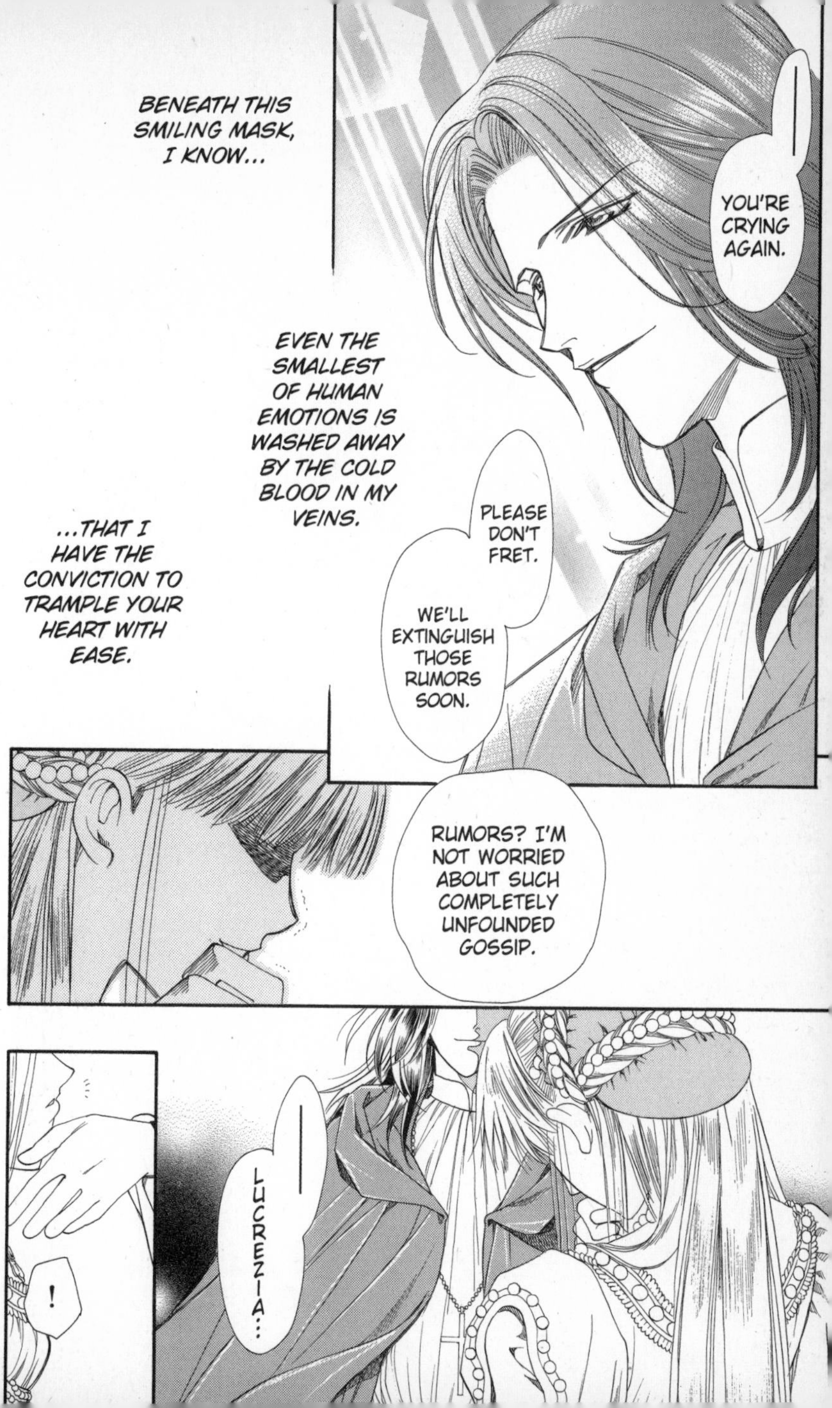
—
YOU'RE CRYING AGAIN.
BENEATH THIS SMILING MASK, I KNOW...
EVEN THE SMALLEST OF HUMAN EMOTIONS IS WASHED AWAY BY THE COLD BLOOD IN MY VEINS.
PLEASE DON'T FRET.
WE'LL EXTINGUISH THOSE RUMORS SOON.
...THAT I HAVE THE CONVICTION TO TRAMPLE YOUR HEART WITH EASE.
RUMORS? I'M NOT WORRIED ABOUT SUCH COMPLETELY UNFOUNDED GOSSIP.
— LUCREZIA...
!

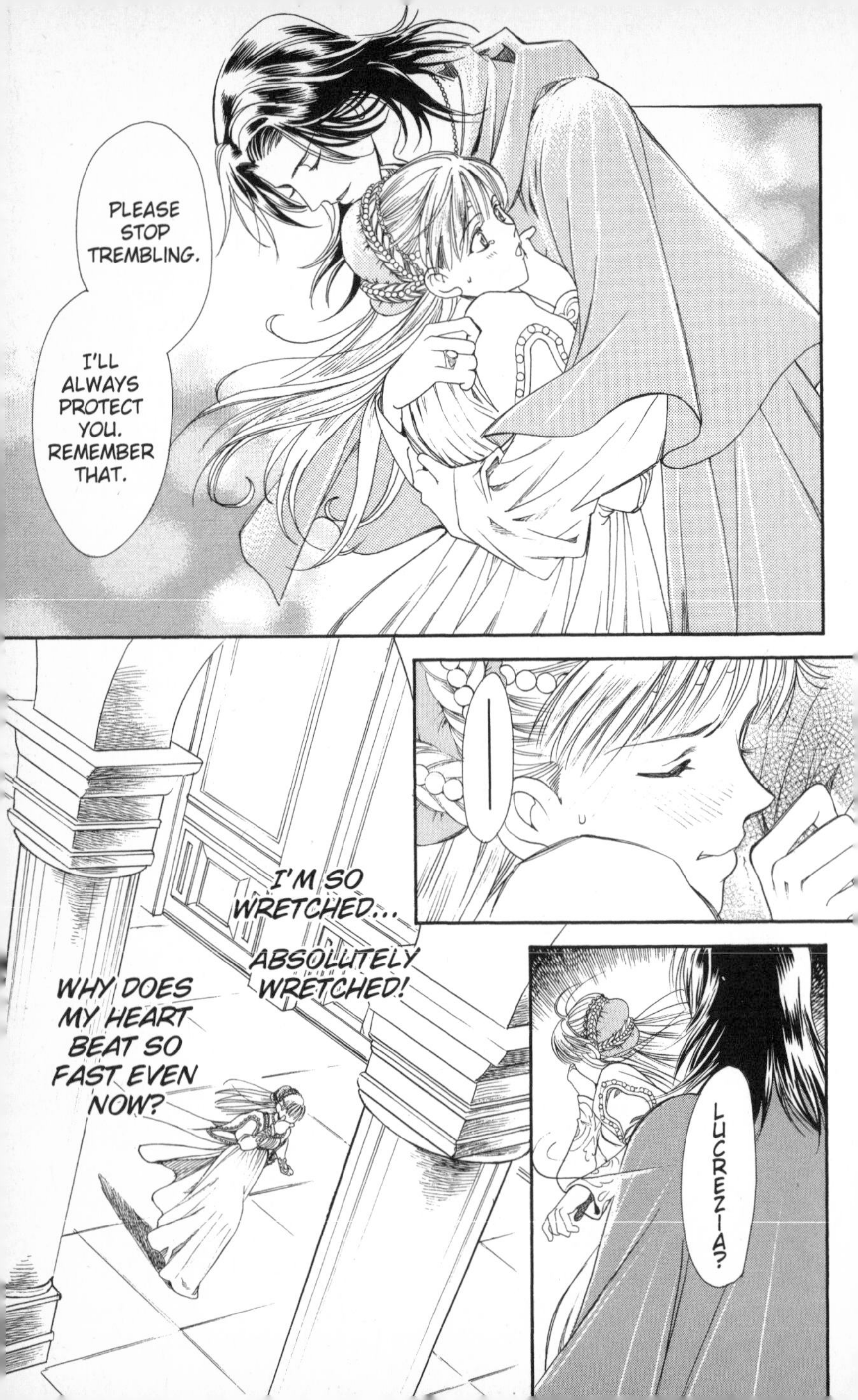
PLEASE STOP TREMBLING.
I'LL ALWAYS PROTECT YOU. REMEMBER THAT.
!
LUCREZIA?
I'M SO WRETCHED...
ABSOLUTELY WRETCHED!
WHY DOES MY HEART BEAT SO FAST EVEN NOW?

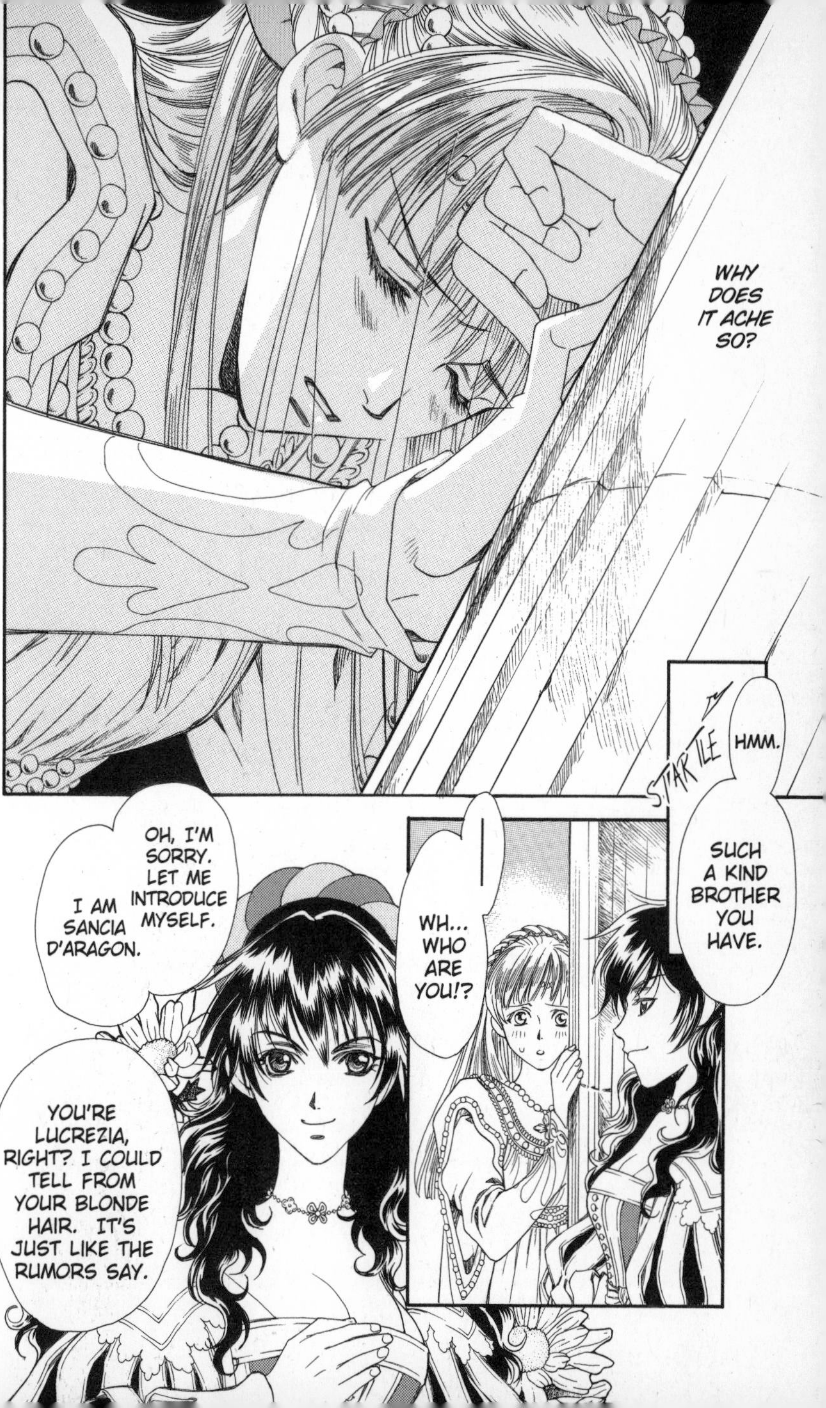
WHY DOES IT ACHE SO?
HMM.
SUCH A KIND BROTHER YOU HAVE.
STARTLE
!
WH... WHO ARE YOU!?
OH, I'M SORRY. LET ME INTRODUCE MYSELF.
I AM SANCIA D'ARAGON.
YOU'RE LUCREZIA, RIGHT? I COULD TELL FROM YOUR BLONDE HAIR. IT'S JUST LIKE THE RUMORS SAY.

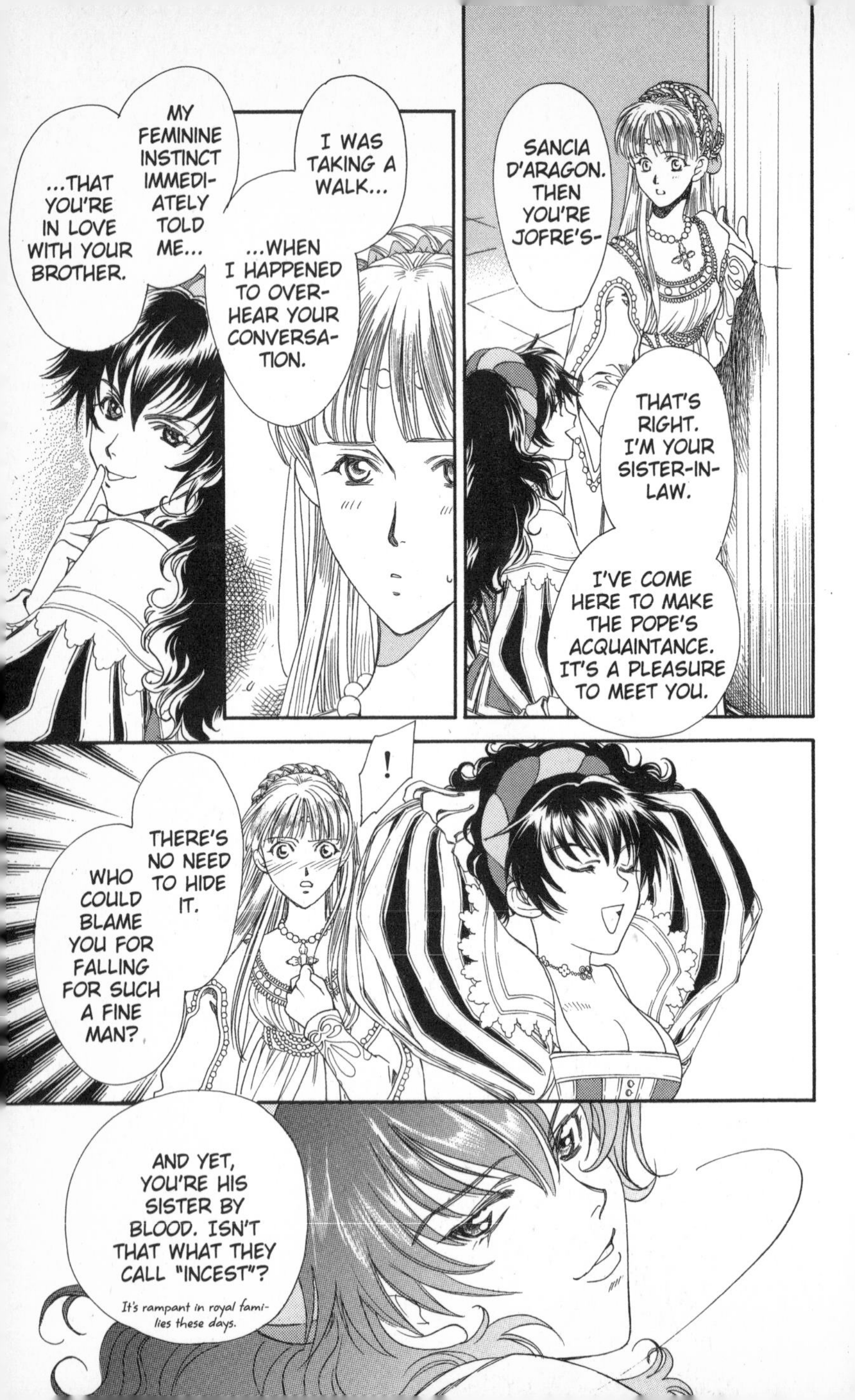
SANCIA D'ARAGON. THEN YOU'RE JOFRE'S-
THAT'S RIGHT. I'M YOUR SISTER-IN-LAW.
I'VE COME HERE TO MAKE THE POPE'S ACQUAINTANCE. IT'S A PLEASURE TO MEET YOU.
I WAS TAKING A WALK...
...WHEN I HAPPENED TO OVERHEAR YOUR CONVERSATION.
MY FEMININE INSTINCT IMMEDIATELY TOLD ME...
...THAT YOU'RE IN LOVE WITH YOUR BROTHER.
!
THERE'S NO NEED TO HIDE IT.
WHO COULD BLAME YOU FOR FALLING FOR SUCH A FINE MAN?
AND YET, YOU'RE HIS SISTER BY BLOOD. ISN'T THAT WHAT THEY CALL "INCEST"?
It's rampant in royal families these days.

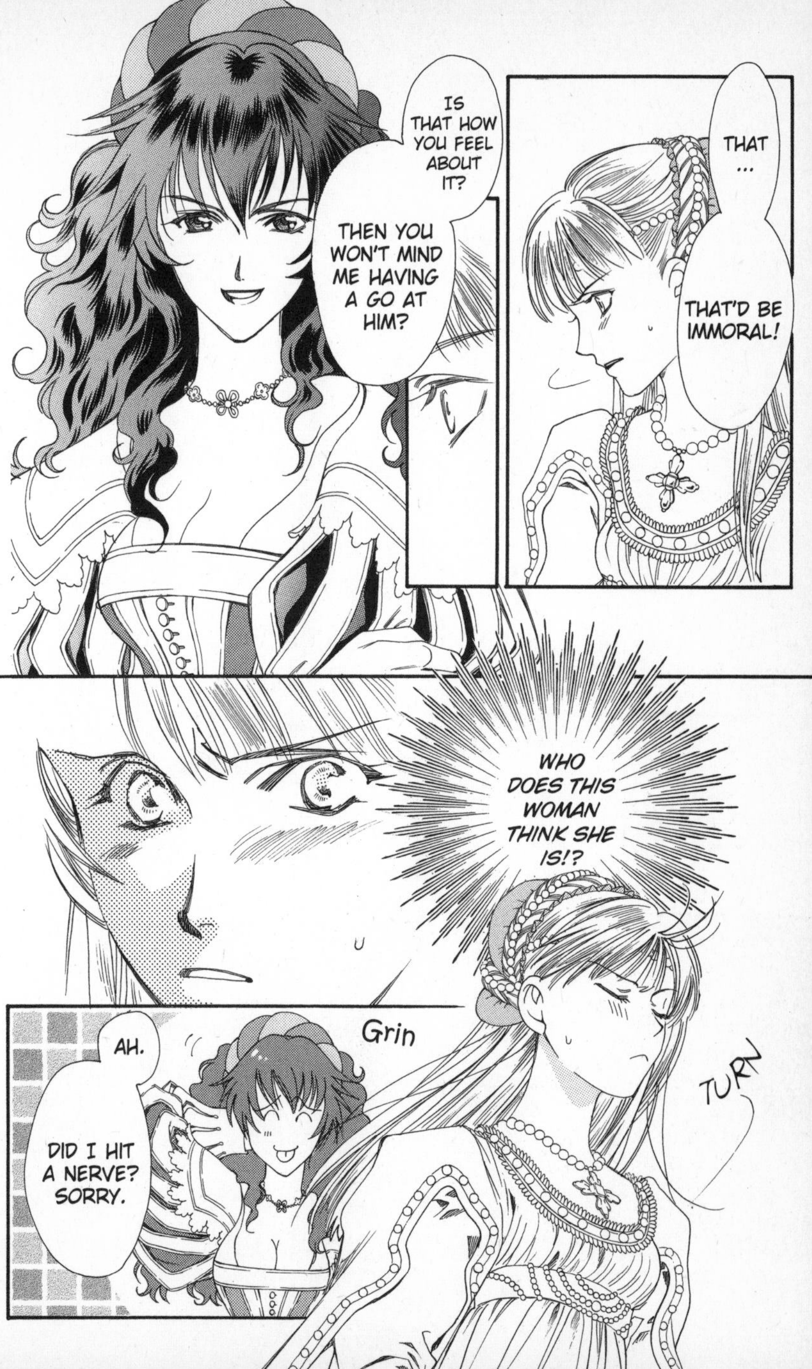
THAT ...
THAT'D BE IMMORAL!
IS THAT HOW YOU FEEL ABOUT IT?
THEN YOU WON'T MIND ME HAVING A GO AT HIM?
WHO DOES THIS WOMAN THINK SHE IS!?
TURN
Grin
AH.
DID I HIT A NERVE? SORRY.

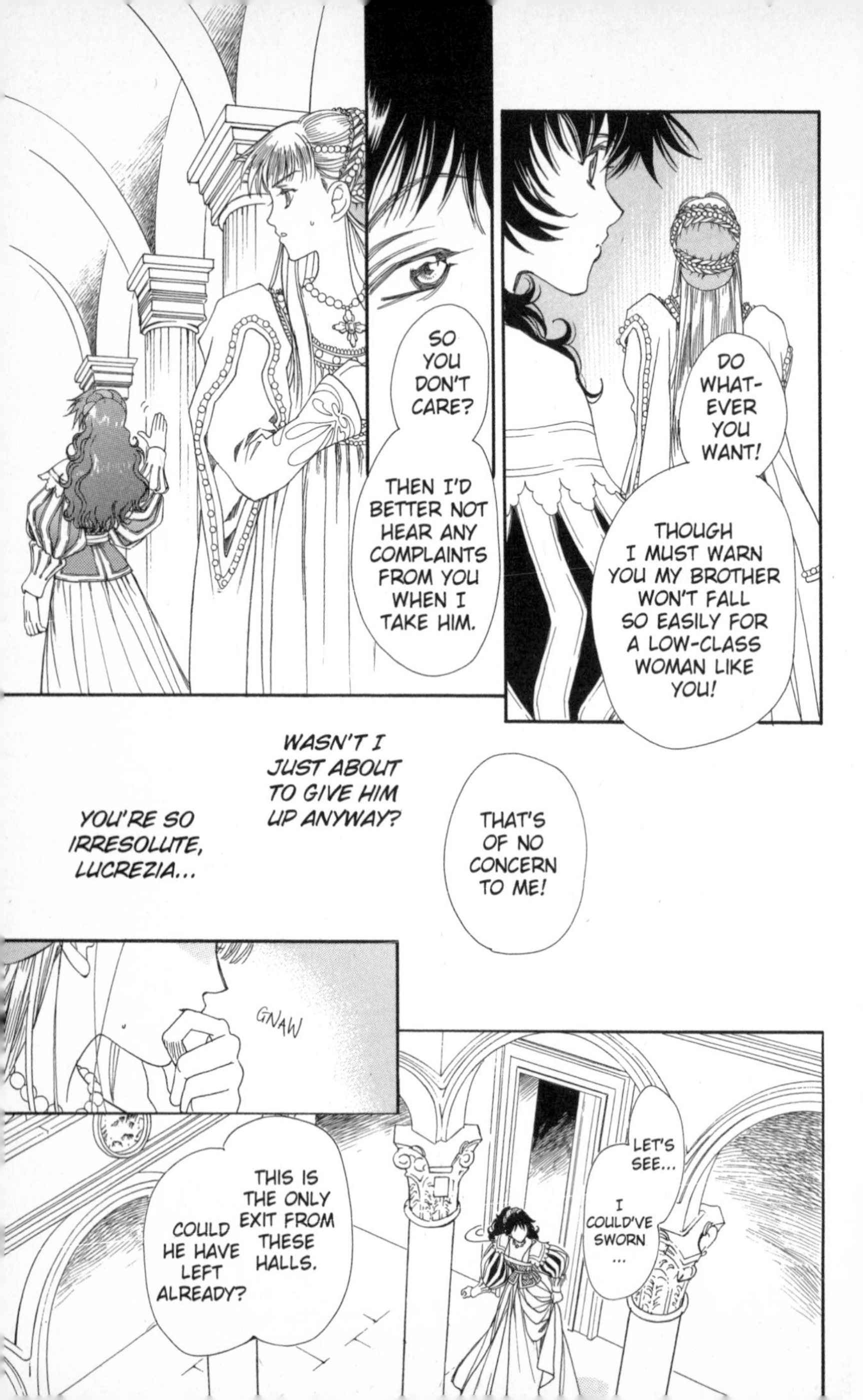
DO WHAT-EVER YOU WANT!
THOUGH I MUST WARN YOU MY BROTHER WON'T FALL SO EASILY FOR A LOW-CLASS WOMAN LIKE YOU!
SO YOU DON'T CARE?
THEN I'D BETTER NOT HEAR ANY COMPLAINTS FROM YOU WHEN I TAKE HIM.
THAT'S OF NO CONCERN TO ME!
WASN'T I JUST ABOUT TO GIVE HIM UP ANYWAY?
YOU'RE SO IRRESOLUTE, LUCREZIA...
GNAW
LET'S SEE...
I COULD'VE SWORN ...
THIS IS THE ONLY EXIT FROM THESE HALLS.
COULD HE HAVE LEFT ALREADY?

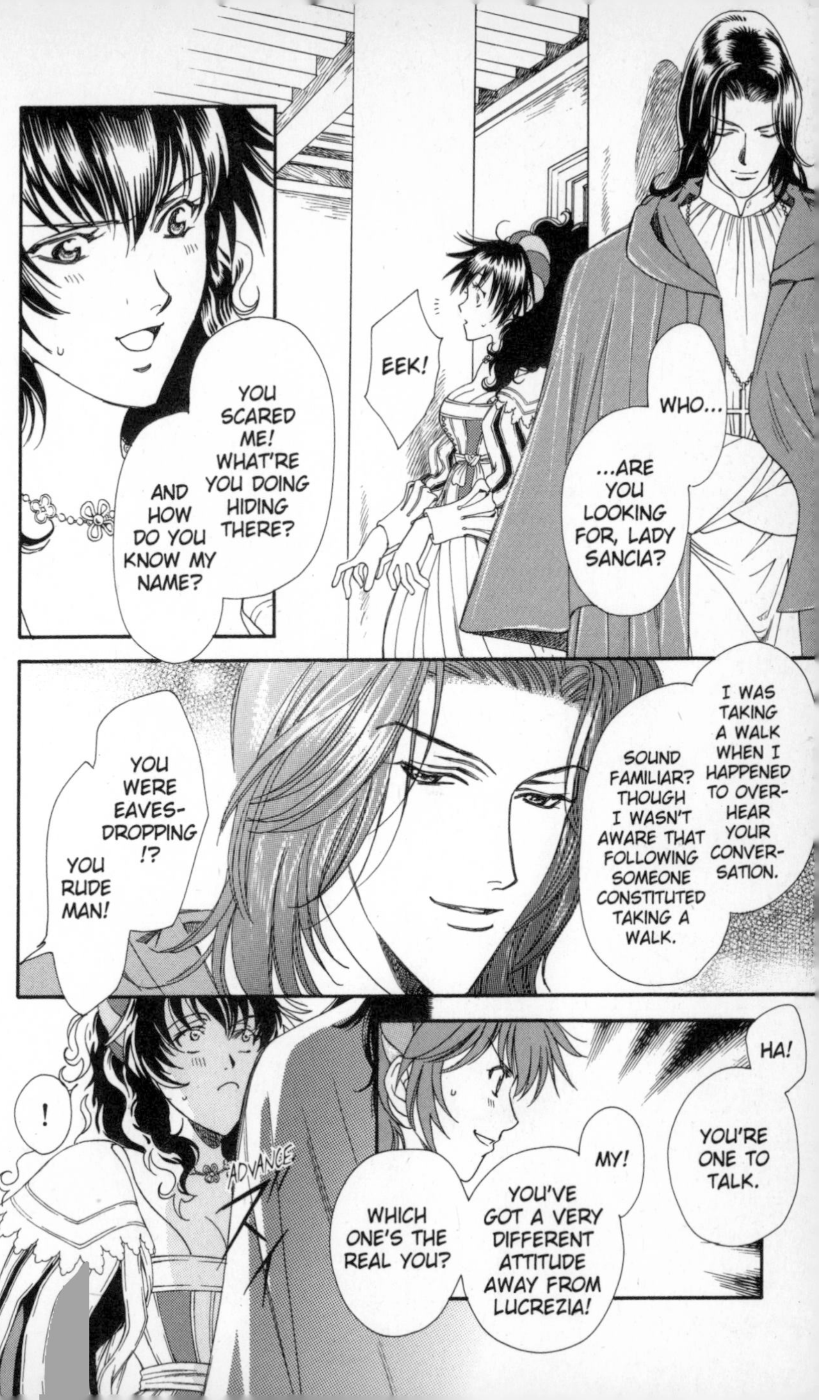

EEK!
WHO...
...ARE YOU LOOKING FOR, LADY SANCIA?
YOU SCARED ME! WHAT'RE YOU DOING HIDING THERE?
AND HOW DO YOU KNOW MY NAME?
I WAS TAKING A WALK WHEN I HAPPENED TO OVERHEAR YOUR CONVERSATION.
SOUND FAMILIAR? THOUGH I WASN'T AWARE THAT FOLLOWING SOMEONE CONSTITUTED TAKING A WALK.
YOU WERE EAVES-DROPPING!?
YOU RUDE MAN!
HA!
YOU'RE ONE TO TALK.
MY!
YOU'VE GOT A VERY DIFFERENT ATTITUDE AWAY FROM LUCREZIA!
WHICH ONE'S THE REAL YOU?
ADVANCE
!

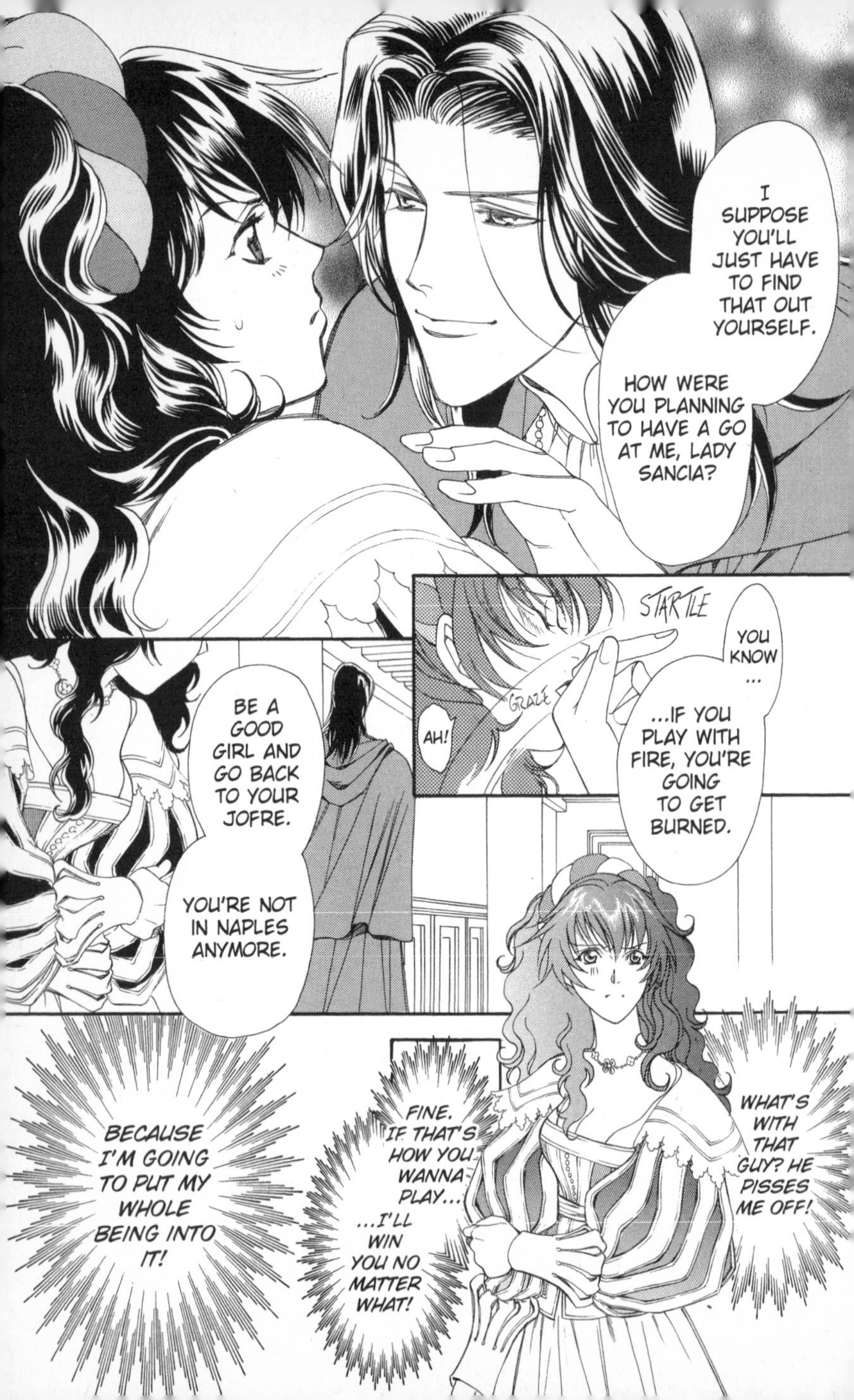
I SUPPOSE YOU'LL JUST HAVE TO FIND THAT OUT YOURSELF.
HOW WERE YOU PLANNING TO HAVE A GO AT ME, LADY SANCIA?
STARTLE
YOU KNOW ...
...IF YOU PLAY WITH FIRE, YOU'RE GOING TO GET BURNED.
GRAZE
AH!
BE A GOOD GIRL AND GO BACK TO YOUR JOFRE.
YOU'RE NOT IN NAPLES ANYMORE.
WHAT'S WITH THAT GUY? HE PISSES ME OFF!
FINE. IF THAT'S HOW YOU WANNA PLAY...
...I'LL WIN YOU NO MATTER WHAT!
BECAUSE I'M GOING TO PUT MY WHOLE BEING INTO IT!

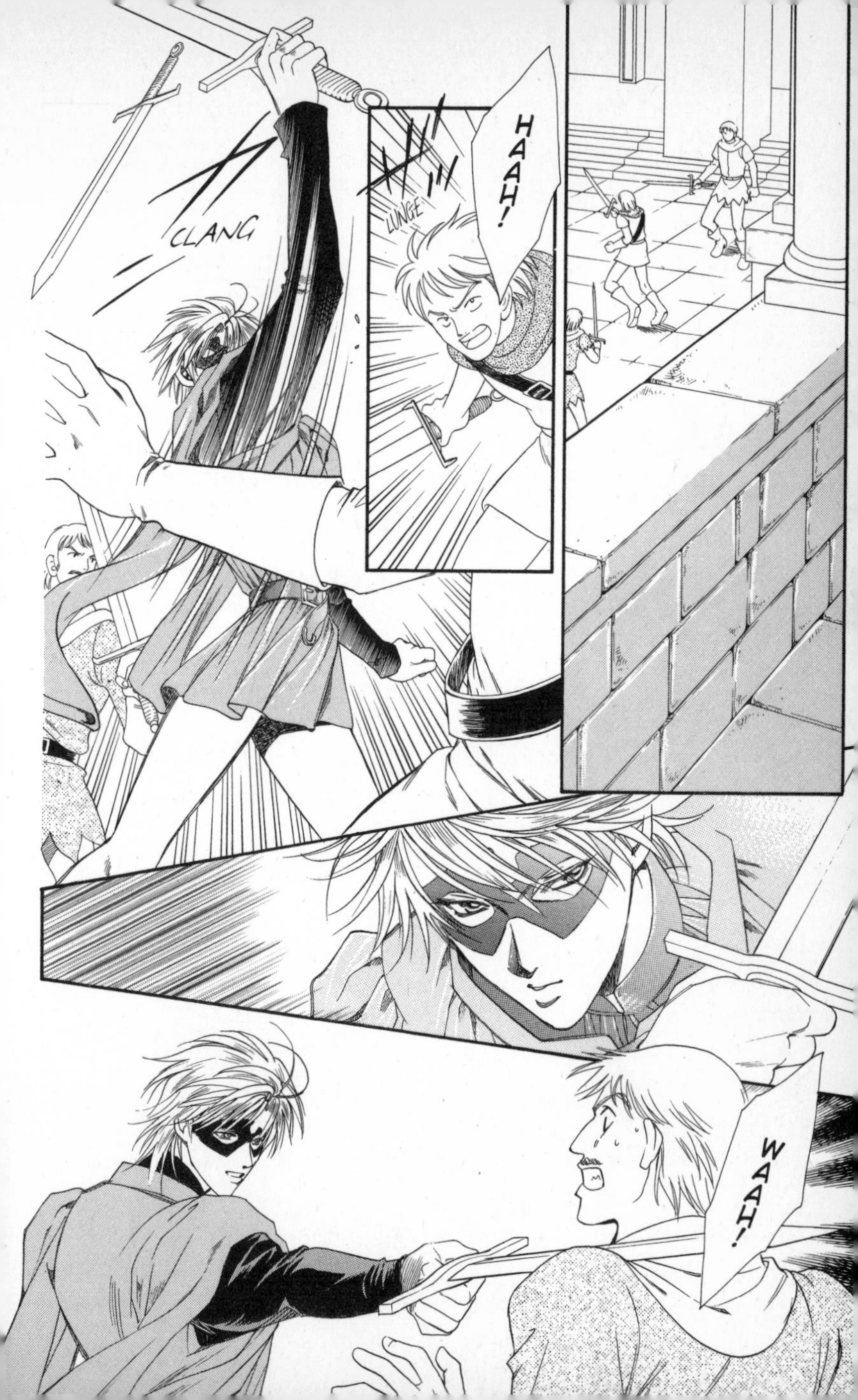
HAAH!
LUNGE
CLANG
WAAH!

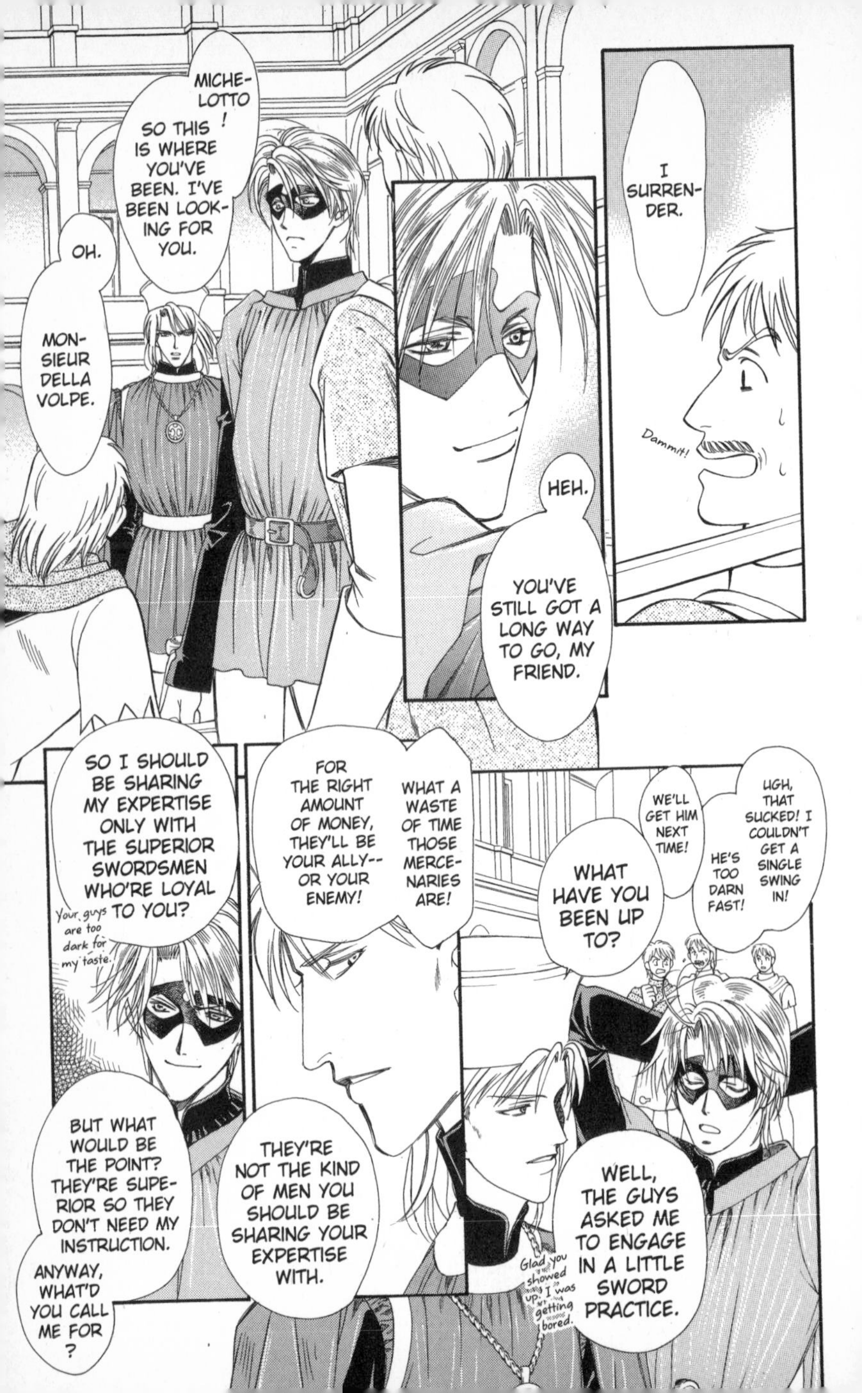
I SURRENDER.
Dammit!
HEH.
YOU'VE STILL GOT A LONG WAY TO GO, MY FRIEND.
MICHELOTTO!
SO THIS IS WHERE YOU'VE BEEN. I'VE BEEN LOOKING FOR YOU.
OH.
MONSIEUR DELLA VOLPE.
UGH, THAT SUCKED! I COULDN'T GET A SINGLE SWING IN!
HE'S TOO DARN FAST!
WE'LL GET HIM NEXT TIME!
WHAT HAVE YOU BEEN UP TO?
WELL, THE GUYS ASKED ME TO ENGAGE IN A LITTLE SWORD PRACTICE.
Glad you showed up. I was getting bored.
WHAT A WASTE OF TIME THOSE MERCENARIES ARE!
FOR THE RIGHT AMOUNT OF MONEY, THEY'LL BE YOUR ALLY--OR YOUR ENEMY!
THEY'RE NOT THE KIND OF MEN YOU SHOULD BE SHARING YOUR EXPERTISE WITH.
SO I SHOULD BE SHARING MY EXPERTISE ONLY WITH THE SUPERIOR SWORDSMEN WHO'RE LOYAL TO YOU?
Your guys are too dark for my taste.
BUT WHAT WOULD BE THE POINT? THEY'RE SUPERIOR SO THEY DON'T NEED MY INSTRUCTION.
ANYWAY, WHAT'D YOU CALL ME FOR?

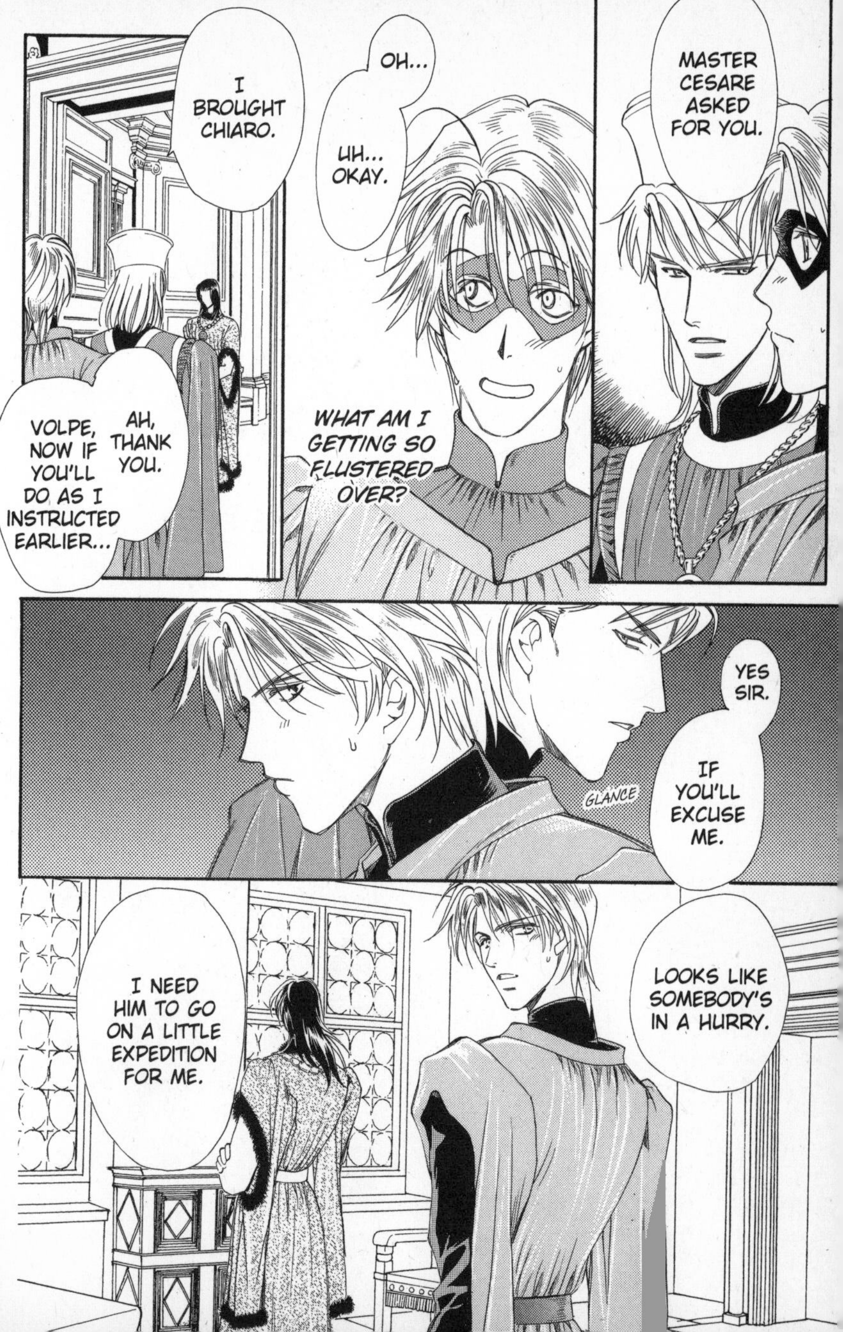
MASTER CESARE ASKED FOR YOU.
OH...
UH... OKAY.
WHAT AM I GETTING SO FLUSTERED OVER?
I BROUGHT CHIARO.
AH, THANK YOU.
VOLPE, NOW IF YOU'LL DO AS I INSTRUCTED EARLIER...
YES SIR.
IF YOU'LL EXCUSE ME.
GLANCE
LOOKS LIKE SOMEBODY'S IN A HURRY.
I NEED HIM TO GO ON A LITTLE EXPEDITION FOR ME.

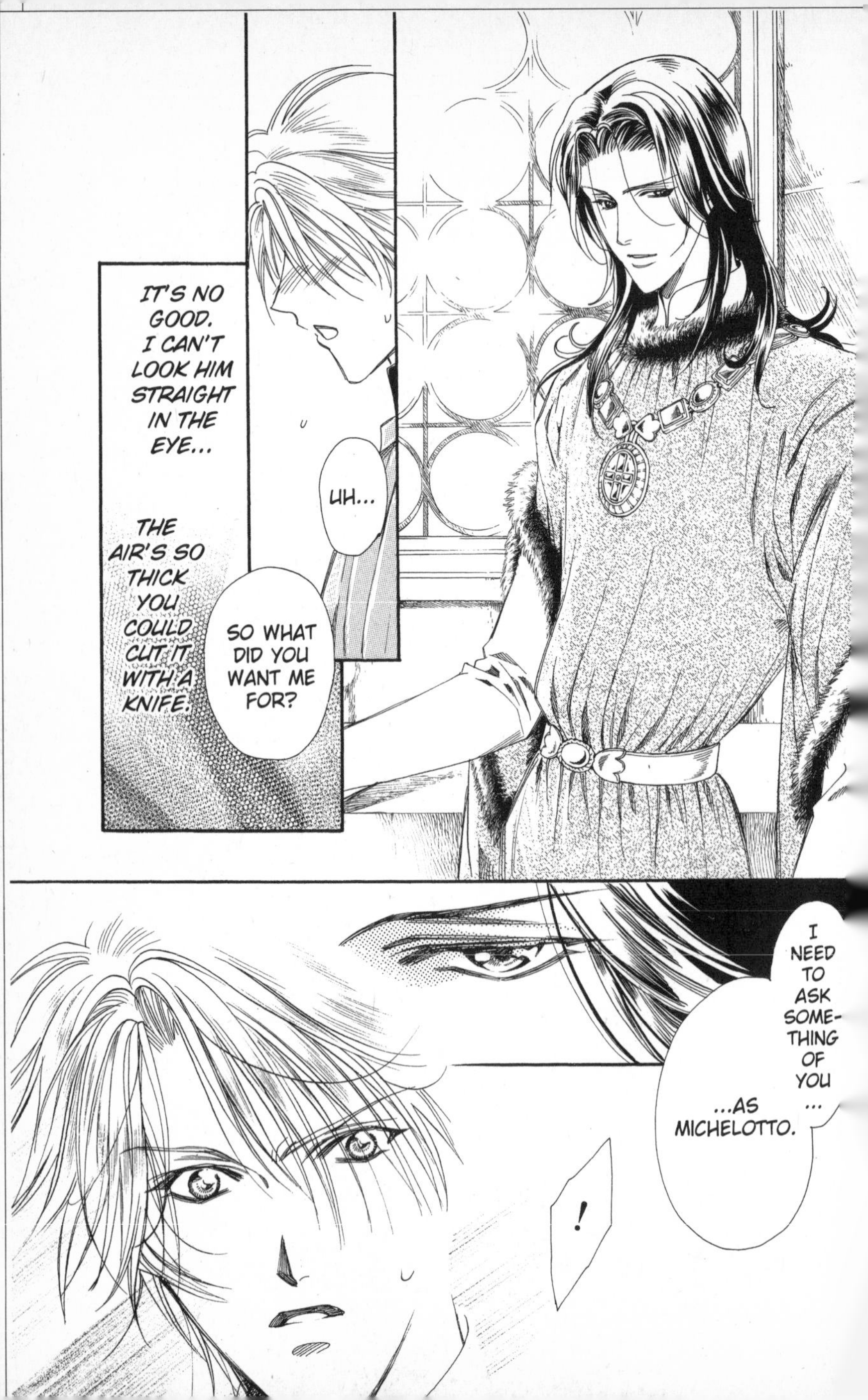
UH...
SO WHAT DID YOU WANT ME FOR?
IT'S NO GOOD. I CAN'T LOOK HIM STRAIGHT IN THE EYE...
THE AIR'S SO THICK YOU COULD CUT IT WITH A KNIFE.
I NEED TO ASK SOME-THING OF YOU ...
...AS MICHELOTTO.
!

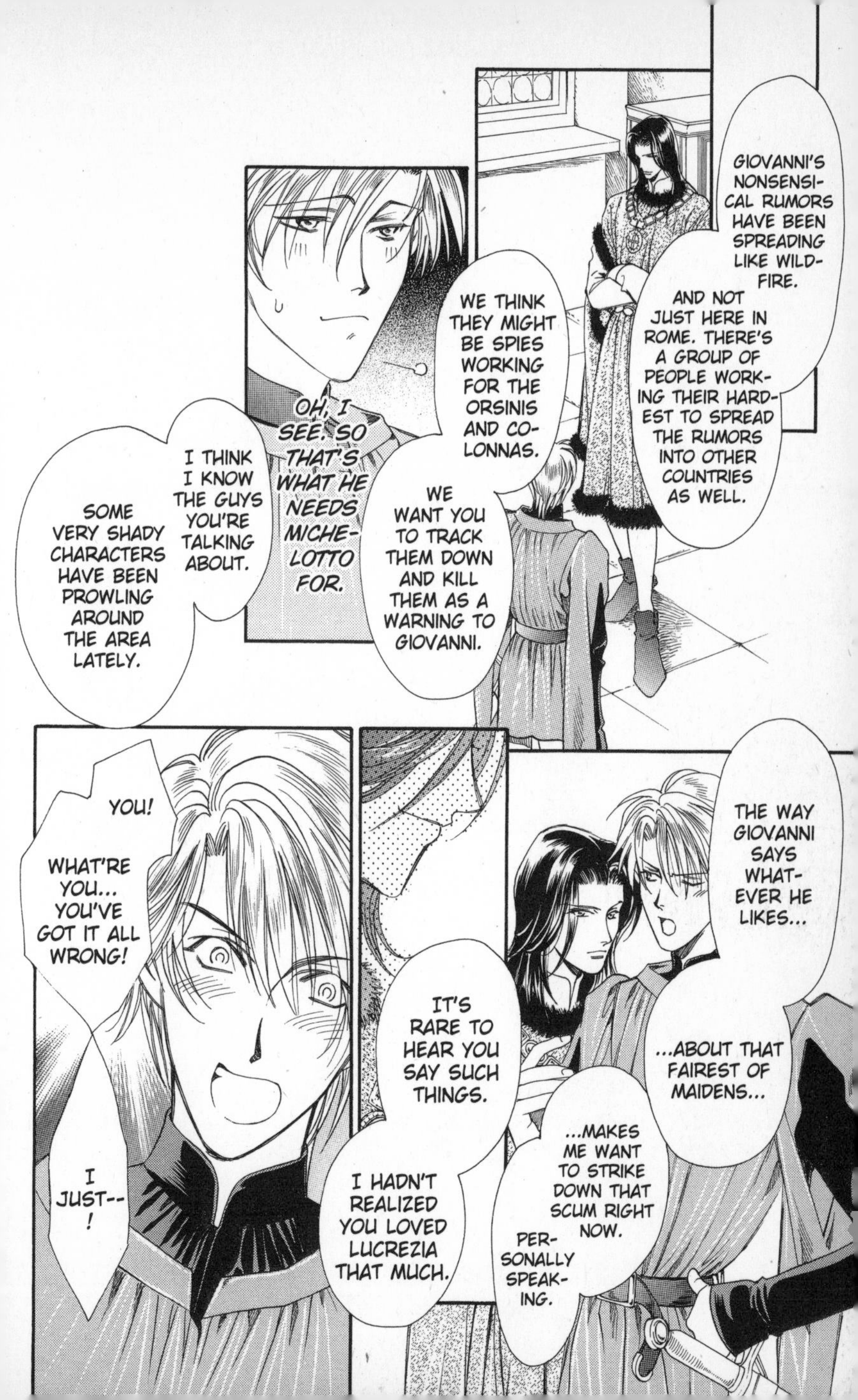
GIOVANNI'S NONSENSICAL RUMORS HAVE BEEN SPREADING LIKE WILDFIRE.
AND NOT JUST HERE IN ROME. THERE'S A GROUP OF PEOPLE WORKING THEIR HARDEST TO SPREAD THE RUMORS INTO OTHER COUNTRIES AS WELL.
WE THINK THEY MIGHT BE SPIES WORKING FOR THE ORSINIS AND COLONNAS.
WE WANT YOU TO TRACK THEM DOWN AND KILL THEM AS A WARNING TO GIOVANNI.
OH, I SEE. SO THAT'S WHAT HE NEEDS MICHELOTTO FOR.
I THINK I KNOW THE GUYS YOU'RE TALKING ABOUT.
SOME VERY SHADY CHARACTERS HAVE BEEN PROWLING AROUND THE AREA LATELY.
THE WAY GIOVANNI SAYS WHATEVER HE LIKES...
...ABOUT THAT FAIREST OF MAIDENS...
...MAKES ME WANT TO STRIKE DOWN THAT SCUM RIGHT NOW.
PERSONALLY SPEAKING.
IT'S RARE TO HEAR YOU SAY SUCH THINGS.
I HADN'T REALIZED YOU LOVED LUCREZIA THAT MUCH.
YOU!
WHAT'RE YOU... YOU'VE GOT IT ALL WRONG!
I JUST--!

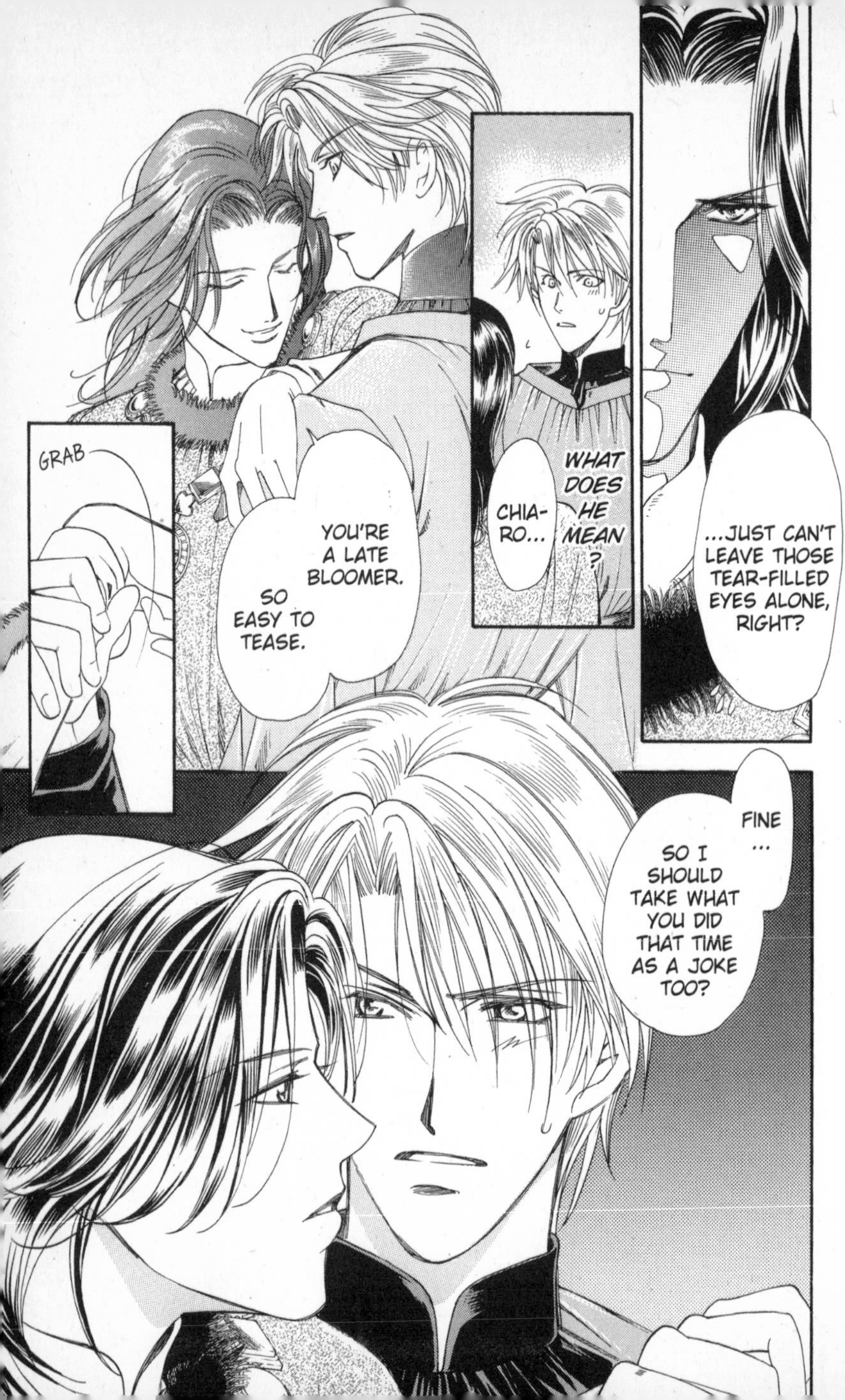
...JUST CAN'T LEAVE THOSE TEAR-FILLED EYES ALONE, RIGHT?
WHAT DOES HE MEAN?
CHIA-RO...
YOU'RE A LATE BLOOMER.
SO EASY TO TEASE.
GRAB
FINE...
SO I SHOULD TAKE WHAT YOU DID THAT TIME AS A JOKE TOO?

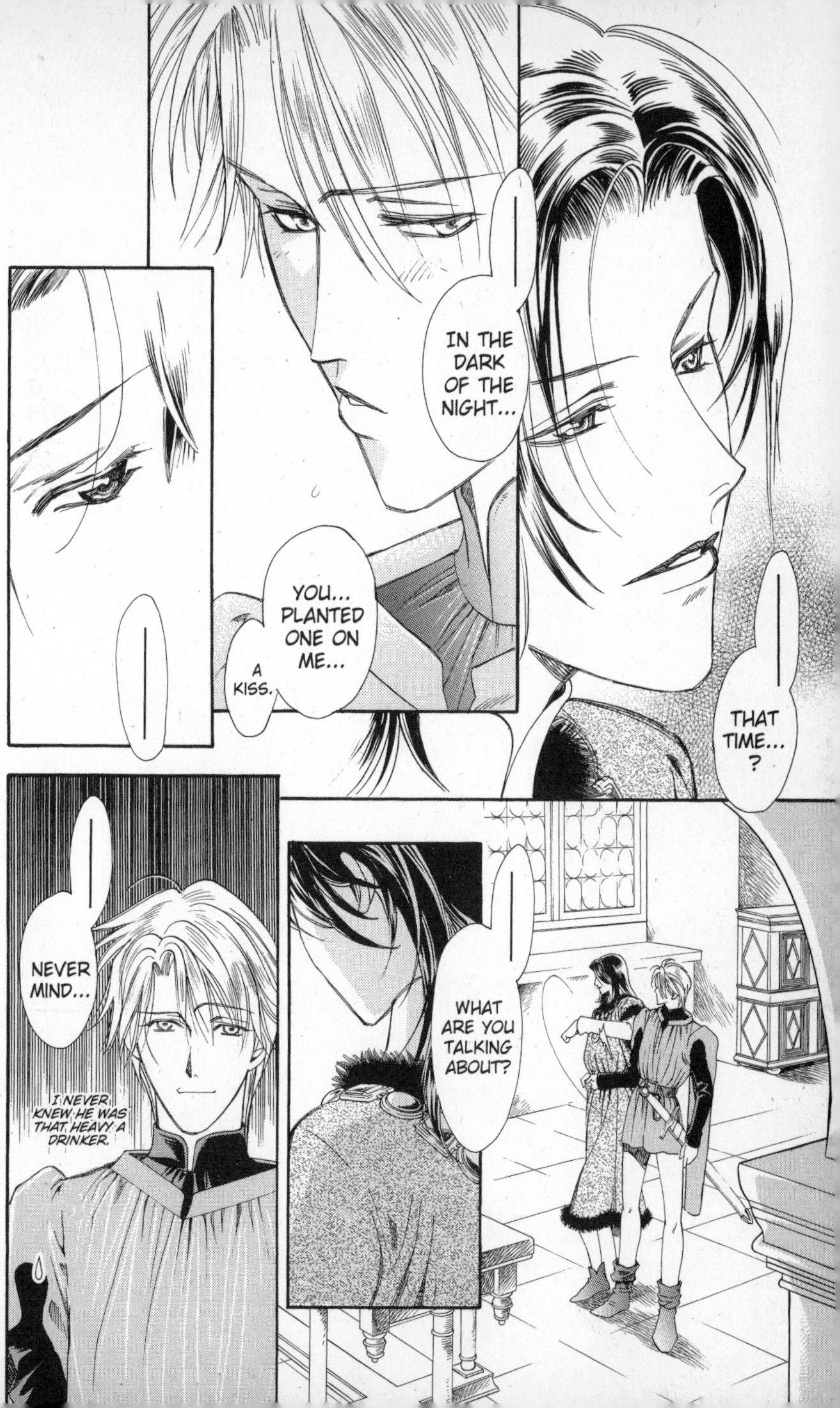
—
THAT TIME...?
—
IN THE DARK OF THE NIGHT...
YOU... PLANTED ONE ON ME...
A KISS.
—
—
WHAT ARE YOU TALKING ABOUT?
—
NEVER MIND...
I NEVER KNEW HE WAS THAT HEAVY A DRINKER.

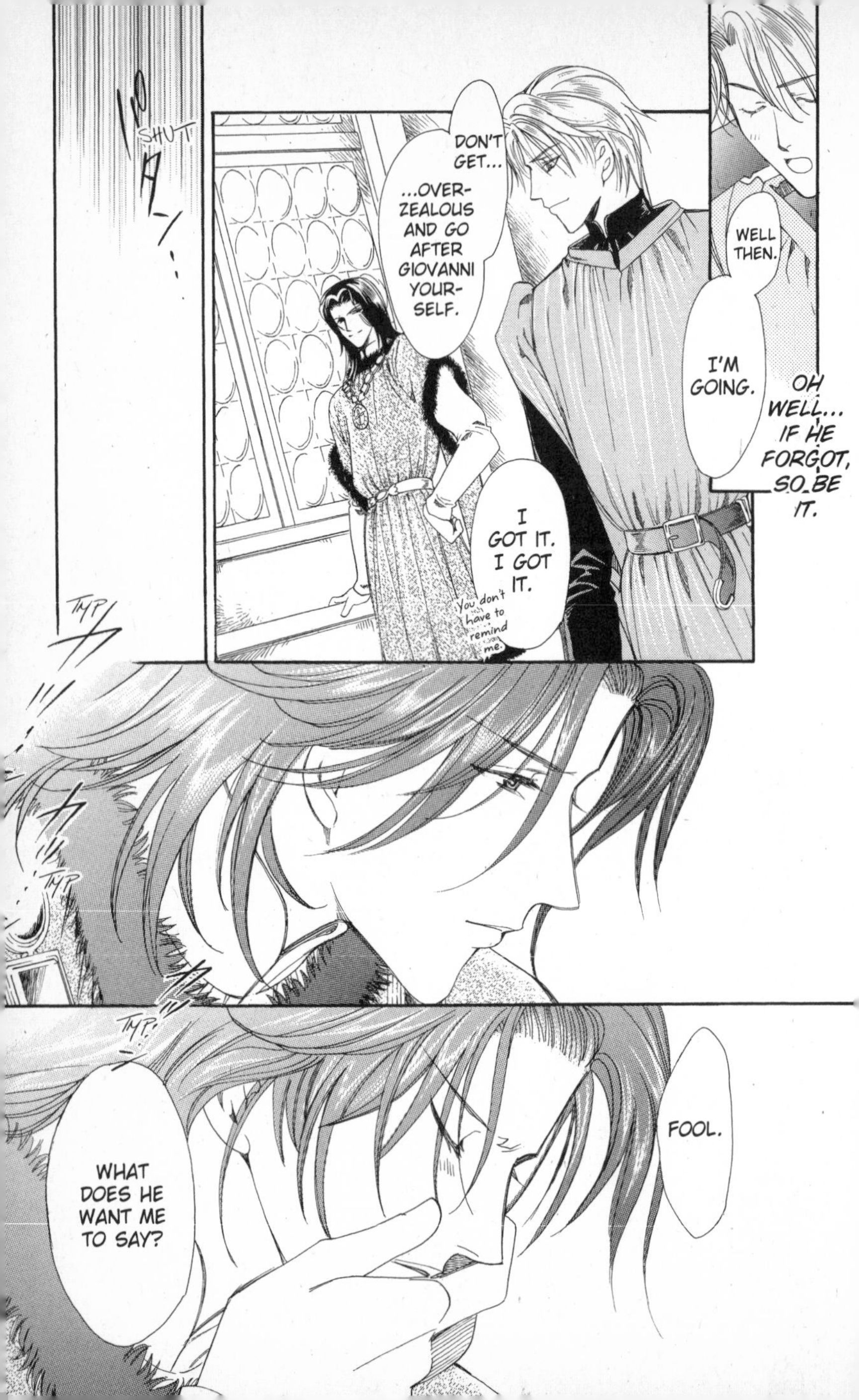
WELL THEN.
I'M GOING.
OH WELL... IF HE FORGOT, SO BE IT.
DON'T GET...
...OVER-ZEALOUS AND GO AFTER GIOVANNI YOUR-SELF.
I GOT IT. I GOT IT.
You don't have to remind me.
SHUT
TMP
TMP
TMP
FOOL.
WHAT DOES HE WANT ME TO SAY?

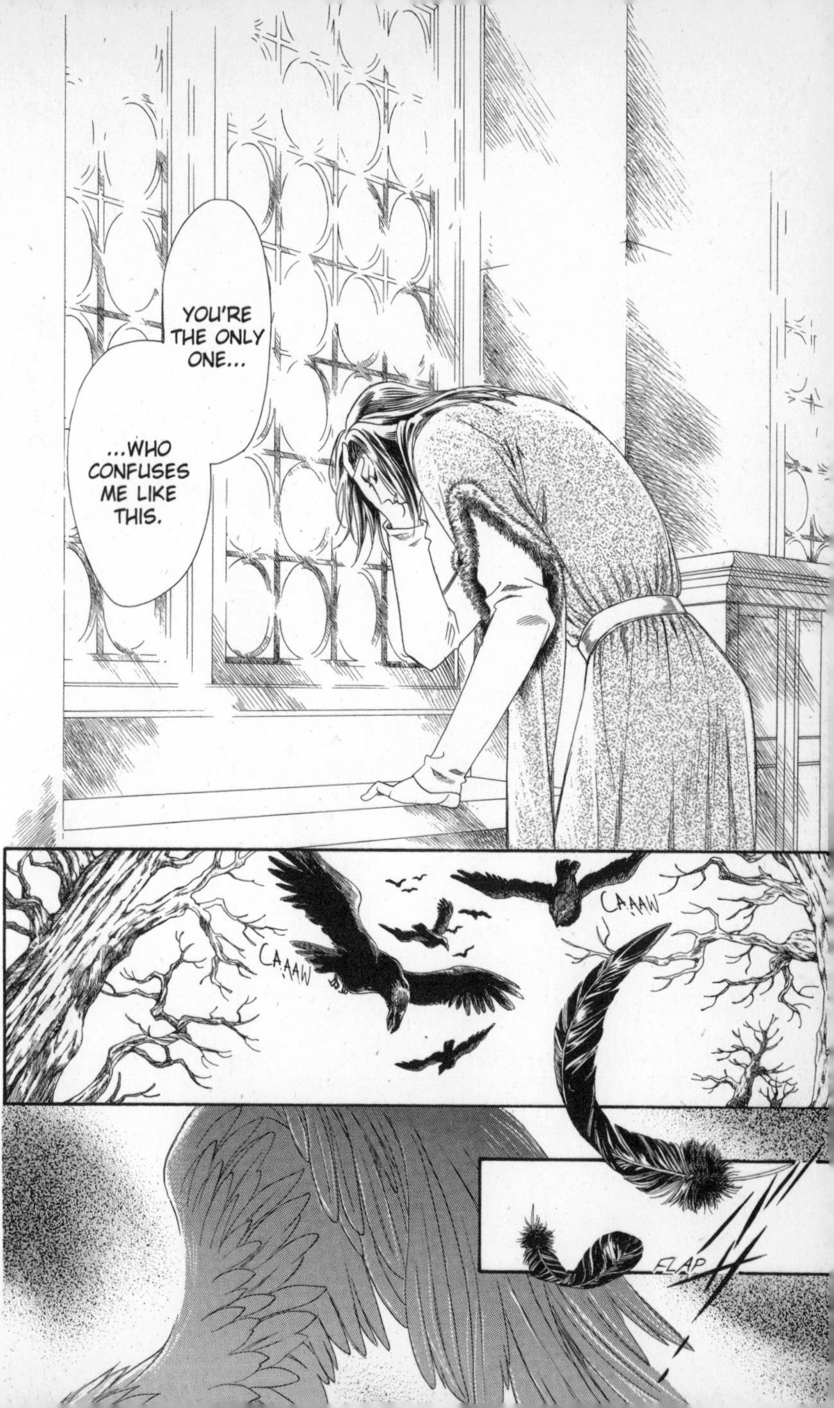
YOU'RE THE ONLY ONE...
...WHO CONFUSES ME LIKE THIS.
CA:AAW
CA:AAW
FLAP

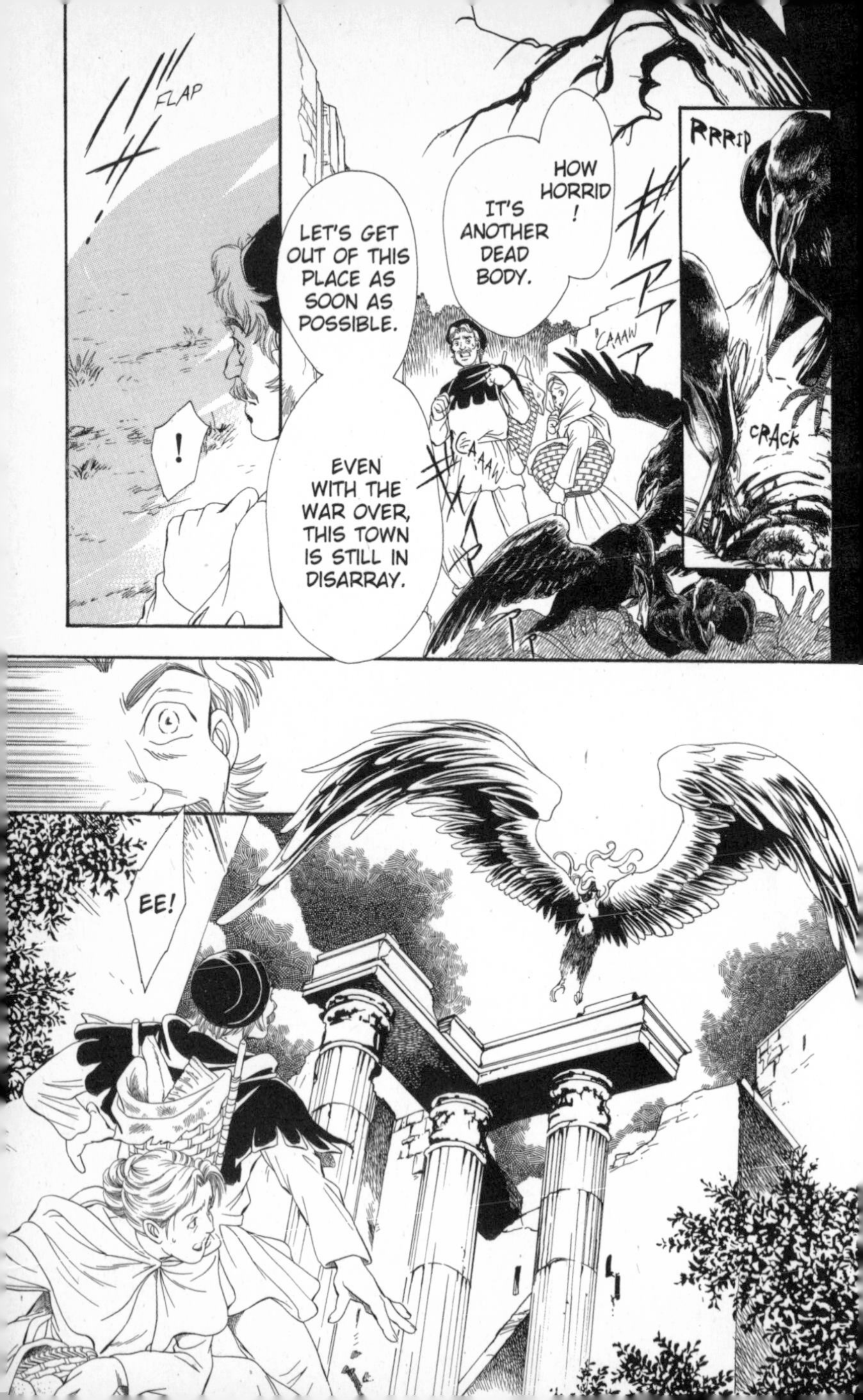
RRRIP
CRACK
HOW HORRID!
IT'S ANOTHER DEAD BODY.
CAAAW
LET'S GET OUT OF THIS PLACE AS SOON AS POSSIBLE.
CAAAW
EVEN WITH THE WAR OVER, THIS TOWN IS STILL IN DISARRAY.
FLAP
!
EE!

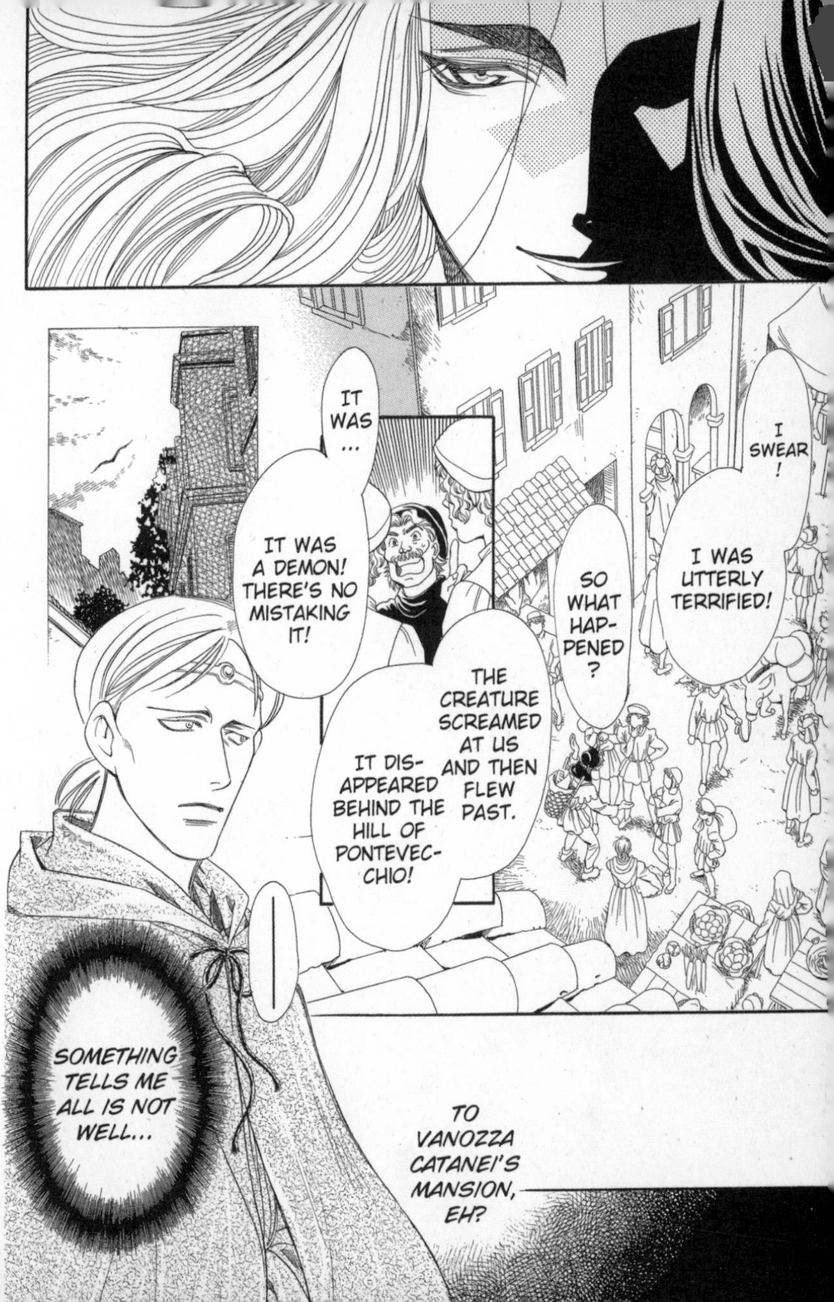
I SWEAR!
I WAS UTTERLY TERRIFIED!
SO WHAT HAP-PENED?
IT WAS...
IT WAS A DEMON! THERE'S NO MISTAKING IT!
THE CREATURE SCREAMED AT US AND THEN FLEW PAST.
IT DIS-APPEARED BEHIND THE HILL OF PONTEVEC-CHIO!
...
TO VANOZZA CATANEI'S MANSION, EH?
SOMETHING TELLS ME ALL IS NOT WELL...

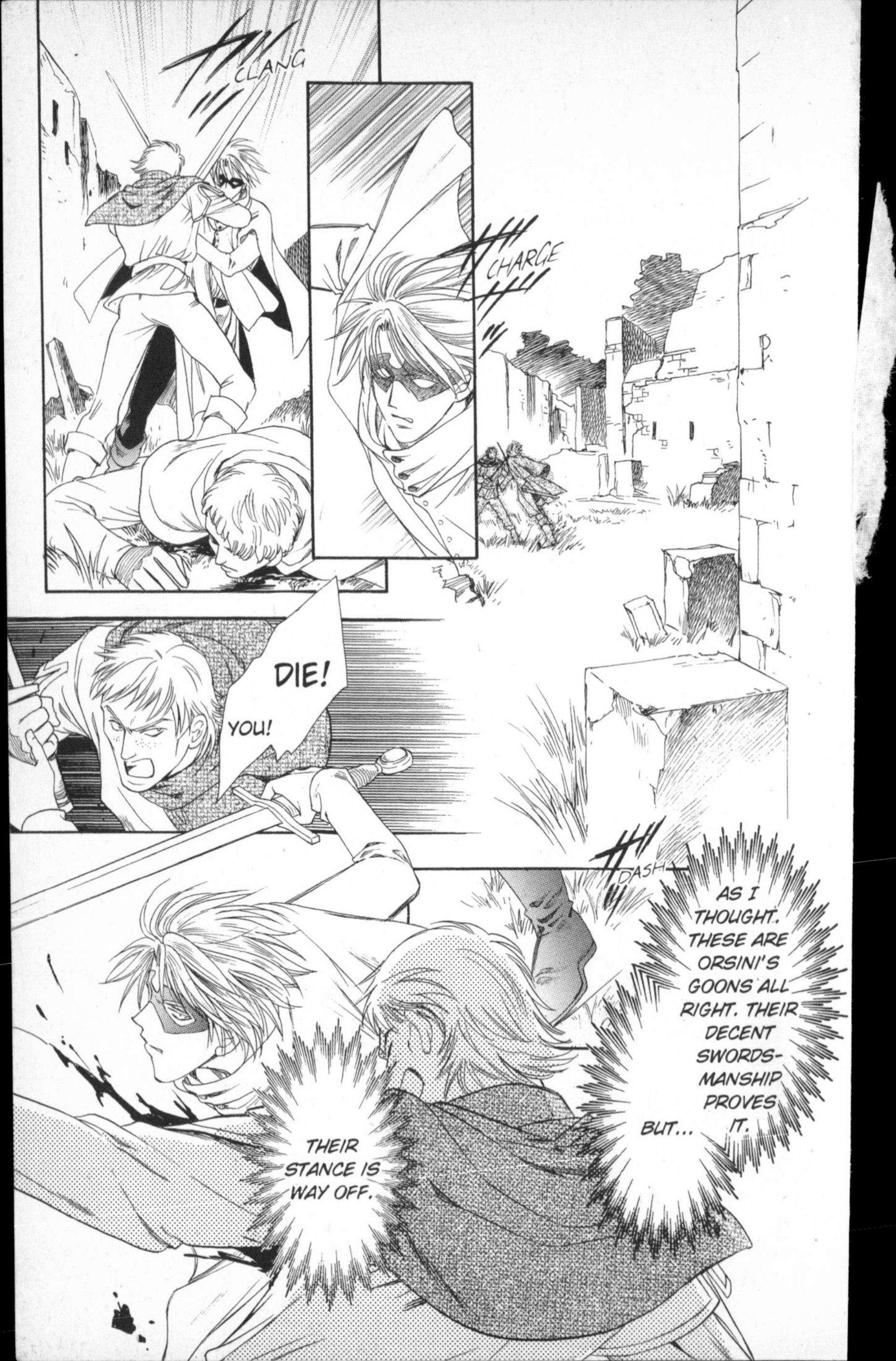
CHARGE
CLANG
DIE!
YOU!
DASH
AS I THOUGHT. THESE ARE ORSINI'S GOONS ALL RIGHT. THEIR DECENT SWORDSMANSHIP PROVES IT.
BUT...
THEIR STANCE IS WAY OFF.

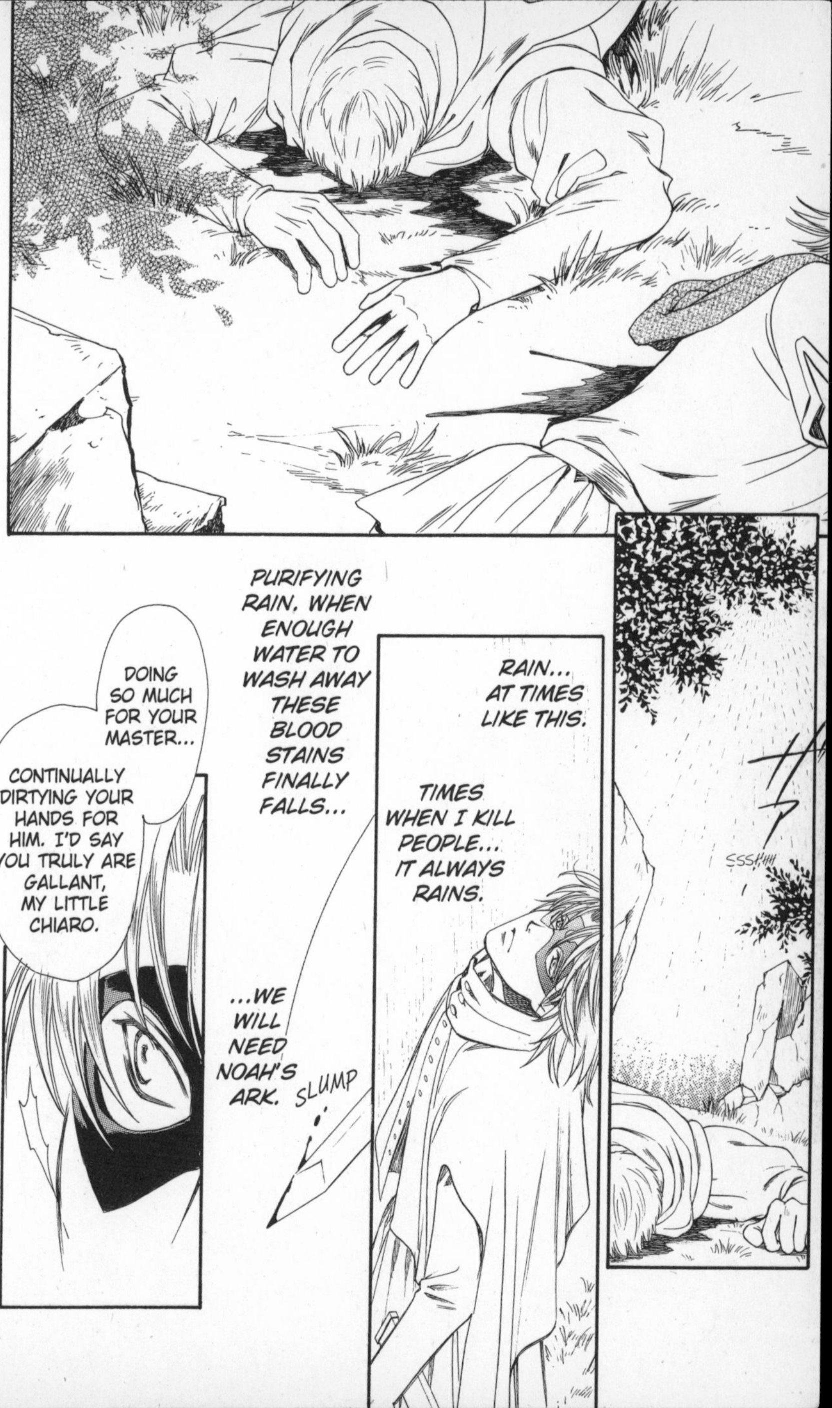
SSSH
RAIN... AT TIMES LIKE THIS.
TIMES WHEN I KILL PEOPLE... IT ALWAYS RAINS.
PURIFYING RAIN. WHEN ENOUGH WATER TO WASH AWAY THESE BLOOD STAINS FINALLY FALLS...
...WE WILL NEED NOAH'S ARK.
SLUMP
DOING SO MUCH FOR YOUR MASTER...
CONTINUALLY DIRTYING YOUR HANDS FOR HIM. I'D SAY YOU TRULY ARE GALLANT, MY LITTLE CHIARO.

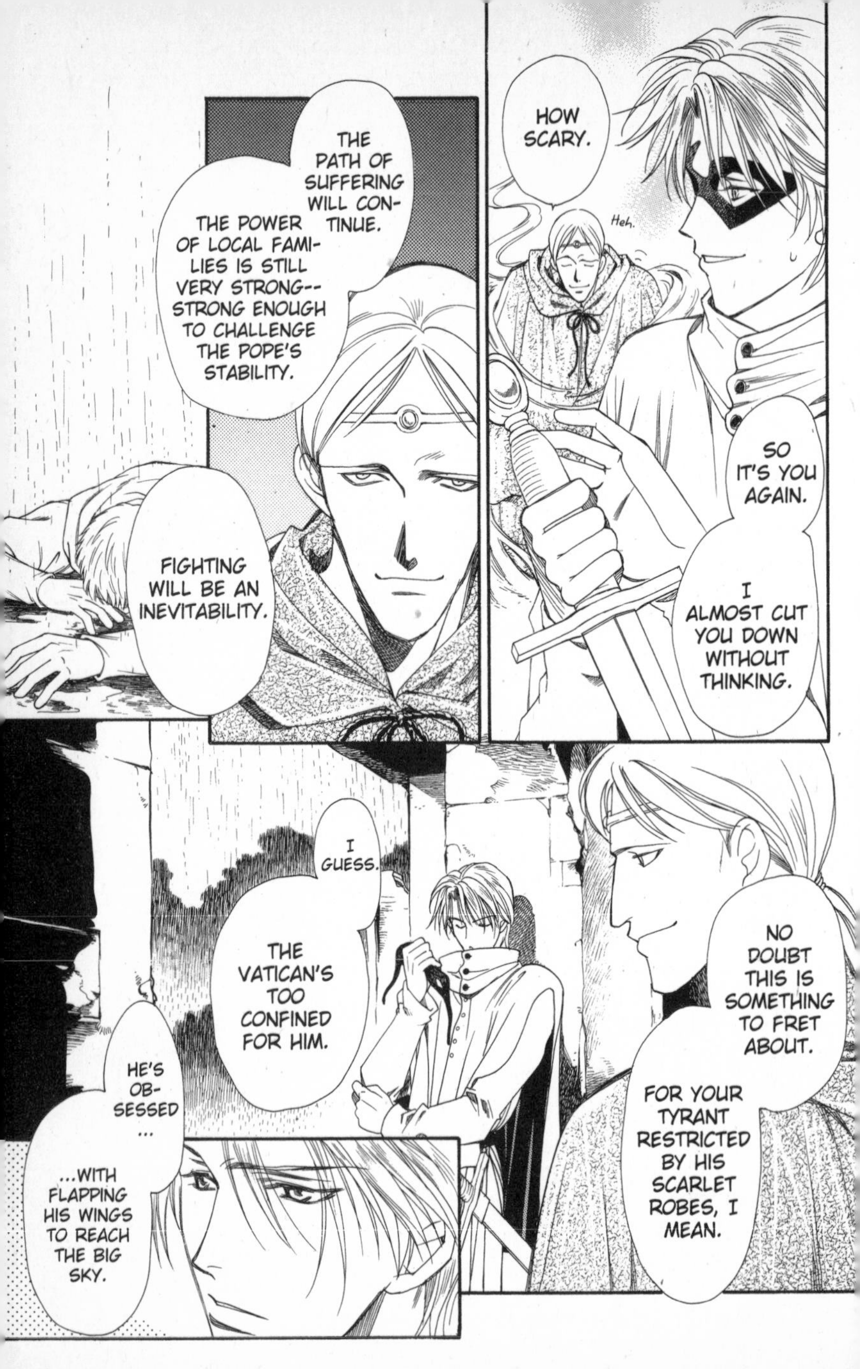
HOW SCARY.
Heh.
SO IT'S YOU AGAIN.
I ALMOST CUT YOU DOWN WITHOUT THINKING.
THE PATH OF SUFFERING WILL CONTINUE.
THE POWER OF LOCAL FAMILIES IS STILL VERY STRONG--STRONG ENOUGH TO CHALLENGE THE POPE'S STABILITY.
FIGHTING WILL BE AN INEVITABILITY.
NO DOUBT THIS IS SOMETHING TO FRET ABOUT.
FOR YOUR TYRANT RESTRICTED BY HIS SCARLET ROBES, I MEAN.
I GUESS.
THE VATICAN'S TOO CONFINED FOR HIM.
HE'S OBSESSED...
...WITH FLAPPING HIS WINGS TO REACH THE BIG SKY.

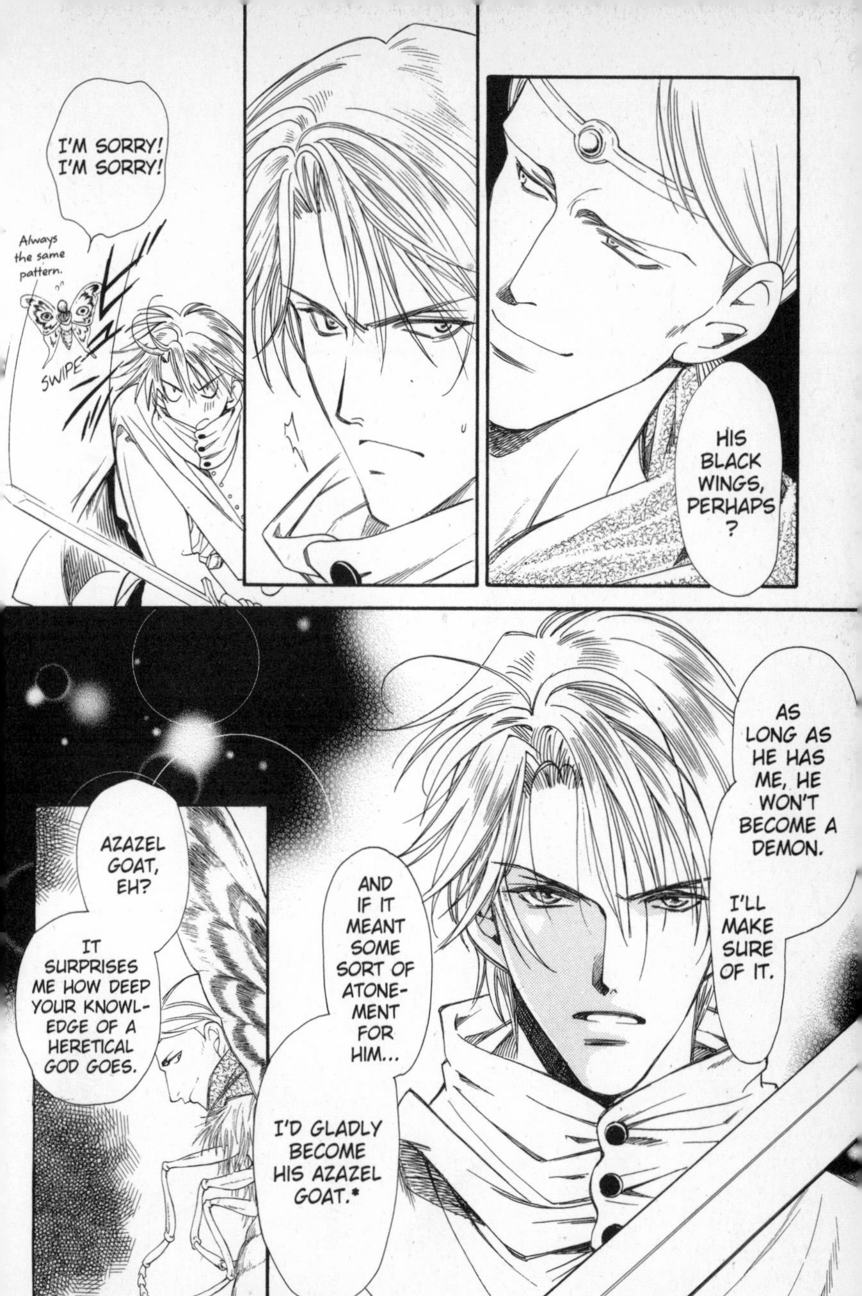
HIS BLACK WINGS, PERHAPS?
I'M SORRY! I'M SORRY!
Always the same pattern.
SWIPE
AS LONG AS HE HAS ME, HE WON'T BECOME A DEMON.
I'LL MAKE SURE OF IT.
AND IF IT MEANT SOME SORT OF ATONEMENT FOR HIM...
I'D GLADLY BECOME HIS AZAZEL GOAT.*
AZAZEL GOAT, EH?
IT SURPRISES ME HOW DEEP YOUR KNOWLEDGE OF A HERETICAL GOD GOES.

*Biblical reference to a ceremony where one goat is sacrificed as atonement while a second goat (Azazel) is forced to wander in a wilderness for its sins.

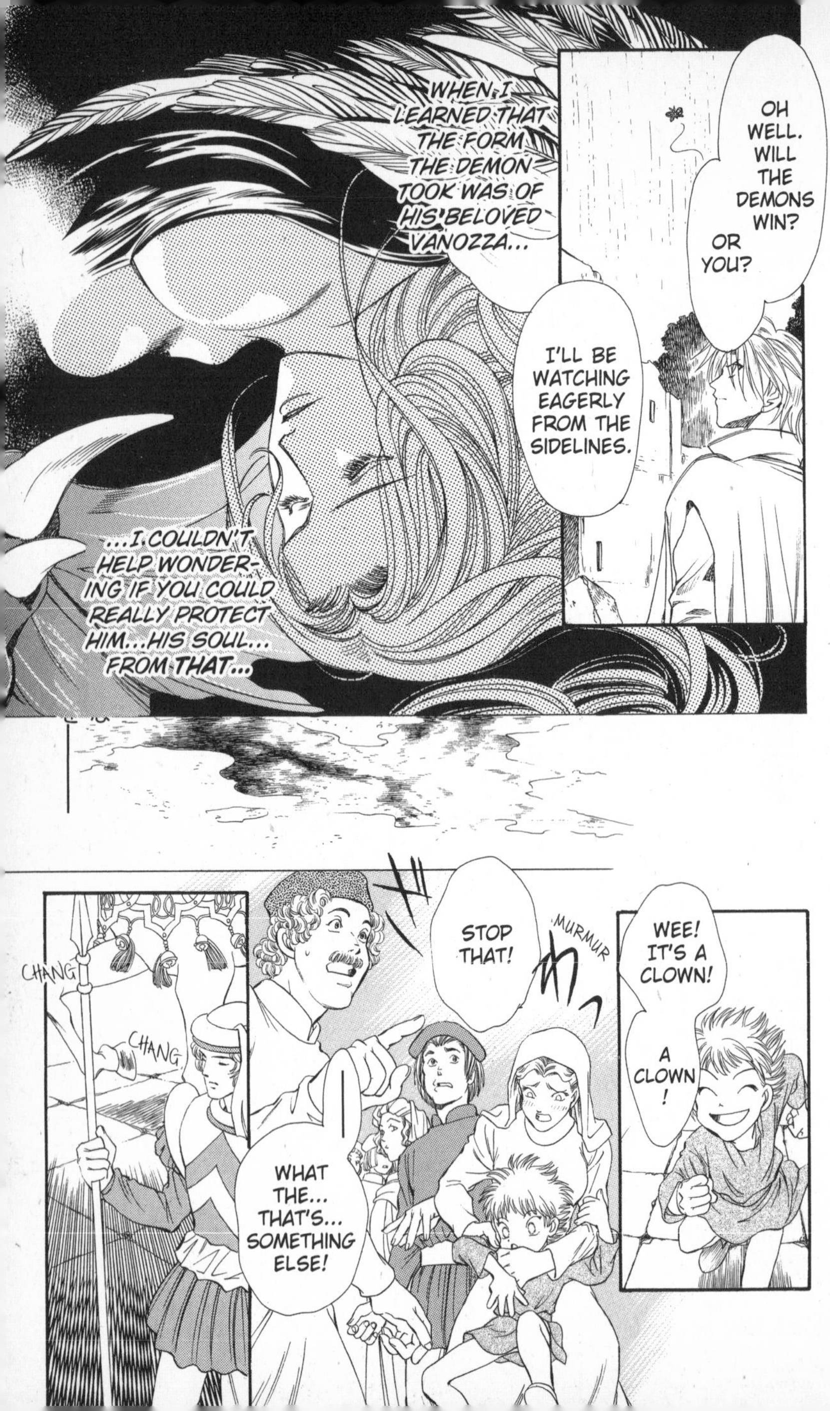
OH WELL. WILL THE DEMONS WIN? OR YOU?
I'LL BE WATCHING EAGERLY FROM THE SIDELINES.
WHEN I LEARNED THAT THE FORM THE DEMON TOOK WAS OF HIS BELOVED VANOZZA...
...I COULDN'T HELP WONDERING IF YOU COULD REALLY PROTECT HIM...HIS SOUL... FROM THAT...
WEE! IT'S A CLOWN!
A CLOWN!
MURMUR
STOP THAT!
WHAT THE... THAT'S... SOMETHING ELSE!
CHANG
CHANG

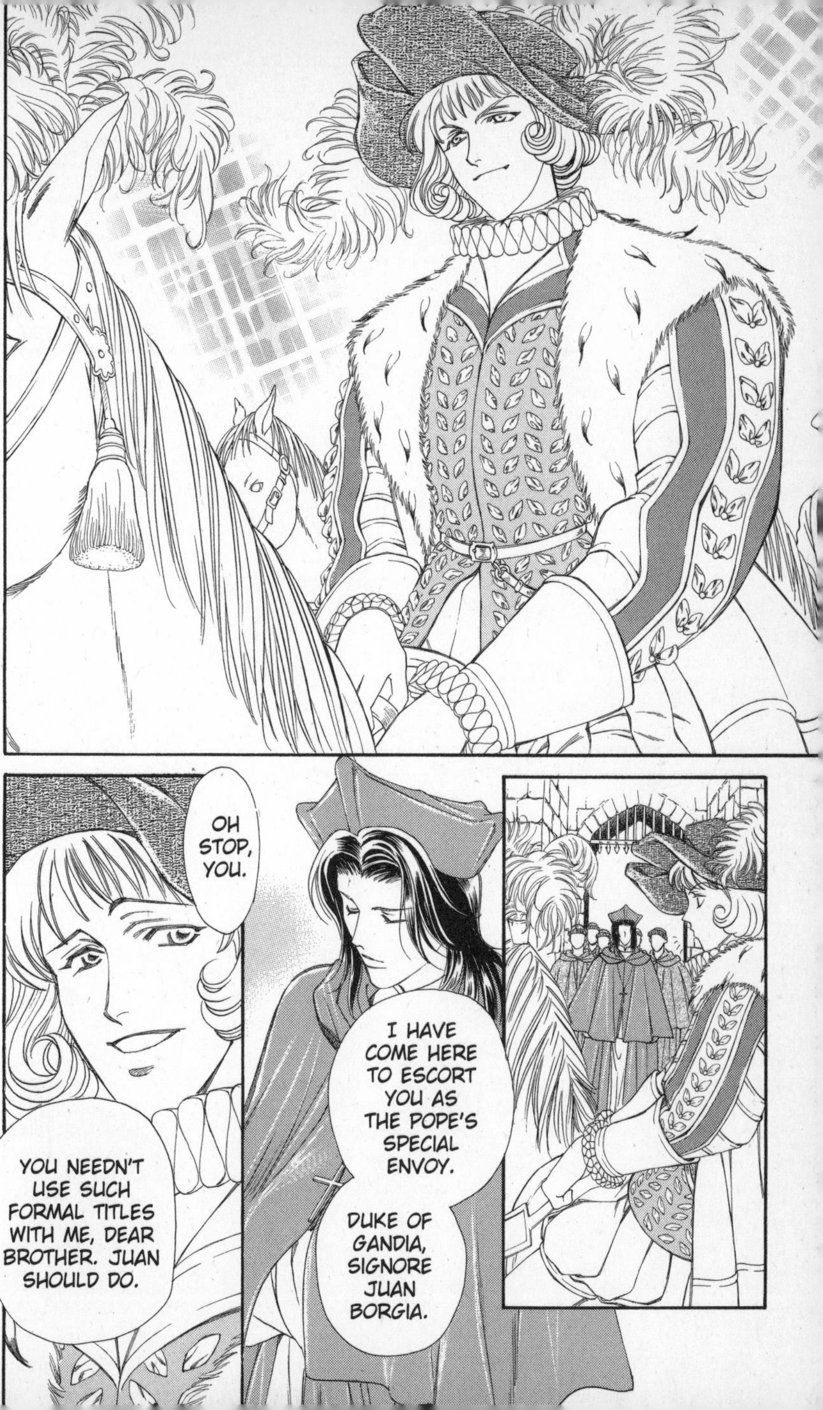
I HAVE COME HERE TO ESCORT YOU AS THE POPE'S SPECIAL ENVOY.
DUKE OF GANDIA, SIGNORE JUAN BORGIA.
OH STOP, YOU.
YOU NEEDN'T USE SUCH FORMAL TITLES WITH ME, DEAR BROTHER. JUAN SHOULD DO.

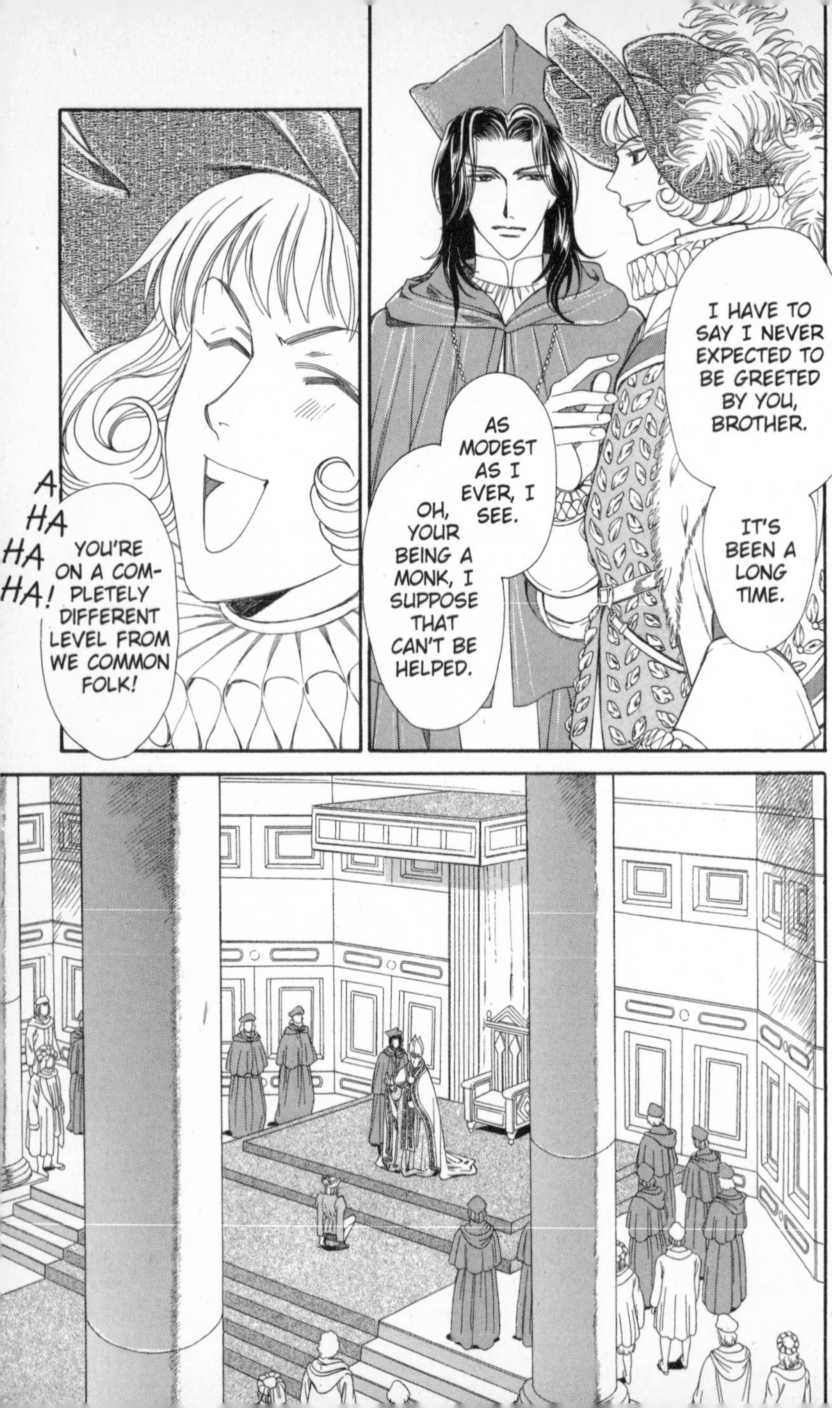
I HAVE TO SAY I NEVER EXPECTED TO BE GREETED BY YOU, BROTHER.
IT'S BEEN A LONG TIME.
AS MODEST AS I EVER, I SEE.
OH, YOUR BEING A MONK, I SUPPOSE THAT CAN'T BE HELPED.
YOU'RE ON A COM-PLETELY DIFFERENT LEVEL FROM WE COMMON FOLK!
A HA HA HA!

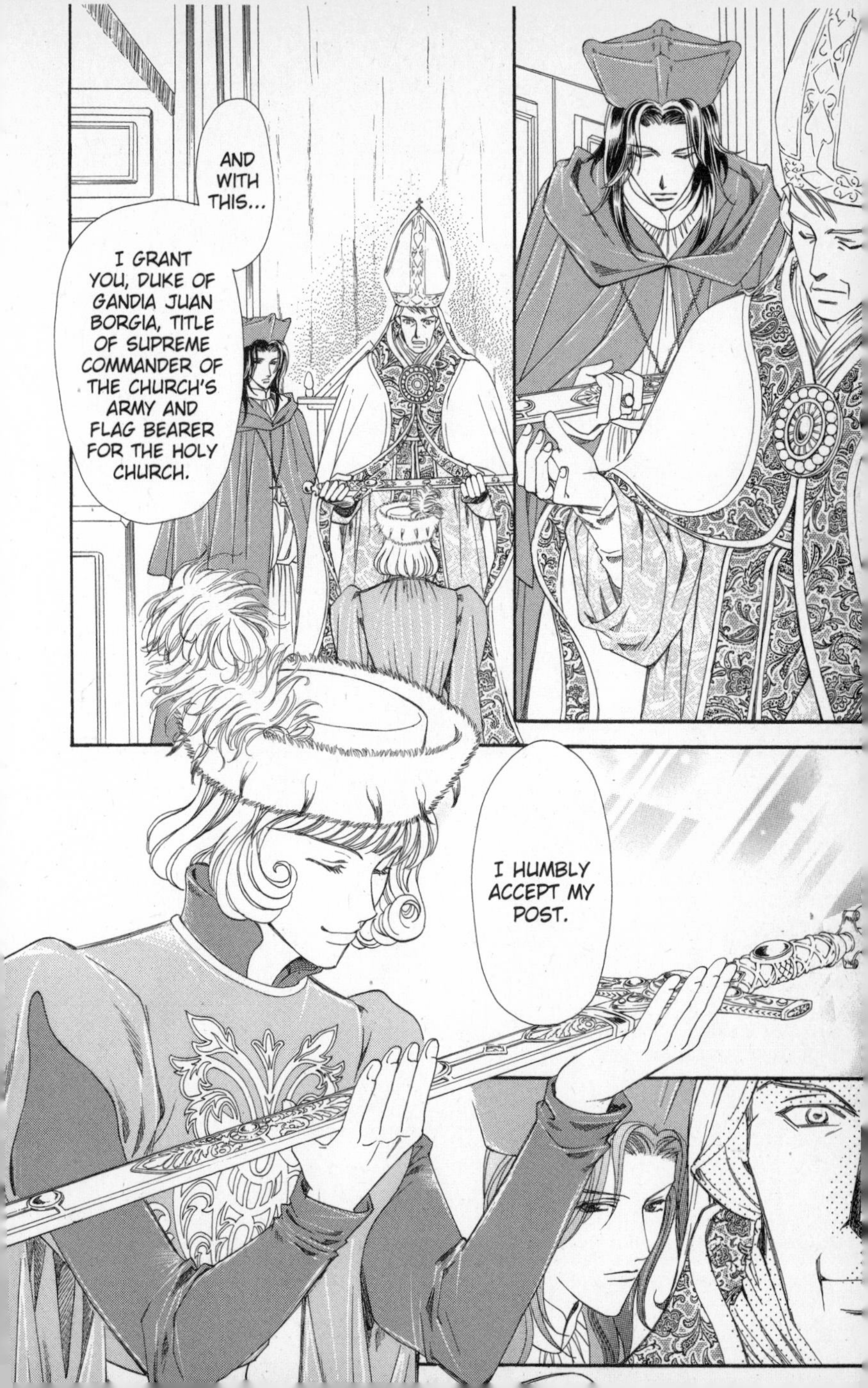
AND WITH THIS...
I GRANT YOU, DUKE OF GANDIA JUAN BORGIA, TITLE OF SUPREME COMMANDER OF THE CHURCH'S ARMY AND FLAG BEARER FOR THE HOLY CHURCH.
I HUMBLY ACCEPT MY POST.

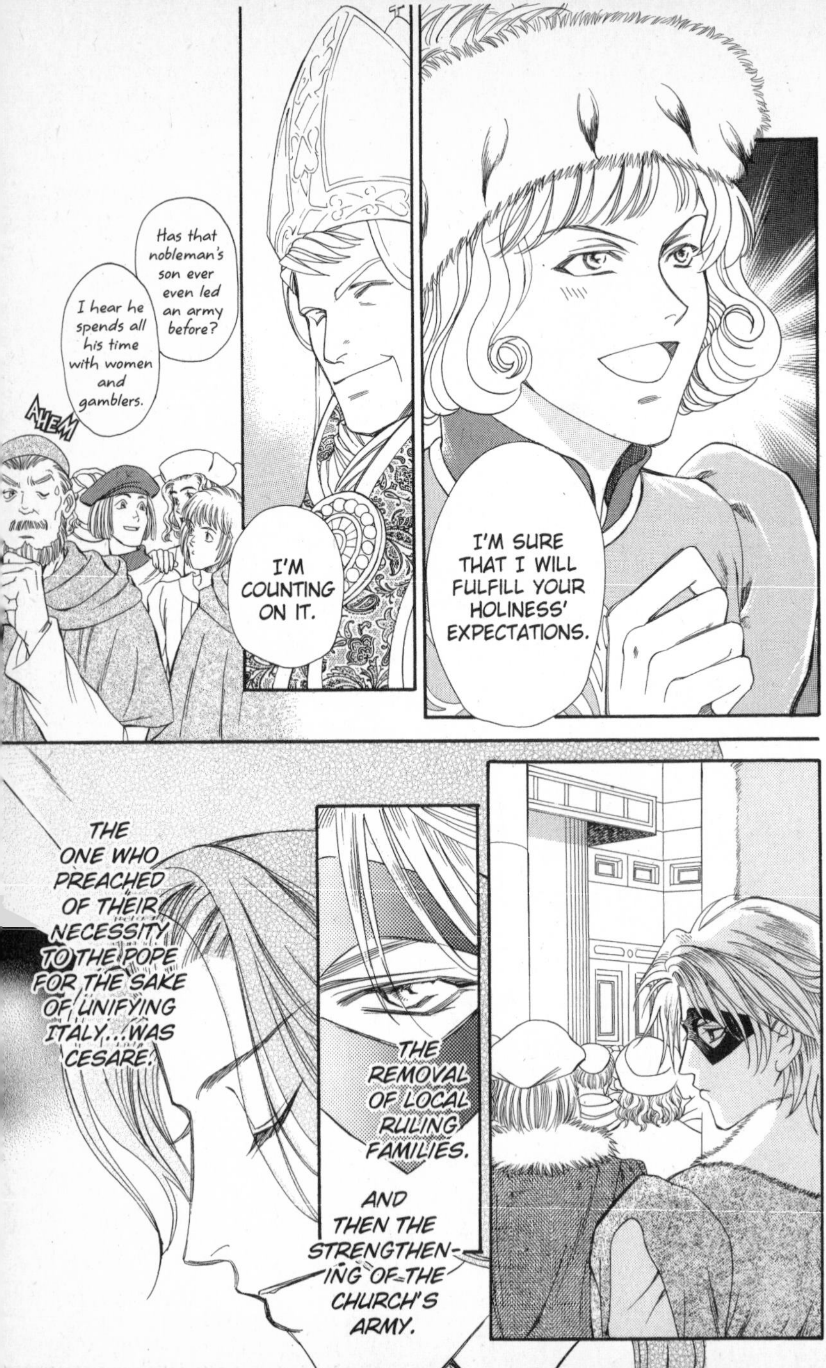

I'M SURE THAT I WILL FULFILL YOUR HOLINESS' EXPECTATIONS.
I'M COUNTING ON IT.
Has that nobleman's son ever even led an army before?
I hear he spends all his time with women and gamblers.
AHEM
THE REMOVAL OF LOCAL RULING FAMILIES.
AND THEN THE STRENGTHEN-ING OF THE CHURCH'S ARMY.
THE ONE WHO PREACHED OF THEIR NECESSITY TO THE POPE FOR THE SAKE OF UNIFYING ITALY...WAS CESARE!

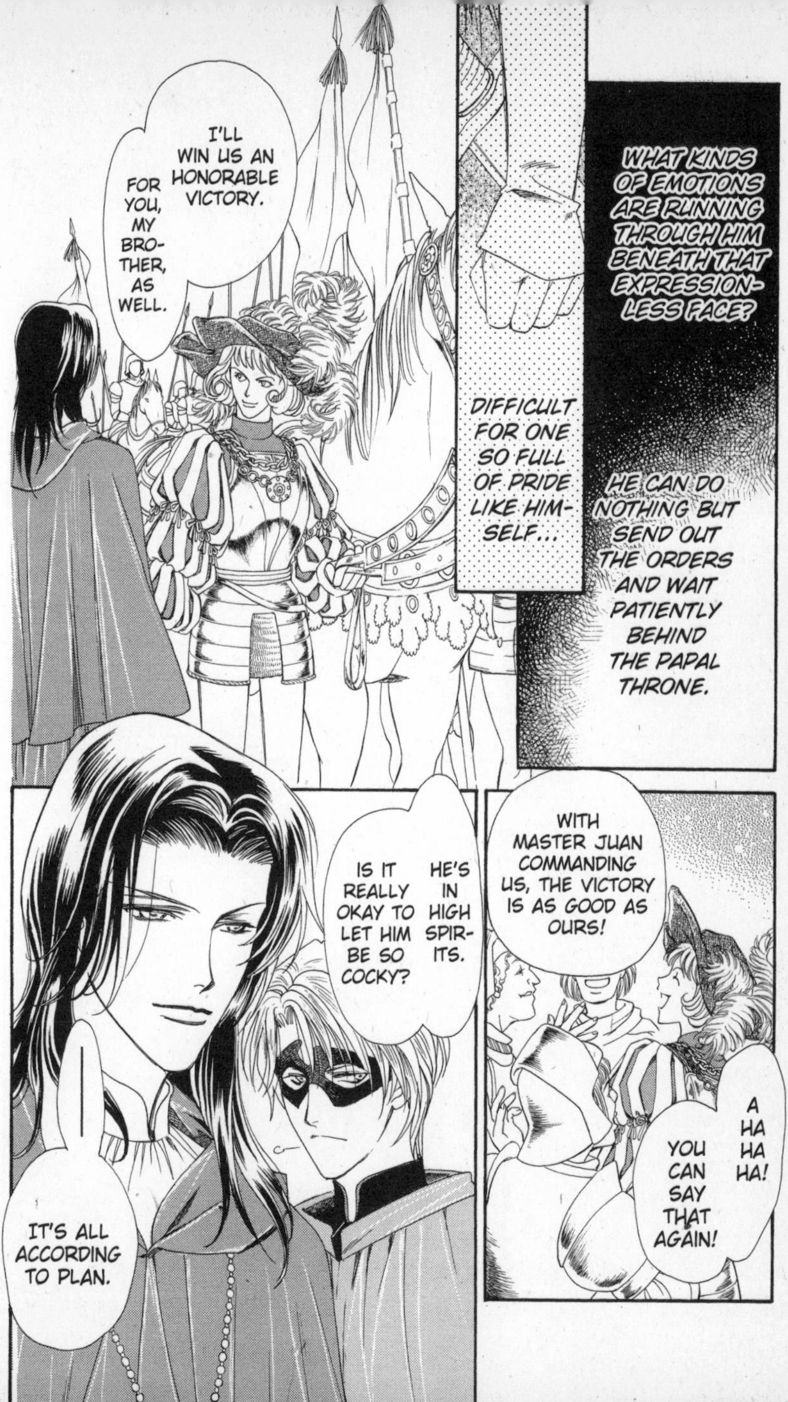
WHAT KINDS OF EMOTIONS ARE RUNNING THROUGH HIM BENEATH THAT EXPRESSIONLESS FACE?
DIFFICULT FOR ONE SO FULL OF PRIDE LIKE HIMSELF...
HE CAN DO NOTHING BUT SEND OUT THE ORDERS AND WAIT PATIENTLY BEHIND THE PAPAL THRONE.
I'LL WIN US AN HONORABLE VICTORY.
FOR YOU, MY BROTHER, AS WELL.
WITH MASTER JUAN COMMANDING US, THE VICTORY IS AS GOOD AS OURS!
A HA HA HA!
YOU CAN SAY THAT AGAIN!
HE'S IN HIGH SPIRITS.
IS IT REALLY OKAY TO LET HIM BE SO COCKY?
IT'S ALL ACCORDING TO PLAN.

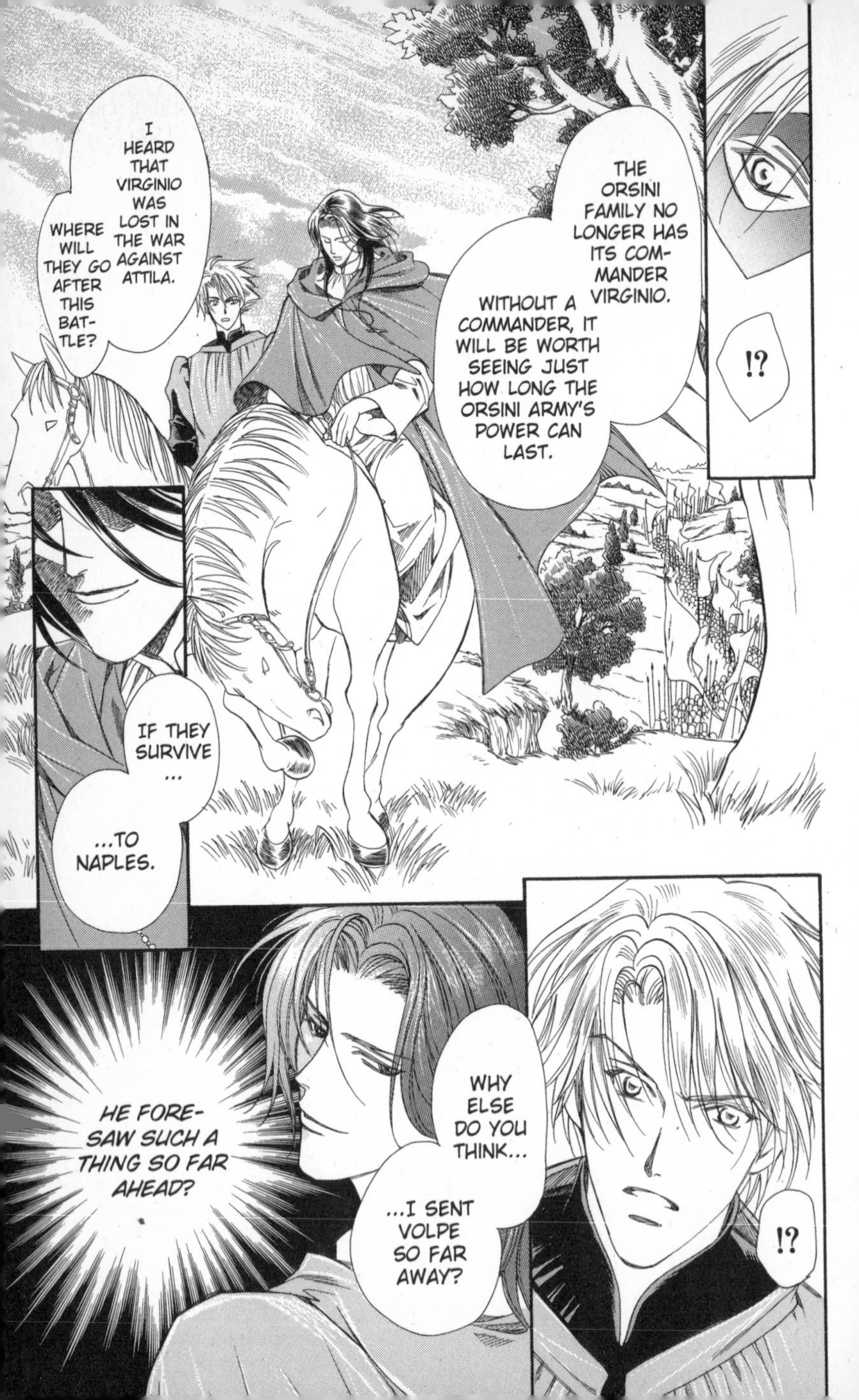
!?
THE ORSINI FAMILY NO LONGER HAS ITS COMMANDER VIRGINIO.
WITHOUT A COMMANDER, IT WILL BE WORTH SEEING JUST HOW LONG THE ORSINI ARMY'S POWER CAN LAST.
I HEARD THAT VIRGINIO WAS LOST IN THE WAR AGAINST ATTILA.
WHERE WILL THEY GO AFTER THIS BATTLE?
IF THEY SURVIVE...
...TO NAPLES.
!?
WHY ELSE DO YOU THINK...
...I SENT VOLPE SO FAR AWAY?
HE FORESAW SUCH A THING SO FAR AHEAD?

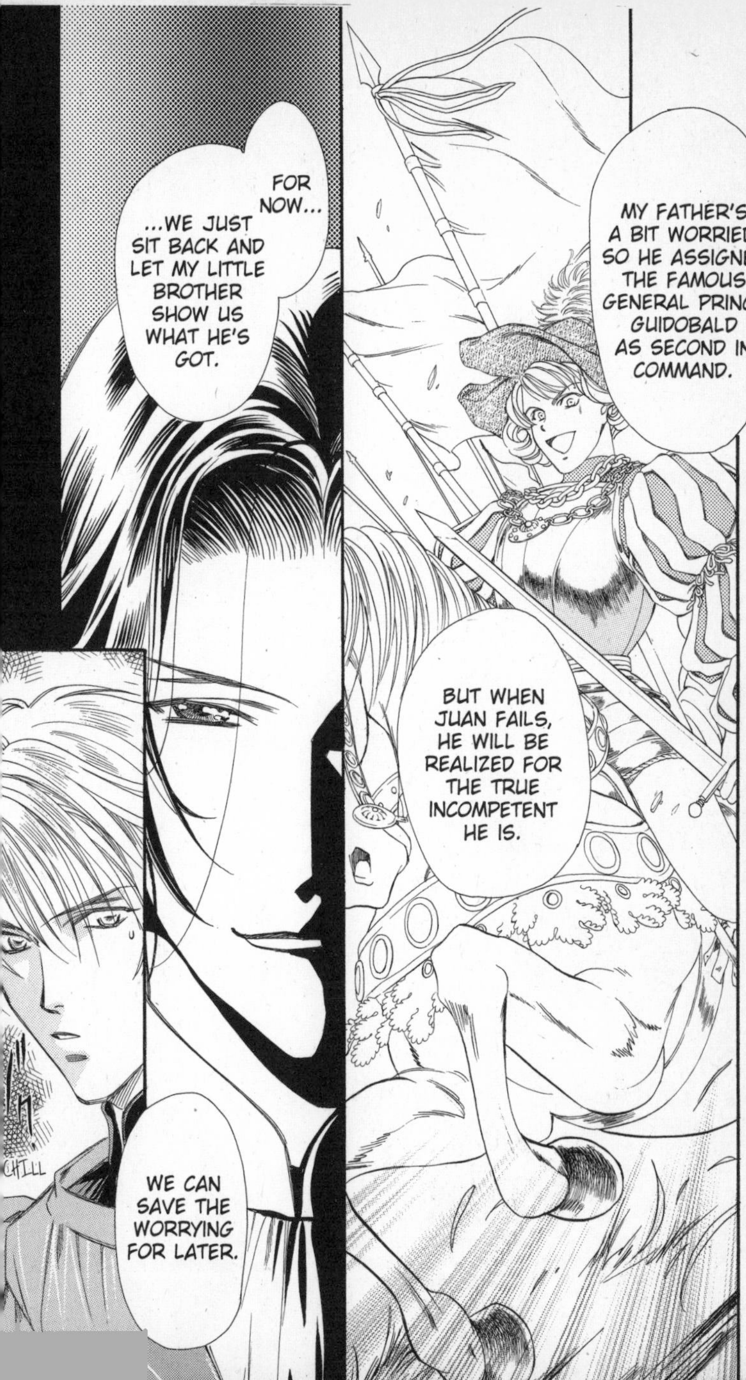
MY FATHER'S A BIT WORRIED, SO HE ASSIGNED THE FAMOUS GENERAL PRINCE GUIDOBALD AS SECOND IN COMMAND.
BUT WHEN JUAN FAILS, HE WILL BE REALIZED FOR THE TRUE INCOMPETENT HE IS.
FOR NOW...
...WE JUST SIT BACK AND LET MY LITTLE BROTHER SHOW US WHAT HE'S GOT.
CHILL
WE CAN SAVE THE WORRYING FOR LATER.

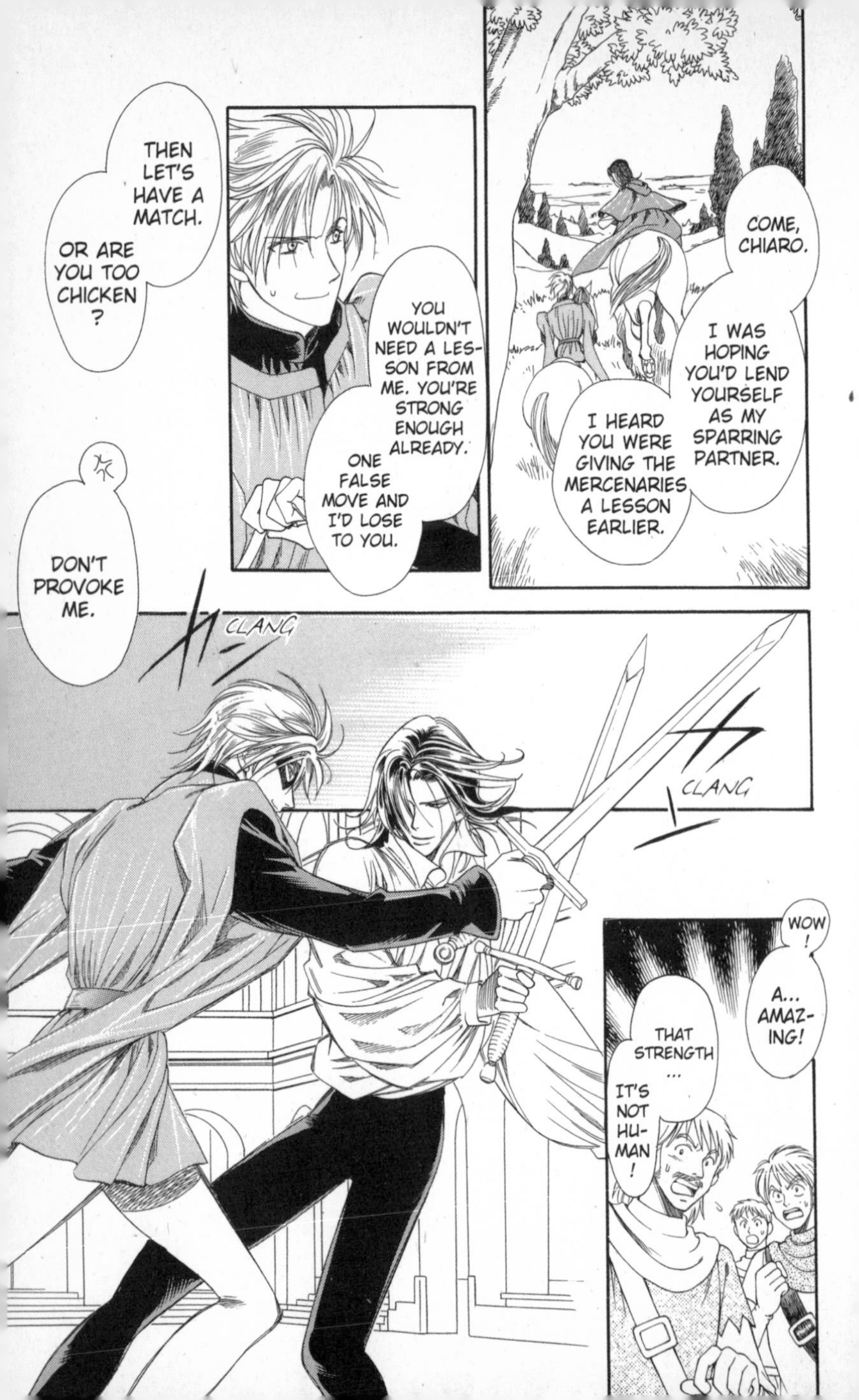
COME, CHIARO.
I WAS HOPING YOU'D LEND YOURSELF AS MY SPARRING PARTNER.
I HEARD YOU WERE GIVING THE MERCENARIES A LESSON EARLIER.
YOU WOULDN'T NEED A LESSON FROM ME. YOU'RE STRONG ENOUGH ALREADY.
ONE FALSE MOVE AND I'D LOSE TO YOU.
THEN LET'S HAVE A MATCH.
OR ARE YOU TOO CHICKEN?
DON'T PROVOKE ME.
CLANG
CLANG
WOW!
A... AMAZING!
THAT STRENGTH...
IT'S NOT HUMAN!

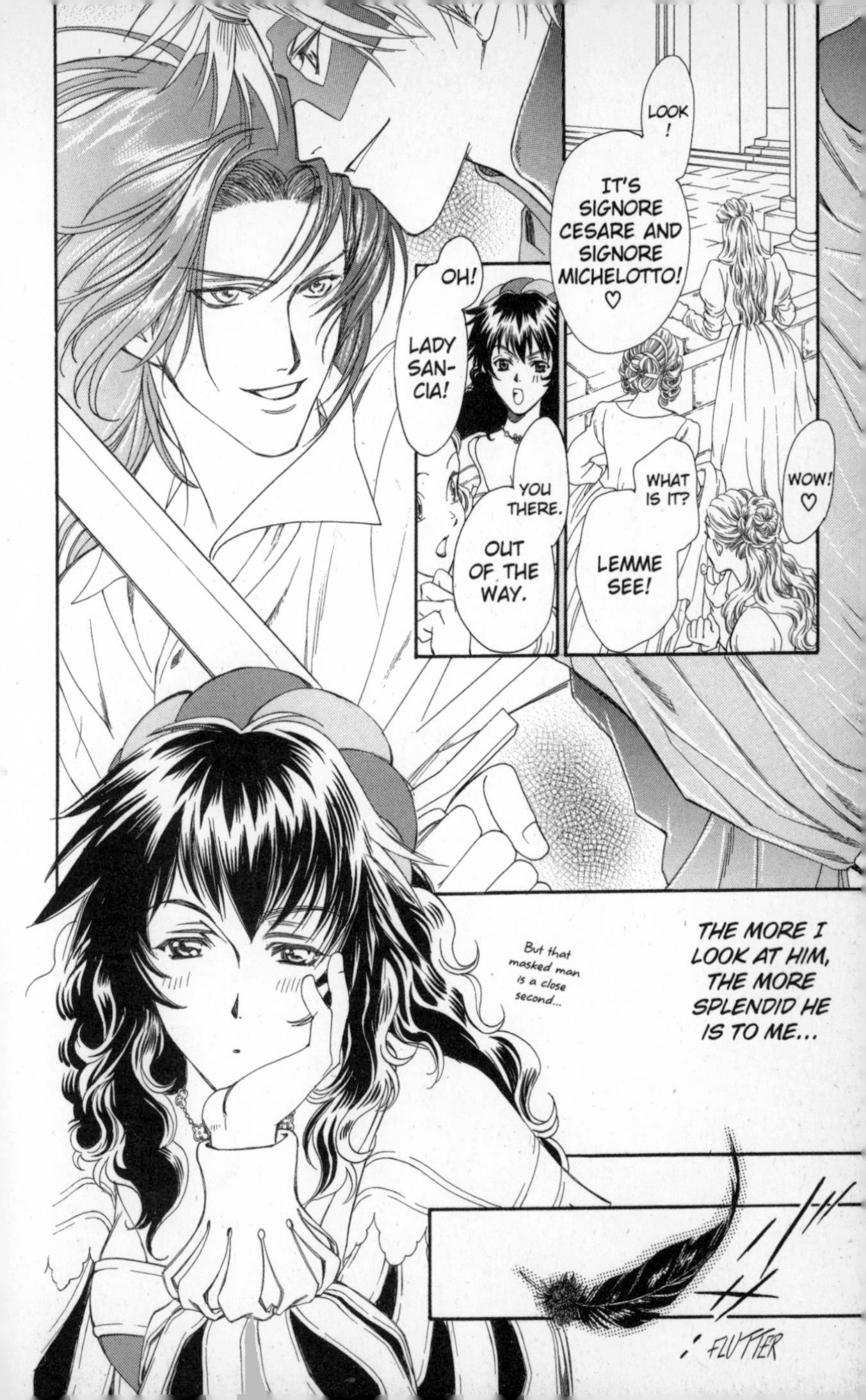

LOOK!
IT'S SIGNORE CESARE AND SIGNORE MICHELOTTO! ♡
WOW! ♡
WHAT IS IT?
LEMME SEE!
OH!
LADY SAN-CIA!
YOU THERE.
OUT OF THE WAY.
THE MORE I LOOK AT HIM, THE MORE SPLENDID HE IS TO ME...
But that masked man is a close second...
FLUTTER

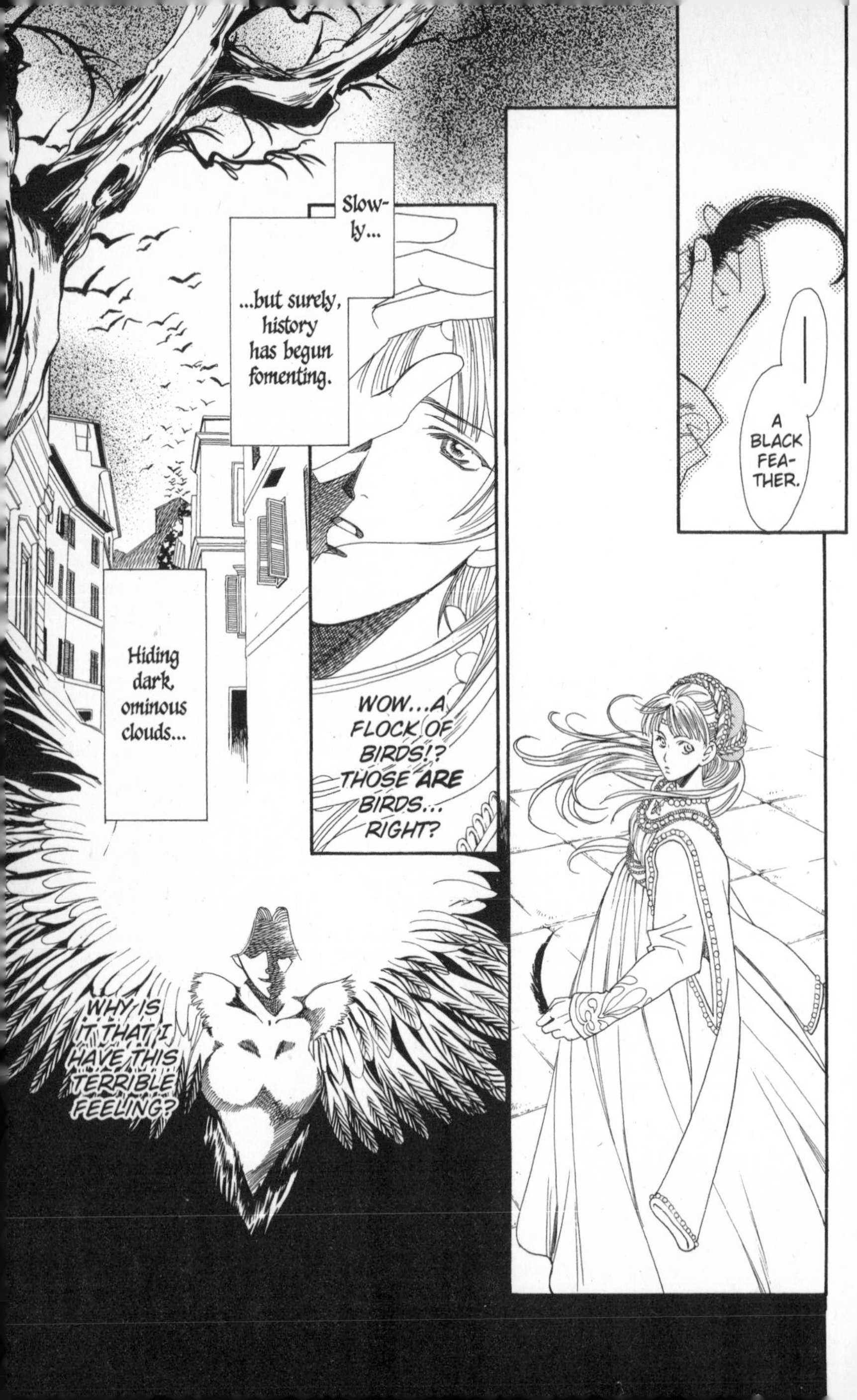
A BLACK FEA-THER.
Slow-ly...
...but surely, history has begun fomenting.
WOW...A FLOCK OF BIRDS!? THOSE ARE BIRDS... RIGHT?
Hiding dark, ominous clouds...
WHY IS IT THAT I HAVE THIS TERRIBLE FEELING?

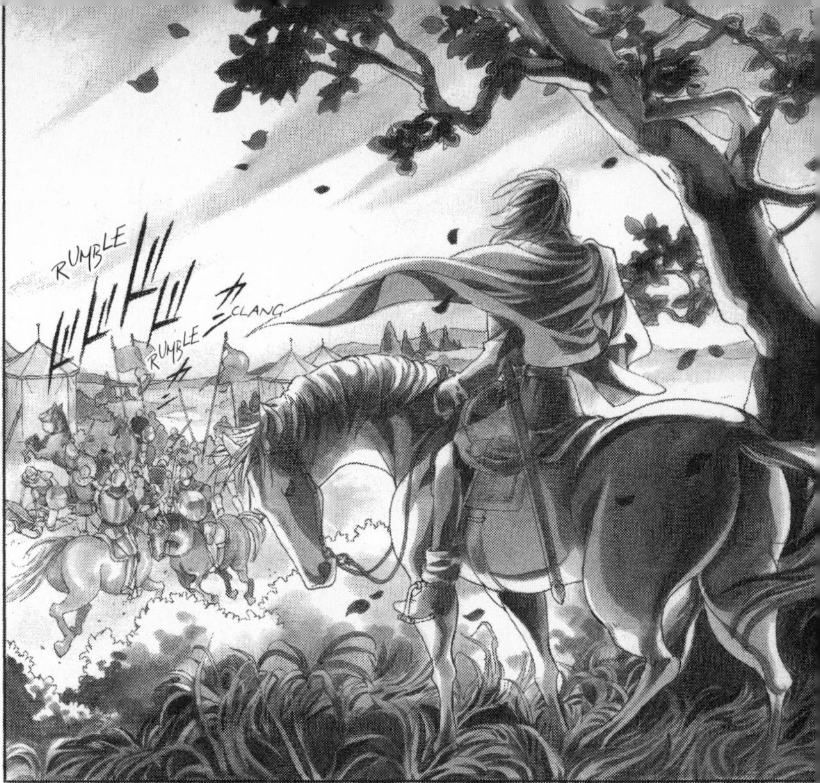
RUMBLE
CLANG
RUMBLE
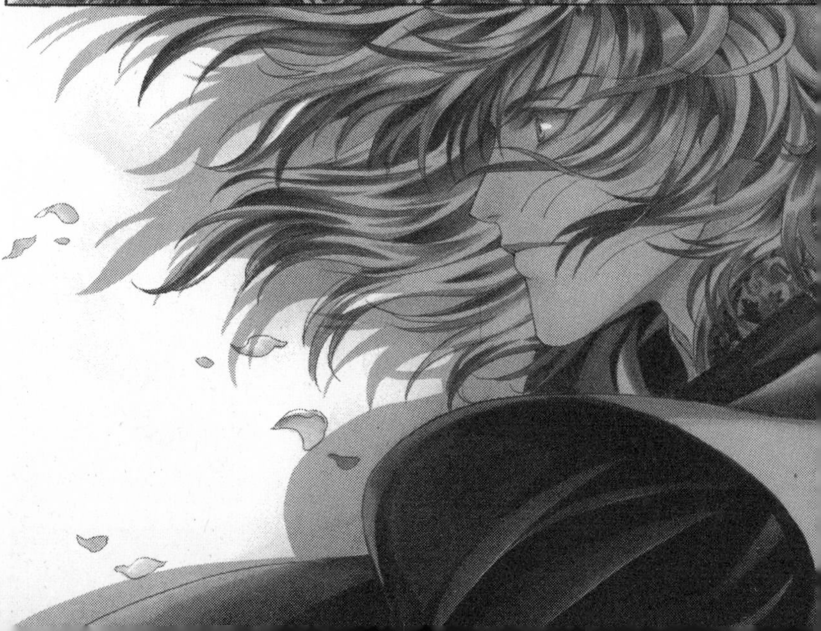

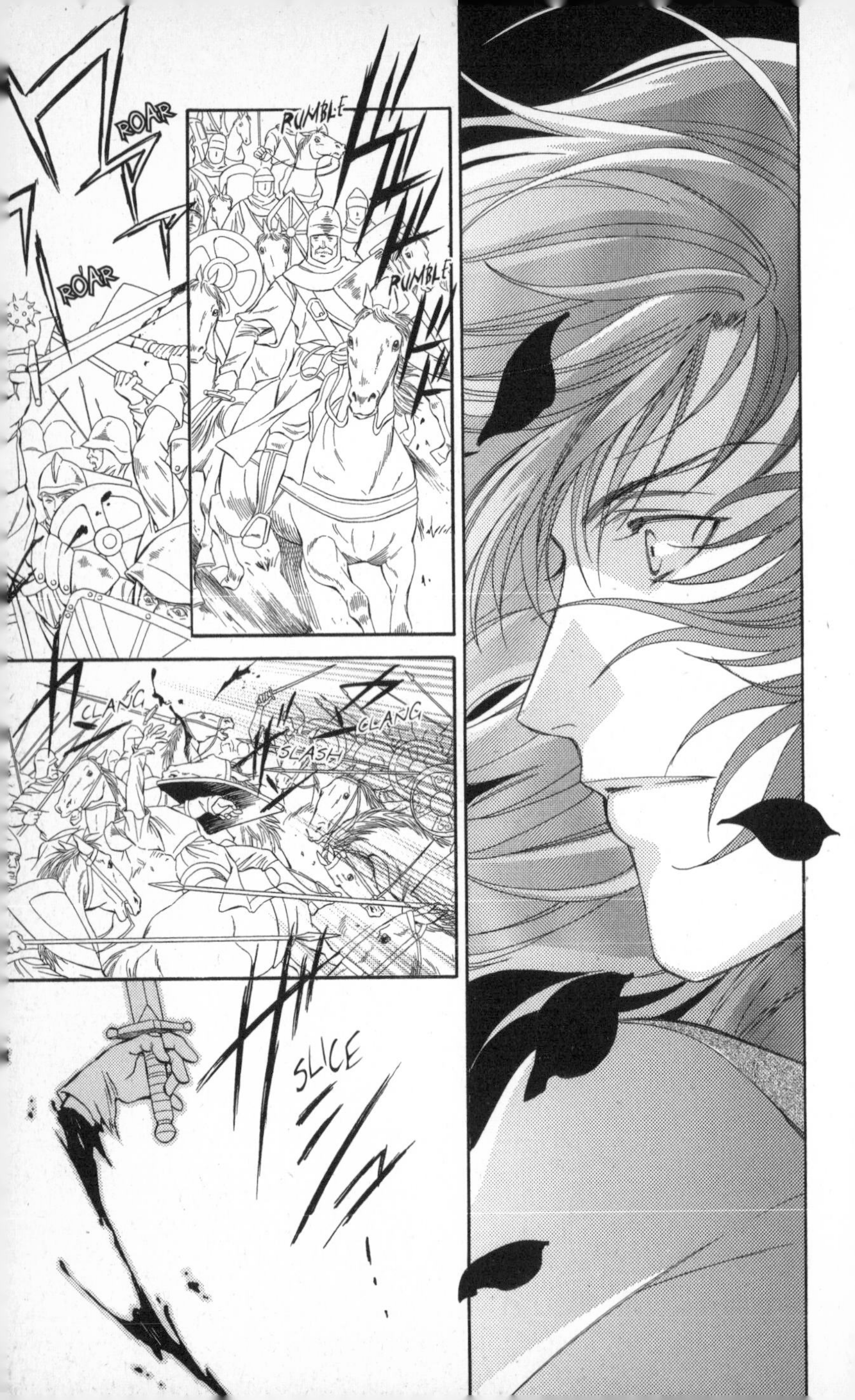
RUMBLE
RUMBLE
ROAR
ROAR
CLANG
SLASH
CLANG
SLICE

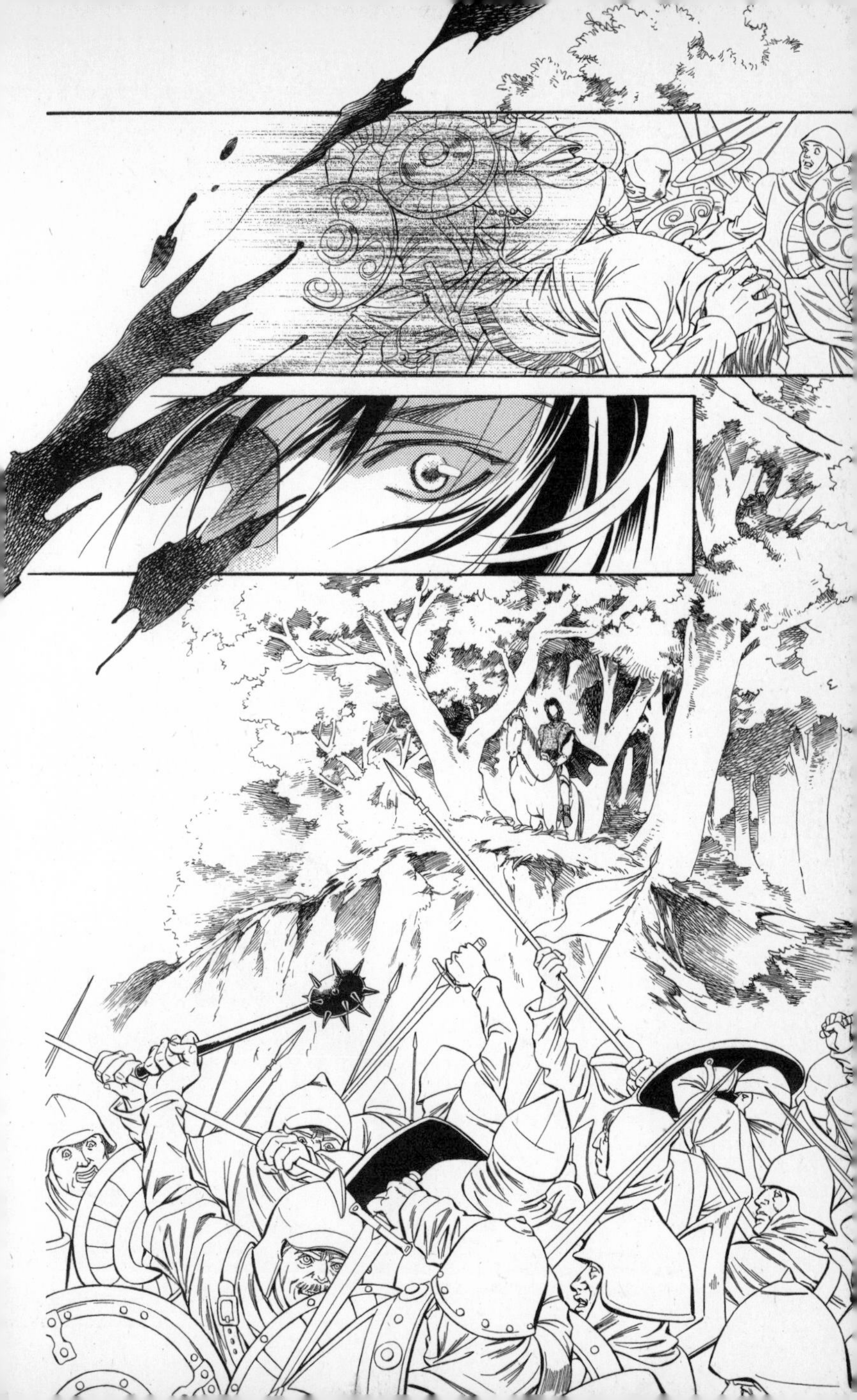

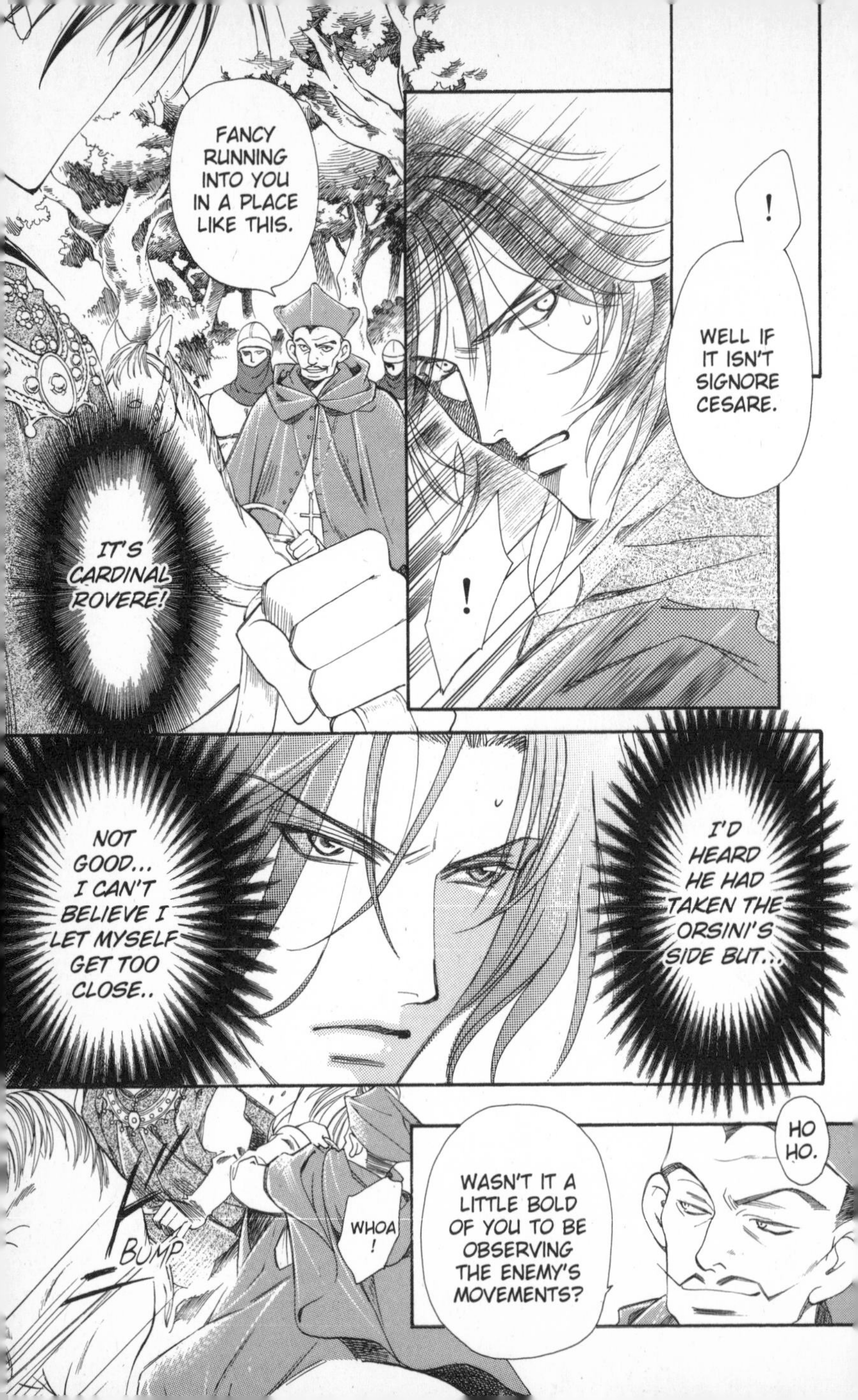
!
WELL IF IT ISN'T SIGNORE CESARE.
!
FANCY RUNNING INTO YOU IN A PLACE LIKE THIS.
IT'S CARDINAL ROVERE!
I'D HEARD HE HAD TAKEN THE ORSINI'S SIDE BUT...
NOT GOOD... I CAN'T BELIEVE I LET MYSELF GET TOO CLOSE..
HO HO.
WASN'T IT A LITTLE BOLD OF YOU TO BE OBSERVING THE ENEMY'S MOVEMENTS?
WHOA !
BUMP

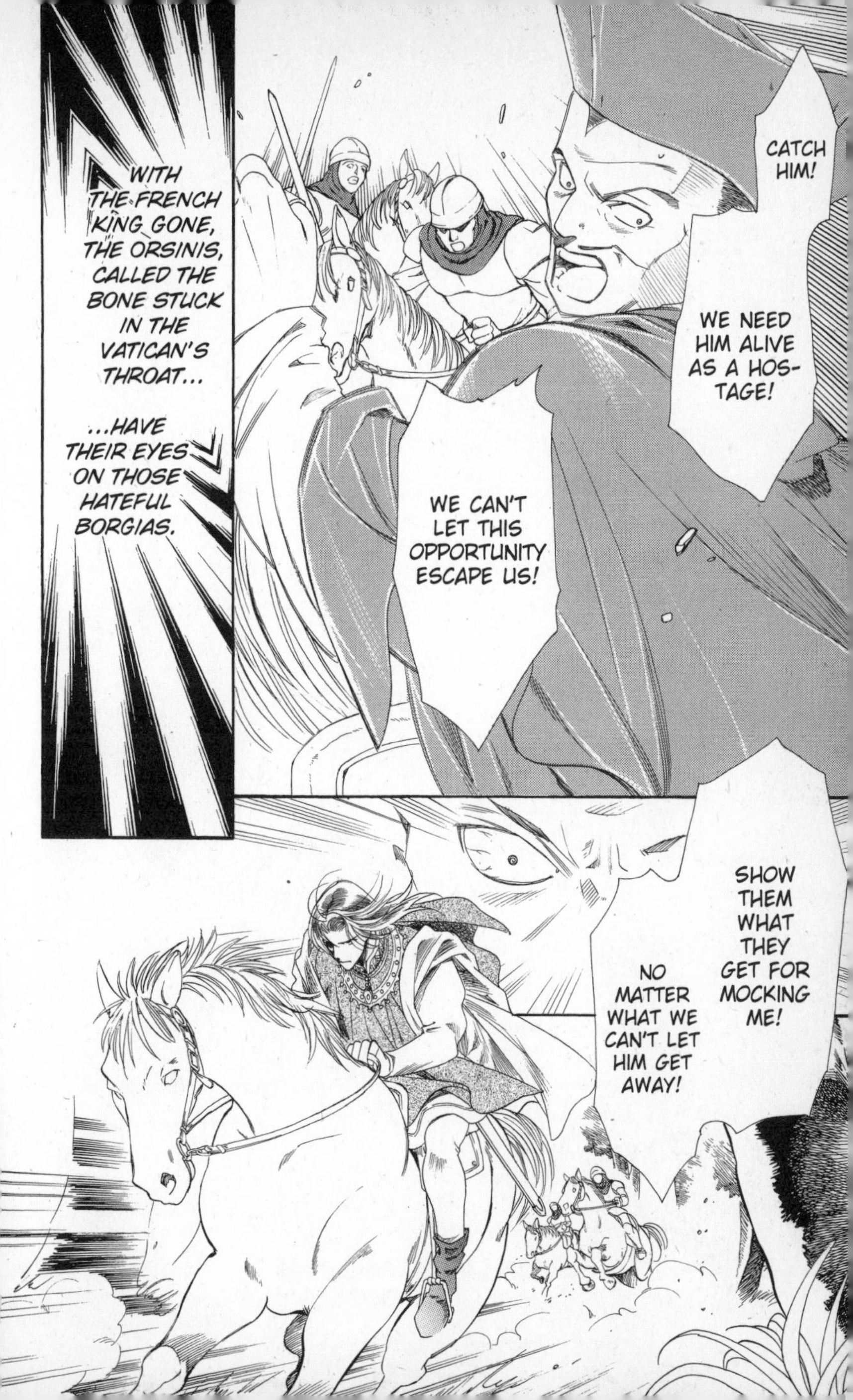
CATCH HIM!
WE NEED HIM ALIVE AS A HOS-TAGE!
WE CAN'T LET THIS OPPORTUNITY ESCAPE US!
WITH THE FRENCH KING GONE, THE ORSINIS, CALLED THE BONE STUCK IN THE VATICAN'S THROAT...
...HAVE THEIR EYES ON THOSE HATEFUL BORGIAS.
SHOW THEM WHAT THEY GET FOR MOCKING ME!
NO MATTER WHAT WE CAN'T LET HIM GET AWAY!

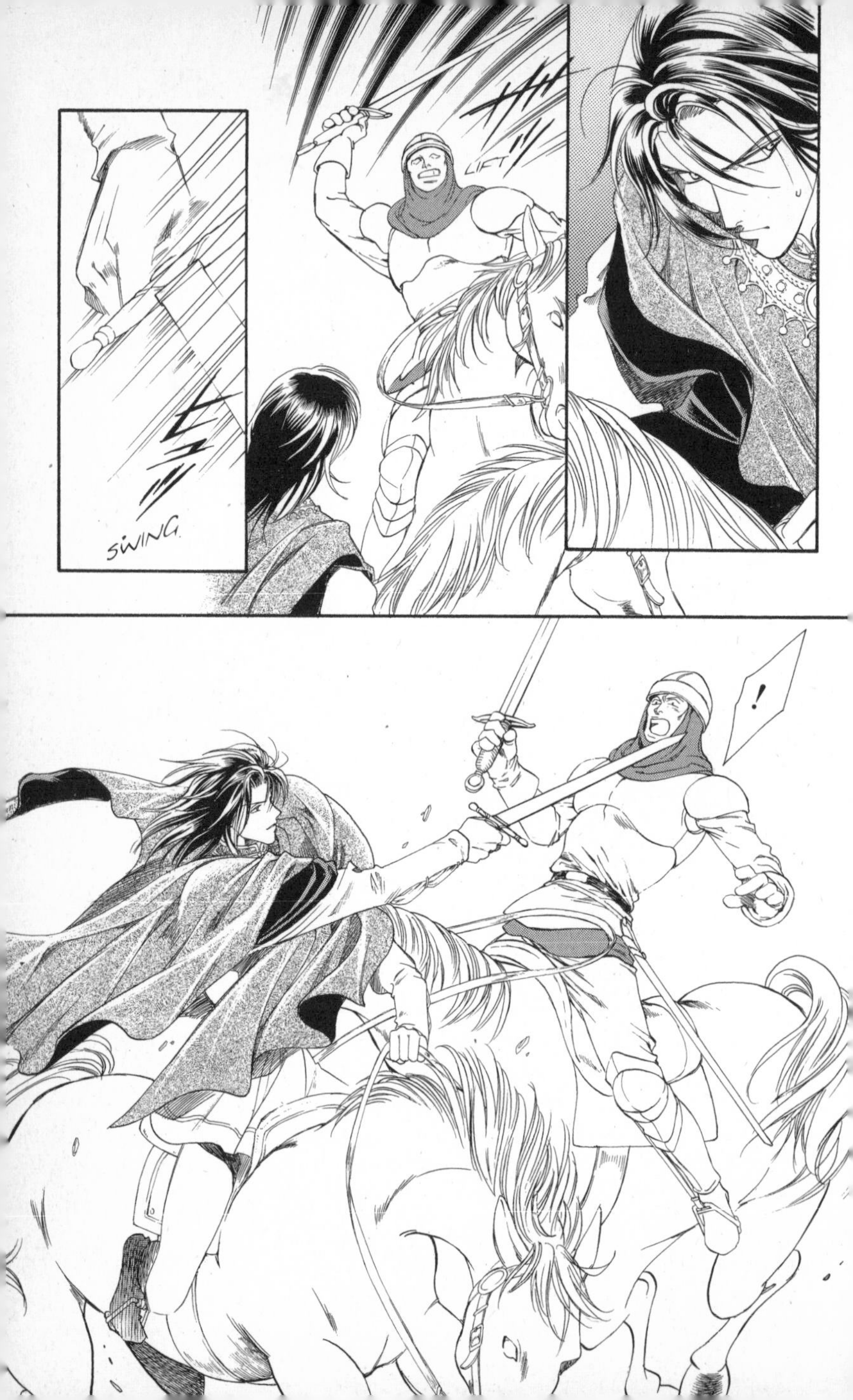
LIFT
SWING
!

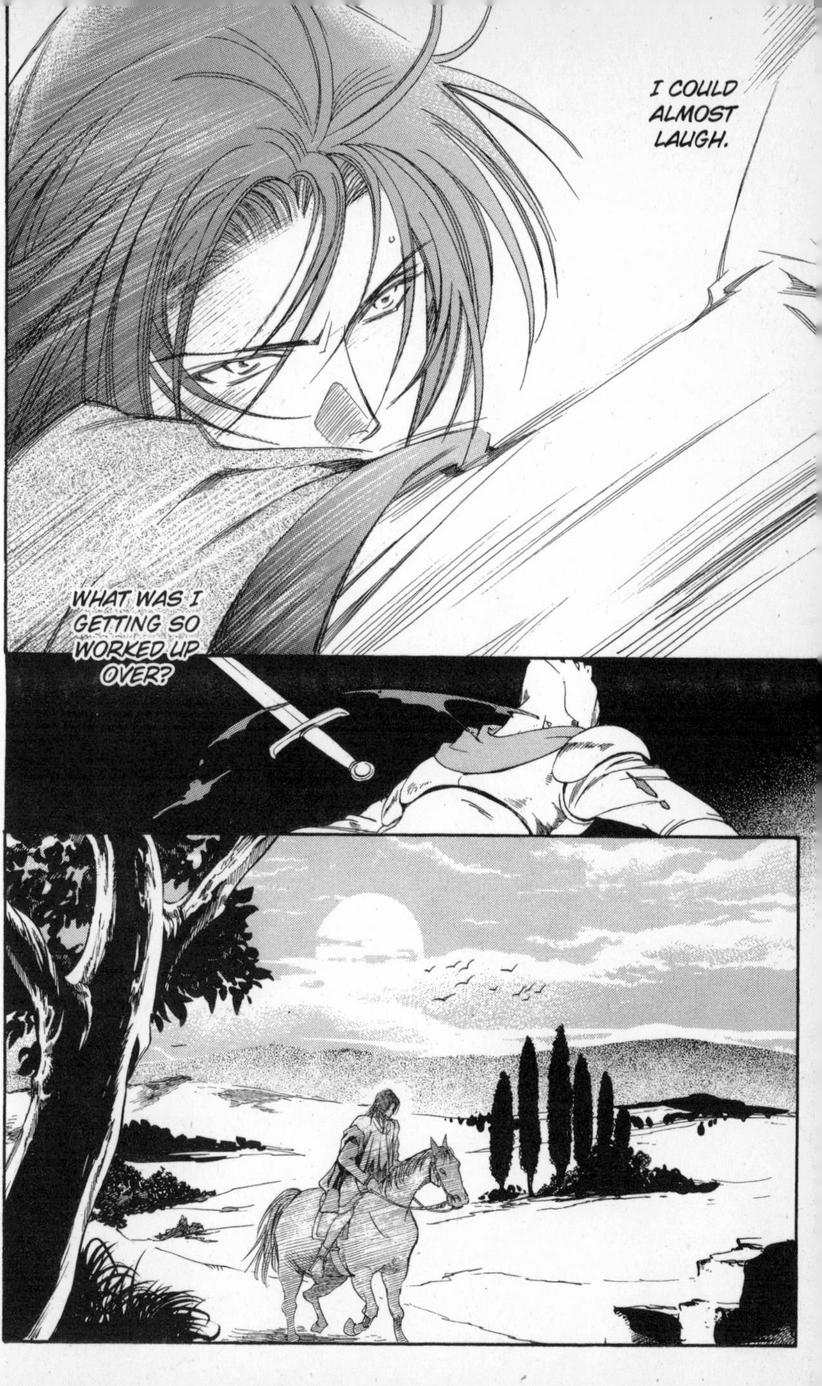
I COULD ALMOST LAUGH.
WHAT WAS I GETTING SO WORKED UP OVER?

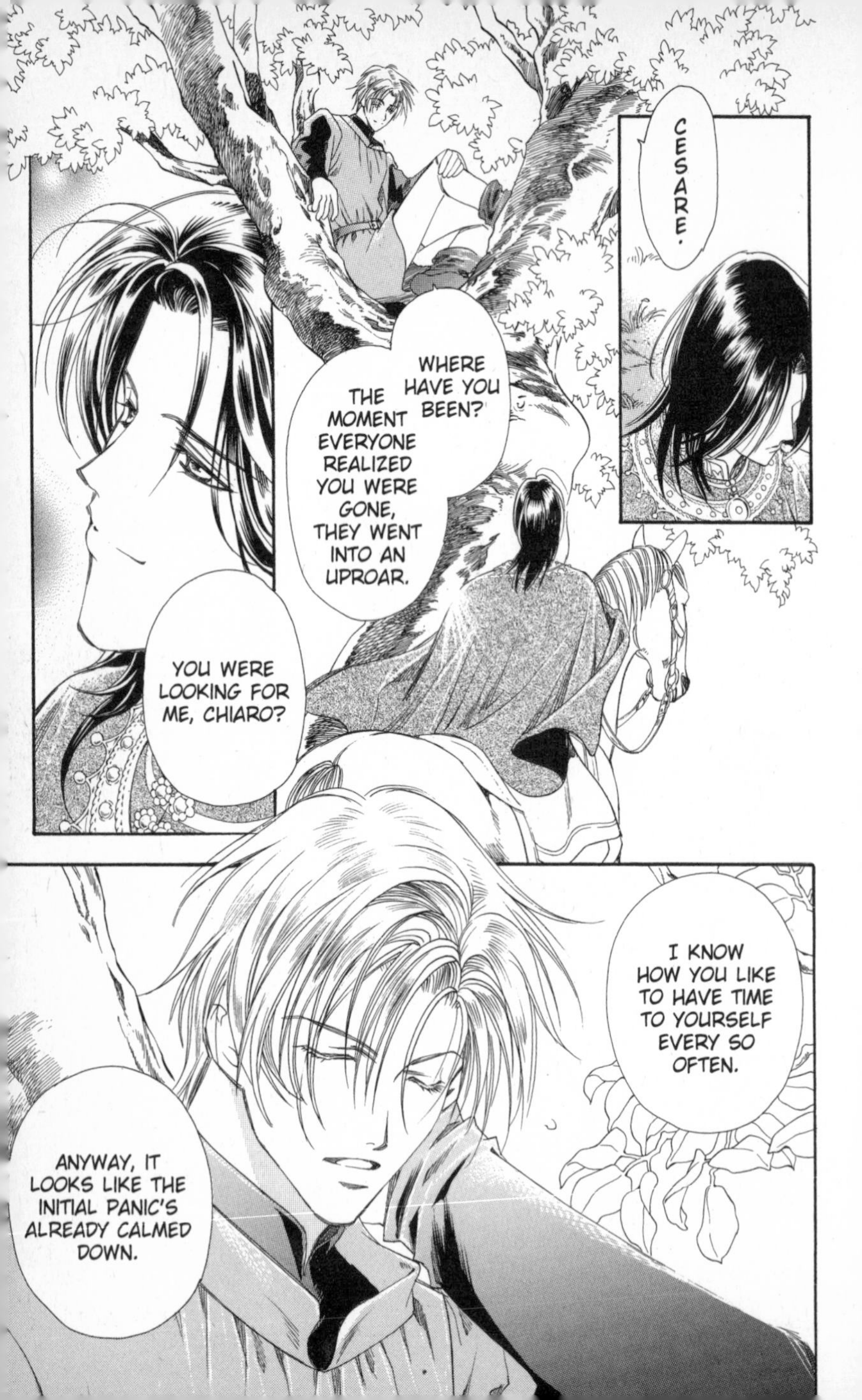
CESARE.
WHERE HAVE YOU BEEN?
THE MOMENT EVERYONE REALIZED YOU WERE GONE, THEY WENT INTO AN UPROAR.
YOU WERE LOOKING FOR ME, CHIARO?
I KNOW HOW YOU LIKE TO HAVE TIME TO YOURSELF EVERY SO OFTEN.
ANYWAY, IT LOOKS LIKE THE INITIAL PANIC'S ALREADY CALMED DOWN.

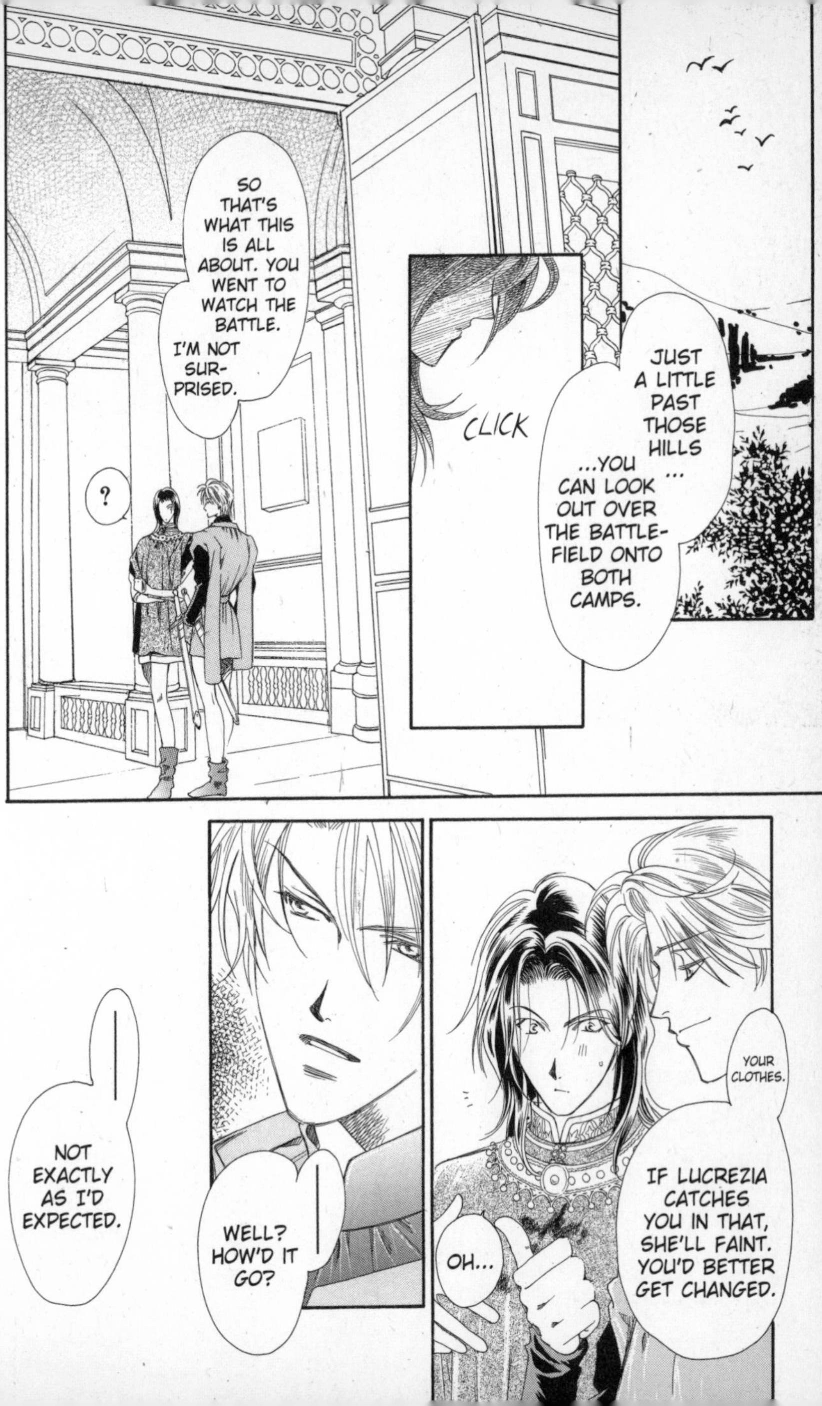
JUST A LITTLE PAST THOSE HILLS ...
...YOU CAN LOOK OUT OVER THE BATTLE-FIELD ONTO BOTH CAMPS.
CLICK
SO THAT'S WHAT THIS IS ALL ABOUT. YOU WENT TO WATCH THE BATTLE.
I'M NOT SUR-PRISED.
?
YOUR CLOTHES.
IF LUCREZIA CATCHES YOU IN THAT, SHE'LL FAINT. YOU'D BETTER GET CHANGED.
OH...
—
WELL? HOW'D IT GO?
—
NOT EXACTLY AS I'D EXPECTED.

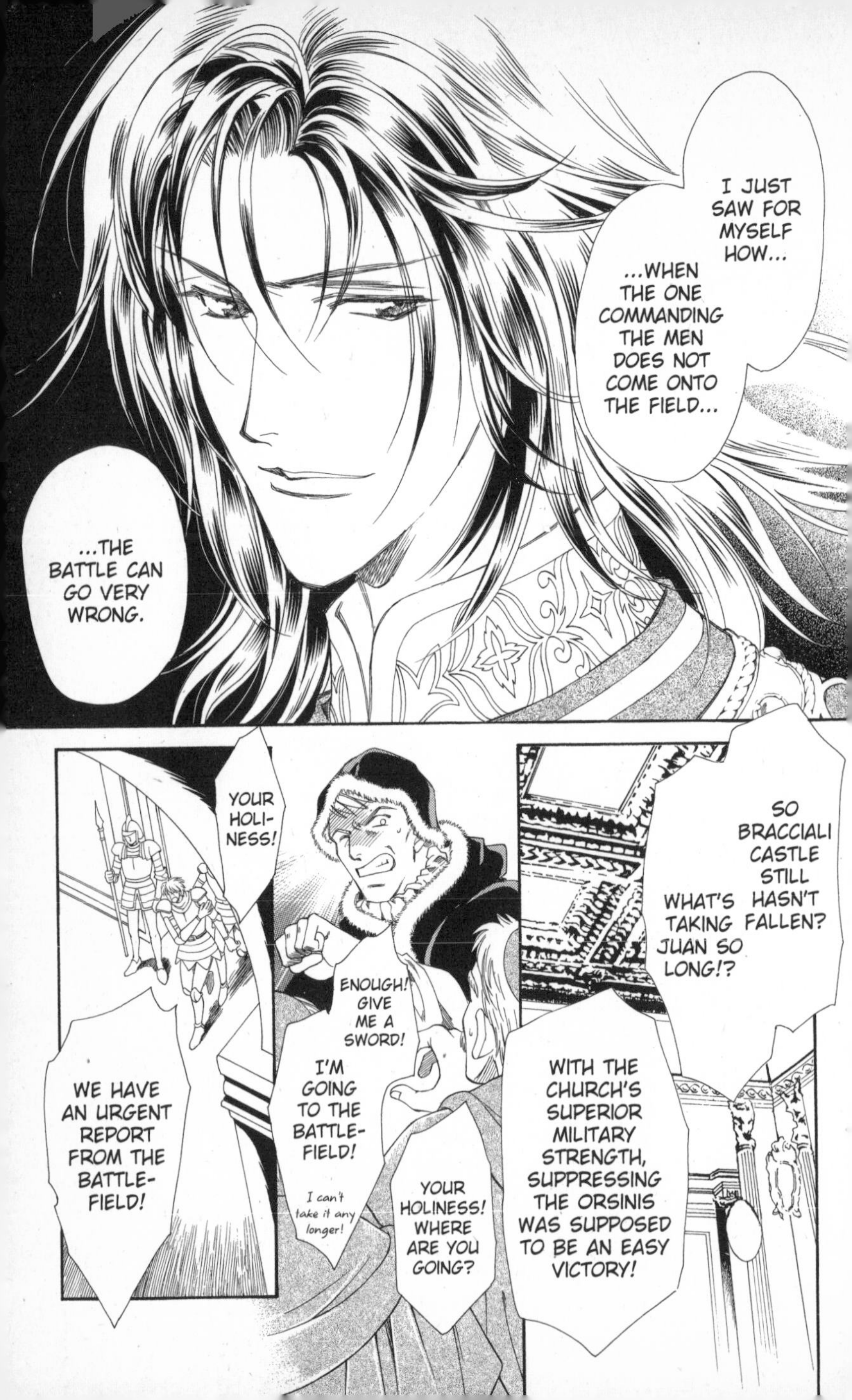
I JUST SAW FOR MYSELF HOW...
...WHEN THE ONE COMMANDING THE MEN DOES NOT COME ONTO THE FIELD...
...THE BATTLE CAN GO VERY WRONG.
SO BRACCIALI CASTLE STILL HASN'T FALLEN?
WHAT'S TAKING JUAN SO LONG!?
WITH THE CHURCH'S SUPERIOR MILITARY STRENGTH, SUPPRESSING THE ORSINIS WAS SUPPOSED TO BE AN EASY VICTORY!
ENOUGH! GIVE ME A SWORD!
I'M GOING TO THE BATTLE-FIELD!
I can't take it any longer!
YOUR HOLINESS! WHERE ARE YOU GOING?
YOUR HOLI-NESS!
WE HAVE AN URGENT REPORT FROM THE BATTLE-FIELD!

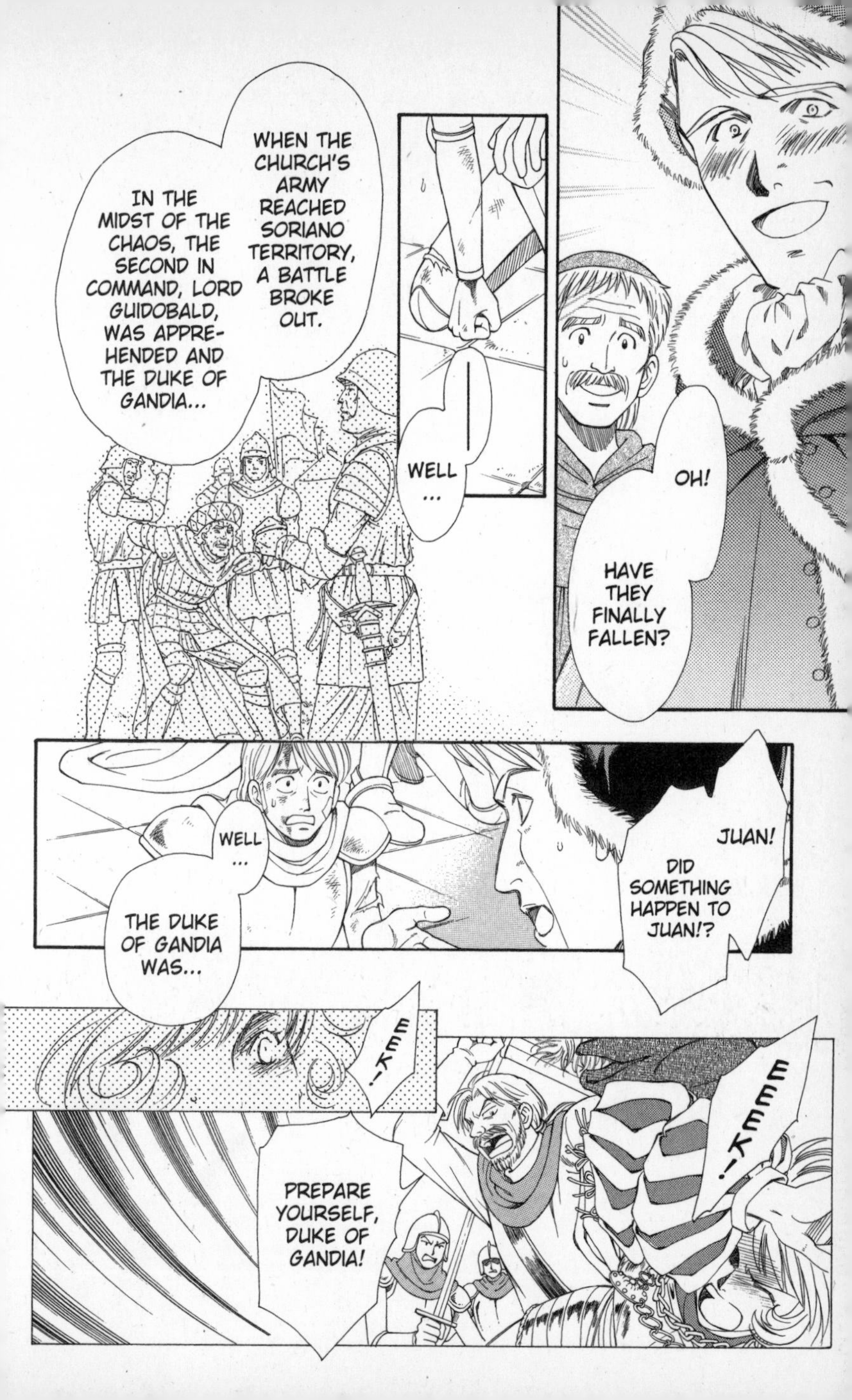
OH!
HAVE THEY FINALLY FALLEN?
WELL ...
WHEN THE CHURCH'S ARMY REACHED SORIANO TERRITORY, A BATTLE BROKE OUT.
IN THE MIDST OF THE CHAOS, THE SECOND IN COMMAND, LORD GUIDOBALD, WAS APPREHENDED AND THE DUKE OF GANDIA...
JUAN!
DID SOMETHING HAPPEN TO JUAN!?
WELL ...
THE DUKE OF GANDIA WAS...
EEEEEK!
PREPARE YOURSELF, DUKE OF GANDIA!
EEK!

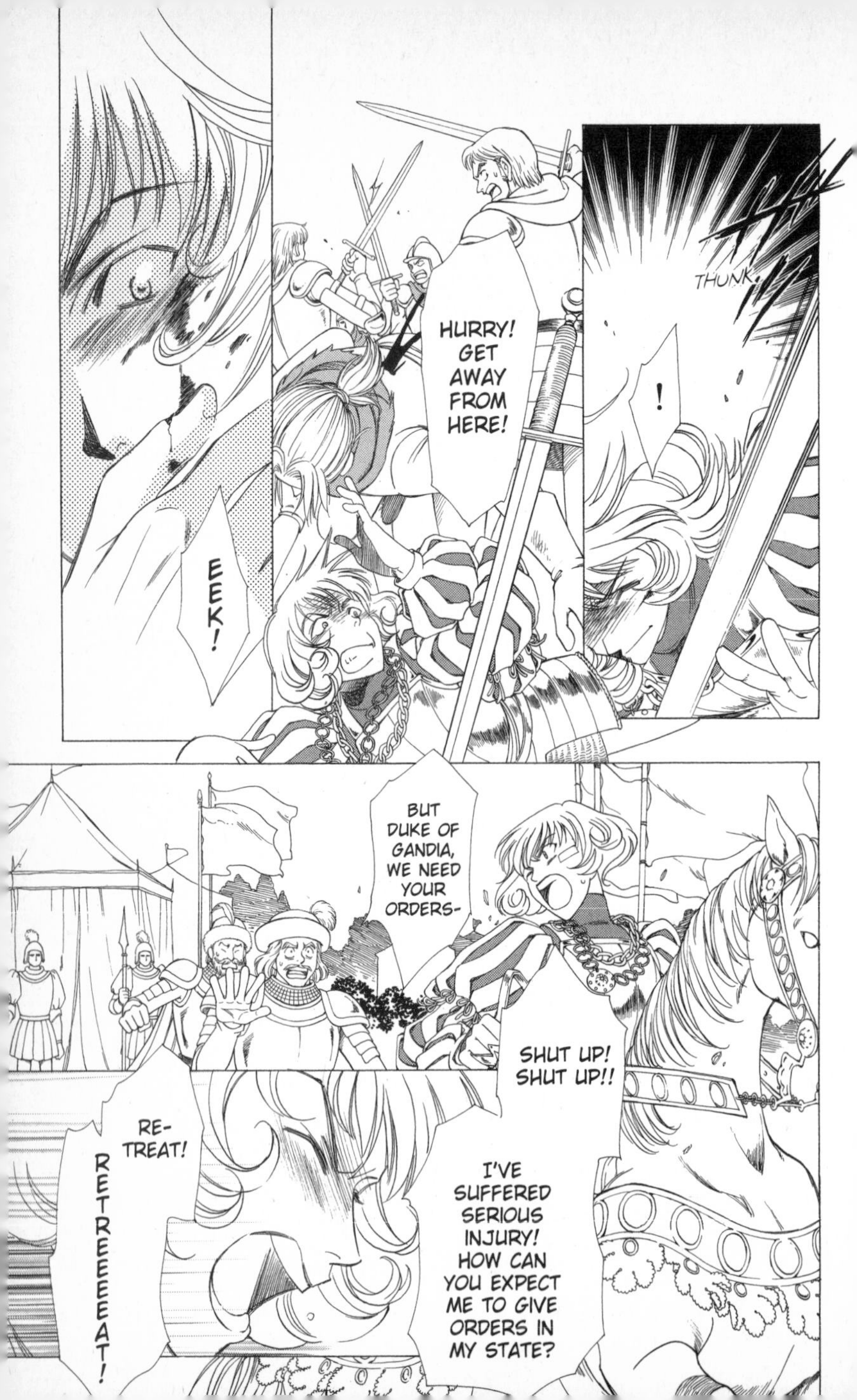
THUNK
!
HURRY! GET AWAY FROM HERE!
EEK!
BUT DUKE OF GANDIA, WE NEED YOUR ORDERS-
SHUT UP! SHUT UP!!
I'VE SUFFERED SERIOUS INJURY! HOW CAN YOU EXPECT ME TO GIVE ORDERS IN MY STATE?
RE-TREAT!
RETREEEEEAT!

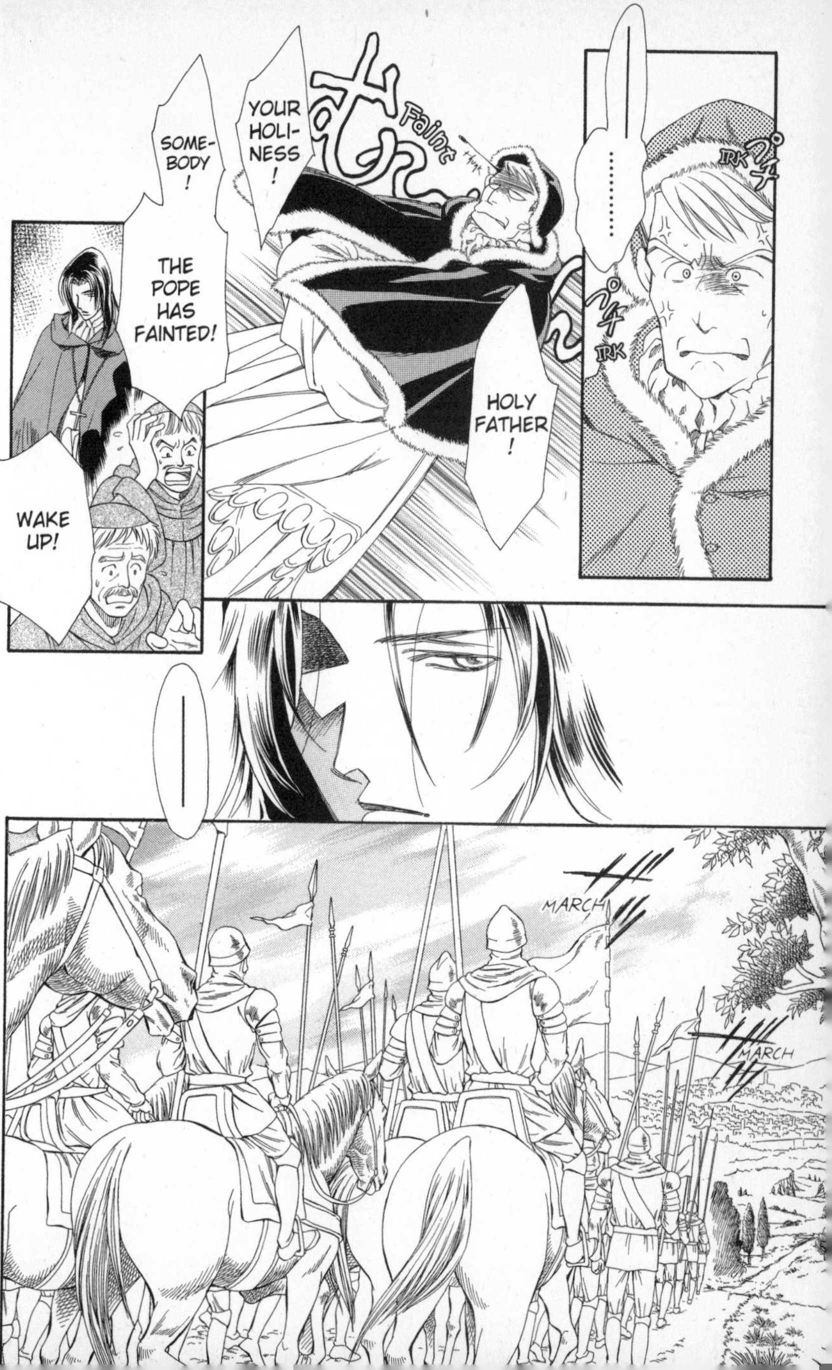
......
IRK
IRK
YOUR HOLI-NESS!
Faint
HOLY FATHER!
SOME-BODY!
THE POPE HAS FAINTED!
WAKE UP!
MARCH
MARCH

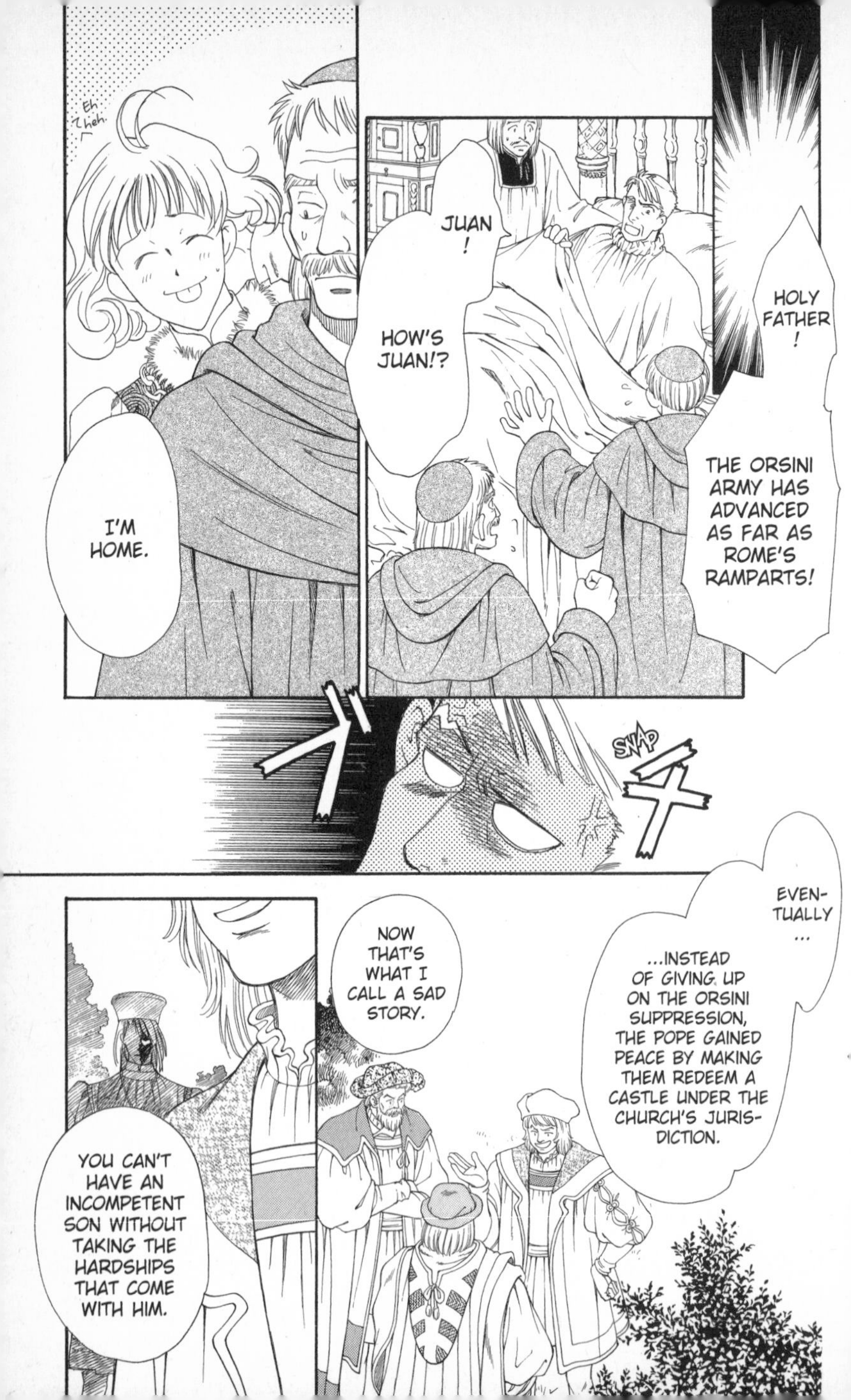
HOLY FATHER!
THE ORSINI ARMY HAS ADVANCED AS FAR AS ROME'S RAMPARTS!
JUAN!
HOW'S JUAN!?
Eh heh.
I'M HOME.
SNAP
EVEN-TUALLY...
...INSTEAD OF GIVING UP ON THE ORSINI SUPPRESSION, THE POPE GAINED PEACE BY MAKING THEM REDEEM A CASTLE UNDER THE CHURCH'S JURIS-DICTION.
NOW THAT'S WHAT I CALL A SAD STORY.
YOU CAN'T HAVE AN INCOMPETENT SON WITHOUT TAKING THE HARDSHIPS THAT COME WITH HIM.

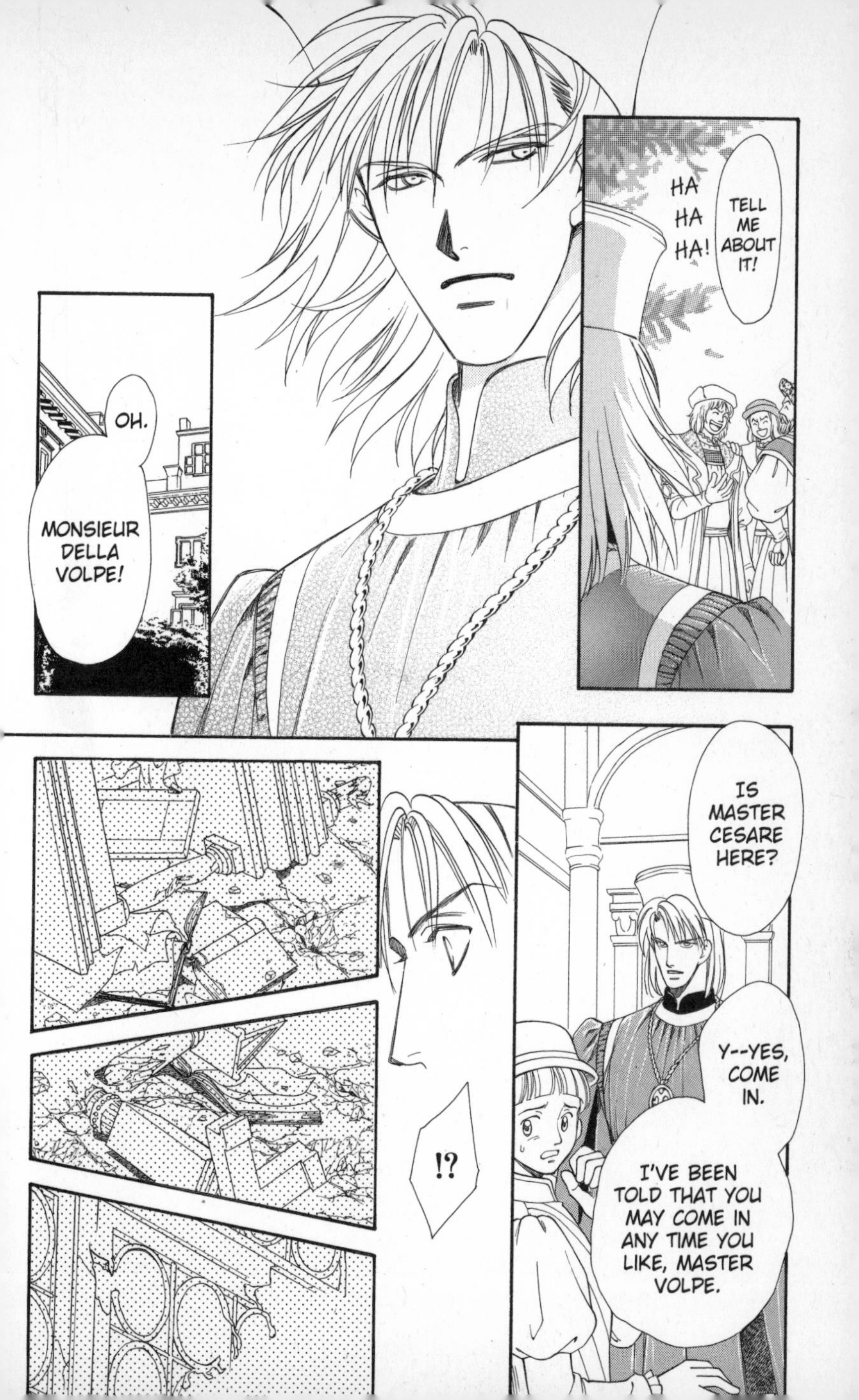
TELL ME ABOUT IT!
HA HA HA!
OH.
MONSIEUR DELLA VOLPE!
IS MASTER CESARE HERE?
Y--YES, COME IN.
I'VE BEEN TOLD THAT YOU MAY COME IN ANY TIME YOU LIKE, MASTER VOLPE.
!?

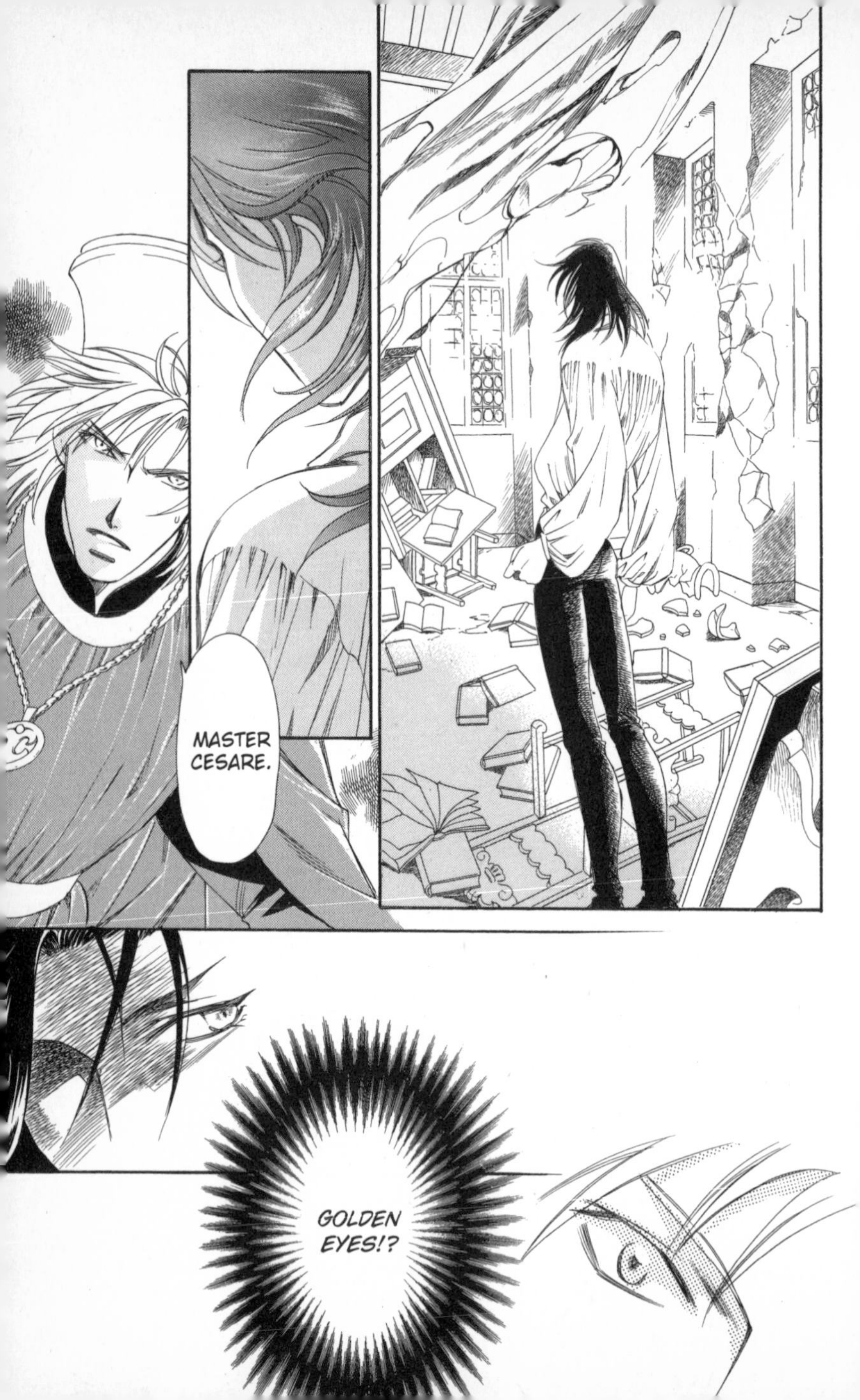
MASTER CESARE.
GOLDEN EYES!?

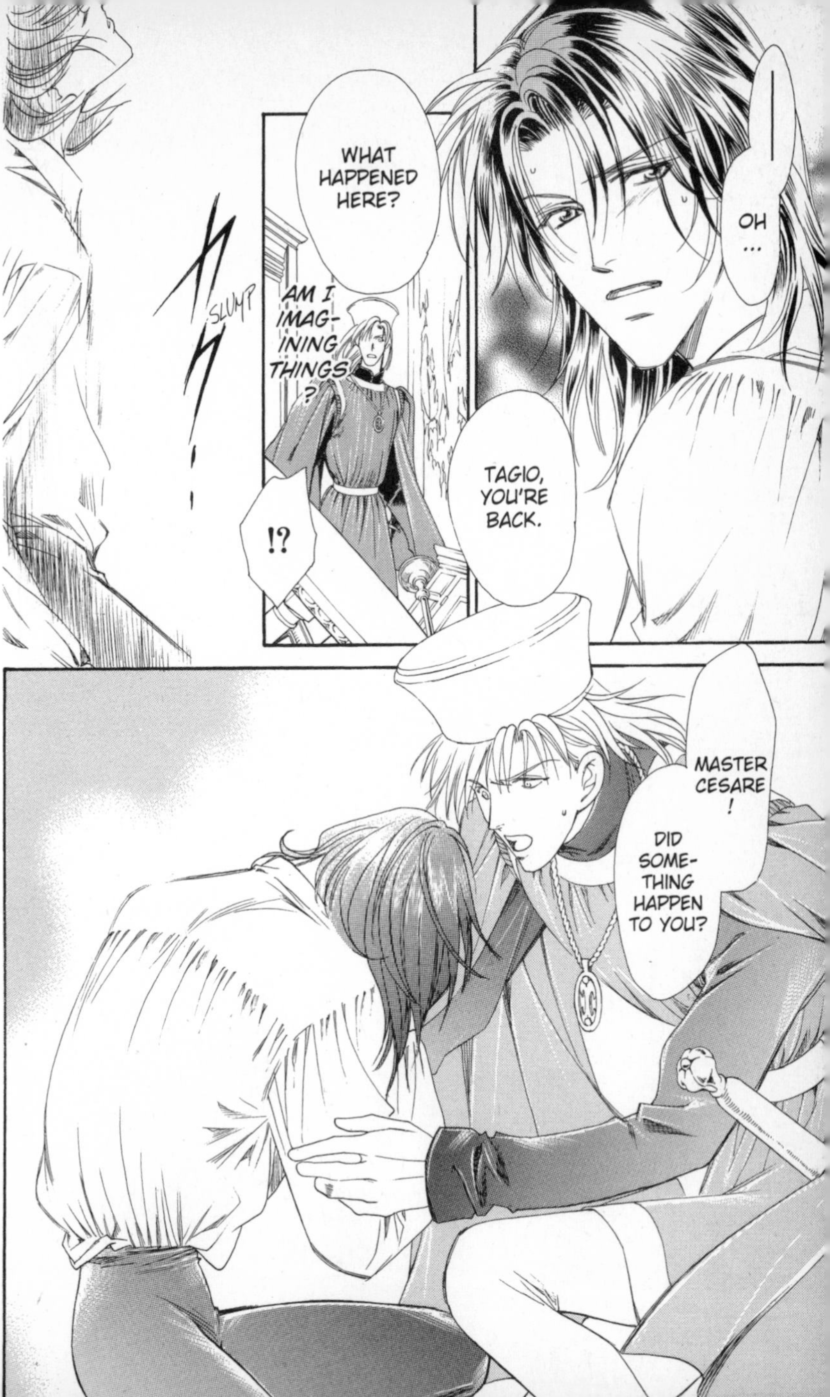
OH ...
TAGIO, YOU'RE BACK.
WHAT HAPPENED HERE?
AM I IMAGINING THINGS?
!?
SLUMP
MASTER CESARE!
DID SOMETHING HAPPEN TO YOU?

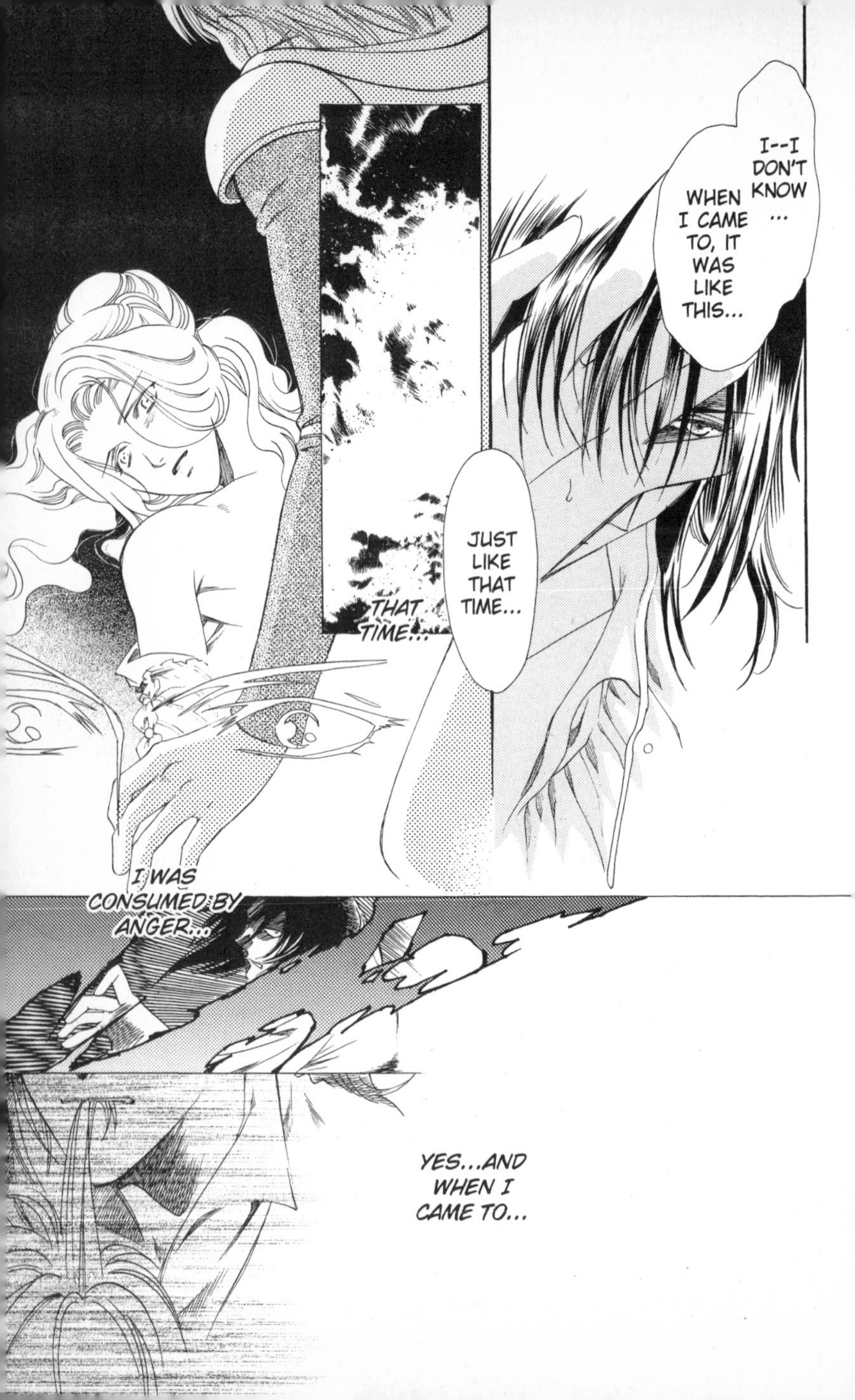
I--I DON'T KNOW ...
WHEN I CAME TO, IT WAS LIKE THIS...
JUST LIKE THAT TIME...
THAT TIME...
I WAS CONSUMED BY ANGER...
YES...AND WHEN I CAME TO...

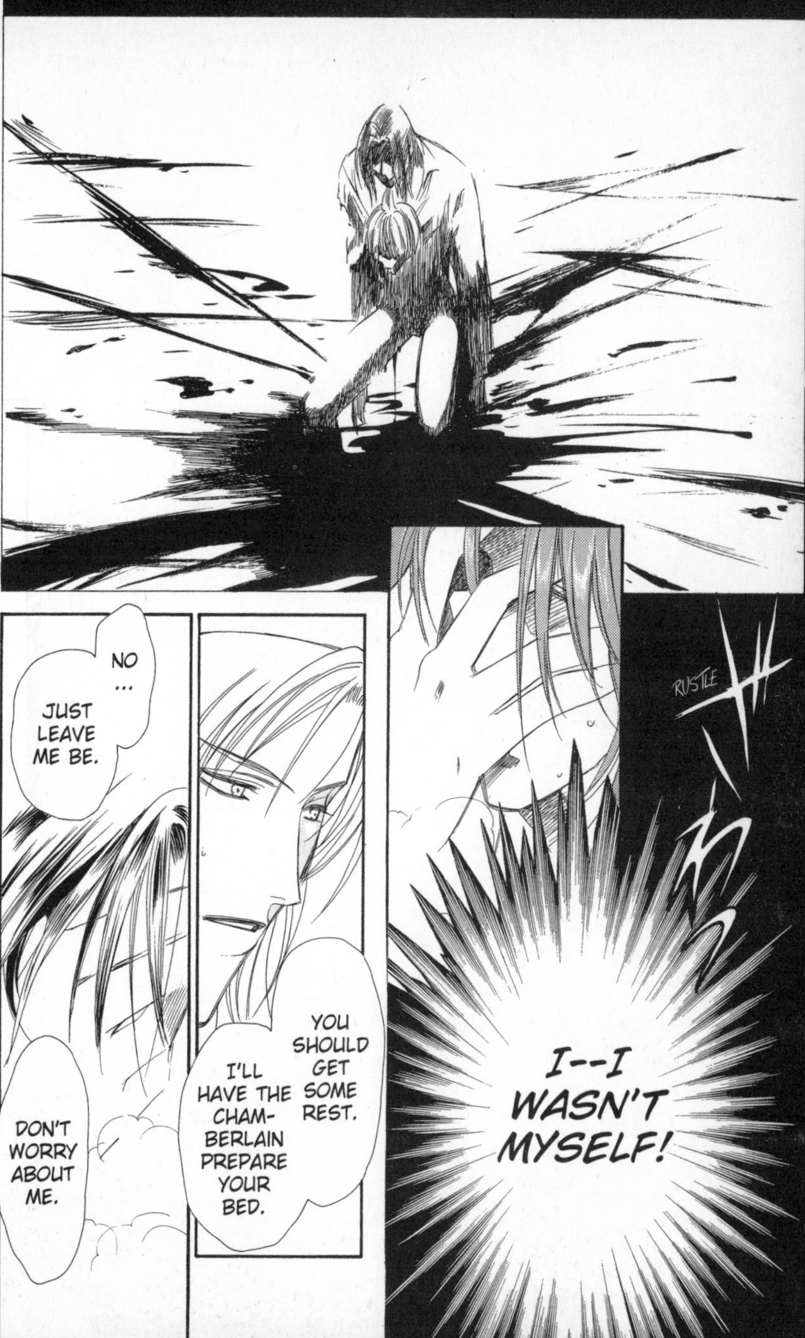
RUSTLE
I--I WASN'T MYSELF!
YOU SHOULD GET SOME REST.
I'LL HAVE THE CHAM-BERLAIN PREPARE YOUR BED.
NO ... JUST LEAVE ME BE.
DON'T WORRY ABOUT ME.

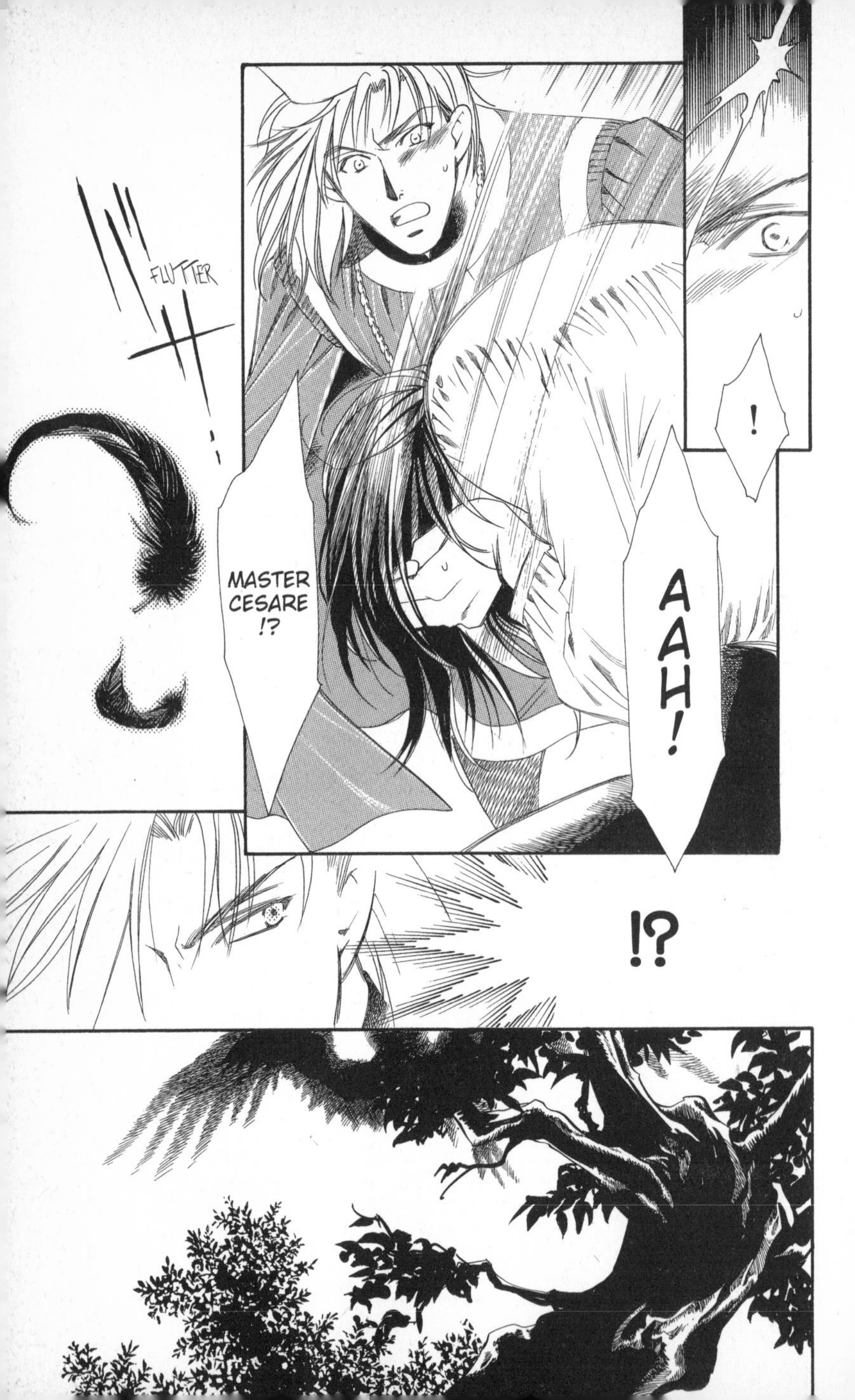
!
AAH!
MASTER CESARE !?
FLUTTER
!?

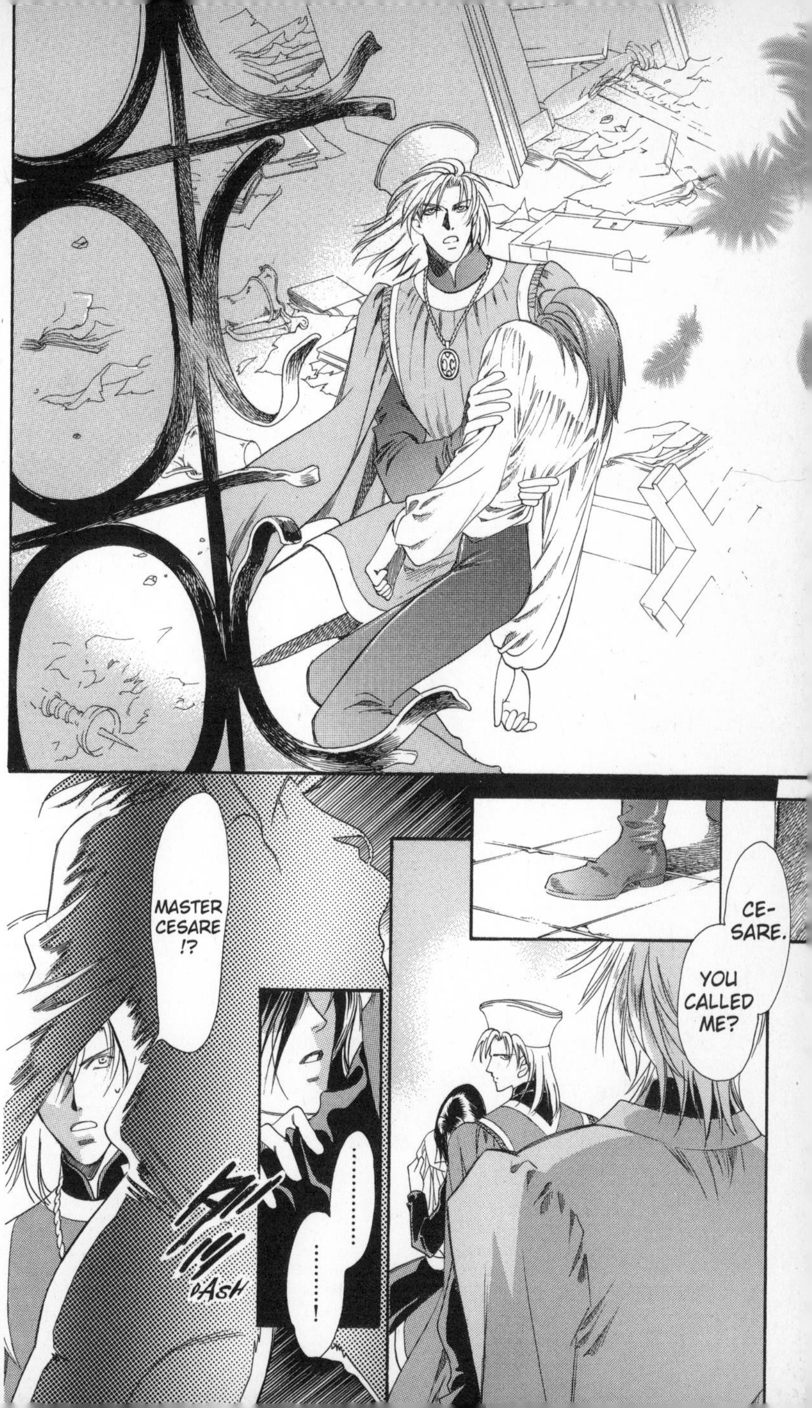
CE-
SARE.
YOU CALLED ME?
......
......!
MASTER CESARE !?
DASH

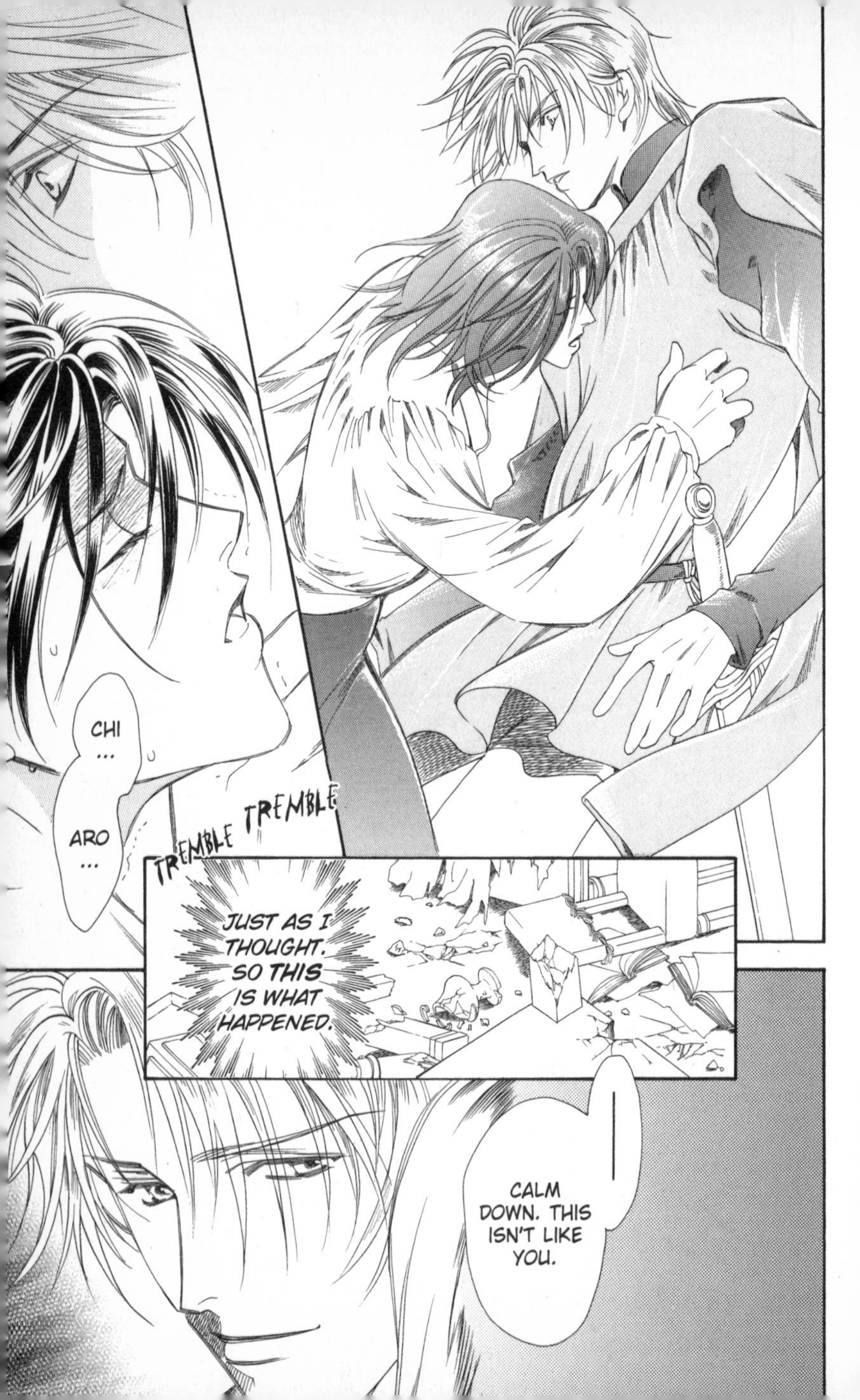
CHI ... ARO ...
TREMBLE TREMBLE
JUST AS I THOUGHT. SO THIS IS WHAT HAPPENED.
CALM DOWN. THIS ISN'T LIKE YOU.

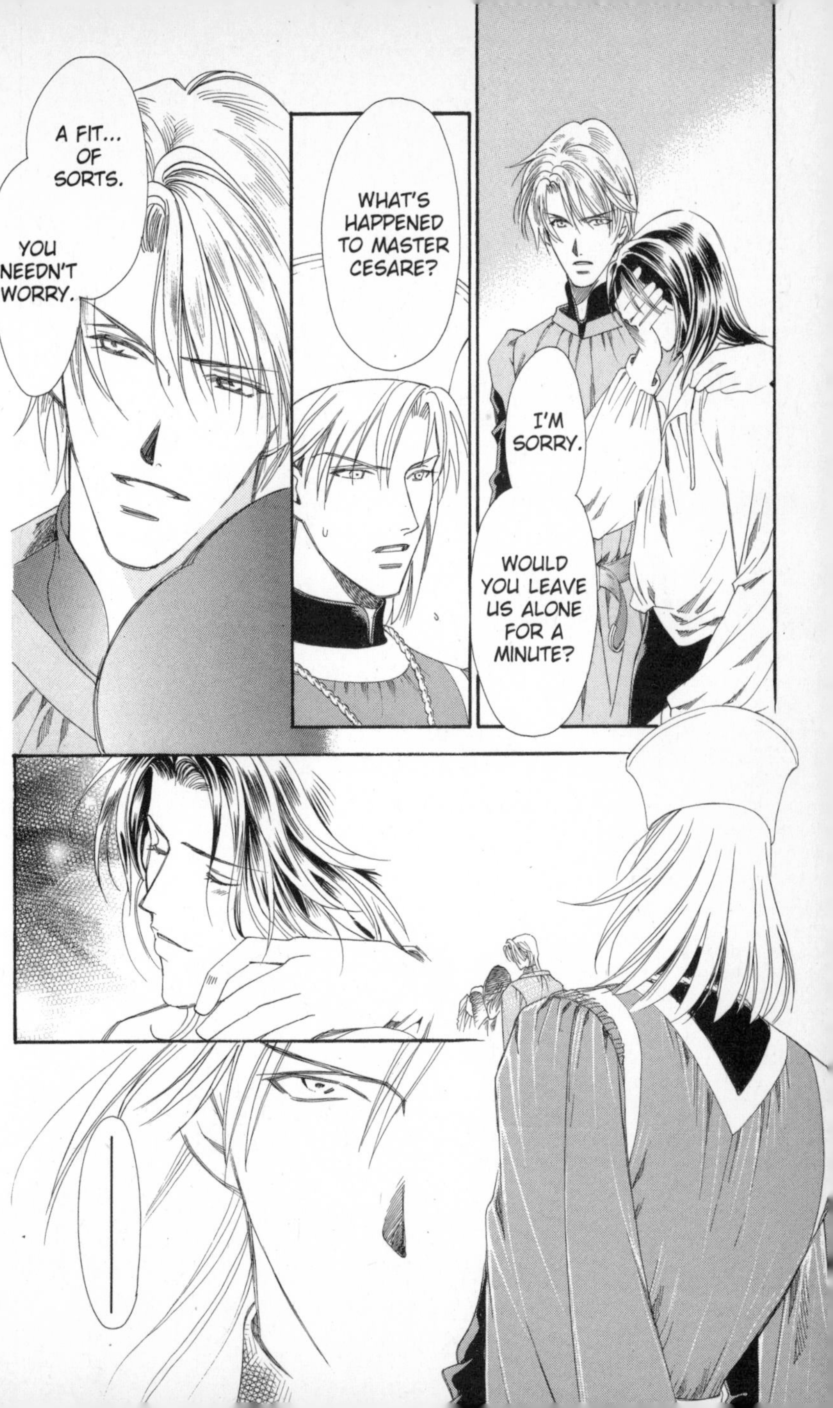
I'M SORRY.
WOULD YOU LEAVE US ALONE FOR A MINUTE?
WHAT'S HAPPENED TO MASTER CESARE?
A FIT... OF SORTS.
YOU NEEDN'T WORRY.
—

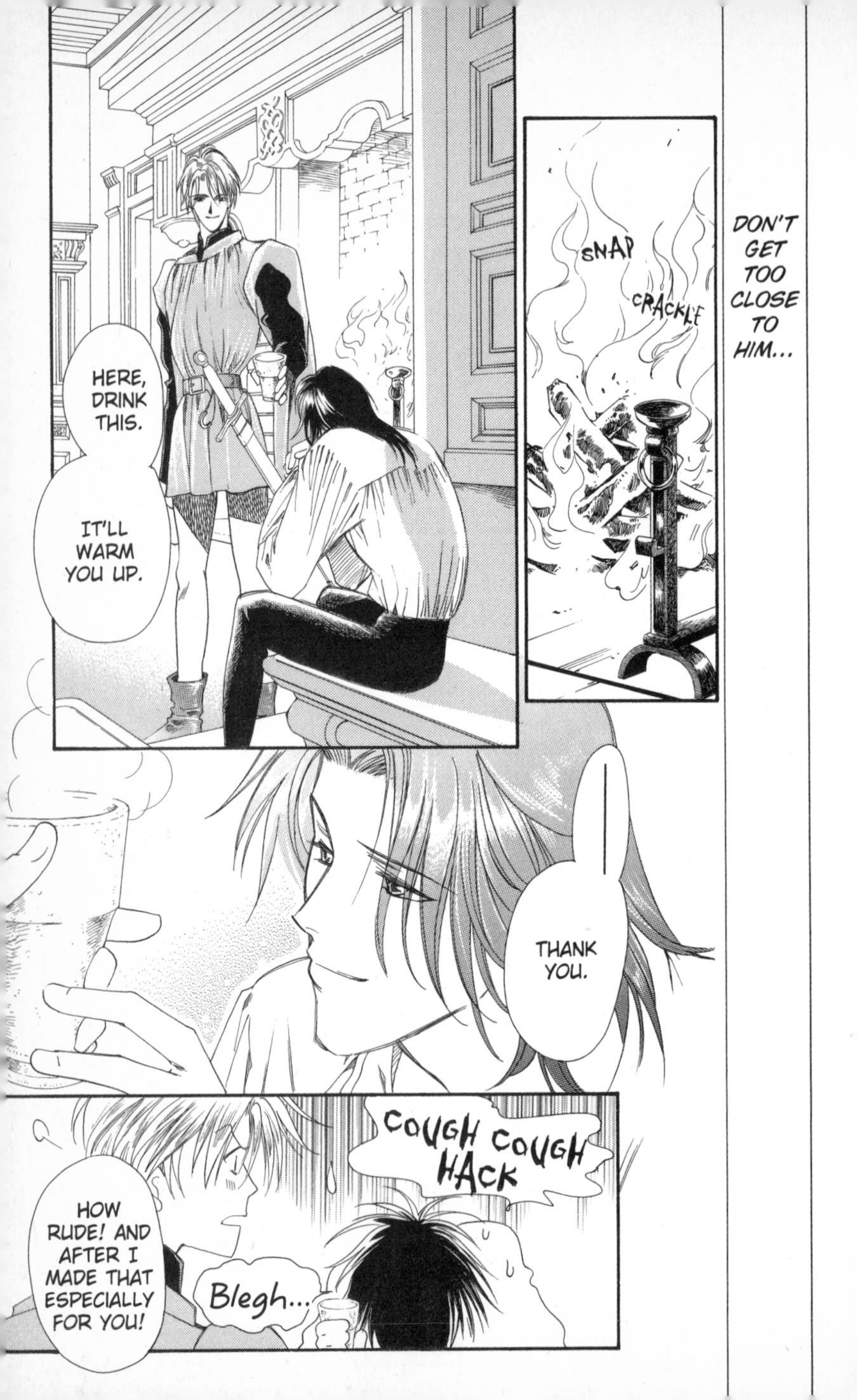

DON'T GET TOO CLOSE TO HIM...
SNAP
CRACKLE
HERE, DRINK THIS.
IT'LL WARM YOU UP.
THANK YOU.
COUGH COUGH HACK
Blegh...
HOW RUDE! AND AFTER I MADE THAT ESPECIALLY FOR YOU!

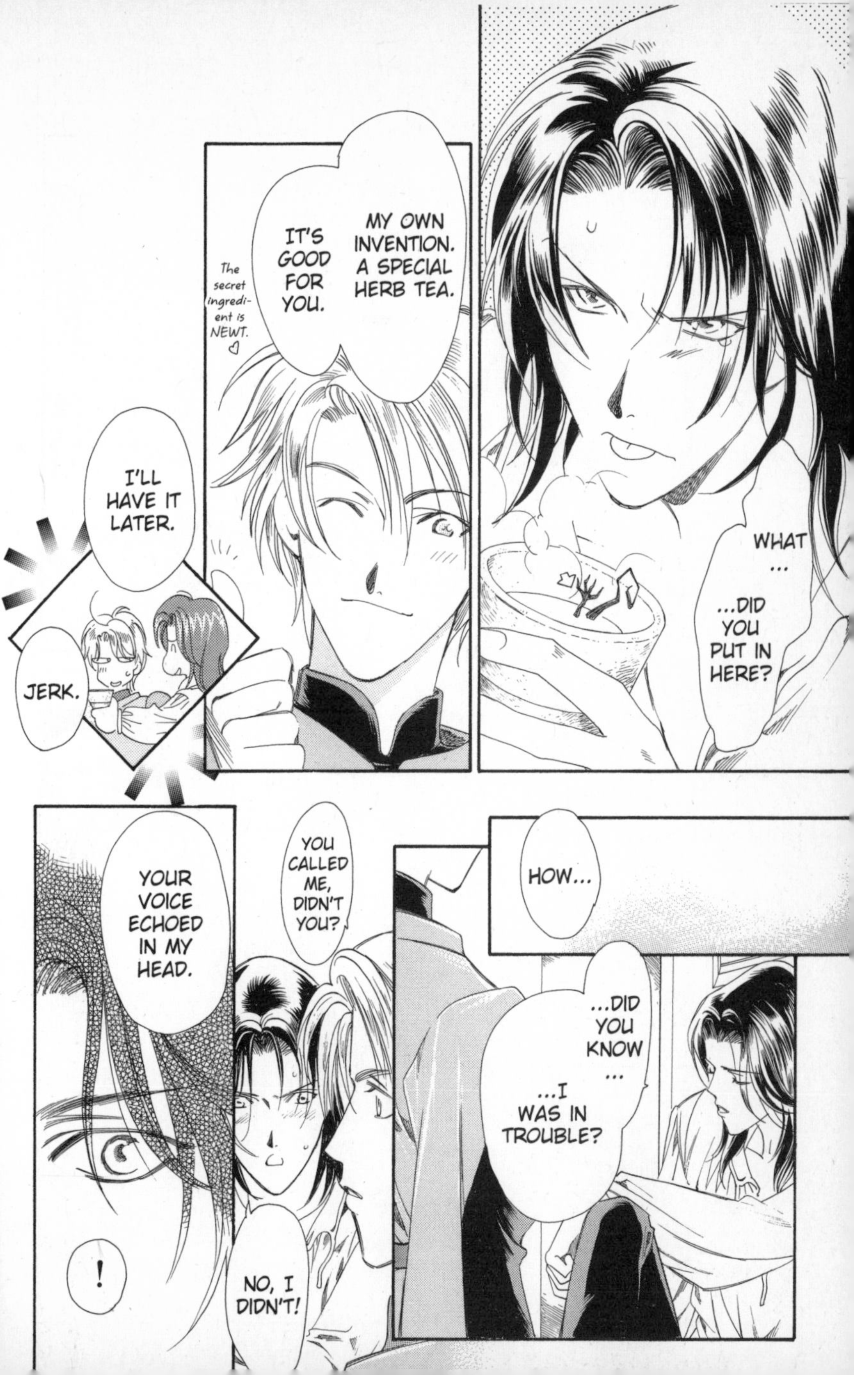
WHAT ...
...DID YOU PUT IN HERE?
MY OWN INVENTION. A SPECIAL HERB TEA.
IT'S GOOD FOR YOU.
The secret ingredient is NEWT. ♡
I'LL HAVE IT LATER.
JERK.
HOW...
...DID YOU KNOW ...
...I WAS IN TROUBLE?
YOU CALLED ME, DIDN'T YOU?
YOUR VOICE ECHOED IN MY HEAD.
NO, I DIDN'T!
!

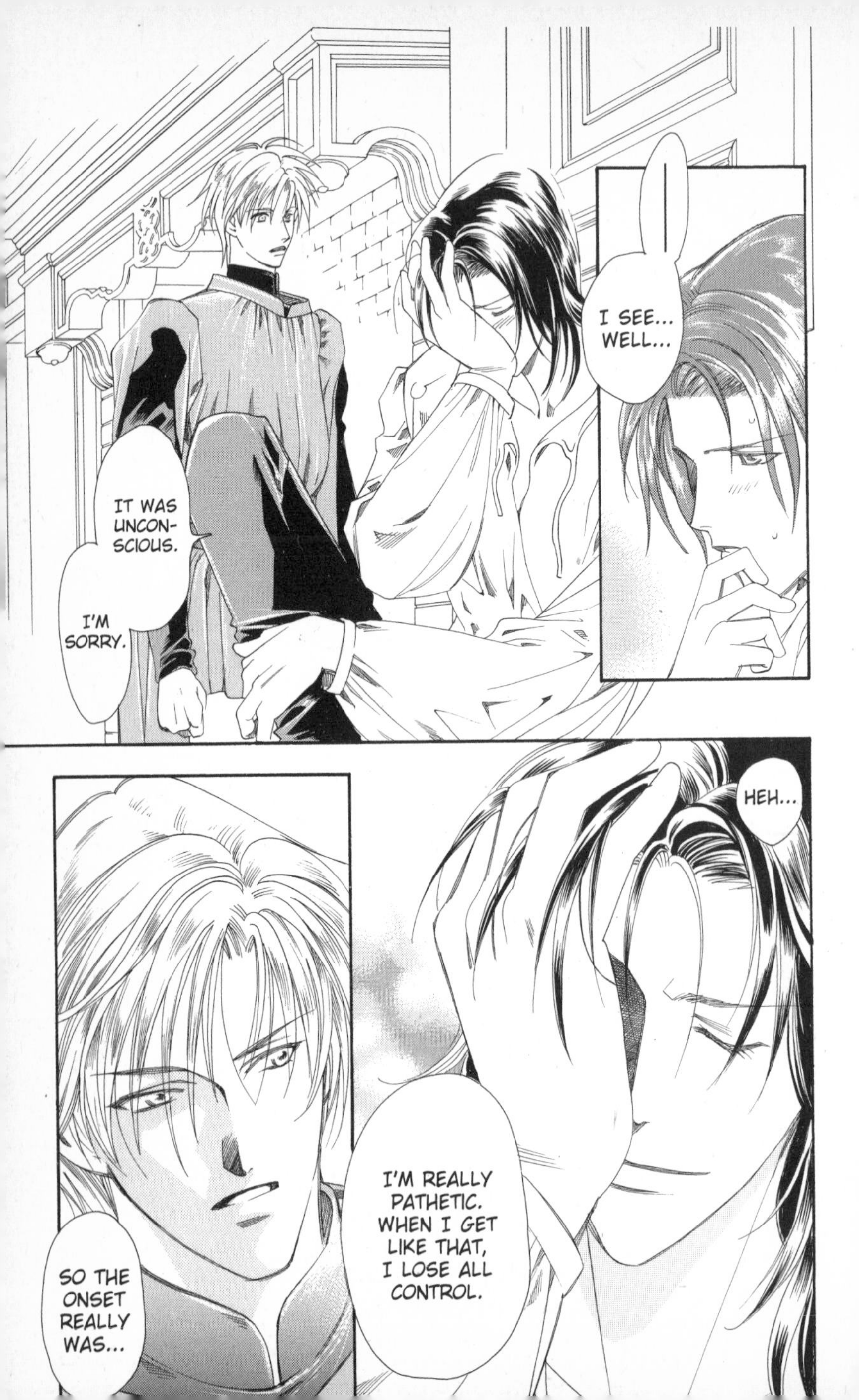
I SEE... WELL...
IT WAS UNCON-SCIOUS.
I'M SORRY.
HEH...
I'M REALLY PATHETIC. WHEN I GET LIKE THAT, I LOSE ALL CONTROL.
SO THE ONSET REALLY WAS...

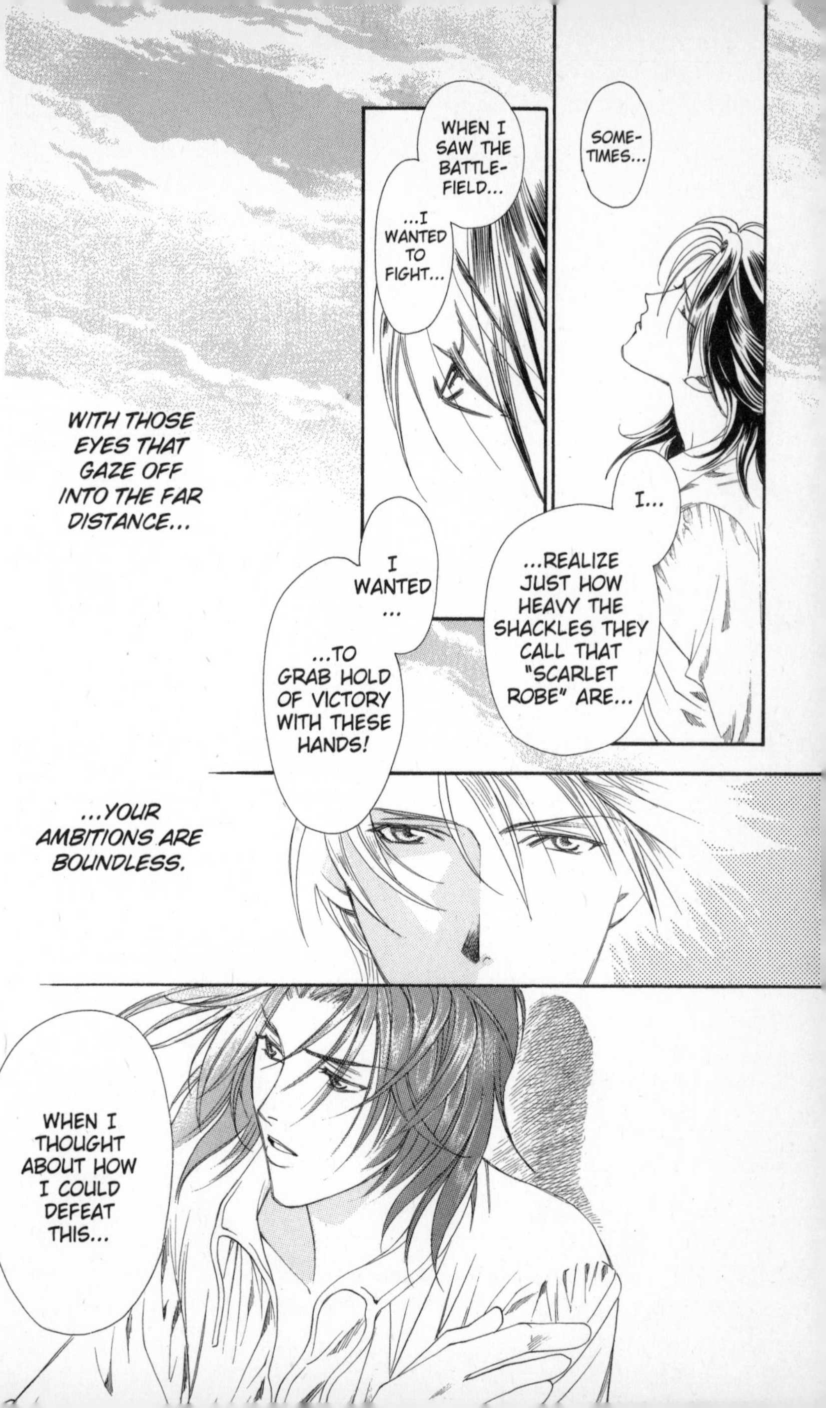
SOME-TIMES...
I...
...REALIZE JUST HOW HEAVY THE SHACKLES THEY CALL THAT "SCARLET ROBE" ARE...
WHEN I SAW THE BATTLE-FIELD...
...I WANTED TO FIGHT...
I WANTED ...
...TO GRAB HOLD OF VICTORY WITH THESE HANDS!
WITH THOSE EYES THAT GAZE OFF INTO THE FAR DISTANCE...
...YOUR AMBITIONS ARE BOUNDLESS.
WHEN I THOUGHT ABOUT HOW I COULD DEFEAT THIS...

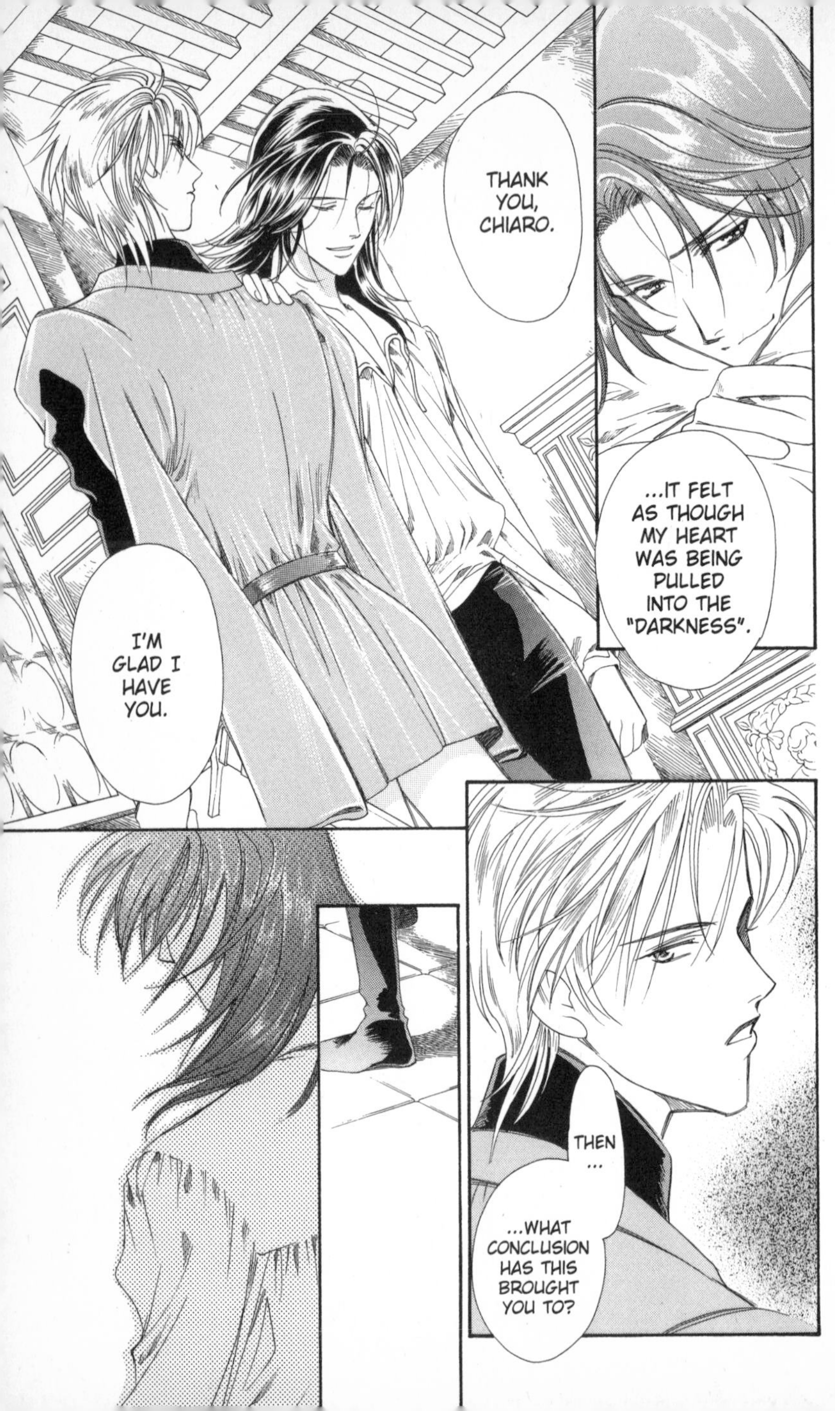
...IT FELT AS THOUGH MY HEART WAS BEING PULLED INTO THE "DARKNESS".
THANK YOU, CHIARO.
I'M GLAD I HAVE YOU.
THEN ...
...WHAT CONCLUSION HAS THIS BROUGHT YOU TO?

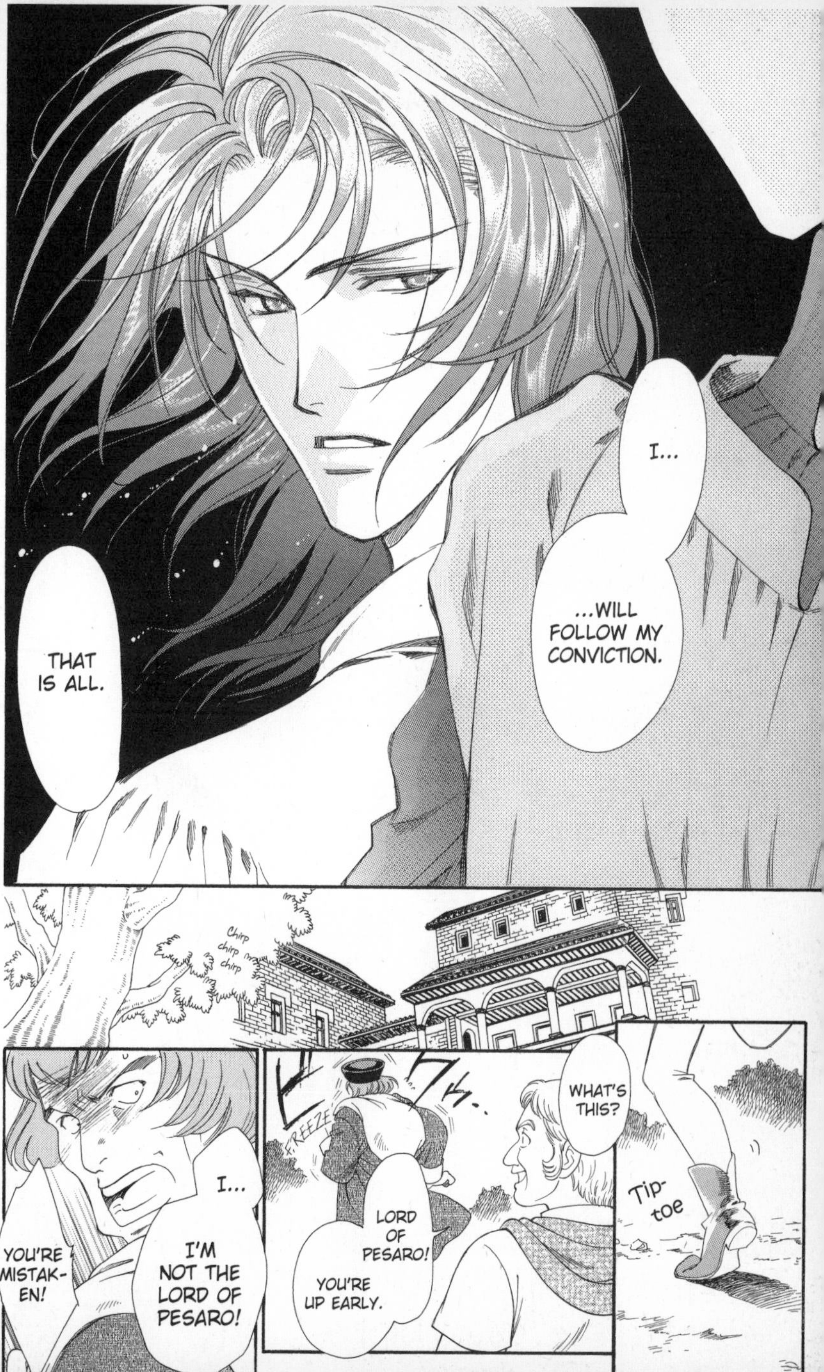
I...
...WILL FOLLOW MY CONVICTION.
THAT IS ALL.
Chirp chirp chirp
Tip-toe
WHAT'S THIS?
FREEZE
LORD OF PESARO!
YOU'RE UP EARLY.
I...
I'M NOT THE LORD OF PESARO!
YOU'RE MISTAKEN!

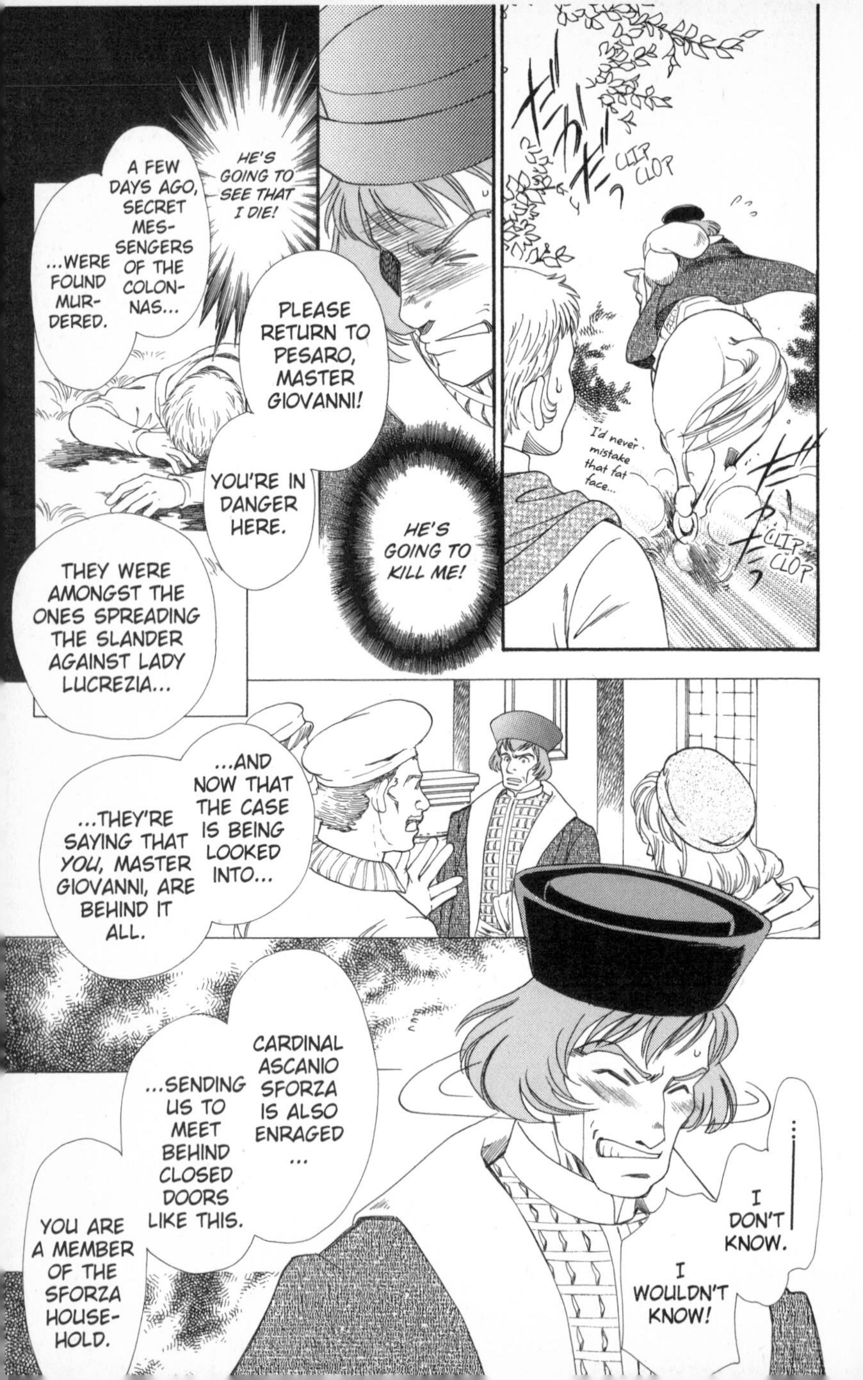
CLIP CLOP
I'd never mistake that fat face...
CLIP CLOP
HE'S GOING TO SEE THAT I DIE!
A FEW DAYS AGO, SECRET MES-SENGERS OF THE COLON-NAS...
...WERE FOUND MUR-DERED.
PLEASE RETURN TO PESARO, MASTER GIOVANNI!
YOU'RE IN DANGER HERE.
HE'S GOING TO KILL ME!
THEY WERE AMONGST THE ONES SPREADING THE SLANDER AGAINST LADY LUCREZIA...
...AND NOW THAT THE CASE IS BEING LOOKED INTO...
...THEY'RE SAYING THAT YOU, MASTER GIOVANNI, ARE BEHIND IT ALL.
CARDINAL ASCANIO SFORZA IS ALSO ENRAGED...
...SENDING US TO MEET BEHIND CLOSED DOORS LIKE THIS.
YOU ARE A MEMBER OF THE SFORZA HOUSE-HOLD.
...I DON'T KNOW.
I WOULDN'T KNOW!

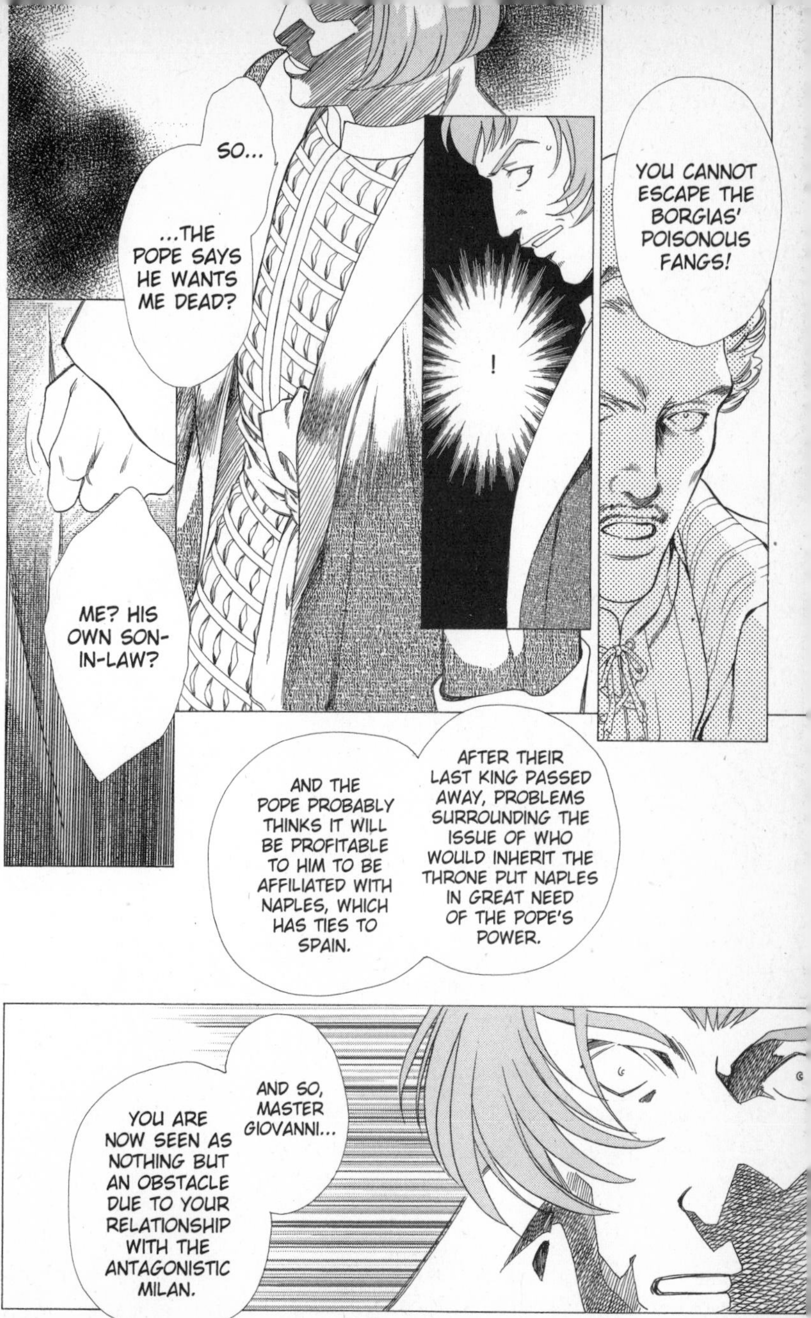
YOU CANNOT ESCAPE THE BORGIAS' POISONOUS FANGS!
!
SO...
...THE POPE SAYS HE WANTS ME DEAD?
ME? HIS OWN SON-IN-LAW?
AFTER THEIR LAST KING PASSED AWAY, PROBLEMS SURROUNDING THE ISSUE OF WHO WOULD INHERIT THE THRONE PUT NAPLES IN GREAT NEED OF THE POPE'S POWER.
AND THE POPE PROBABLY THINKS IT WILL BE PROFITABLE TO HIM TO BE AFFILIATED WITH NAPLES, WHICH HAS TIES TO SPAIN.
AND SO, MASTER GIOVANNI...
YOU ARE NOW SEEN AS NOTHING BUT AN OBSTACLE DUE TO YOUR RELATIONSHIP WITH THE ANTAGONISTIC MILAN.

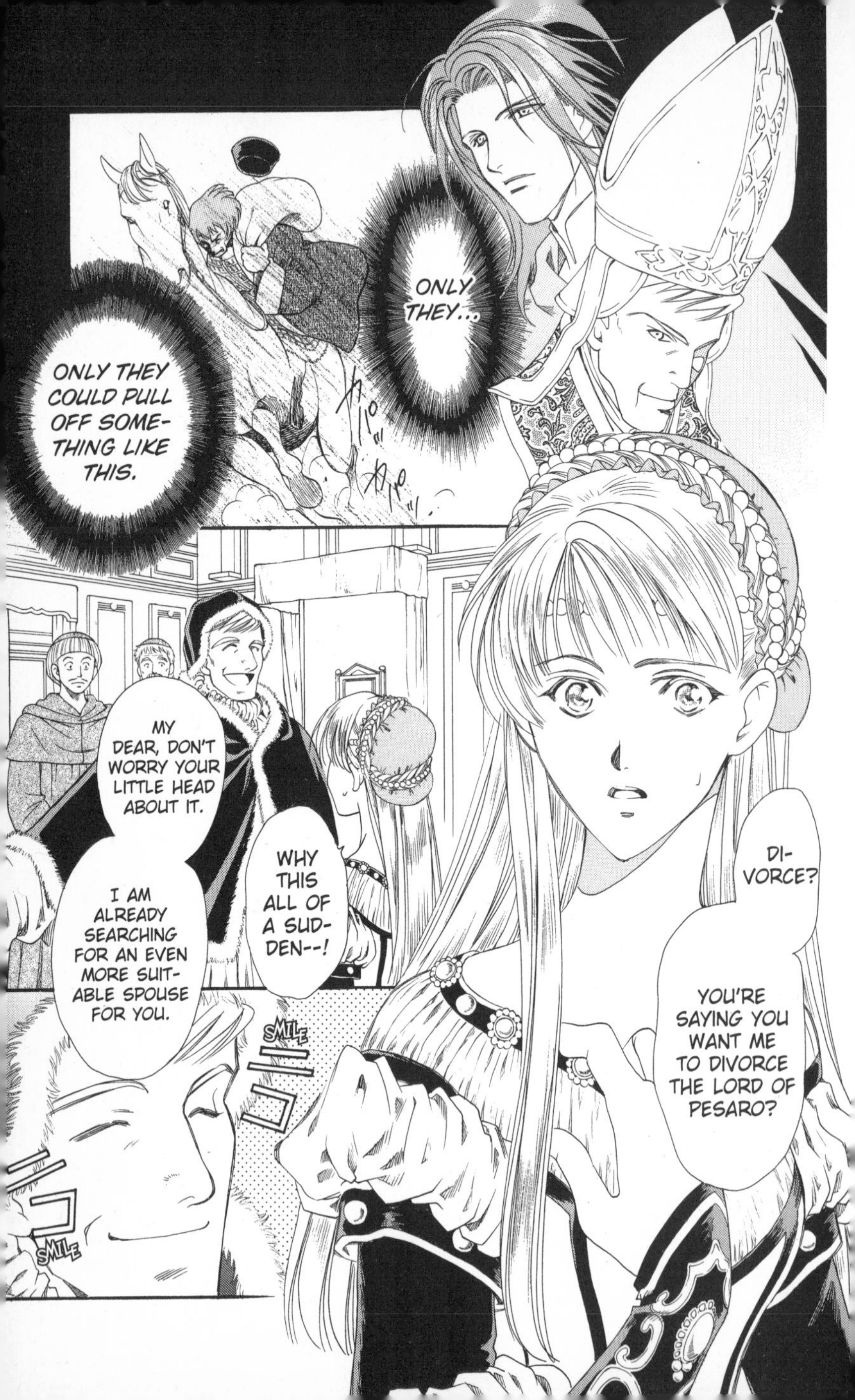
ONLY THEY...
ONLY THEY COULD PULL OFF SOME-THING LIKE THIS.
DI-VORCE?
YOU'RE SAYING YOU WANT ME TO DIVORCE THE LORD OF PESARO?
WHY THIS ALL OF A SUD-DEN--!
MY DEAR, DON'T WORRY YOUR LITTLE HEAD ABOUT IT.
I AM ALREADY SEARCHING FOR AN EVEN MORE SUIT-ABLE SPOUSE FOR YOU.
SMILE
SMILE

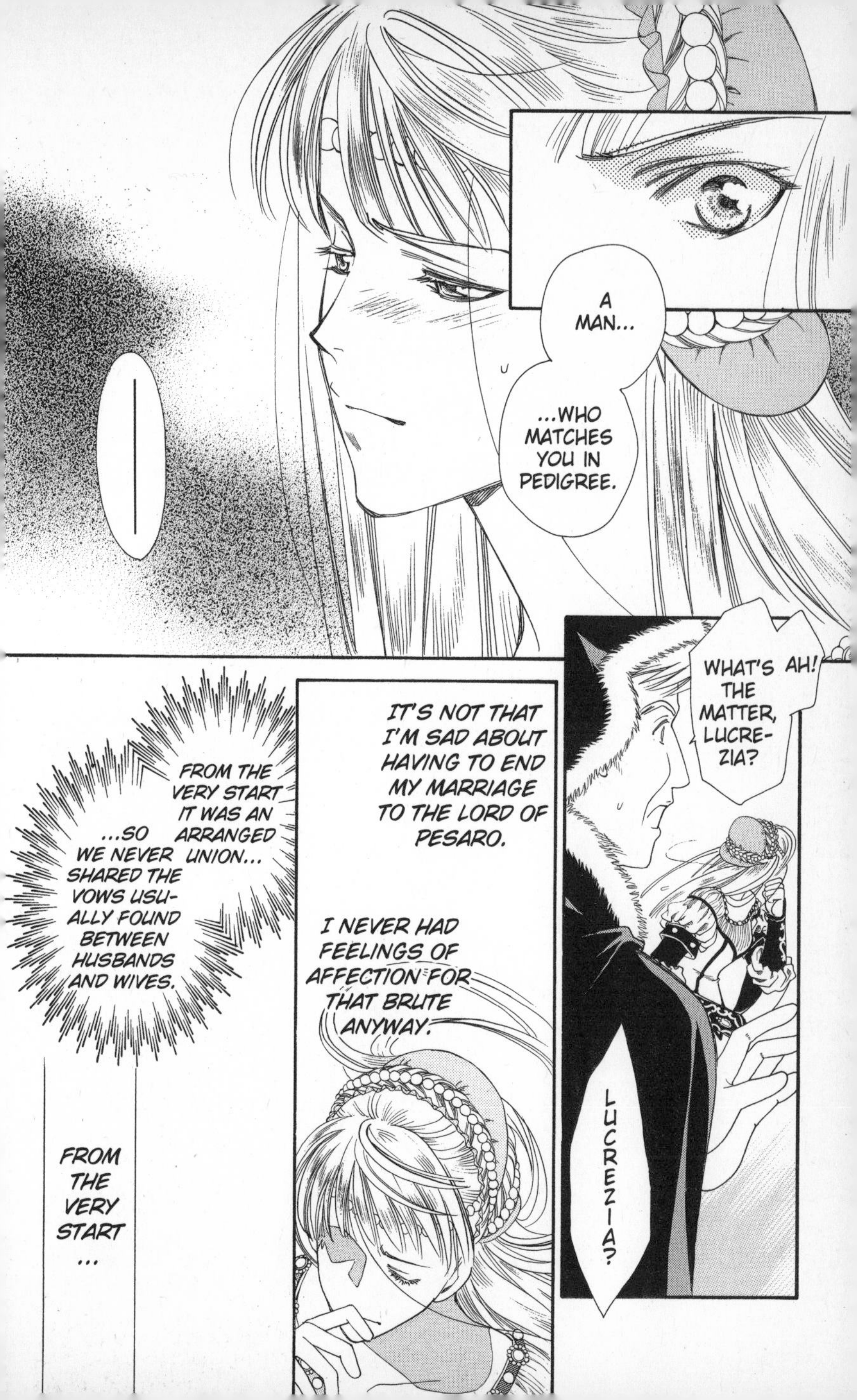
A MAN...
...WHO MATCHES YOU IN PEDIGREE.
—
AH!
WHAT'S THE MATTER, LUCREZIA?
LUCREZIA?
IT'S NOT THAT I'M SAD ABOUT HAVING TO END MY MARRIAGE TO THE LORD OF PESARO.
I NEVER HAD FEELINGS OF AFFECTION FOR THAT BRUTE ANYWAY.
FROM THE VERY START IT WAS AN ARRANGED UNION...
...SO WE NEVER SHARED THE VOWS USUALLY FOUND BETWEEN HUSBANDS AND WIVES.
FROM THE VERY START...

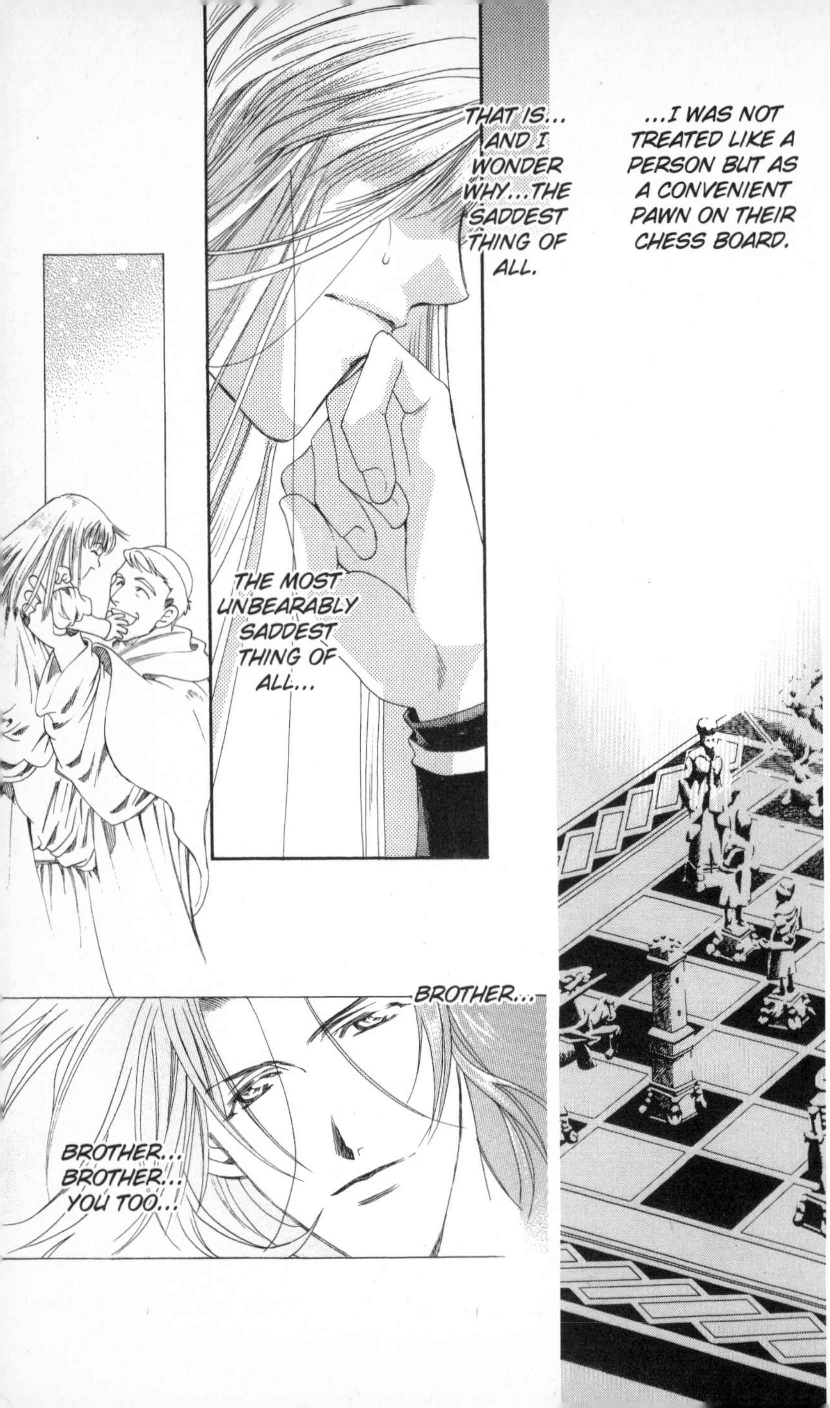
...I WAS NOT TREATED LIKE A PERSON BUT AS A CONVENIENT PAWN ON THEIR CHESS BOARD.
THAT IS... AND I WONDER WHY...THE SADDEST THING OF ALL.
THE MOST UNBEARABLY SADDEST THING OF ALL...
BROTHER...
BROTHER... BROTHER... YOU TOO...

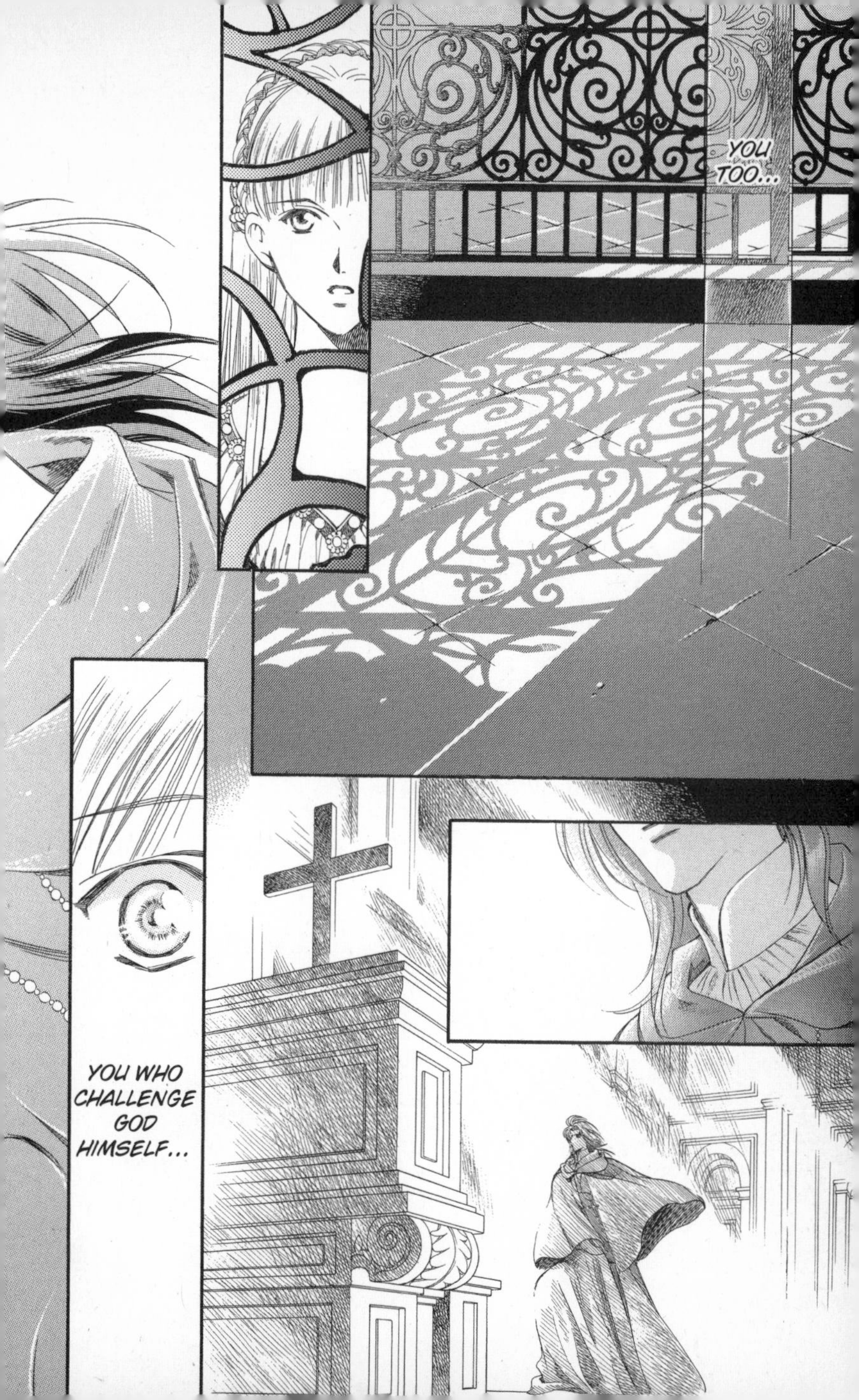
YOU TOO...
YOU WHO CHALLENGE GOD HIMSELF...

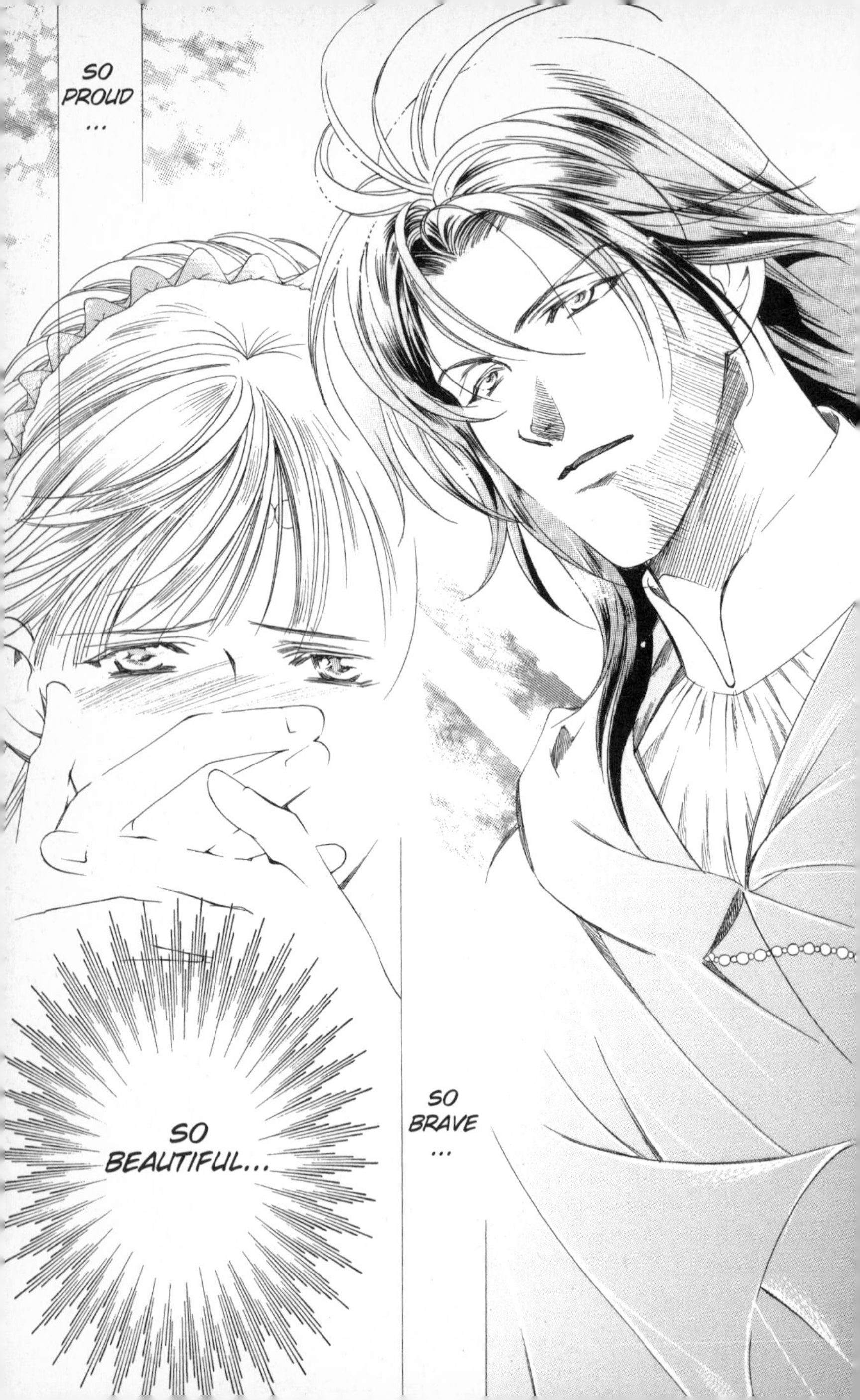
SO PROUD ...
SO BRAVE ...
SO BEAUTIFUL...

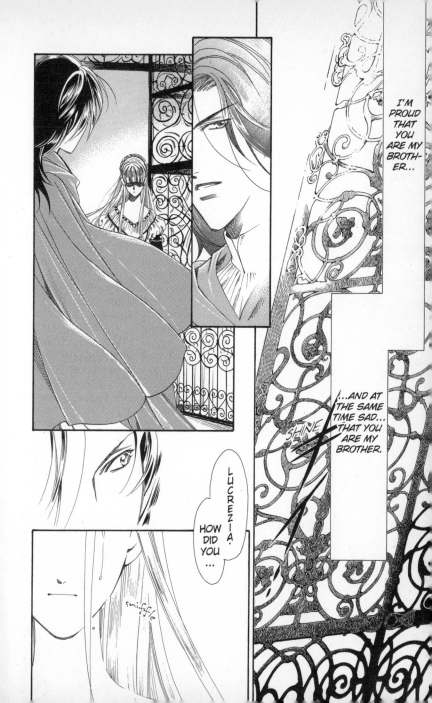

I'M PROUD THAT YOU ARE MY BROTHER...

...AND AT THE SAME TIME SAD... THAT YOU ARE MY BROTHER.

SHINE

LUCREZIA.

HOW DID YOU ...

sniffle

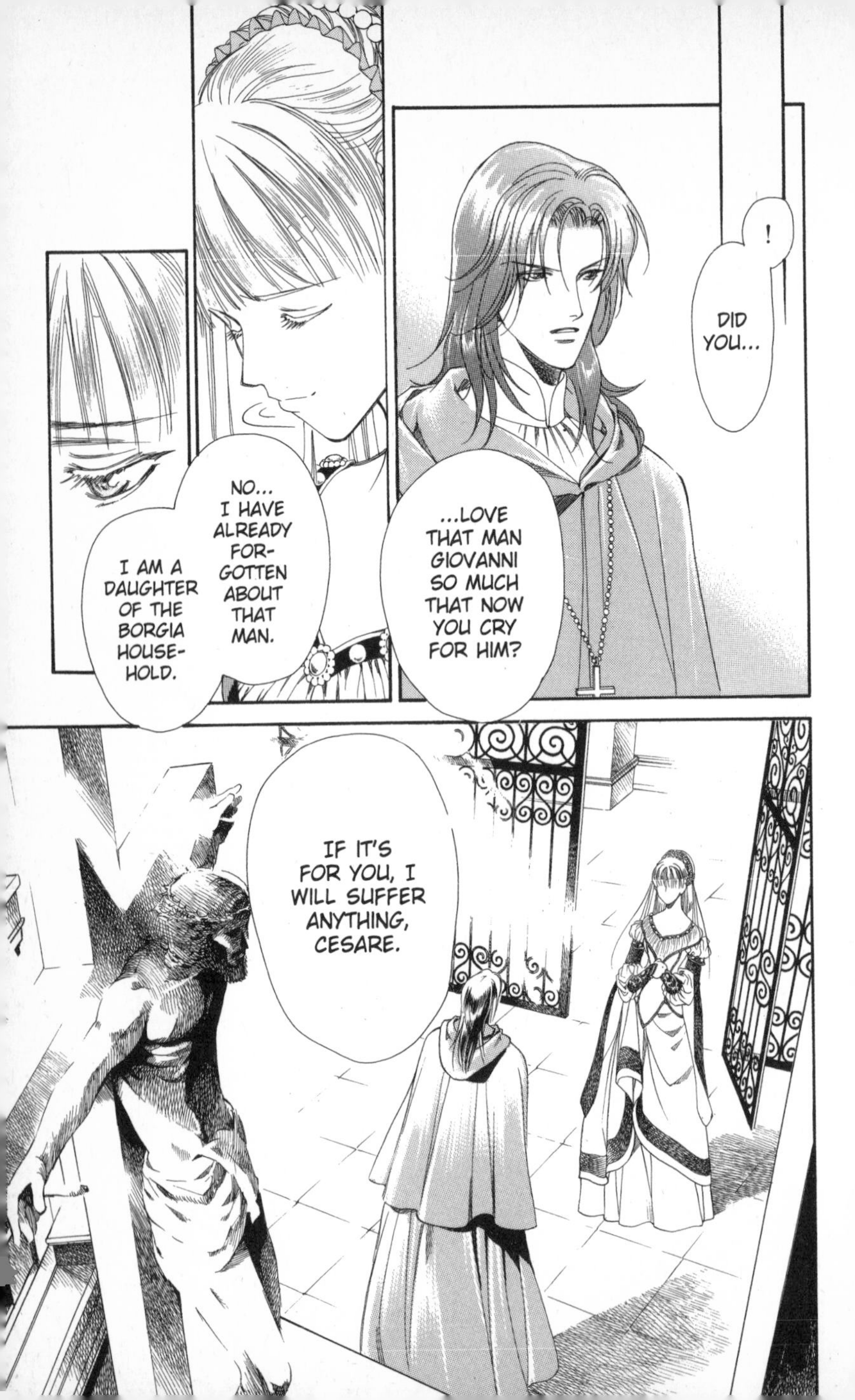
!
DID YOU...
...LOVE THAT MAN GIOVANNI SO MUCH THAT NOW YOU CRY FOR HIM?
NO... I HAVE ALREADY FOR-GOTTEN ABOUT THAT MAN.
I AM A DAUGHTER OF THE BORGIA HOUSE-HOLD.
IF IT'S FOR YOU, I WILL SUFFER ANYTHING, CESARE.

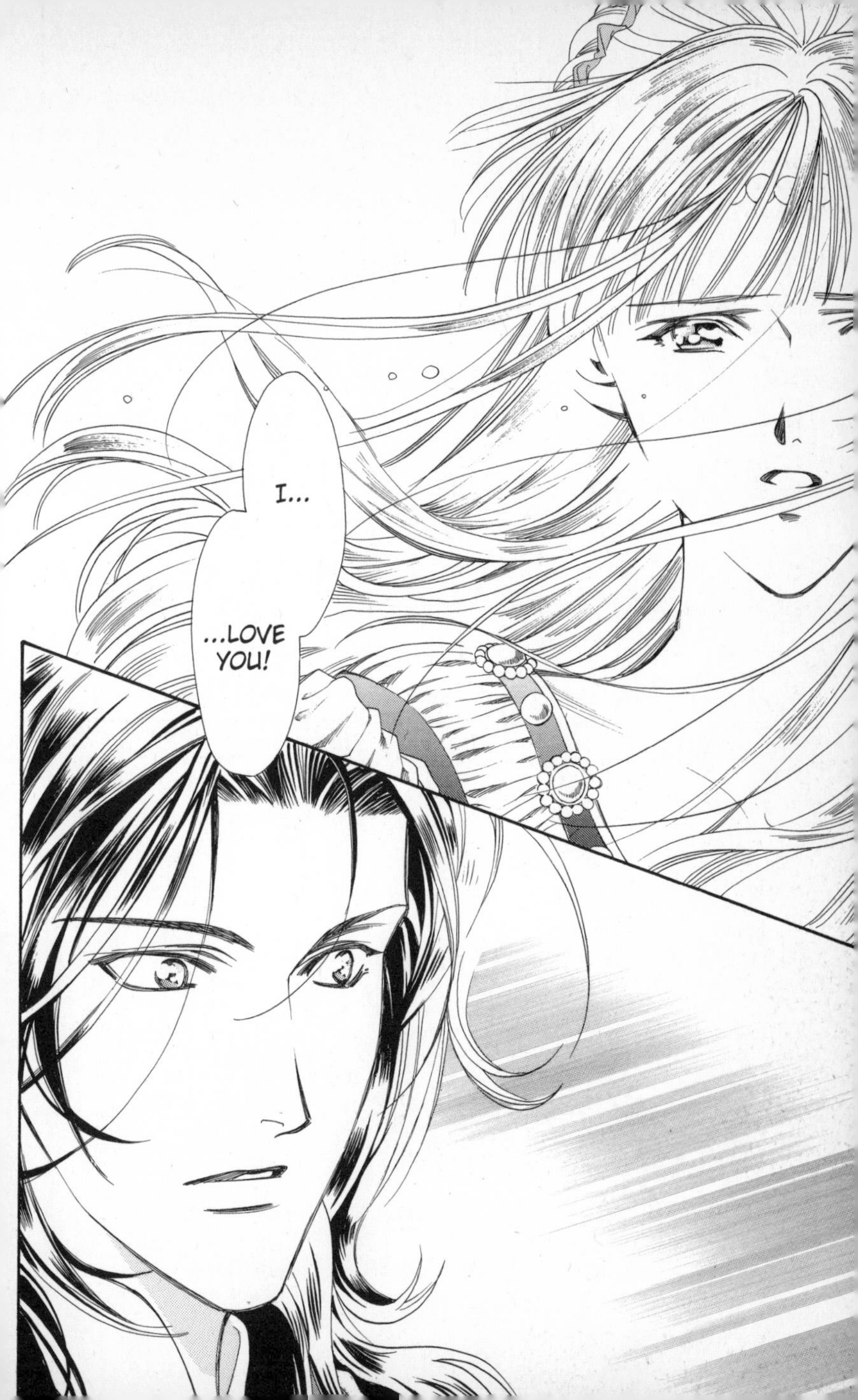
I...
...LOVE YOU!

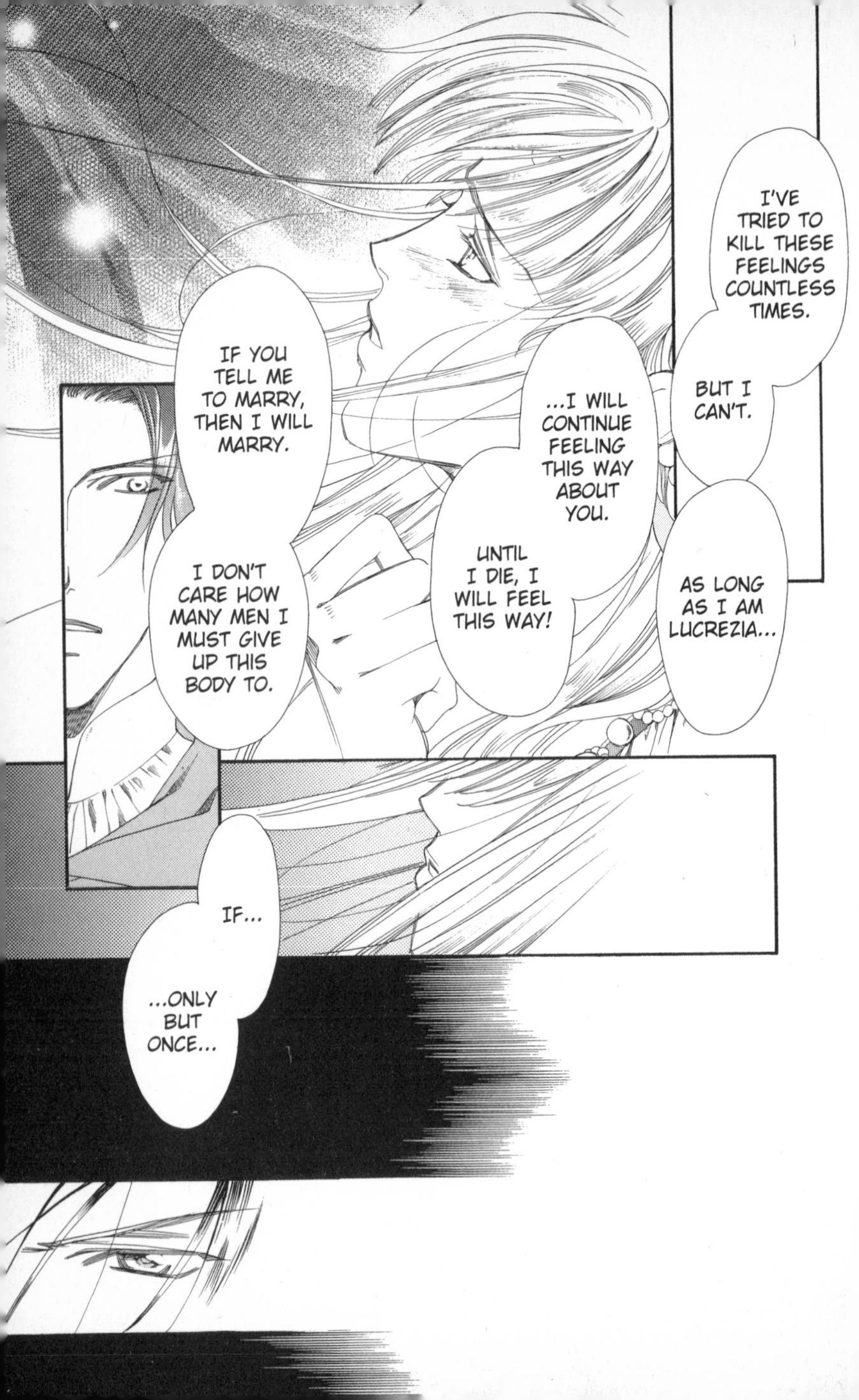
I'VE TRIED TO KILL THESE FEELINGS COUNTLESS TIMES.
BUT I CAN'T.
IF YOU TELL ME TO MARRY, THEN I WILL MARRY.
I DON'T CARE HOW MANY MEN I MUST GIVE UP THIS BODY TO.
...I WILL CONTINUE FEELING THIS WAY ABOUT YOU.
AS LONG AS I AM LUCREZIA...
UNTIL I DIE, I WILL FEEL THIS WAY!
IF...
...ONLY BUT ONCE...

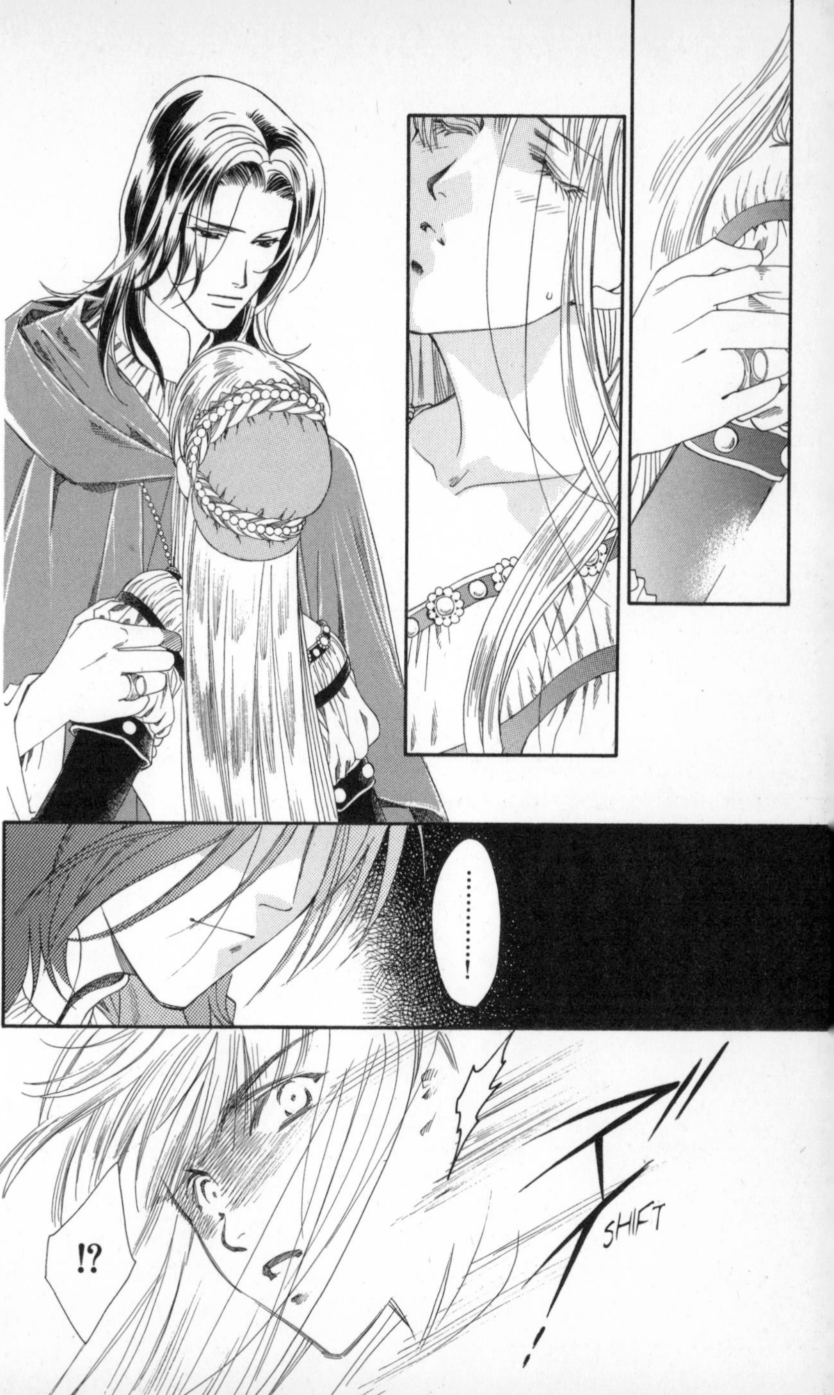

.........!
!?
SHIFT
!

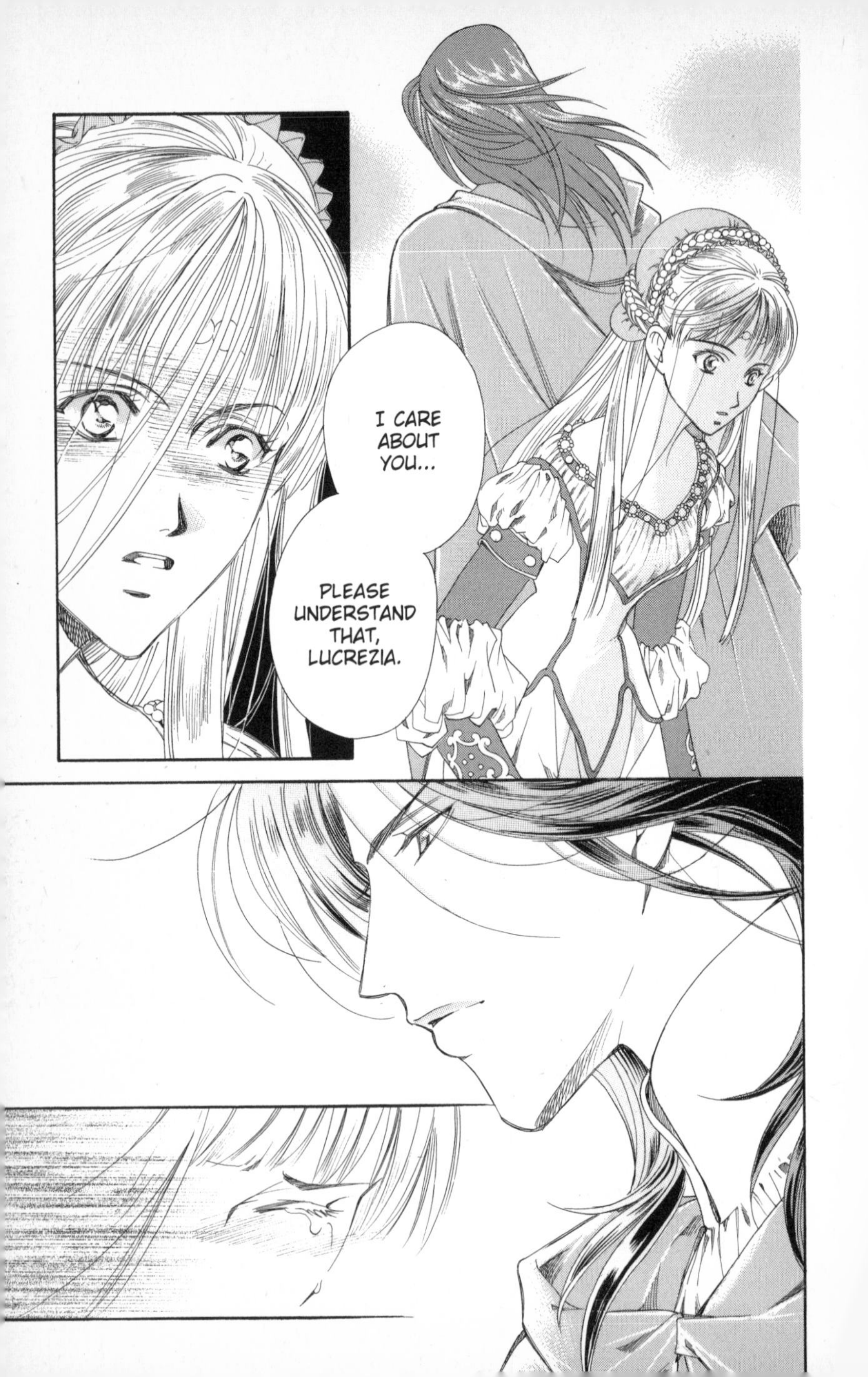
I CARE ABOUT YOU...
PLEASE UNDERSTAND THAT, LUCREZIA.

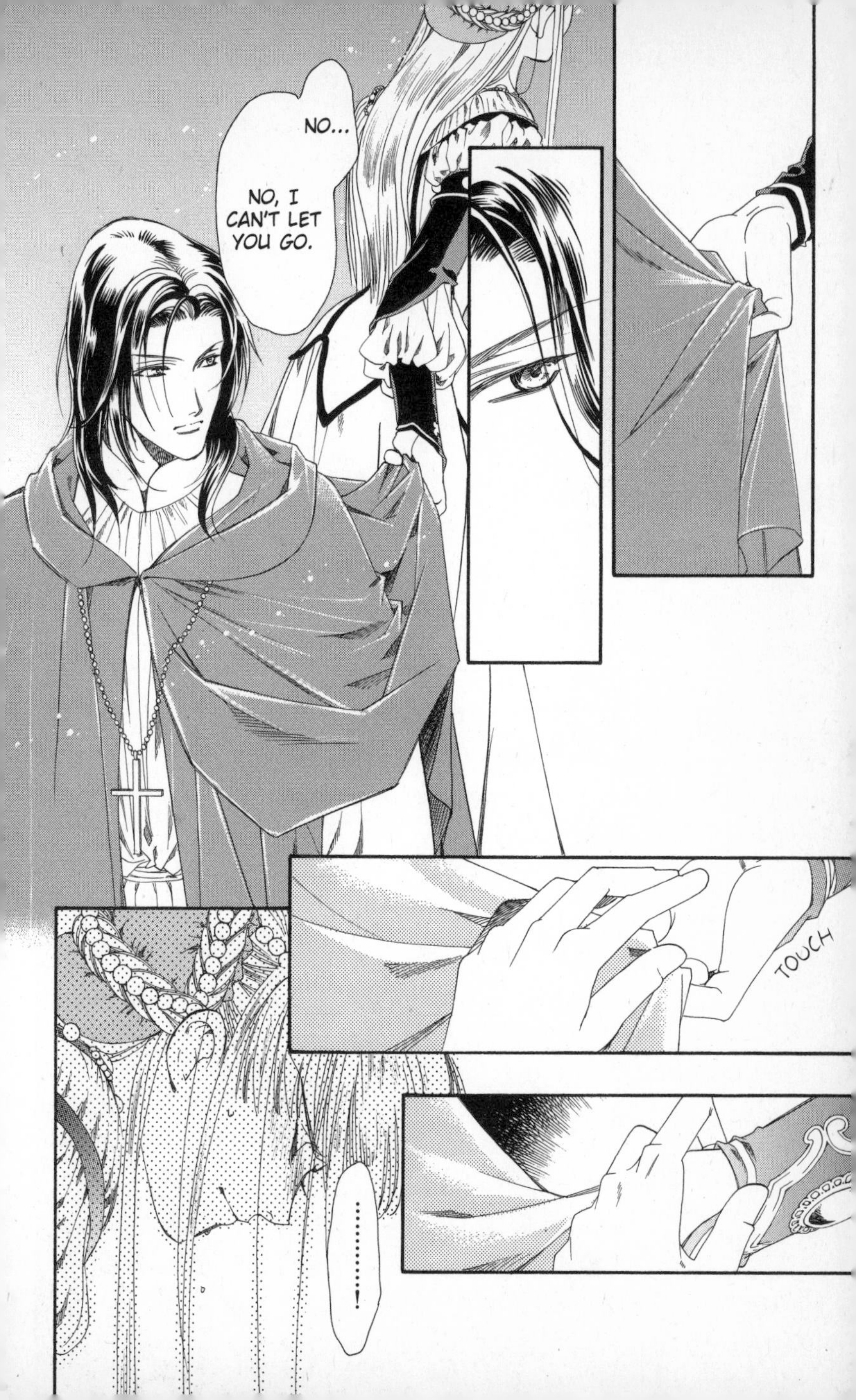
NO...
NO, I CAN'T LET YOU GO.
TOUCH
......!

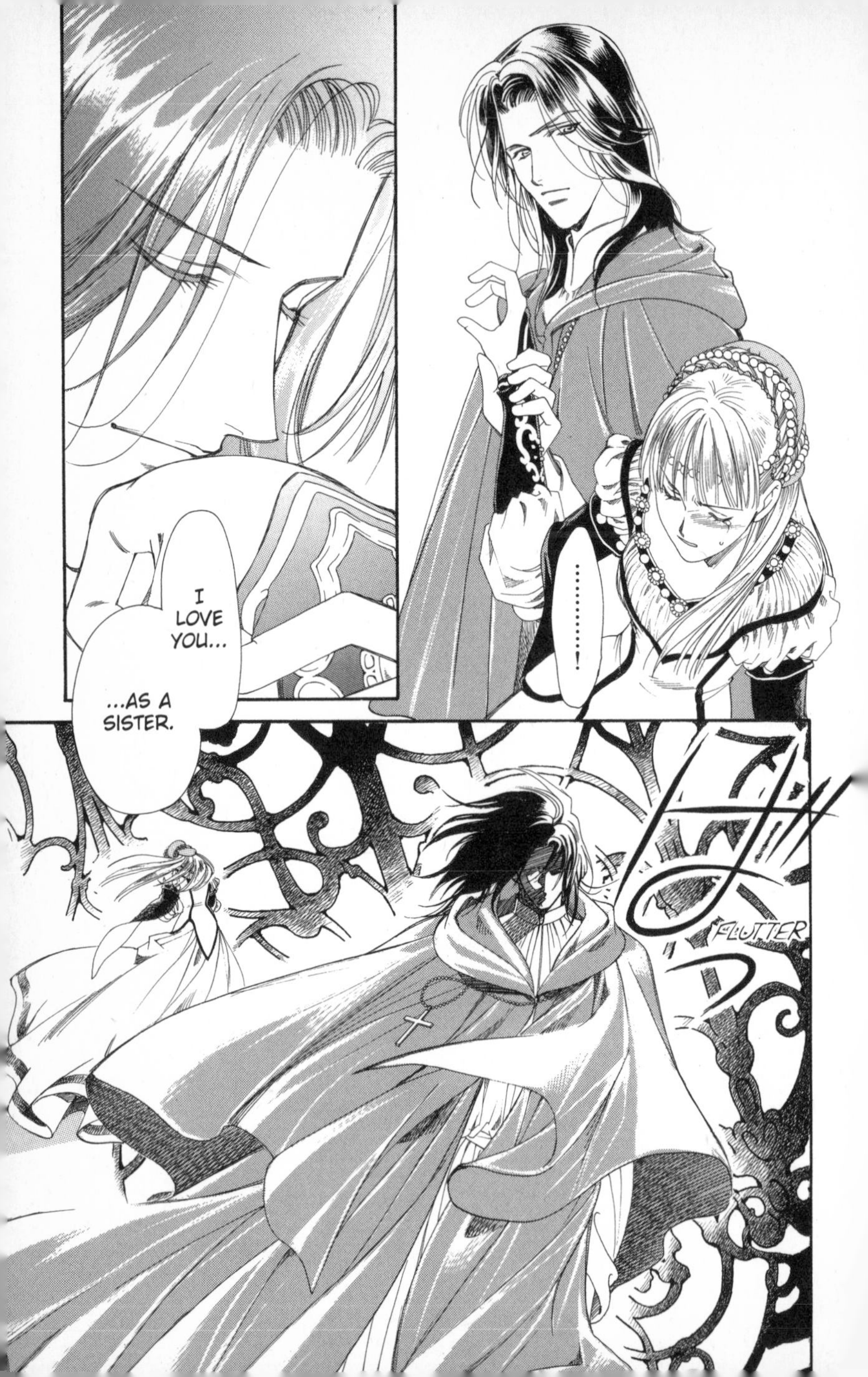
......!
I LOVE YOU...
...AS A SISTER.
FLUTTER

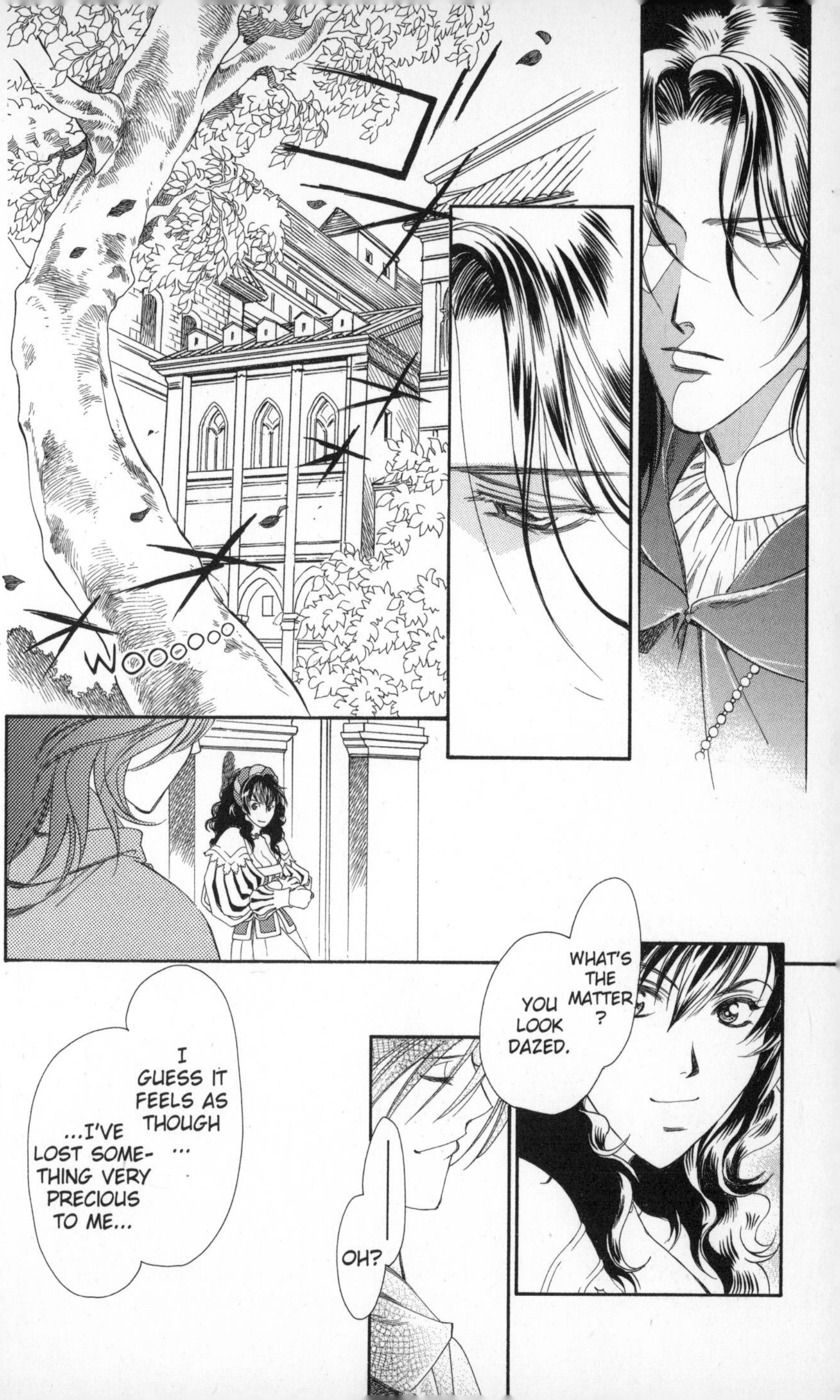
WOOOOOO
WHAT'S THE MATTER?
YOU LOOK DAZED.
——
OH?
I GUESS IT FEELS AS THOUGH...
...I'VE LOST SOMETHING VERY PRECIOUS TO ME...

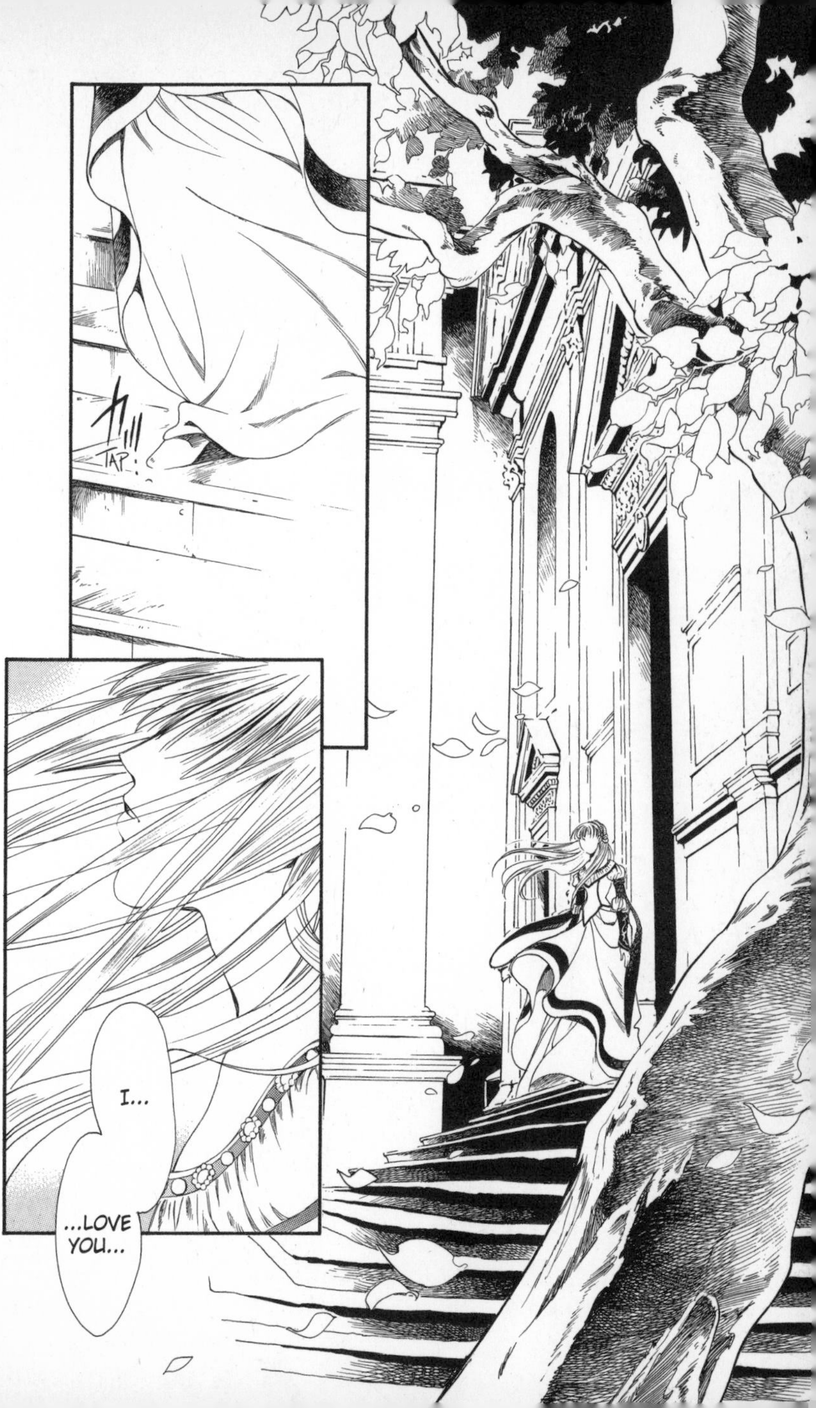
TAP!
I...
...LOVE YOU...

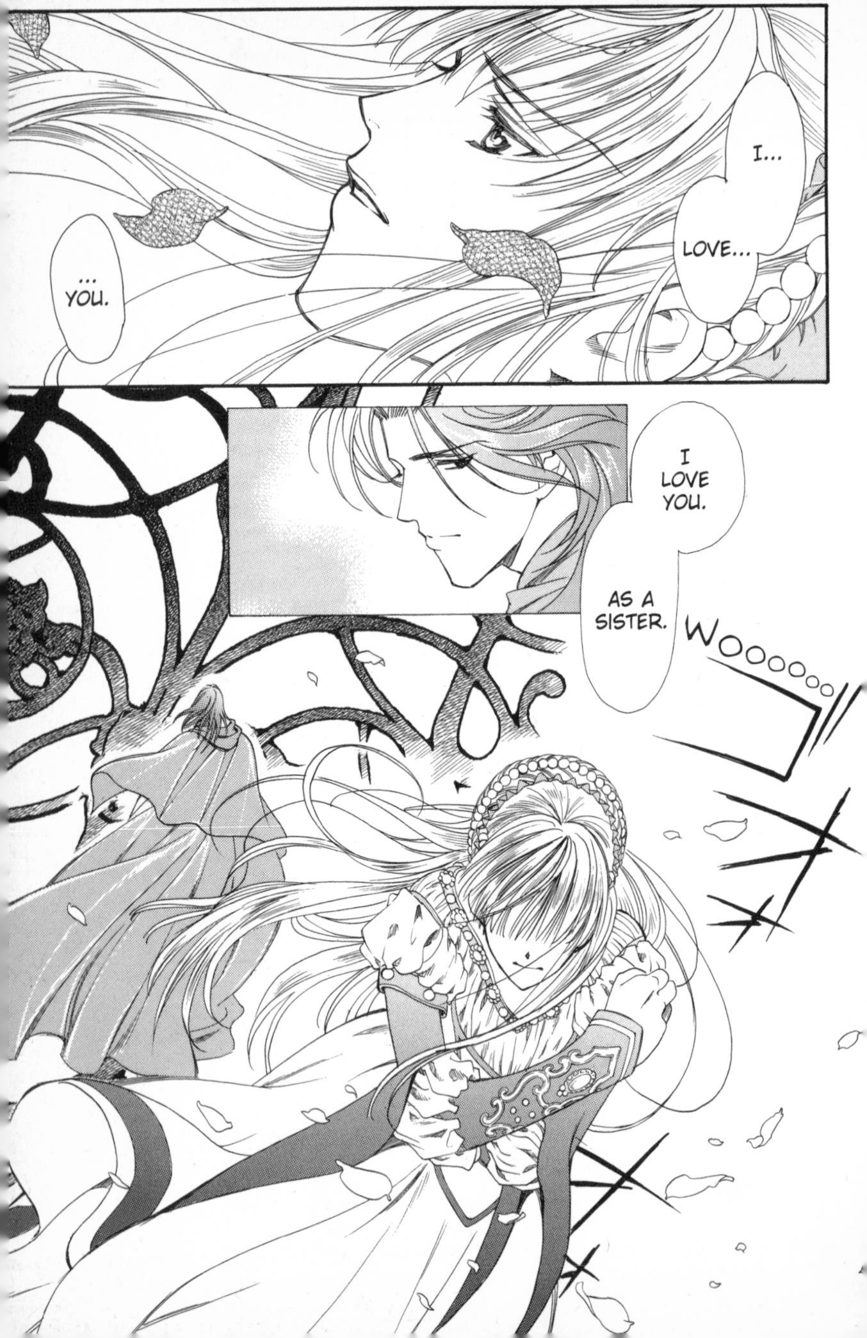
I...
LOVE...
... YOU.
I LOVE YOU.
AS A SISTER.
WOOOOOOO

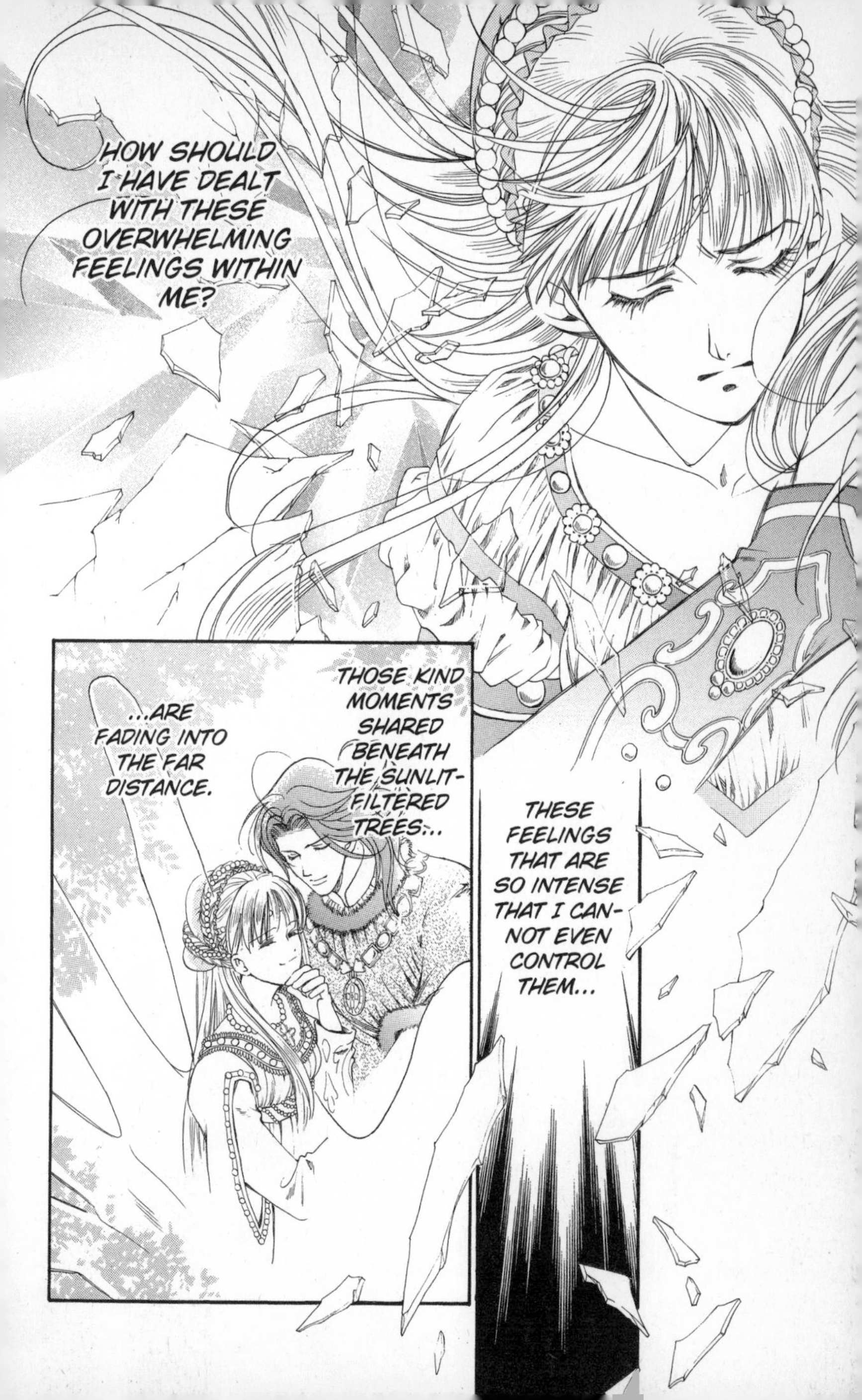
HOW SHOULD I HAVE DEALT WITH THESE OVERWHELMING FEELINGS WITHIN ME?
THESE FEELINGS THAT ARE SO INTENSE THAT I CAN-NOT EVEN CONTROL THEM...
THOSE KIND MOMENTS SHARED BENEATH THE SUNLIT-FILTERED TREES...
...ARE FADING INTO THE FAR DISTANCE.

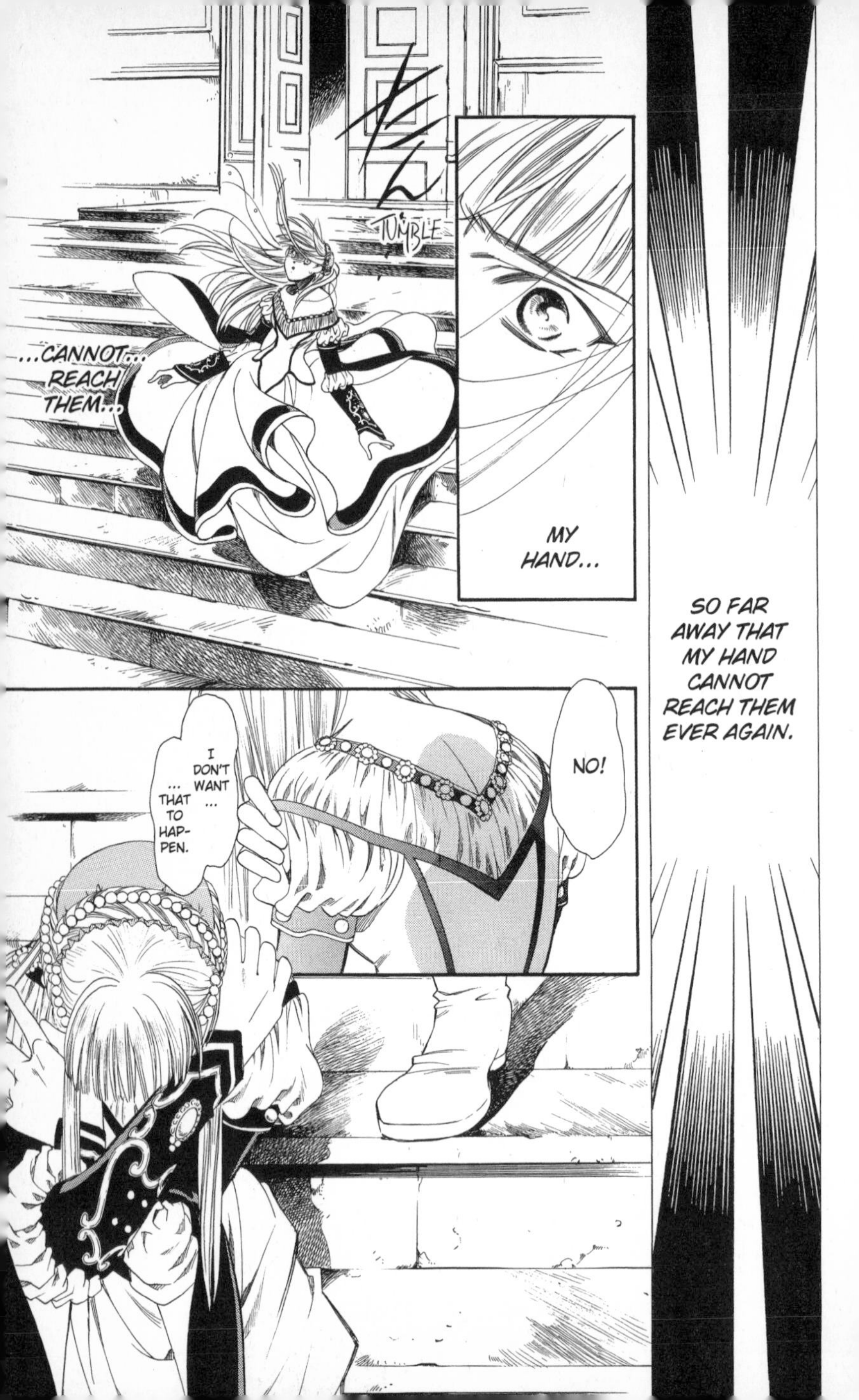
SO FAR AWAY THAT MY HAND CANNOT REACH THEM EVER AGAIN.
MY HAND...
TUMBLE
...CANNOT... REACH THEM...
NO!
I DON'T WANT ... ... THAT TO HAPPEN.

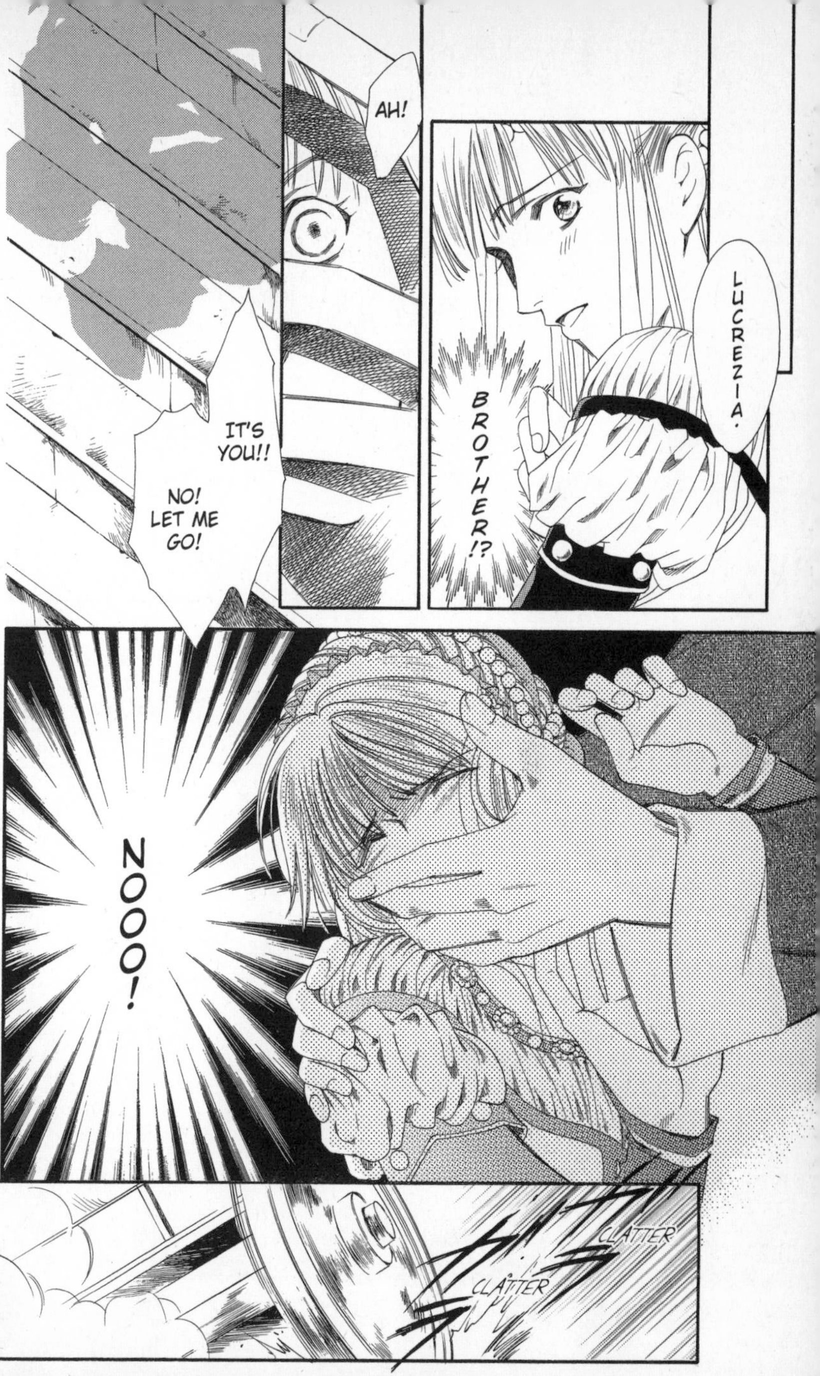
LUCREZIA.
BROTHER!?
AH!
IT'S YOU!!
NO! LET ME GO!
NOOOO!
CLATTER
CLATTER

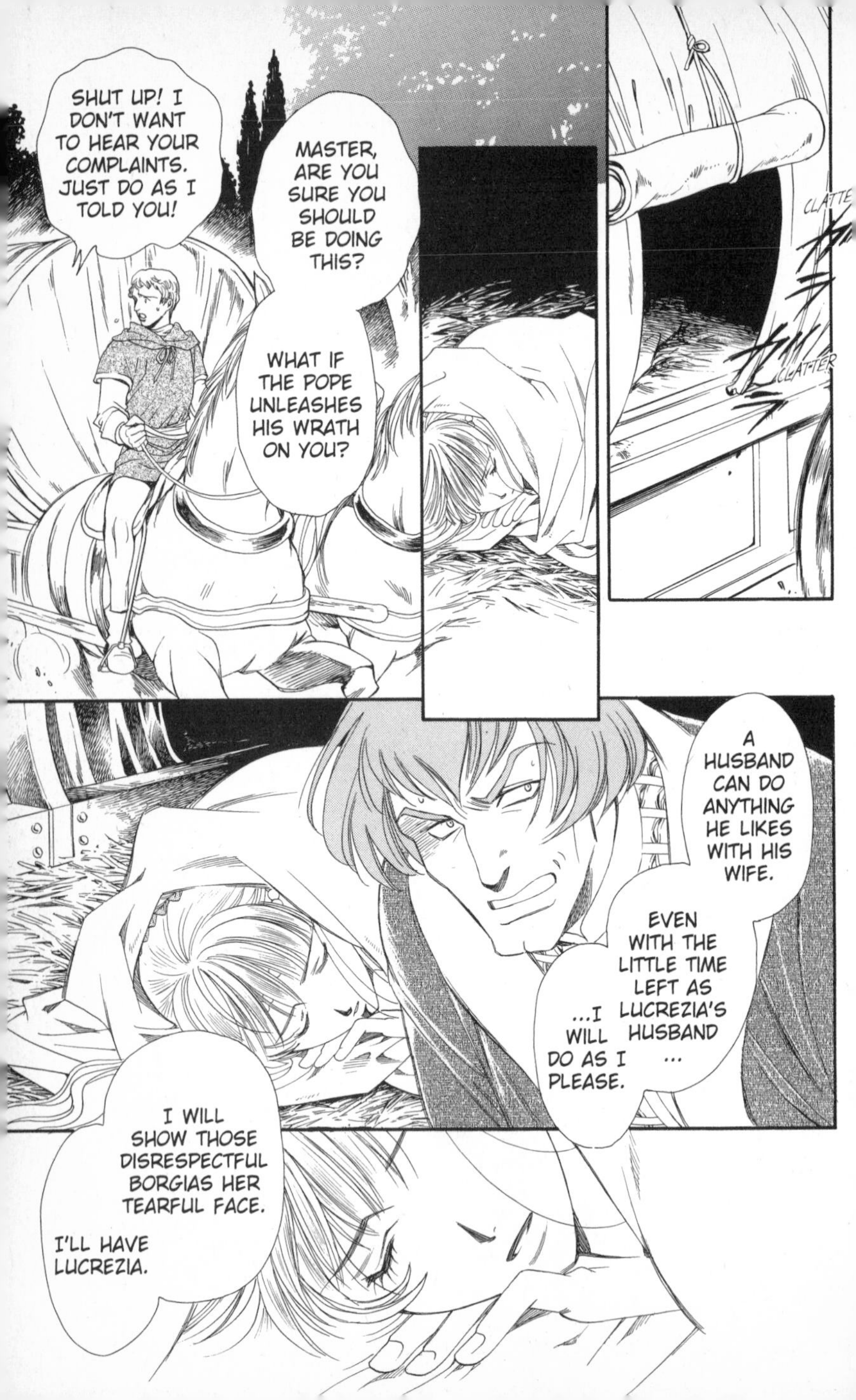
CLATTE
CLATTER
MASTER, ARE YOU SURE YOU SHOULD BE DOING THIS?
WHAT IF THE POPE UNLEASHES HIS WRATH ON YOU?
SHUT UP! I DON'T WANT TO HEAR YOUR COMPLAINTS. JUST DO AS I TOLD YOU!
A HUSBAND CAN DO ANYTHING HE LIKES WITH HIS WIFE.
EVEN WITH THE LITTLE TIME LEFT AS LUCREZIA'S HUSBAND ...
...I WILL DO AS I PLEASE.
I WILL SHOW THOSE DISRESPECTFUL BORGIAS HER TEARFUL FACE.
I'LL HAVE LUCREZIA.

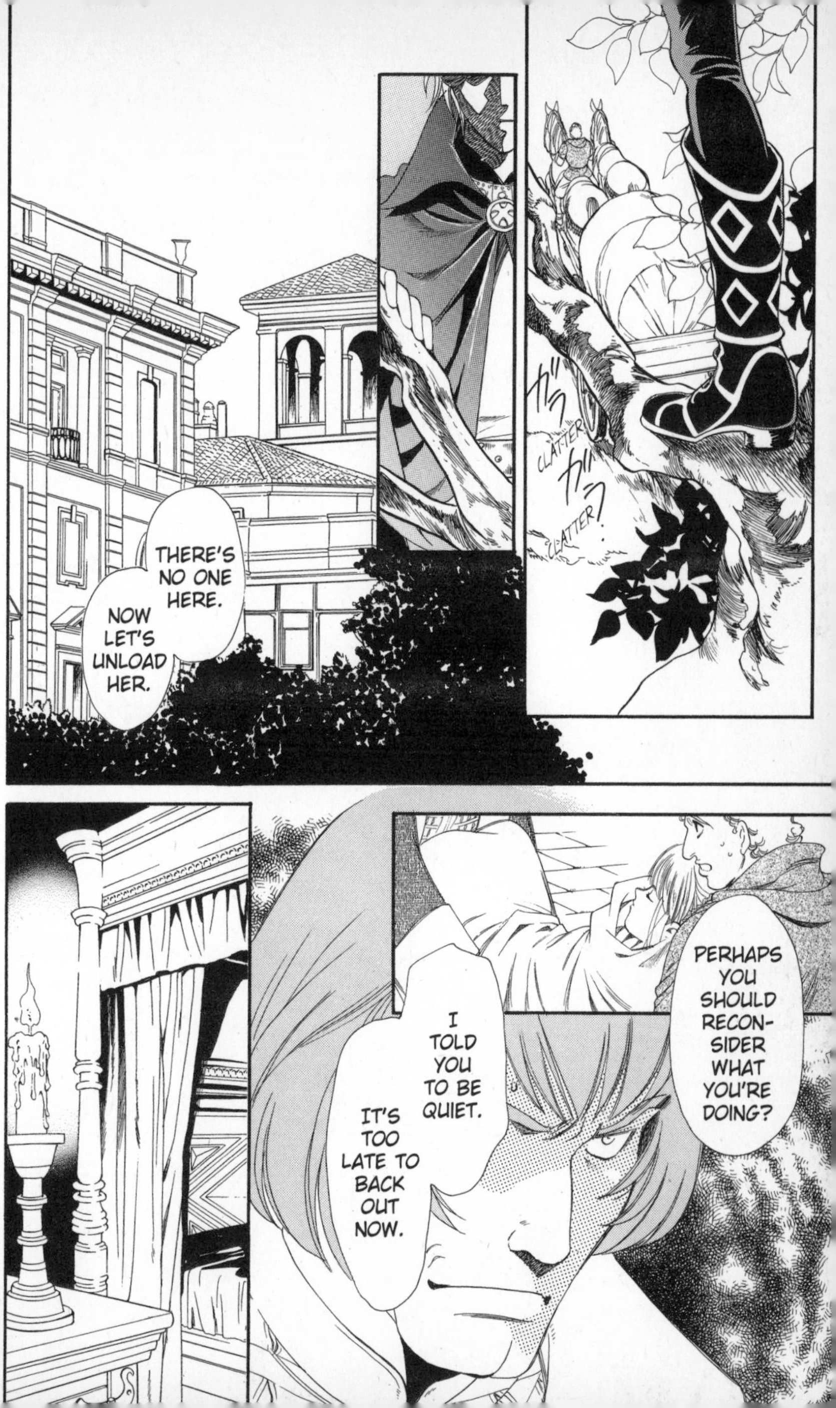
CLATTER
CLATTER
THERE'S NO ONE HERE.
NOW LET'S UNLOAD HER.
PERHAPS YOU SHOULD RECONSIDER WHAT YOU'RE DOING?
I TOLD YOU TO BE QUIET.
IT'S TOO LATE TO BACK OUT NOW.

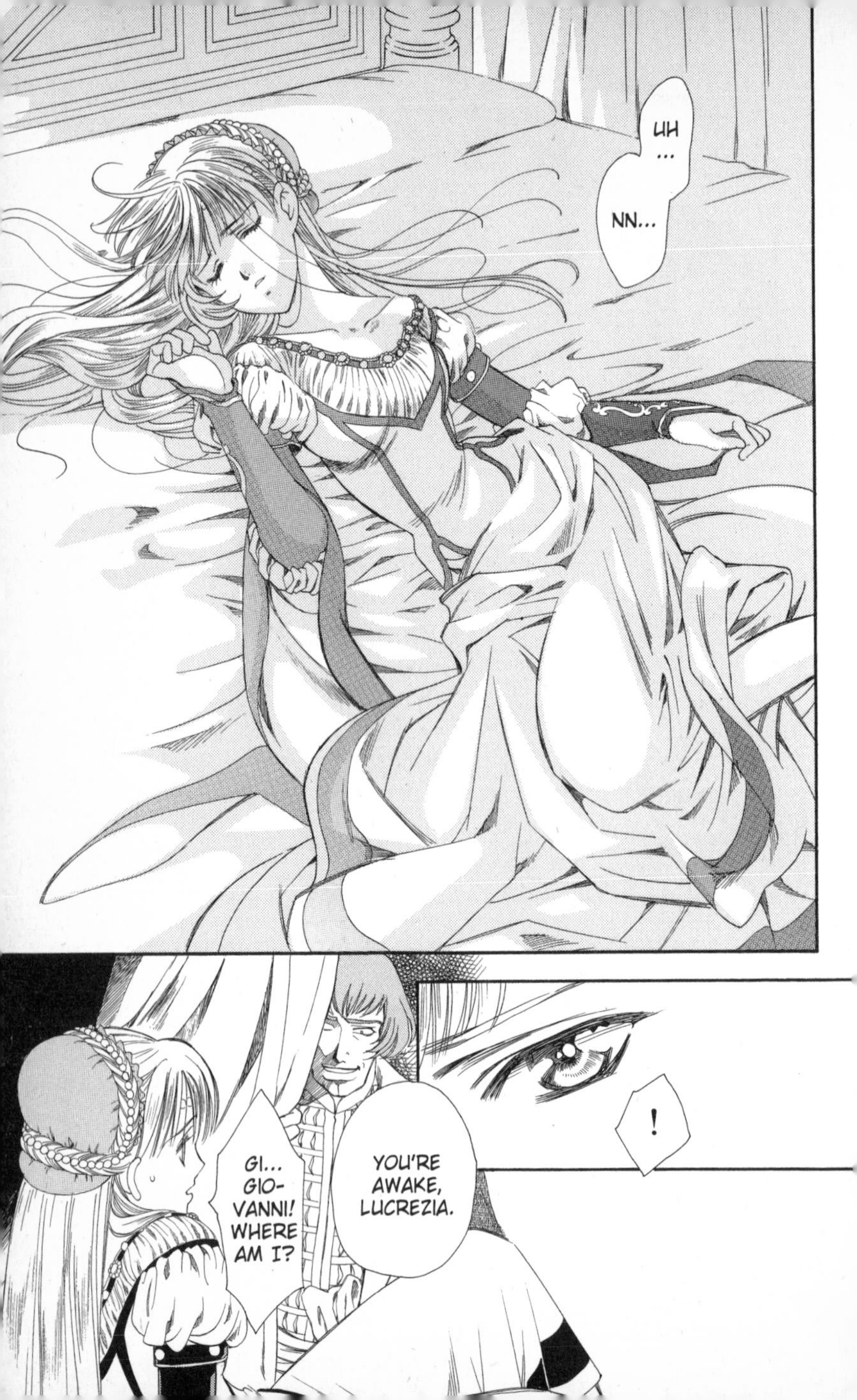
UH ...
NN...
!
YOU'RE AWAKE, LUCREZIA.
GI... GIO-VANNI! WHERE AM I?

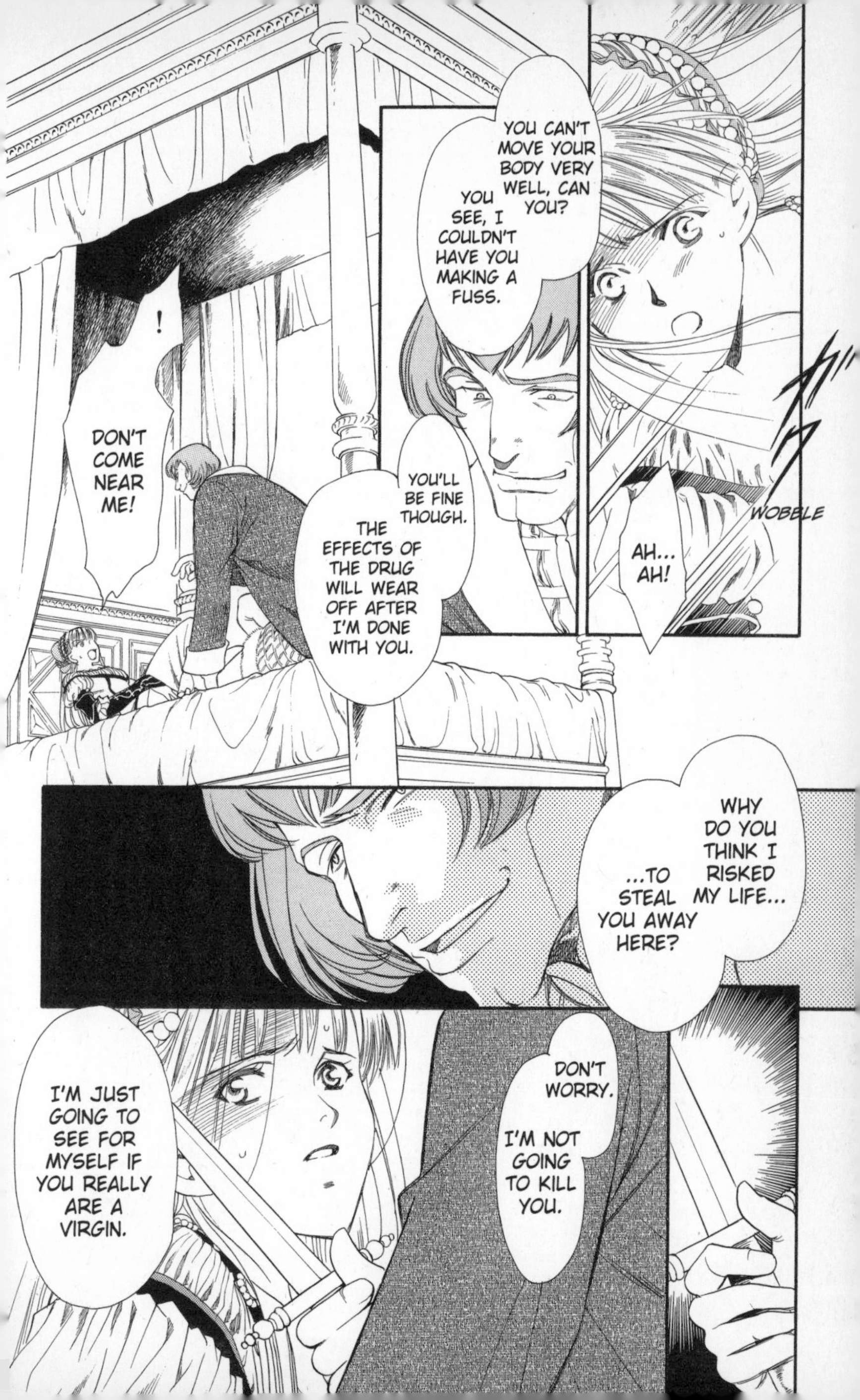

AH... AH!
WOBBLE
YOU CAN'T MOVE YOUR BODY VERY WELL, CAN YOU?
YOU SEE, I COULDN'T HAVE YOU MAKING A FUSS.
!
DON'T COME NEAR ME!
YOU'LL BE FINE THOUGH.
THE EFFECTS OF THE DRUG WILL WEAR OFF AFTER I'M DONE WITH YOU.
WHY DO YOU THINK I RISKED MY LIFE...
...TO STEAL YOU AWAY HERE?
DON'T WORRY.
I'M NOT GOING TO KILL YOU.
I'M JUST GOING TO SEE FOR MYSELF IF YOU REALLY ARE A VIRGIN.

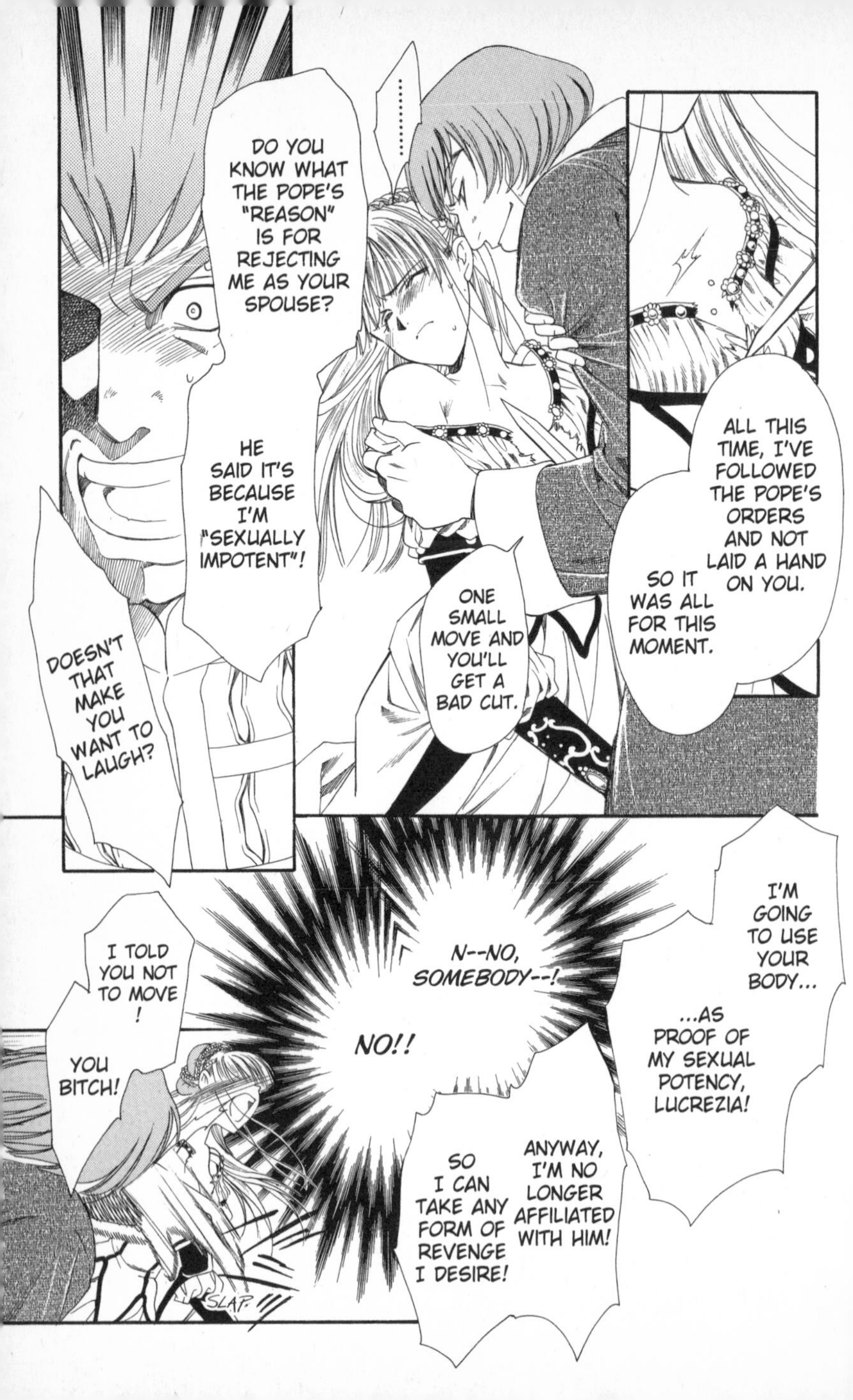
ALL THIS TIME, I'VE FOLLOWED THE POPE'S ORDERS AND NOT LAID A HAND ON YOU.
SO IT WAS ALL FOR THIS MOMENT.
......
ONE SMALL MOVE AND YOU'LL GET A BAD CUT.
DO YOU KNOW WHAT THE POPE'S "REASON" IS FOR REJECTING ME AS YOUR SPOUSE?
HE SAID IT'S BECAUSE I'M "SEXUALLY IMPOTENT"!
DOESN'T THAT MAKE YOU WANT TO LAUGH?
I'M GOING TO USE YOUR BODY...
...AS PROOF OF MY SEXUAL POTENCY, LUCREZIA!
ANYWAY, I'M NO LONGER AFFILIATED WITH HIM!
SO I CAN TAKE ANY FORM OF REVENGE I DESIRE!
N--NO, SOMEBODY--!
NO!!
I TOLD YOU NOT TO MOVE!
YOU BITCH!
SLAP!!!

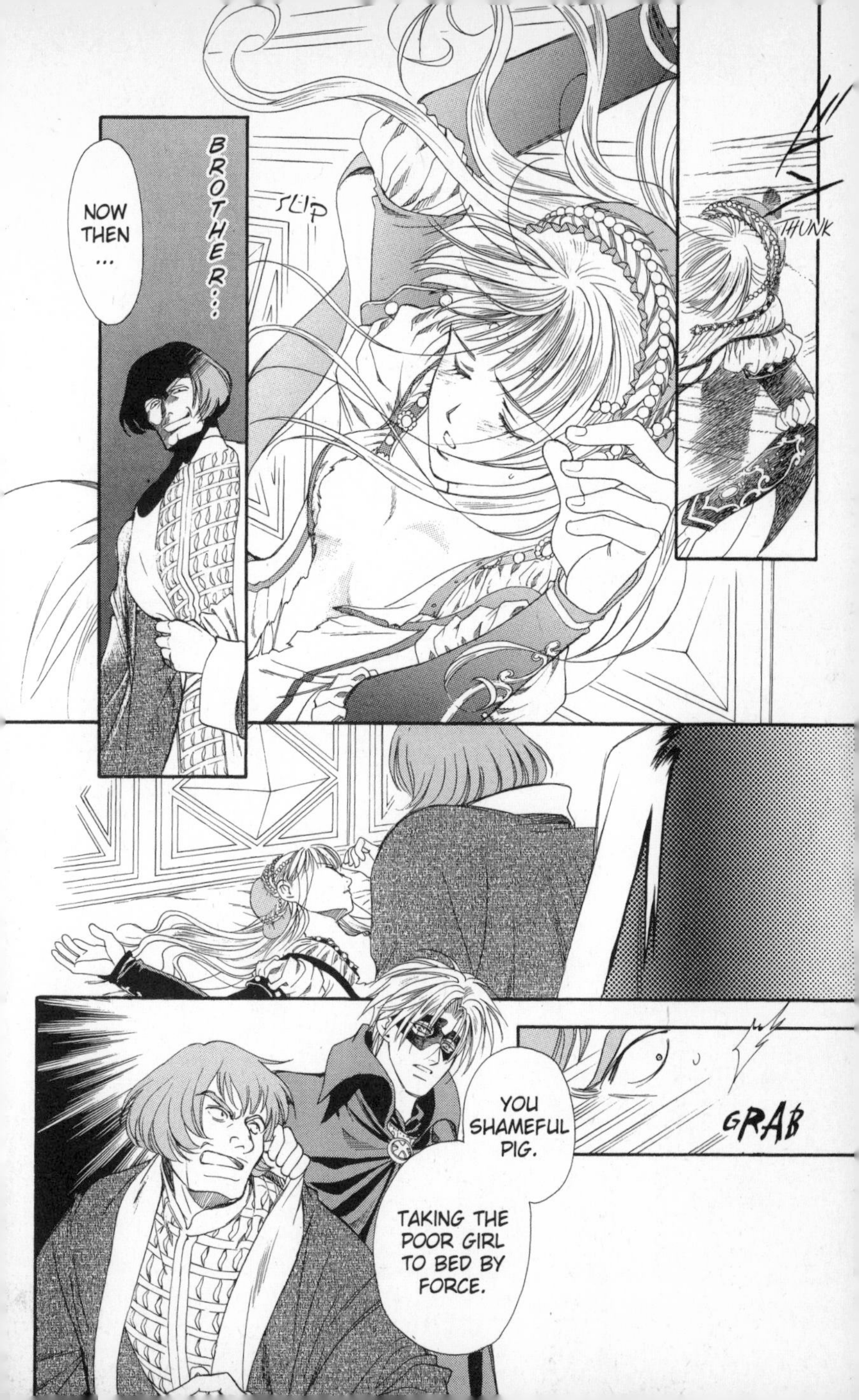
THUNK
SLIP
BROTHER...
NOW THEN ...
GRAB
YOU SHAMEFUL PIG.
TAKING THE POOR GIRL TO BED BY FORCE.

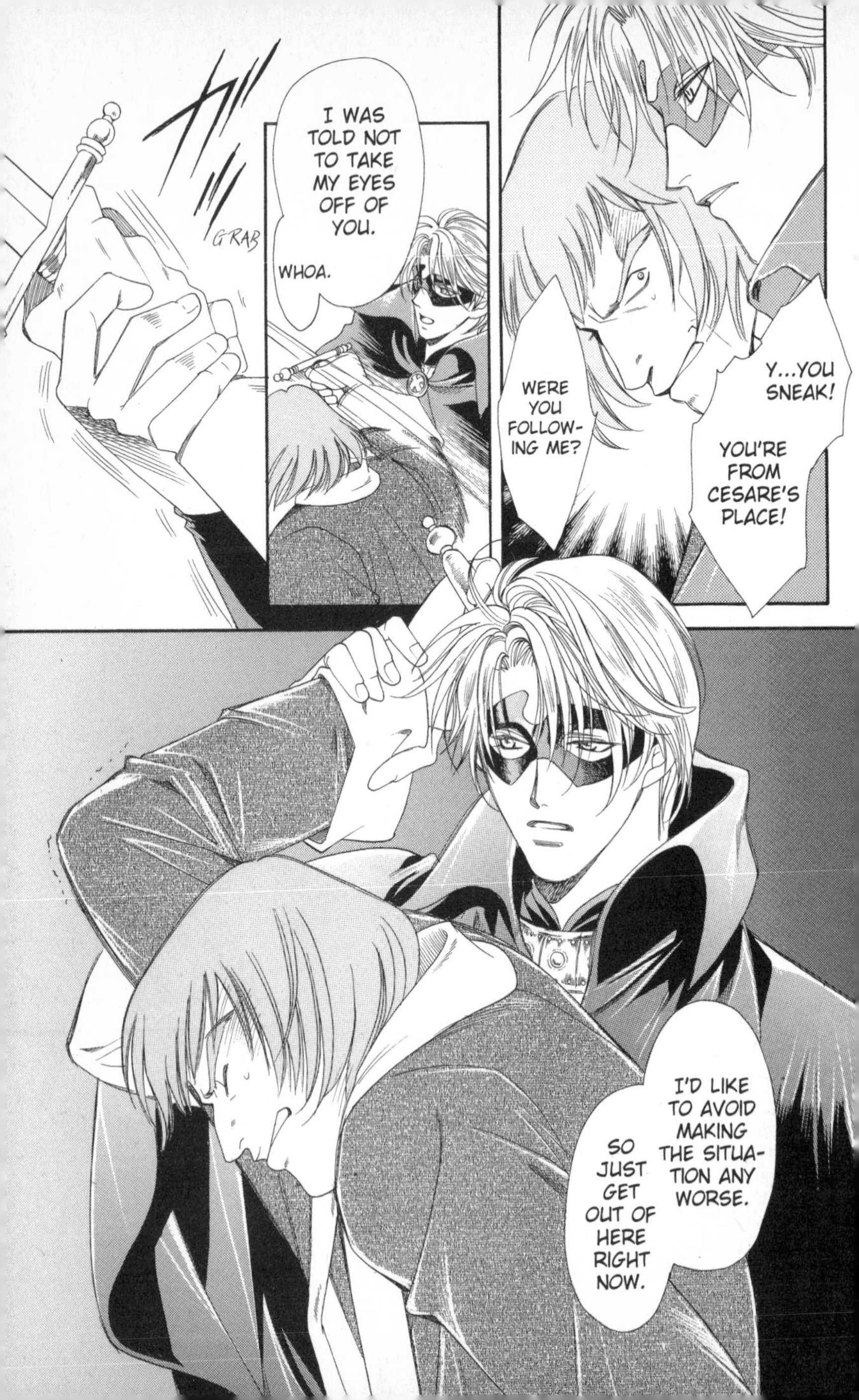
Y...YOU SNEAK!
YOU'RE FROM CESARE'S PLACE!
WERE YOU FOLLOWING ME?
I WAS TOLD NOT TO TAKE MY EYES OFF OF YOU.
WHOA.
GRAB
I'D LIKE TO AVOID MAKING THE SITUATION ANY WORSE.
SO JUST GET OUT OF HERE RIGHT NOW.

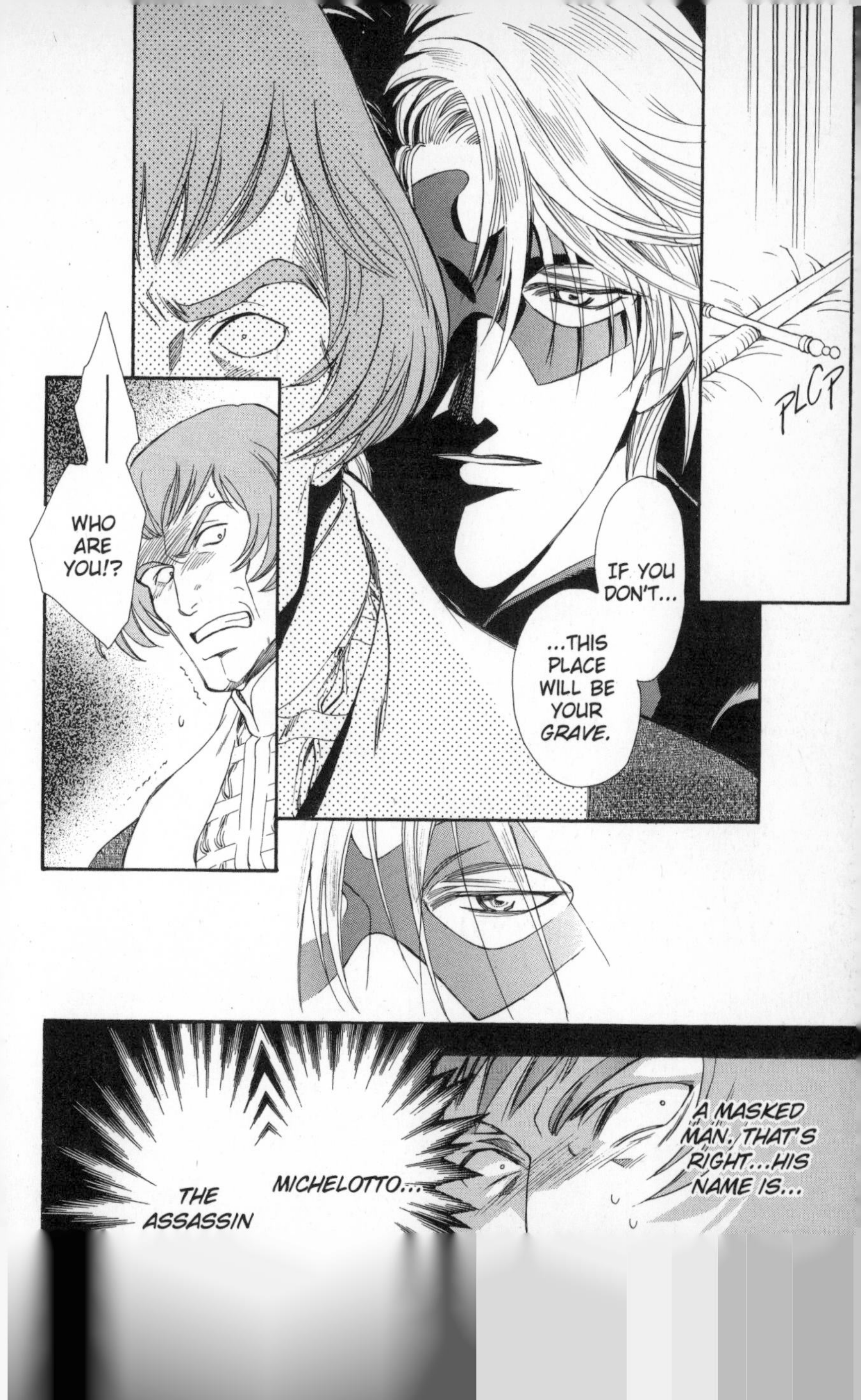
PLCP
IF YOU DON'T...
...THIS PLACE WILL BE YOUR GRAVE.
WHO ARE YOU!?
A MASKED MAN. THAT'S RIGHT...HIS NAME IS...
MICHELOTTO...
THE ASSASSIN

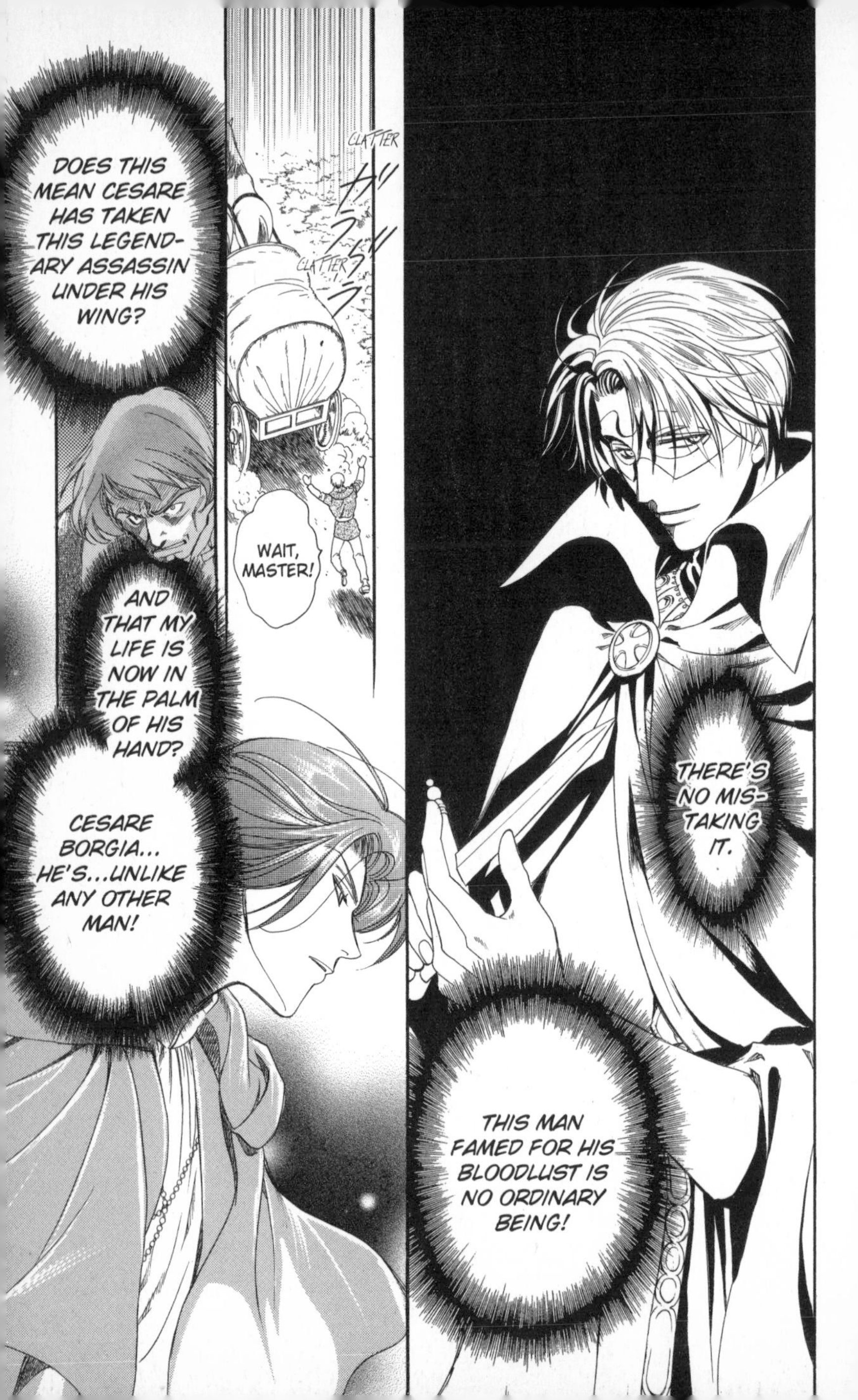
THERE'S NO MIS-TAKING IT.
THIS MAN FAMED FOR HIS BLOODLUST IS NO ORDINARY BEING!
CLATTER
CLATTER
WAIT, MASTER!
DOES THIS MEAN CESARE HAS TAKEN THIS LEGEND-ARY ASSASSIN UNDER HIS WING?
AND THAT MY LIFE IS NOW IN THE PALM OF HIS HAND?
CESARE BORGIA... HE'S...UNLIKE ANY OTHER MAN!

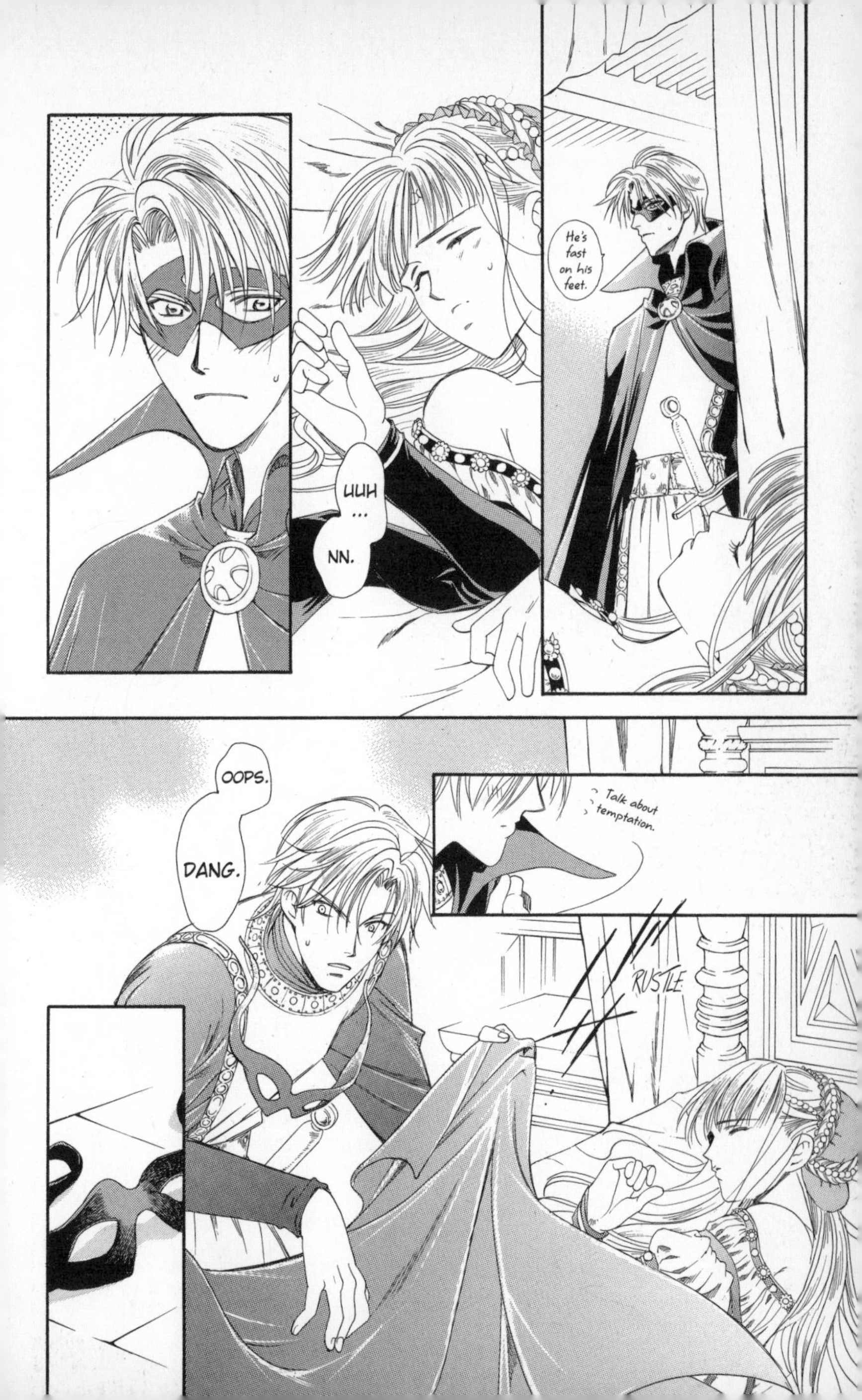
He's fast on his feet.
UUH ...
NN.
Talk about temptation.
RUSTLE
OOPS.
DANG.

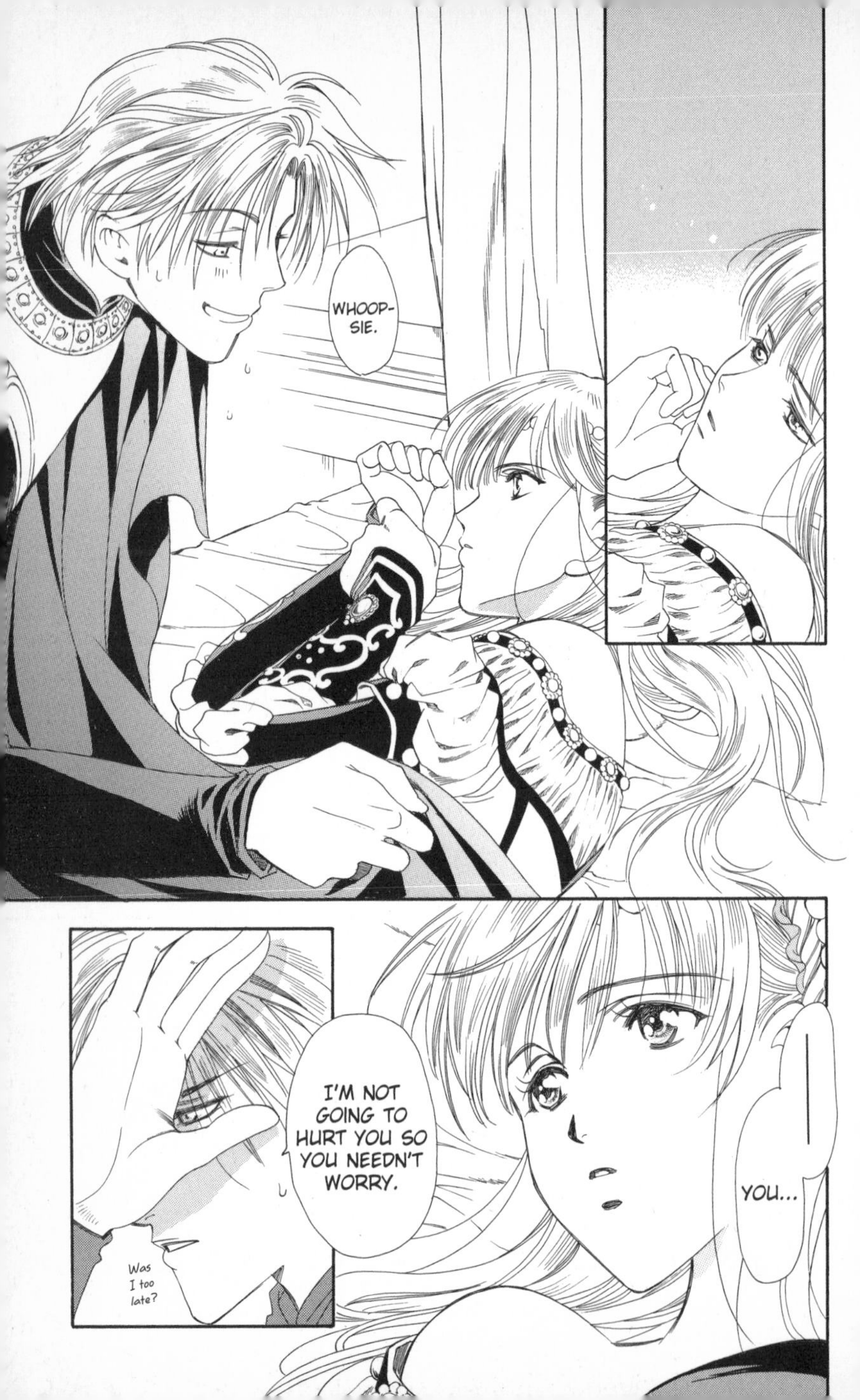
WHOOP-SIE.
YOU...
I'M NOT GOING TO HURT YOU SO YOU NEEDN'T WORRY.
Was I too late?

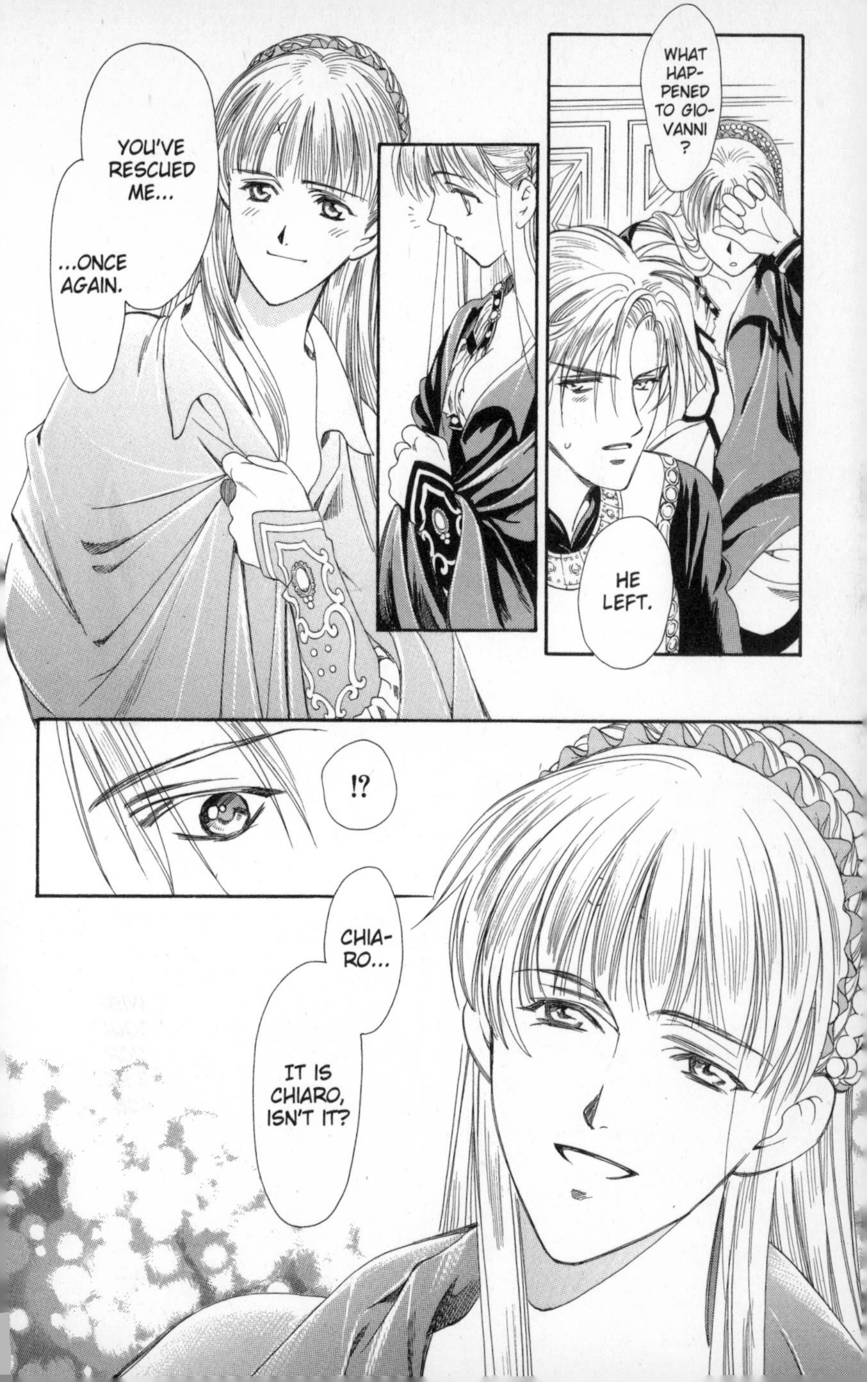
WHAT HAPPENED TO GIOVANNI?
HE LEFT.
YOU'VE RESCUED ME...
...ONCE AGAIN.
!?
CHIARO...
IT IS CHIARO, ISN'T IT?

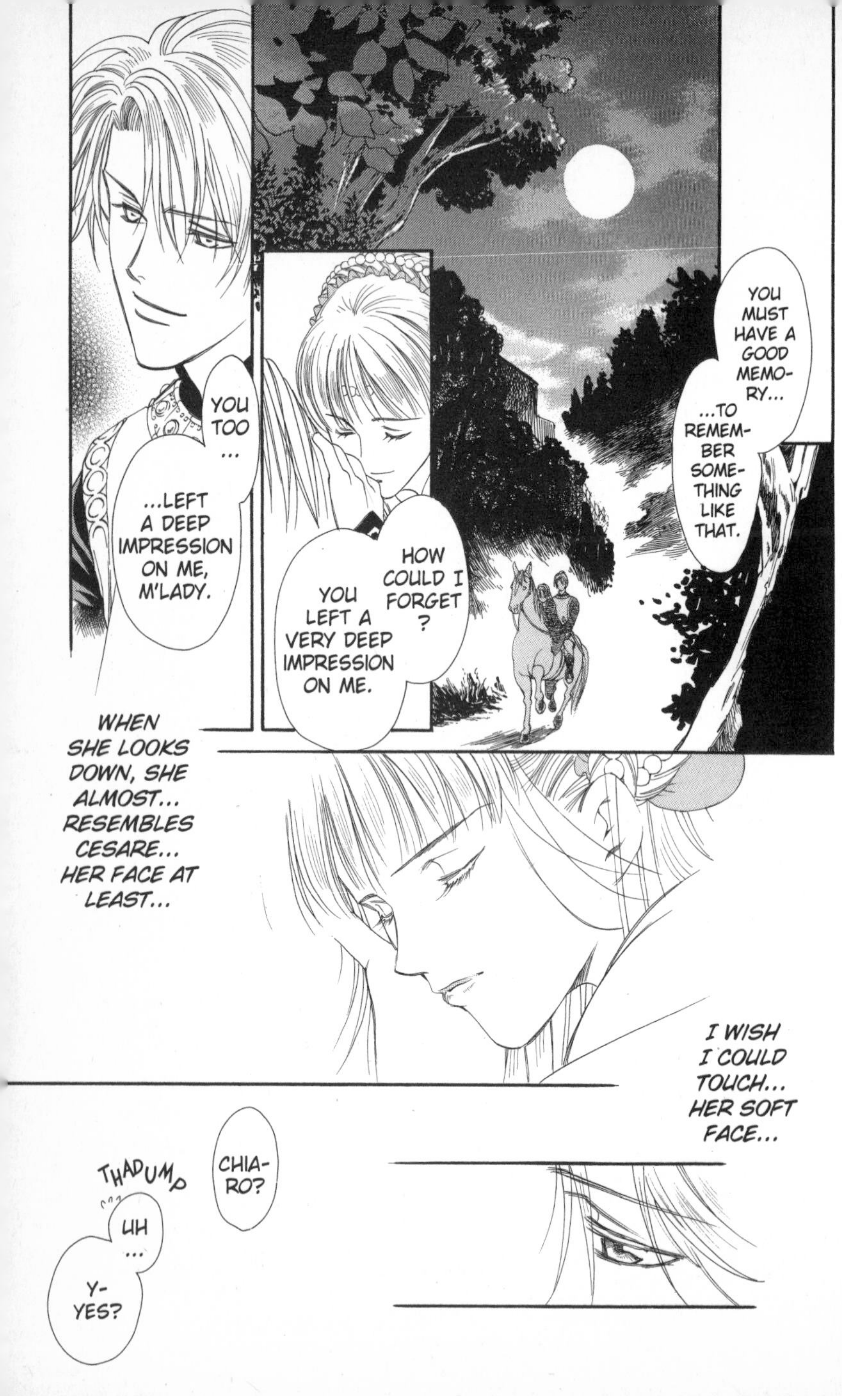
YOU MUST HAVE A GOOD MEMORY...
...TO REMEMBER SOMETHING LIKE THAT.
HOW COULD I FORGET?
YOU LEFT A VERY DEEP IMPRESSION ON ME.
YOU TOO...
...LEFT A DEEP IMPRESSION ON ME, M'LADY.
WHEN SHE LOOKS DOWN, SHE ALMOST... RESEMBLES CESARE... HER FACE AT LEAST...
I WISH I COULD TOUCH... HER SOFT FACE...
CHIARO?
THADUMP
UH... Y-YES?

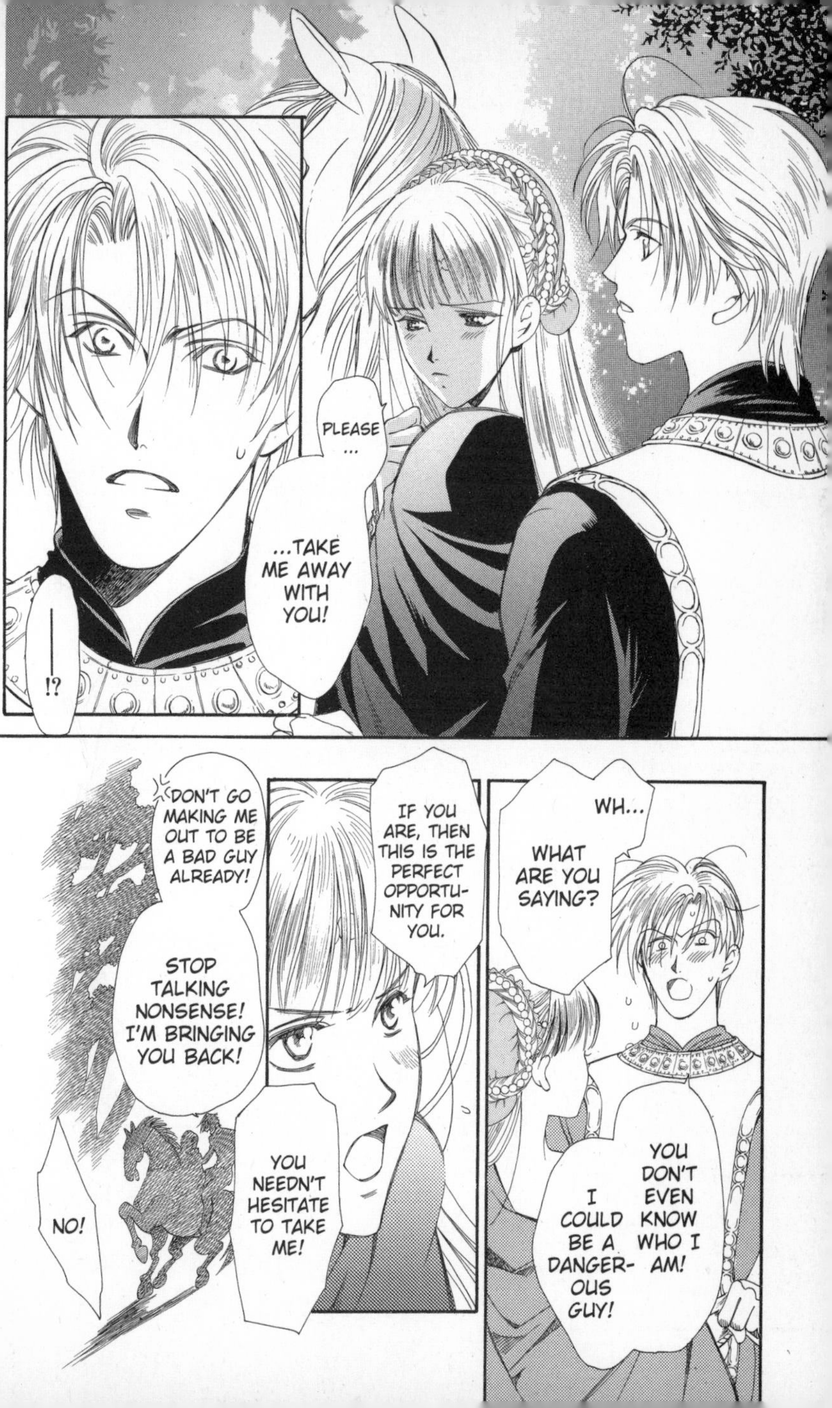
PLEASE ...
...TAKE ME AWAY WITH YOU!
——!?
WH...
WHAT ARE YOU SAYING?
YOU DON'T EVEN KNOW WHO I AM!
I COULD BE A DANGEROUS GUY!
IF YOU ARE, THEN THIS IS THE PERFECT OPPORTUNITY FOR YOU.
YOU NEEDN'T HESITATE TO TAKE ME!
DON'T GO MAKING ME OUT TO BE A BAD GUY ALREADY!
STOP TALKING NONSENSE! I'M BRINGING YOU BACK!
NO!

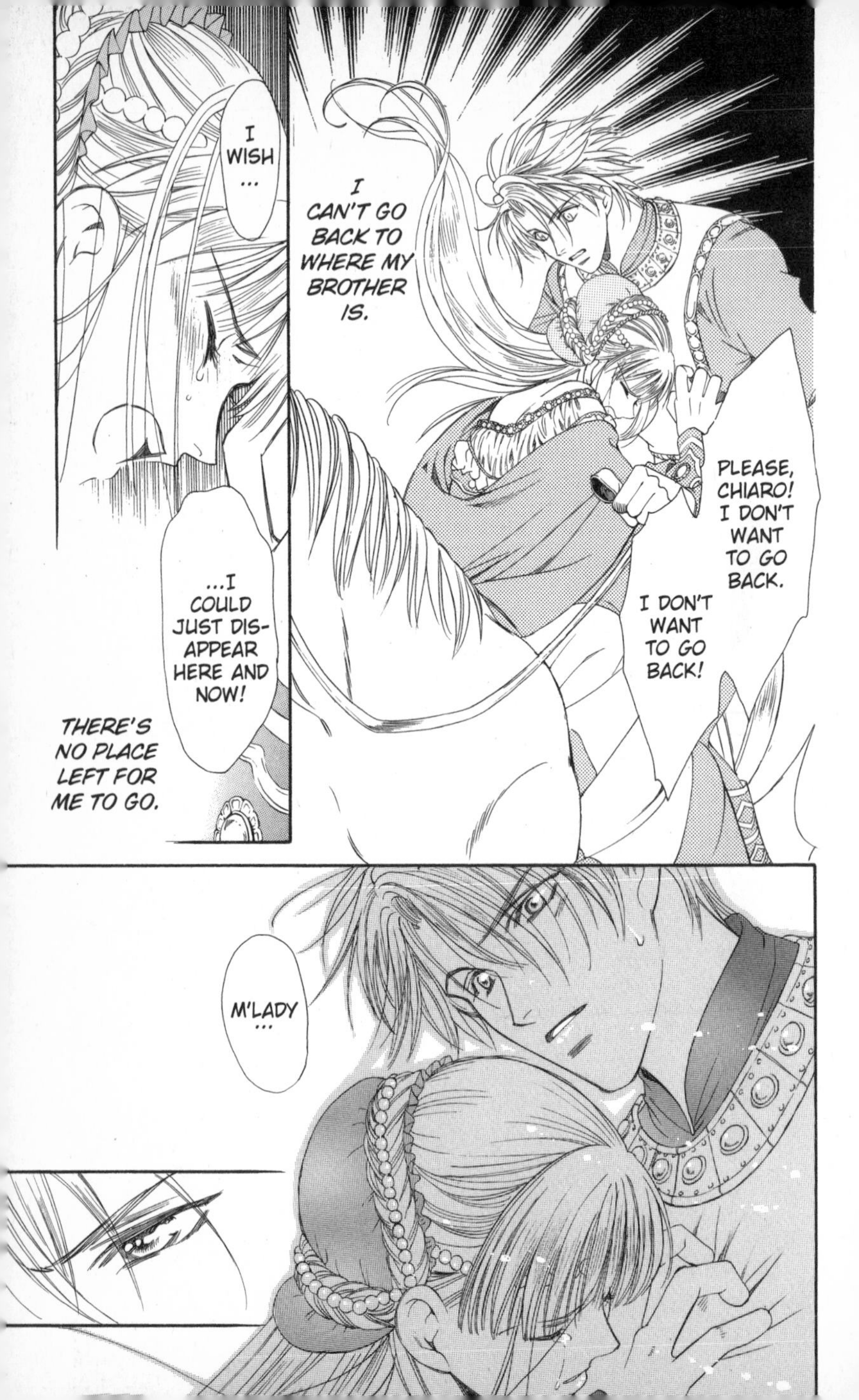
PLEASE, CHIARO! I DON'T WANT TO GO BACK.
I DON'T WANT TO GO BACK!
I CAN'T GO BACK TO WHERE MY BROTHER IS.
I WISH ...
...I COULD JUST DIS-APPEAR HERE AND NOW!
THERE'S NO PLACE LEFT FOR ME TO GO.
M'LADY ...

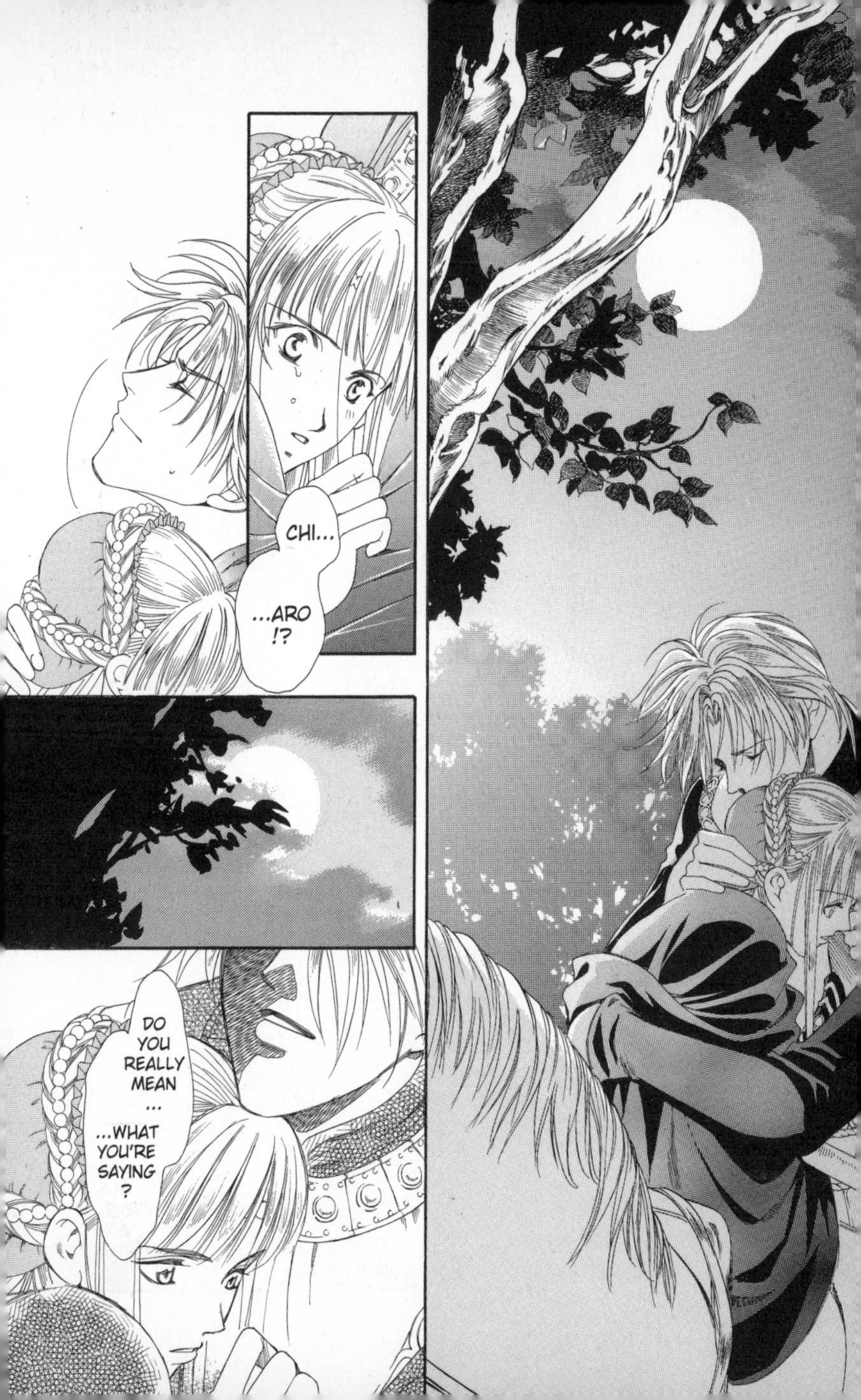
CHI...
...ARO !?
DO YOU REALLY MEAN ...
...WHAT YOU'RE SAYING ?

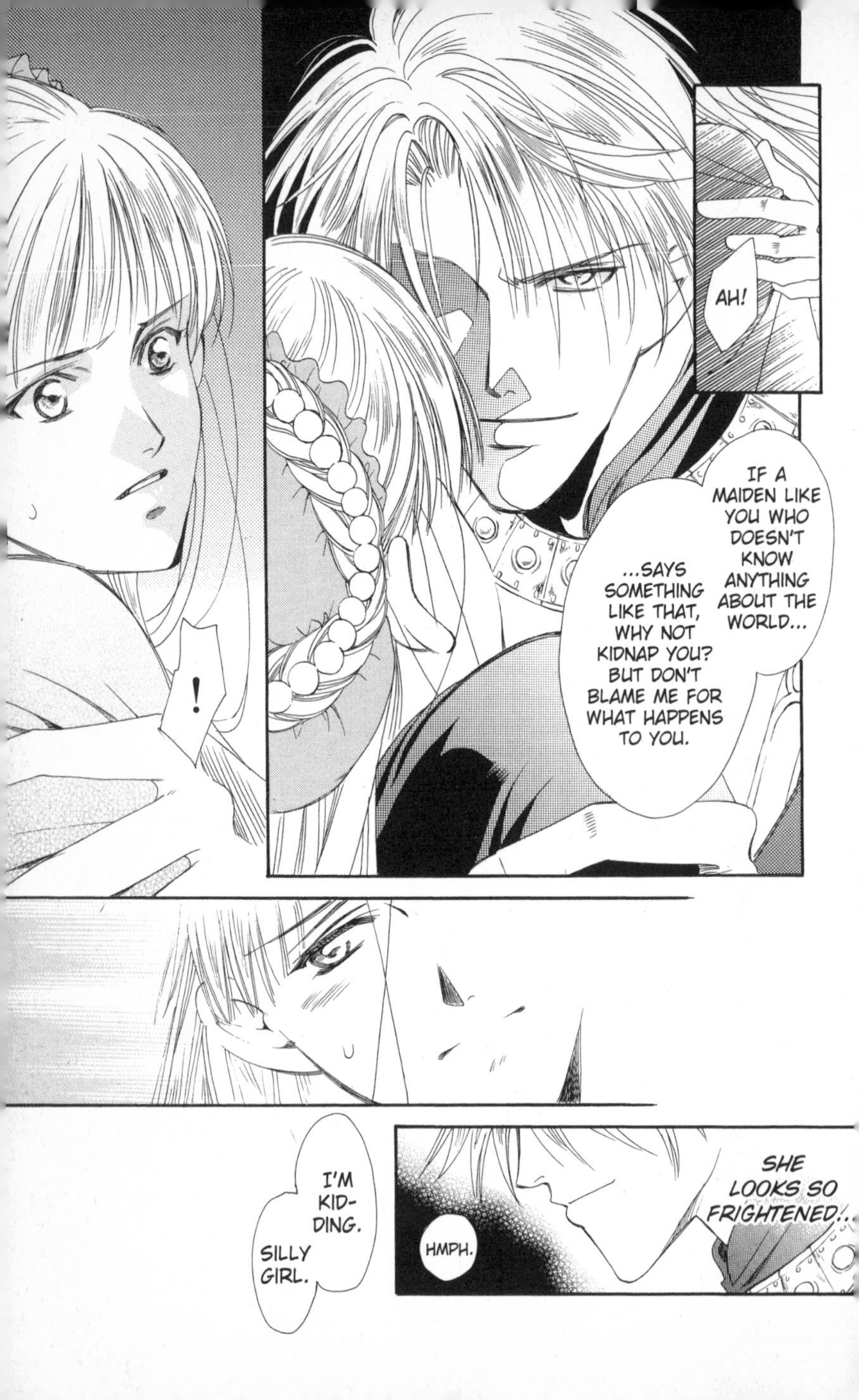
AH!
IF A MAIDEN LIKE YOU WHO DOESN'T KNOW ANYTHING ABOUT THE WORLD...
...SAYS SOMETHING LIKE THAT, WHY NOT KIDNAP YOU? BUT DON'T BLAME ME FOR WHAT HAPPENS TO YOU.
!
SHE LOOKS SO FRIGHTENED...
HMPH.
I'M KID-DING. SILLY GIRL.

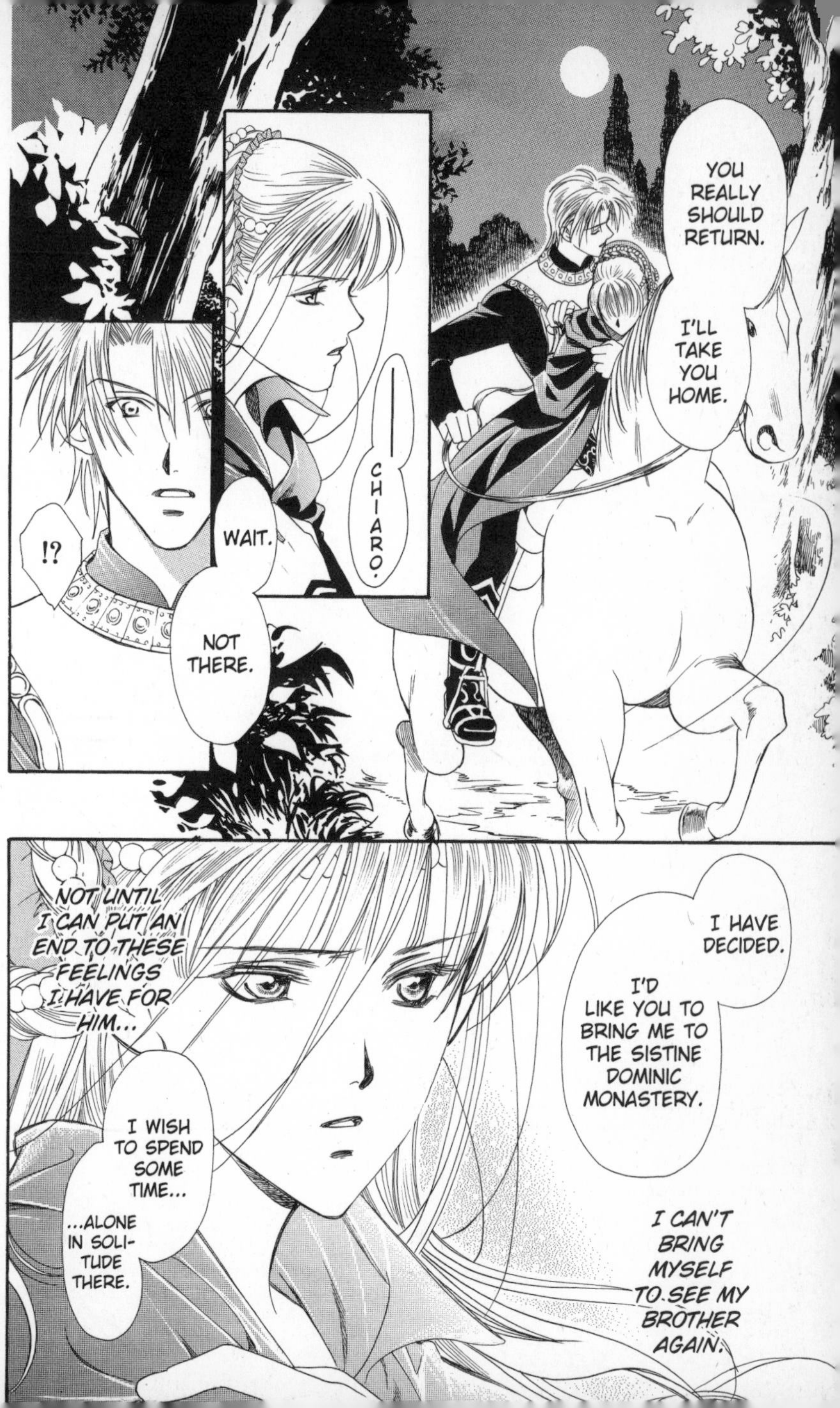
YOU REALLY SHOULD RETURN.
I'LL TAKE YOU HOME.
——CHIARO.
WAIT.
!?
NOT THERE.
I HAVE DECIDED.
I'D LIKE YOU TO BRING ME TO THE SISTINE DOMINIC MONASTERY.
I CAN'T BRING MYSELF TO SEE MY BROTHER AGAIN.
I WISH TO SPEND SOME TIME...
...ALONE IN SOLI-TUDE THERE.
NOT UNTIL I CAN PUT AN END TO THESE FEELINGS I HAVE FOR HIM...

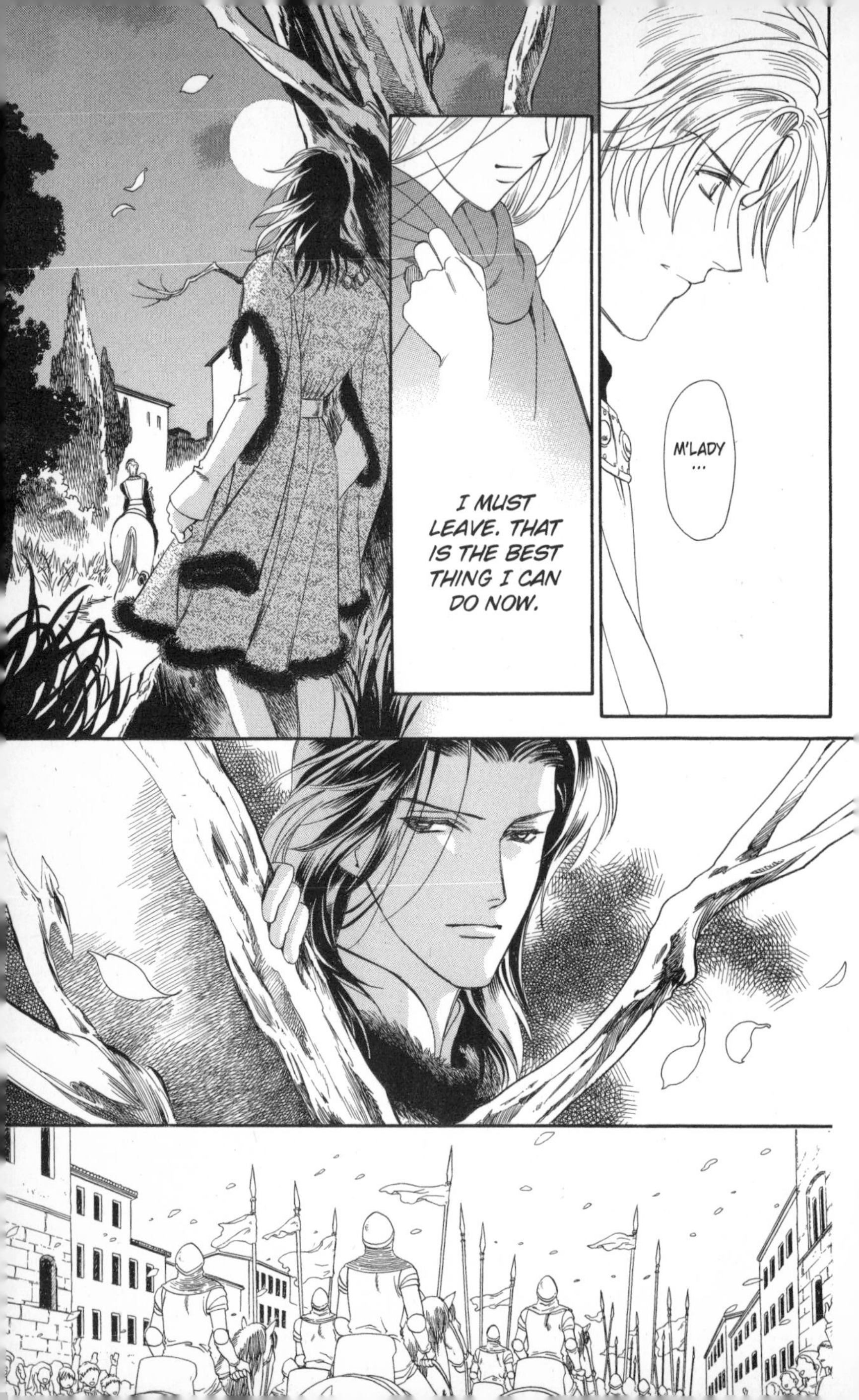
M'LADY ...
I MUST LEAVE. THAT IS THE BEST THING I CAN DO NOW.

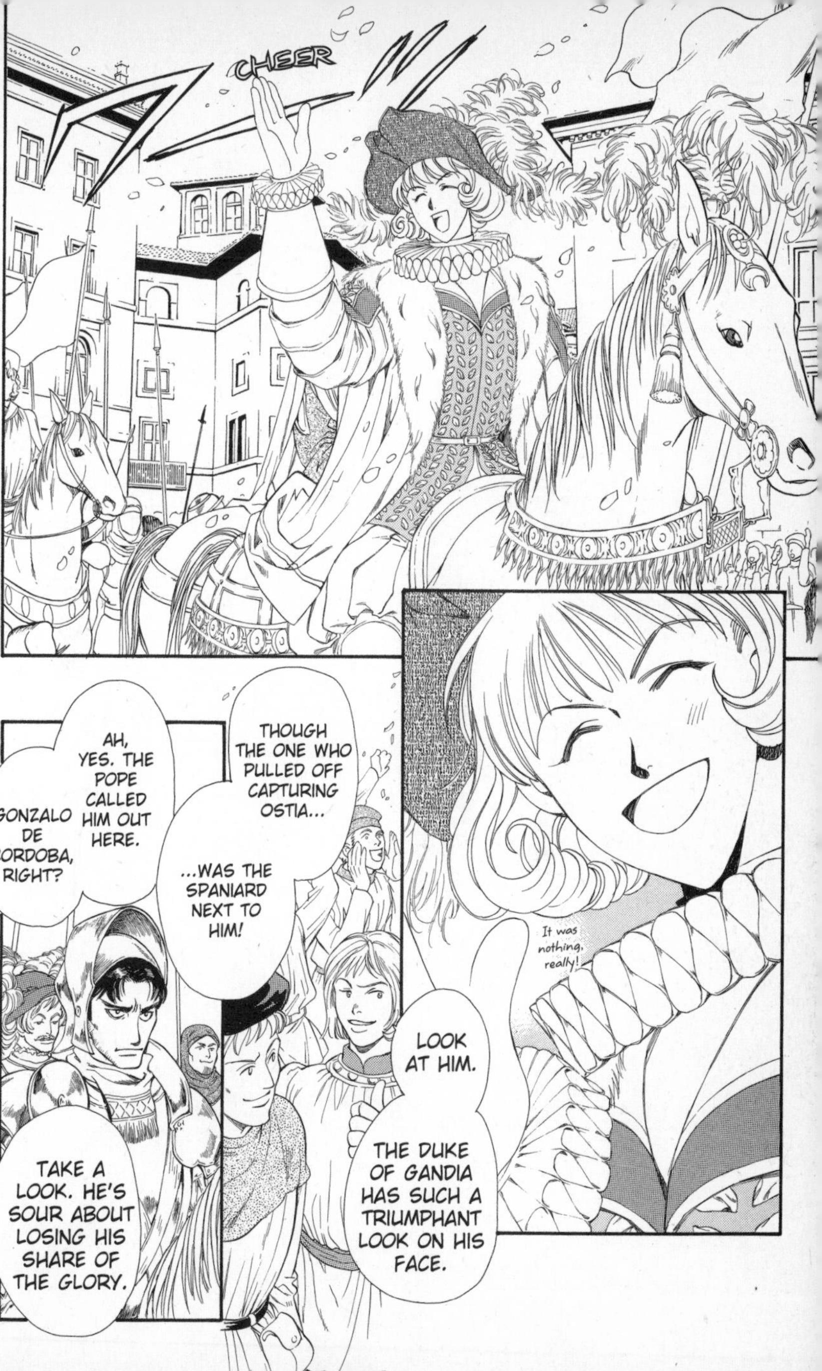
CHEER
It was nothing, really!
LOOK AT HIM.
THE DUKE OF GANDIA HAS SUCH A TRIUMPHANT LOOK ON HIS FACE.
THOUGH THE ONE WHO PULLED OFF CAPTURING OSTIA...
...WAS THE SPANIARD NEXT TO HIM!
GONZALO DE CORDOBA, RIGHT?
AH, YES. THE POPE CALLED HIM OUT HERE.
TAKE A LOOK. HE'S SOUR ABOUT LOSING HIS SHARE OF THE GLORY.

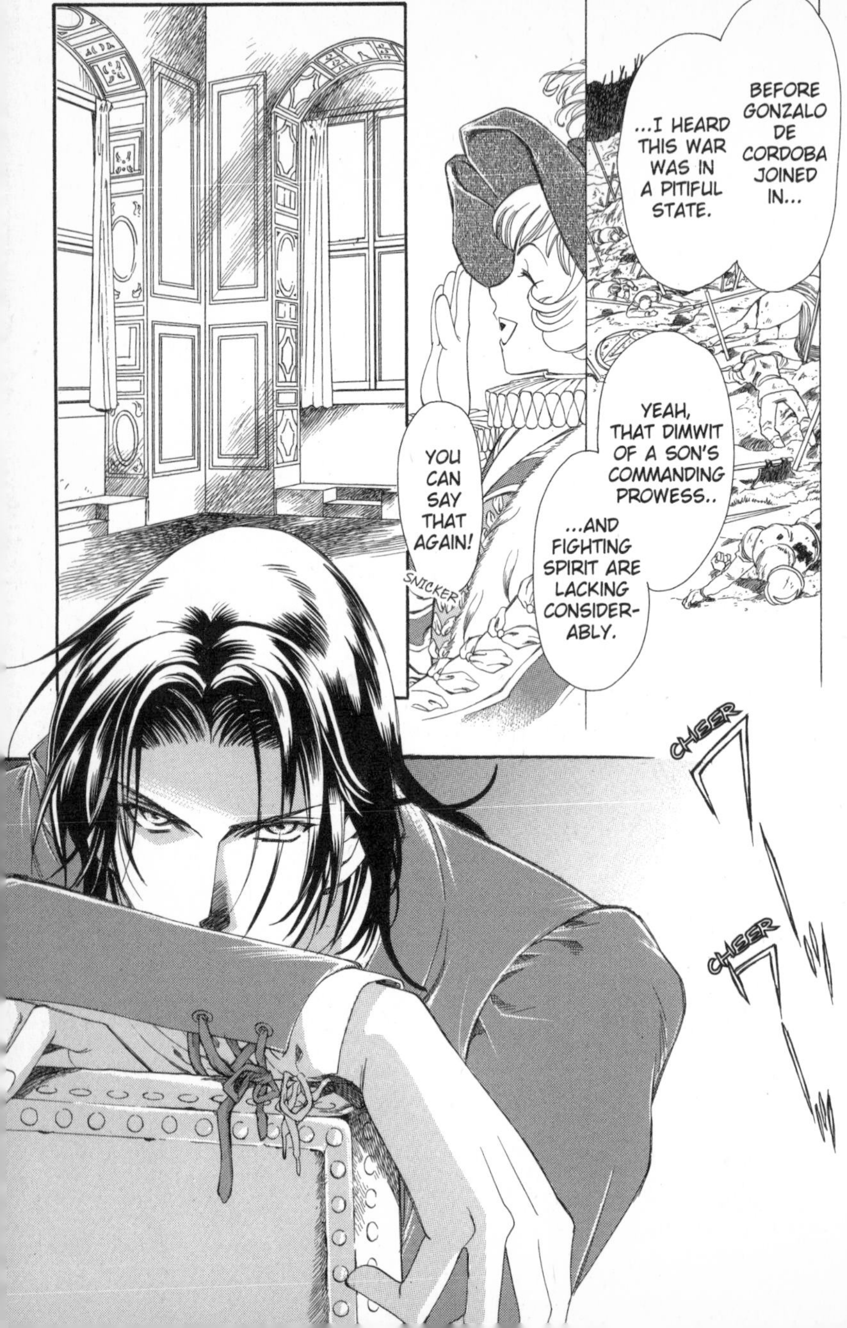
BEFORE GONZALO DE CORDOBA JOINED IN...
...I HEARD THIS WAR WAS IN A PITIFUL STATE.
YEAH, THAT DIMWIT OF A SON'S COMMANDING PROWESS..
...AND FIGHTING SPIRIT ARE LACKING CONSIDERABLY.
YOU CAN SAY THAT AGAIN!
SNICKER
CHEER
CHEER

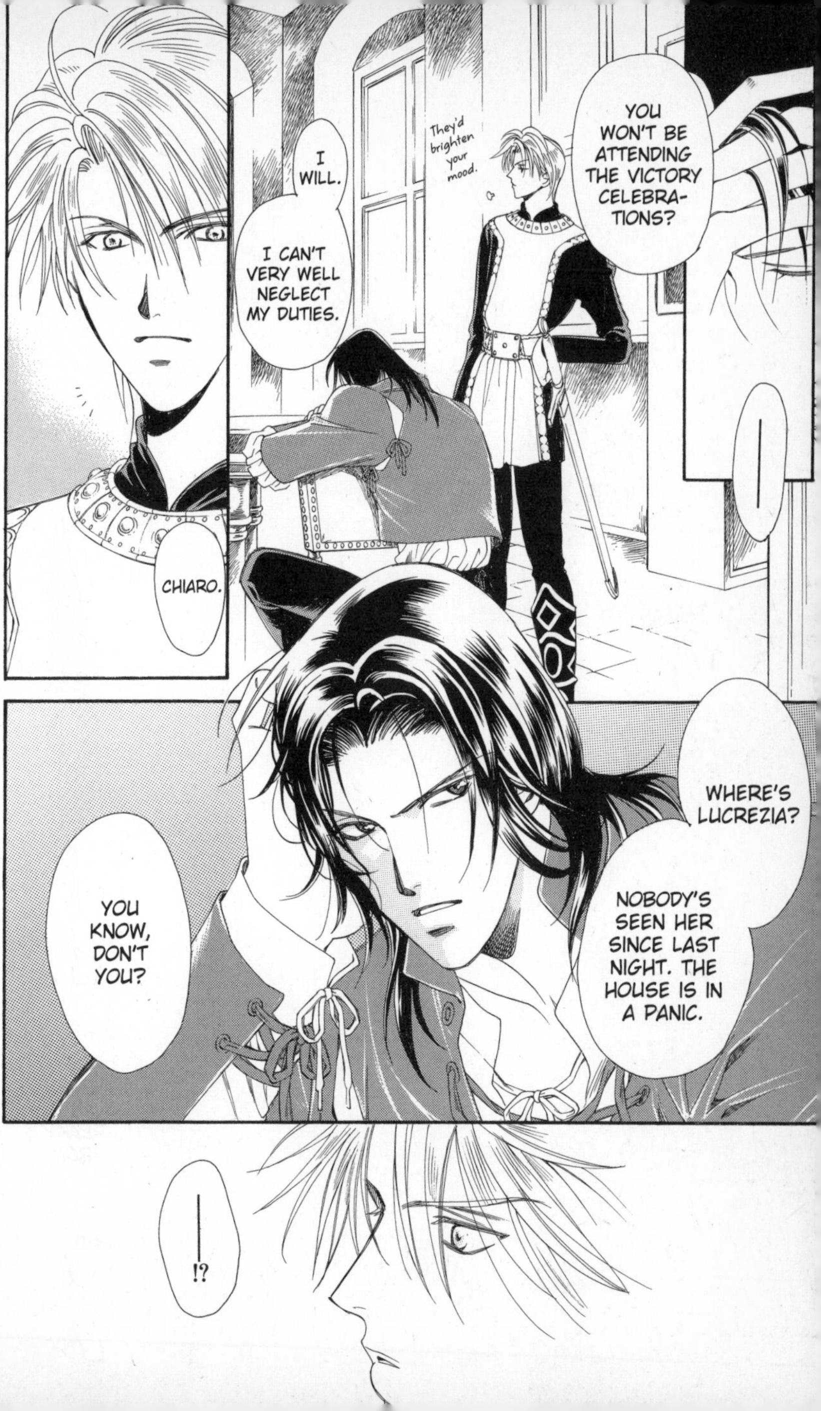

YOU WON'T BE ATTENDING THE VICTORY CELEBRATIONS?
—
They'd brighten your mood.
I WILL.
I CAN'T VERY WELL NEGLECT MY DUTIES.
CHIARO.
WHERE'S LUCREZIA?
NOBODY'S SEEN HER SINCE LAST NIGHT. THE HOUSE IS IN A PANIC.
YOU KNOW, DON'T YOU?
—!?

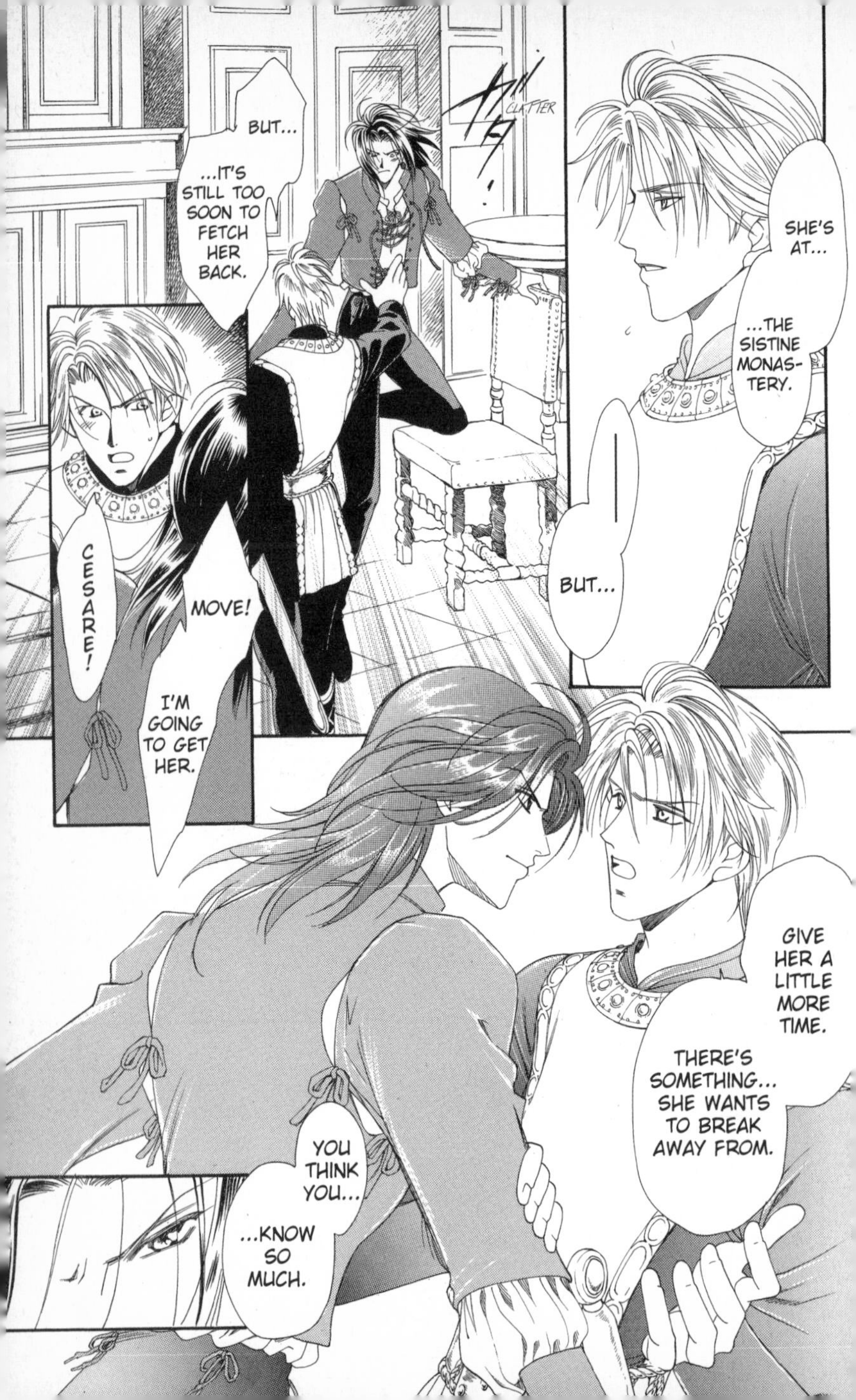
SHE'S AT...
...THE SISTINE MONASTERY.
BUT...
CLATTER
BUT...
...IT'S STILL TOO SOON TO FETCH HER BACK.
CESARE!
MOVE!
I'M GOING TO GET HER.
GIVE HER A LITTLE MORE TIME.
THERE'S SOMETHING... SHE WANTS TO BREAK AWAY FROM.
YOU THINK YOU...
...KNOW SO MUCH.

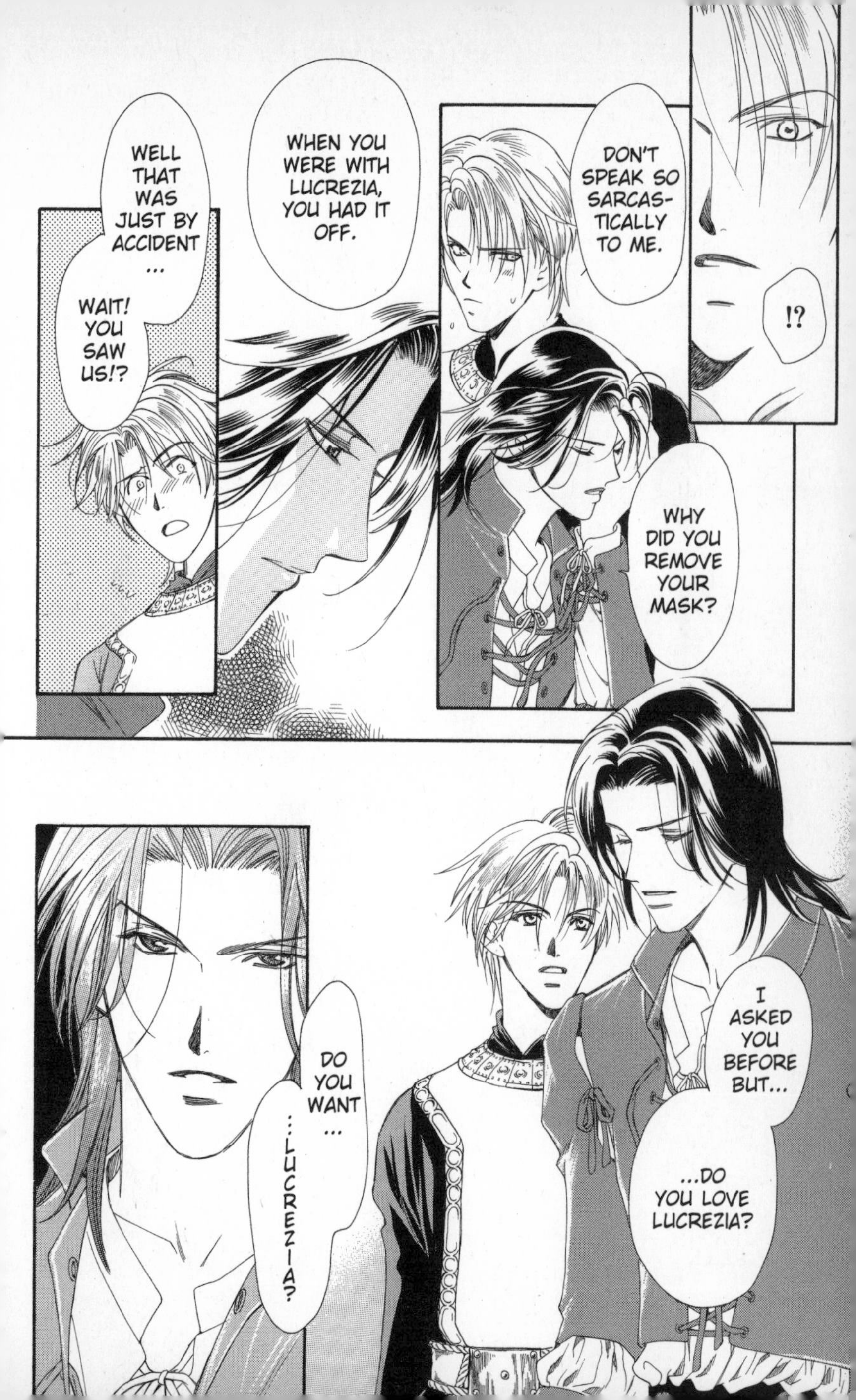
!?
DON'T SPEAK SO SARCAS-TICALLY TO ME.
WHY DID YOU REMOVE YOUR MASK?
WHEN YOU WERE WITH LUCREZIA, YOU HAD IT OFF.
WELL THAT WAS JUST BY ACCIDENT ...
WAIT! YOU SAW US!?
I ASKED YOU BEFORE BUT...
...DO YOU LOVE LUCREZIA?
DO YOU WANT ...
...LUCREZIA?

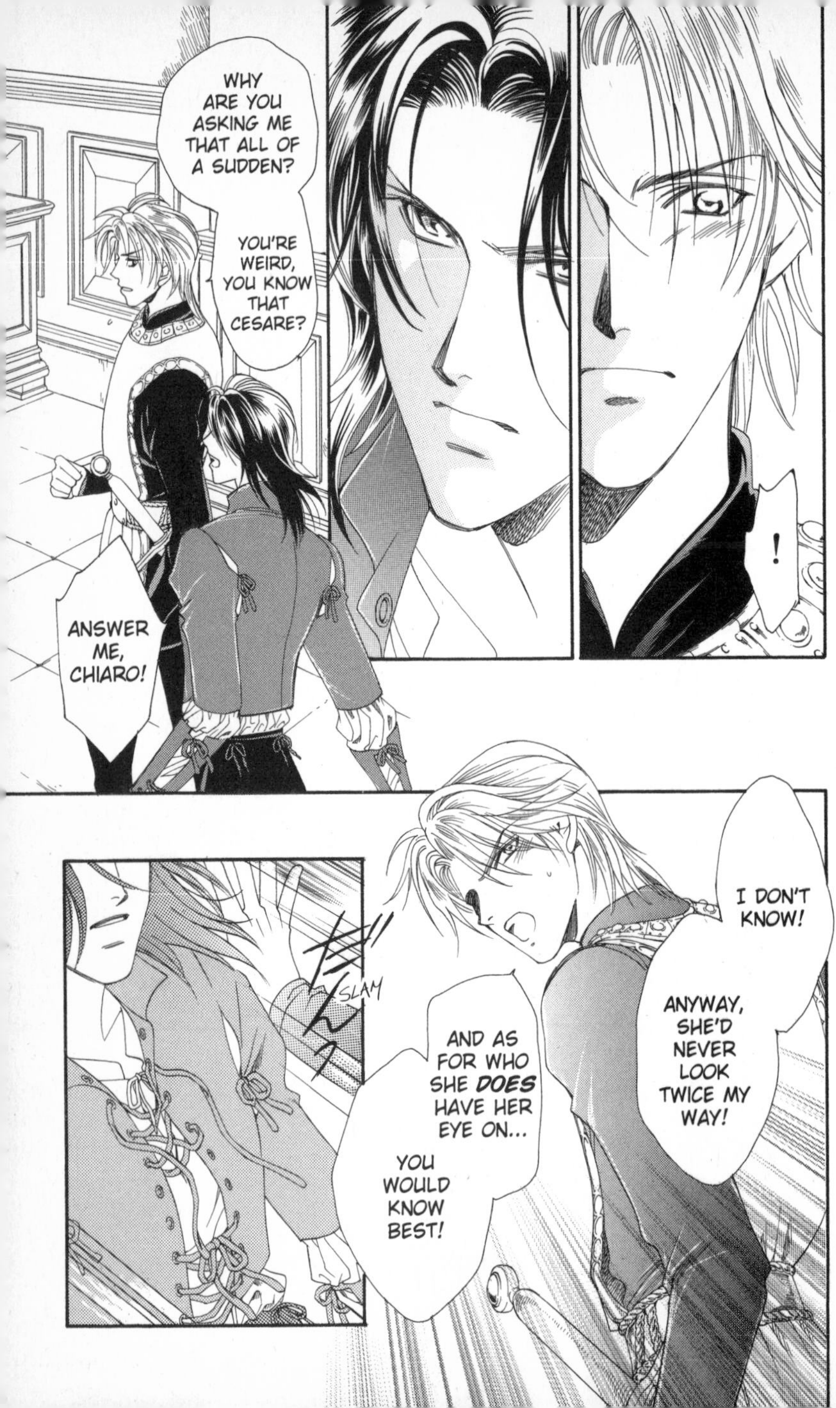
!
WHY ARE YOU ASKING ME THAT ALL OF A SUDDEN?
YOU'RE WEIRD, YOU KNOW THAT CESARE?
ANSWER ME, CHIARO!
I DON'T KNOW!
ANYWAY, SHE'D NEVER LOOK TWICE MY WAY!
SLAM
AND AS FOR WHO SHE ***DOES*** HAVE HER EYE ON...
YOU WOULD KNOW BEST!

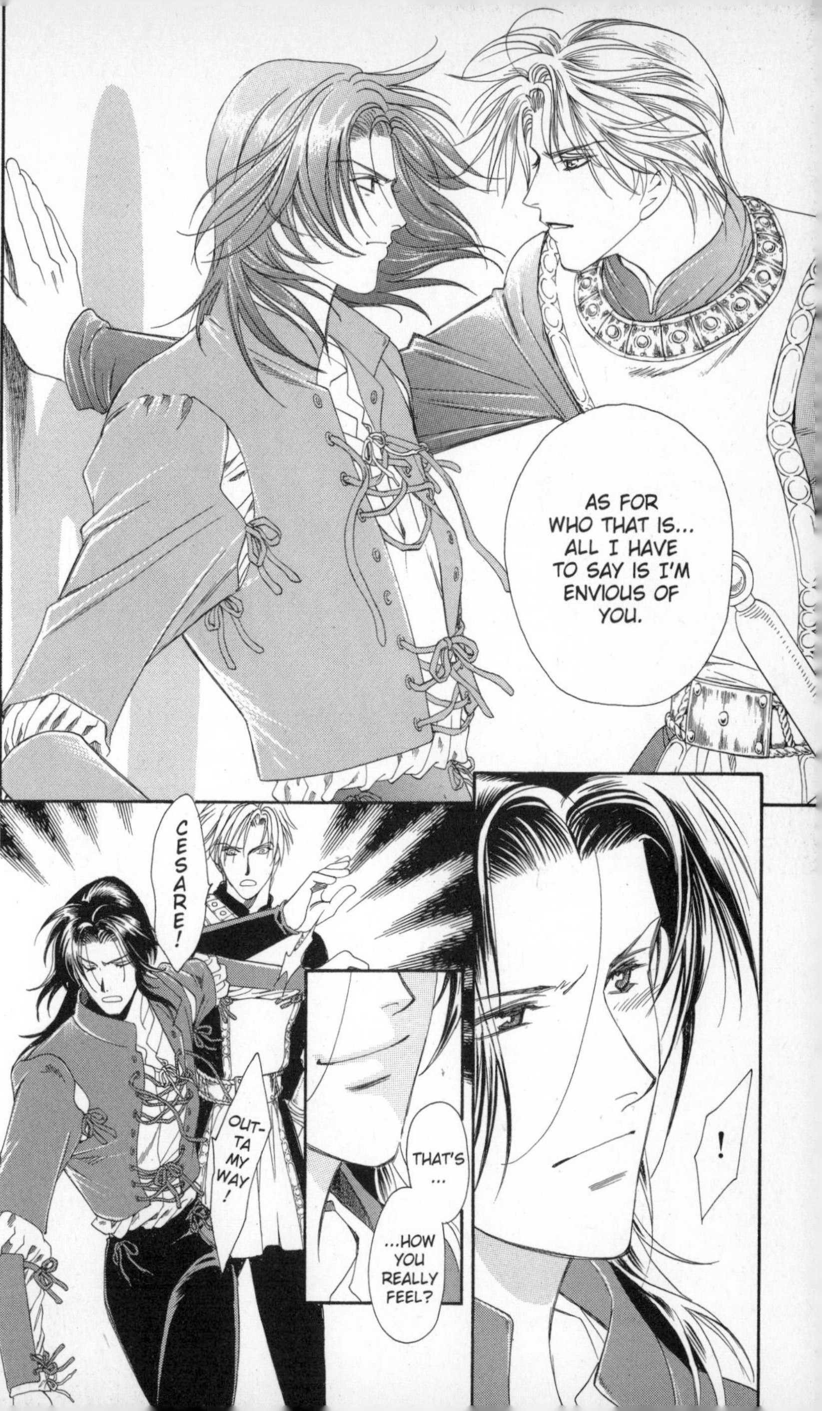
AS FOR WHO THAT IS... ALL I HAVE TO SAY IS I'M ENVIOUS OF YOU.
!
THAT'S ...
...HOW YOU REALLY FEEL?
CESARE!
OUT-TA MY WAY!

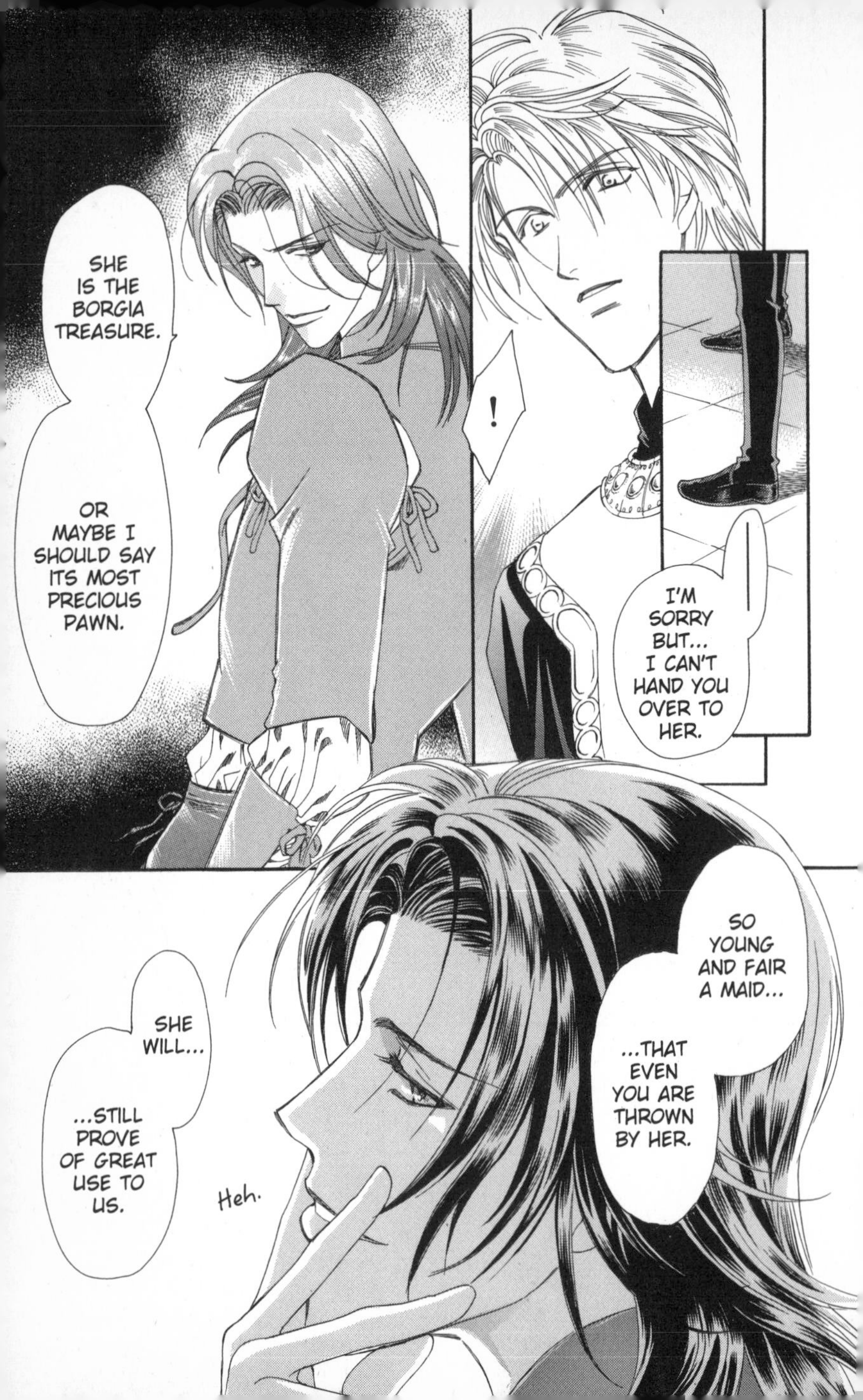
!
I'M SORRY BUT... I CAN'T HAND YOU OVER TO HER.
SHE IS THE BORGIA TREASURE.
OR MAYBE I SHOULD SAY ITS MOST PRECIOUS PAWN.
SO YOUNG AND FAIR A MAID...
...THAT EVEN YOU ARE THROWN BY HER.
SHE WILL...
...STILL PROVE OF GREAT USE TO US.
Heh.

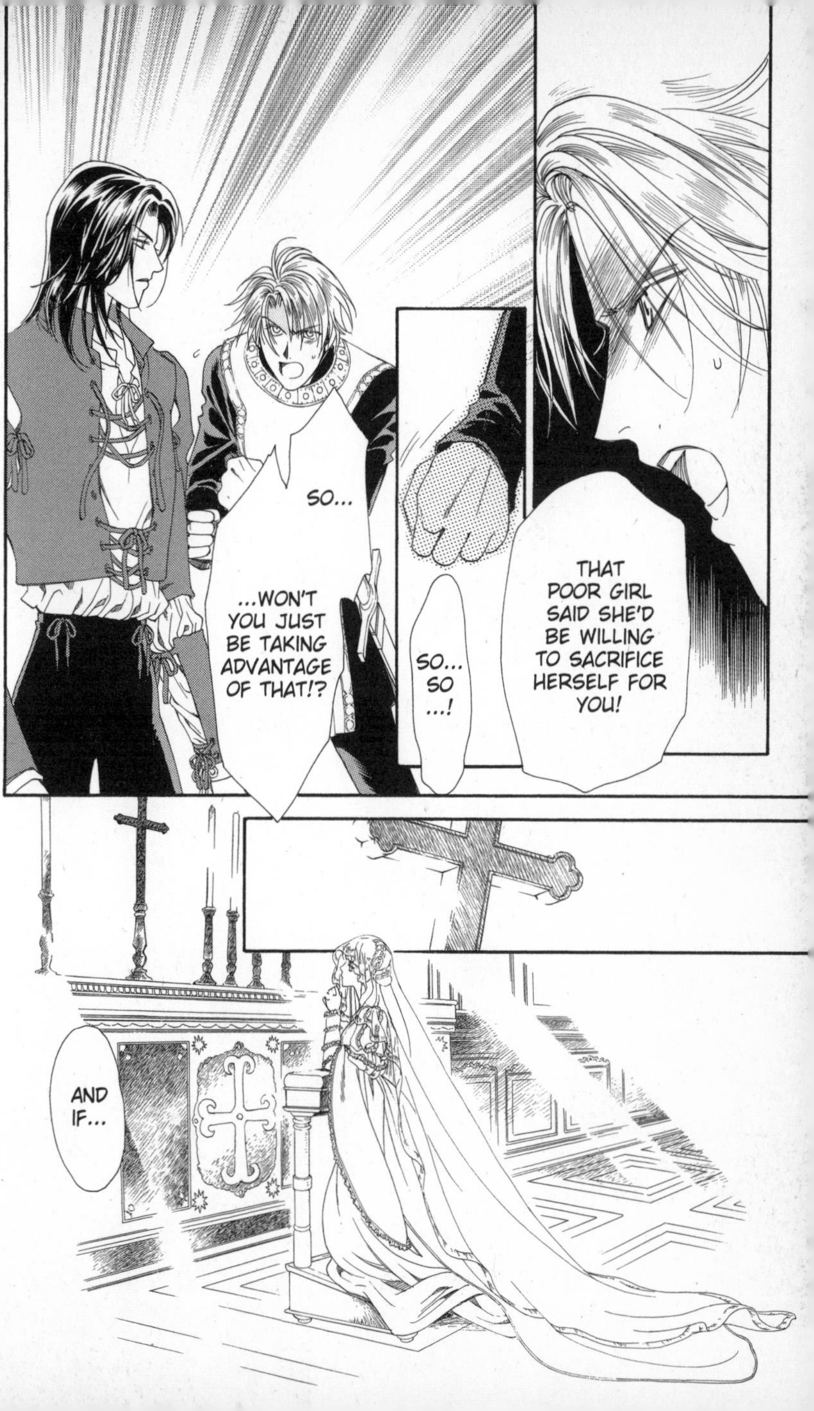
THAT POOR GIRL SAID SHE'D BE WILLING TO SACRIFICE HERSELF FOR YOU!
SO... SO ...!
SO...
...WON'T YOU JUST BE TAKING ADVANTAGE OF THAT!?
AND IF...

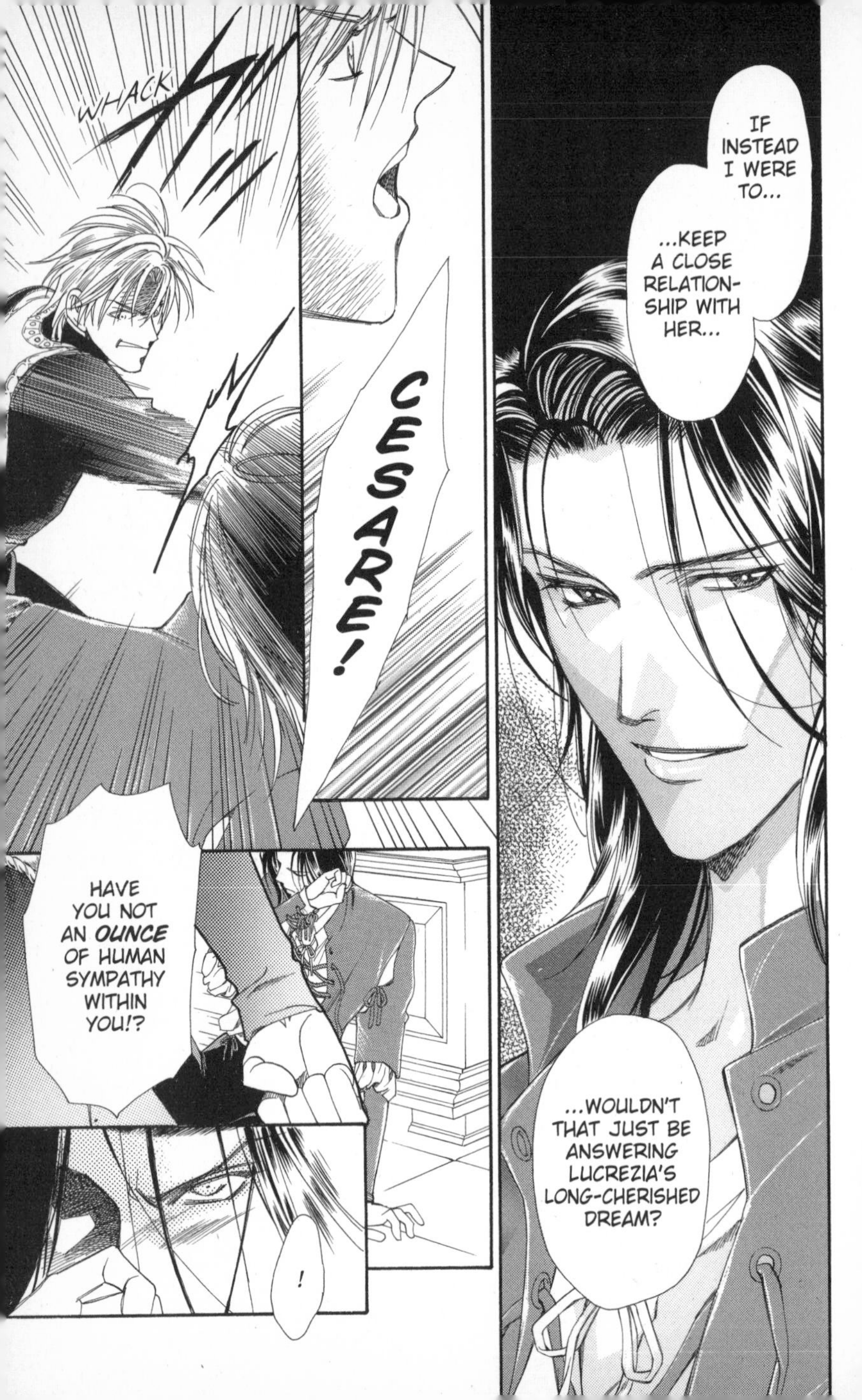
IF INSTEAD I WERE TO...
...KEEP A CLOSE RELATION-SHIP WITH HER...
...WOULDN'T THAT JUST BE ANSWERING LUCREZIA'S LONG-CHERISHED DREAM?
CESARE!
WHACK
HAVE YOU NOT AN OUNCE OF HUMAN SYMPATHY WITHIN YOU!?
!

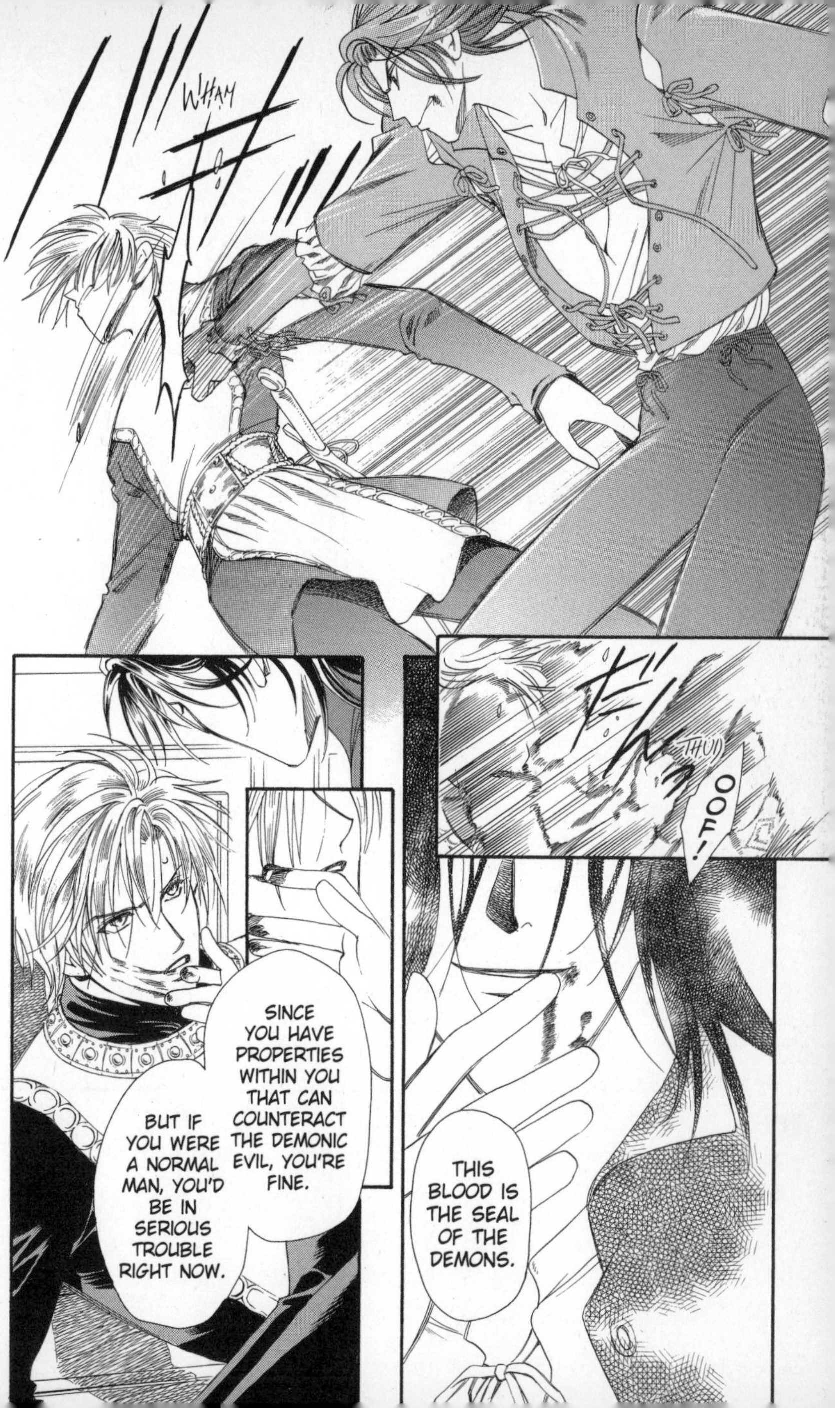
WHAM
THUD
OOF!
THIS BLOOD IS THE SEAL OF THE DEMONS.
SINCE YOU HAVE PROPERTIES WITHIN YOU THAT CAN COUNTERACT THE DEMONIC EVIL, YOU'RE FINE.
BUT IF YOU WERE A NORMAL MAN, YOU'D BE IN SERIOUS TROUBLE RIGHT NOW.

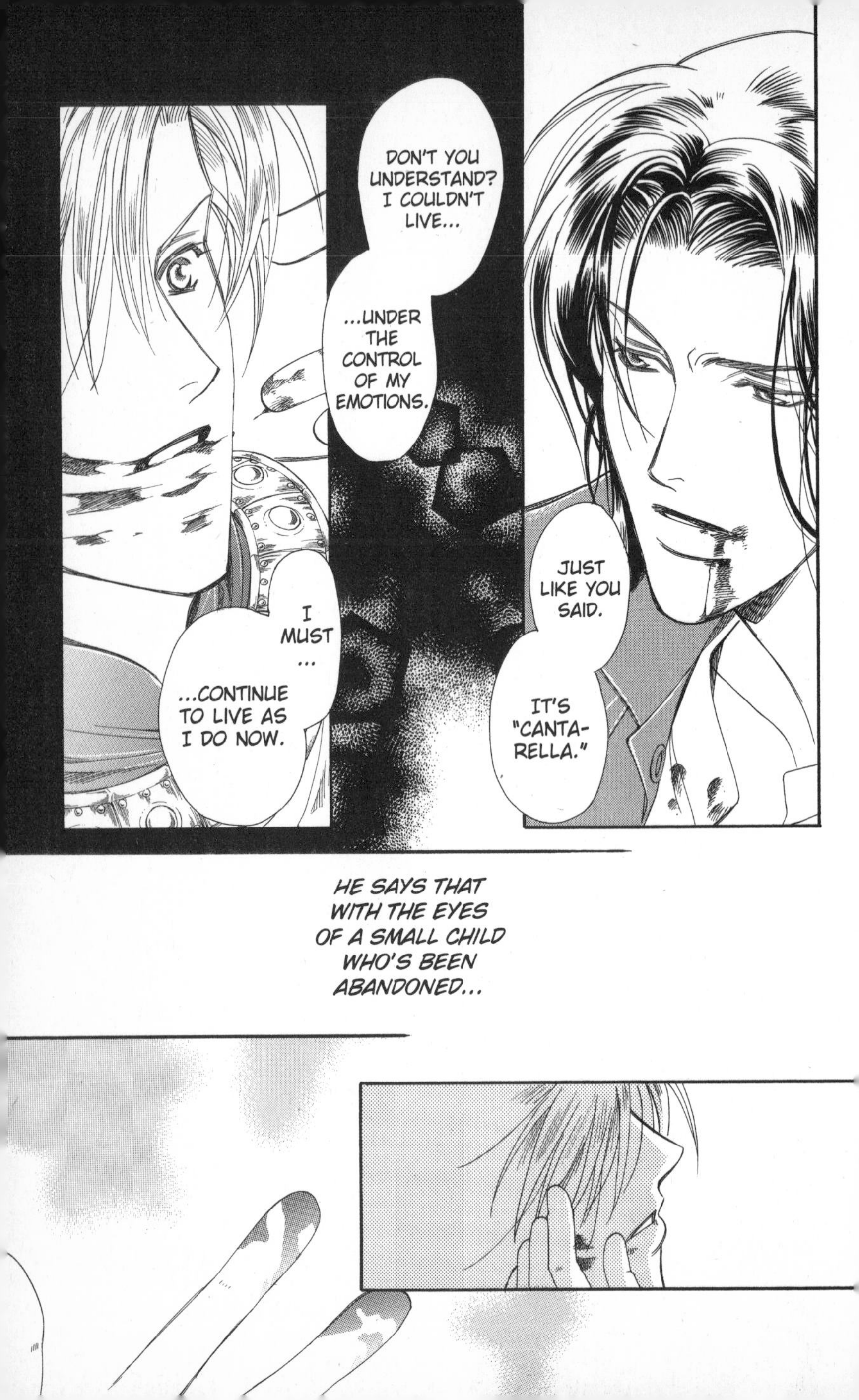
JUST LIKE YOU SAID.
IT'S "CANTA-RELLA."
DON'T YOU UNDERSTAND? I COULDN'T LIVE...
...UNDER THE CONTROL OF MY EMOTIONS.
I MUST...
...CONTINUE TO LIVE AS I DO NOW.
HE SAYS THAT WITH THE EYES OF A SMALL CHILD WHO'S BEEN ABANDONED...

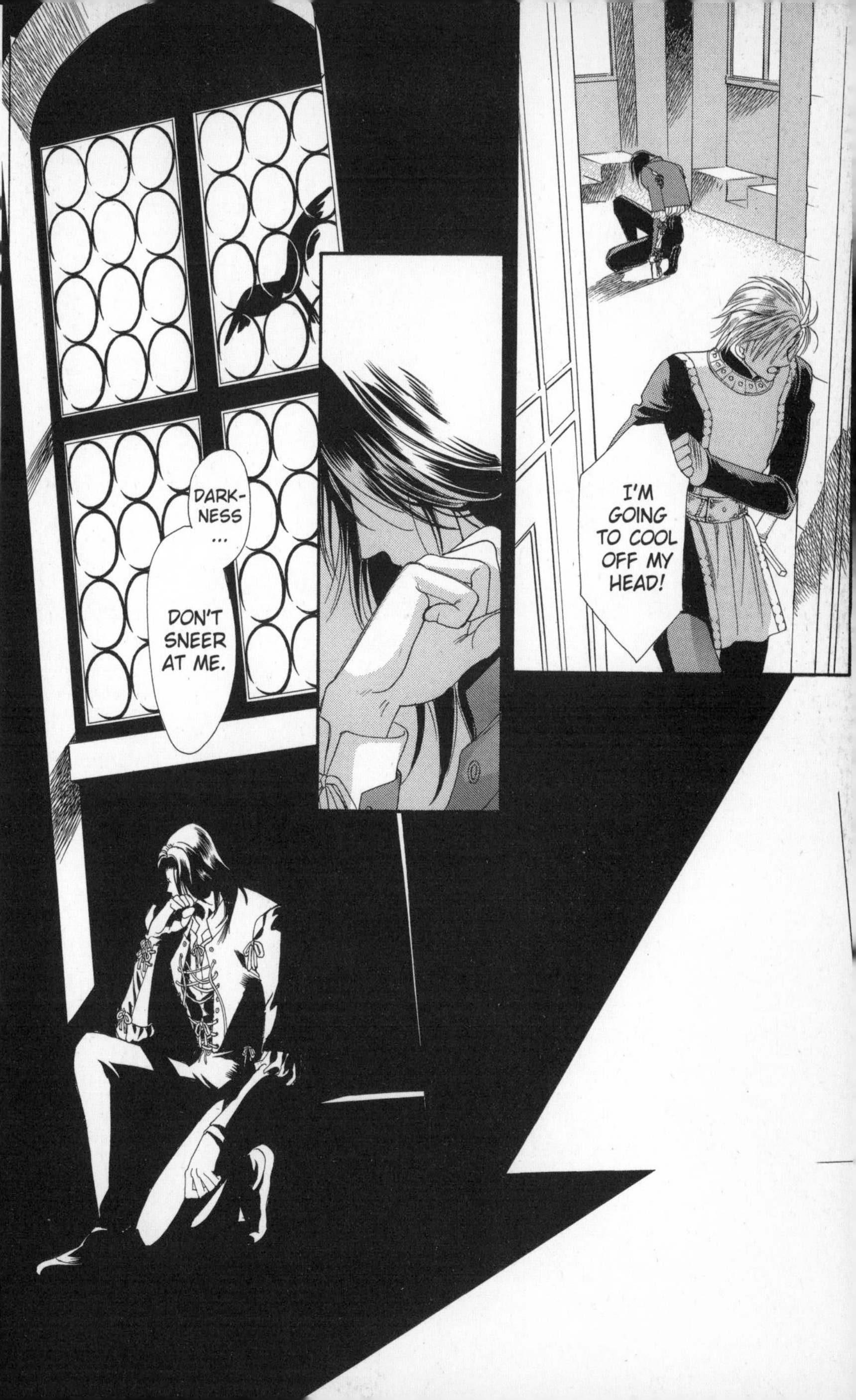
I'M GOING TO COOL OFF MY HEAD!
DARK-NESS ...
DON'T SNEER AT ME.

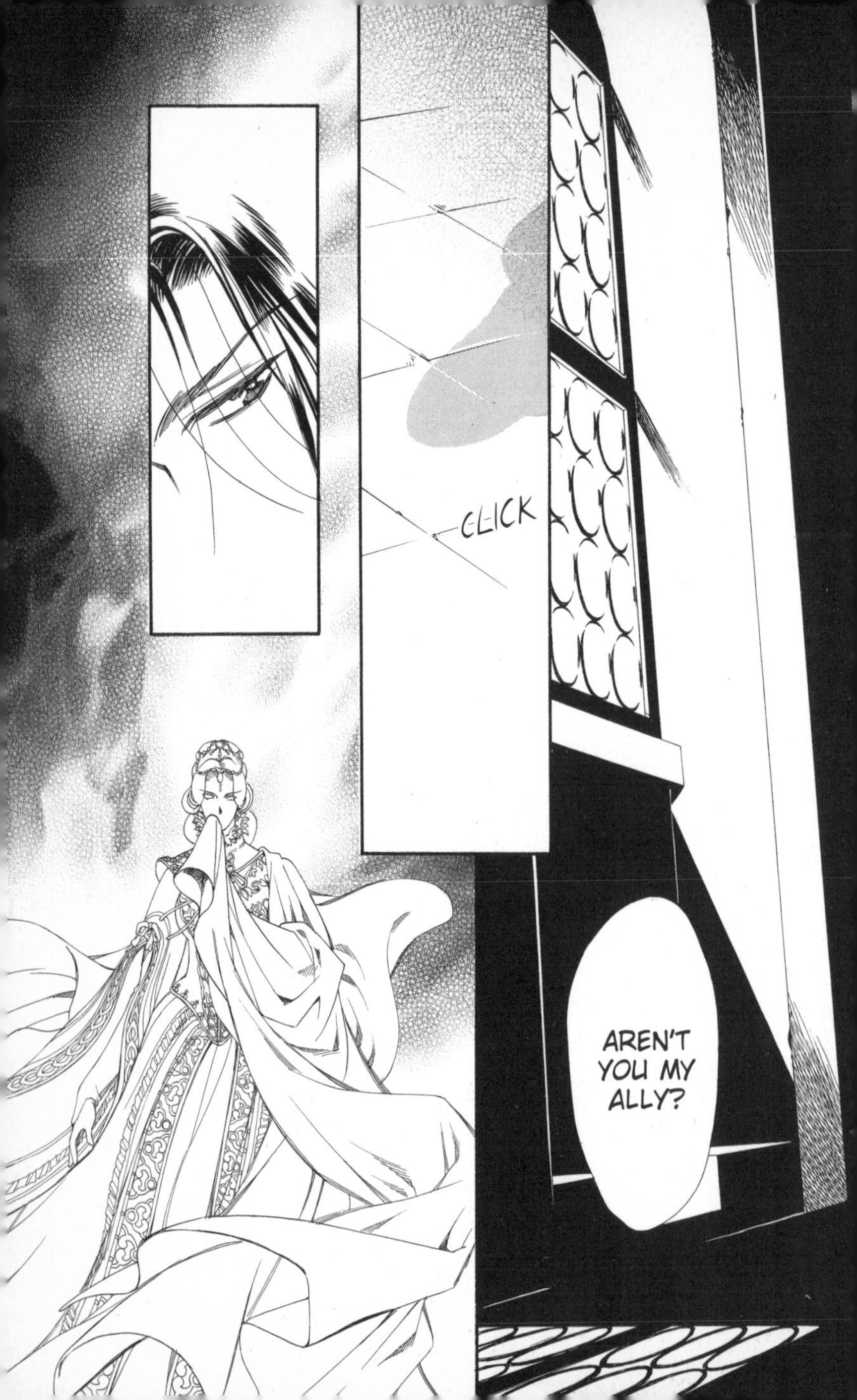
CLICK
AREN'T YOU MY ALLY?

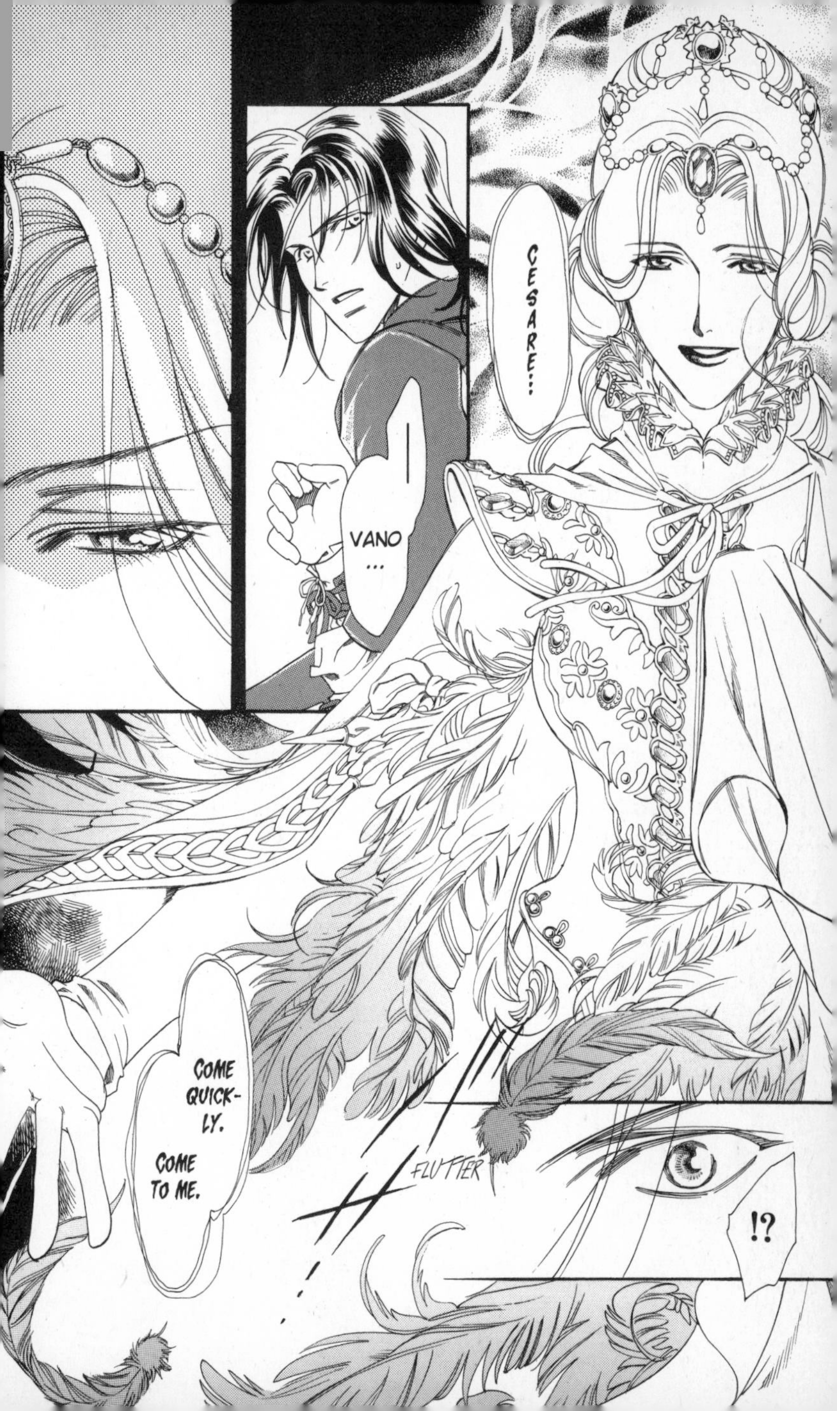
CESARE...!
VANO...
COME QUICKLY. COME TO ME.
FLUTTER
!?

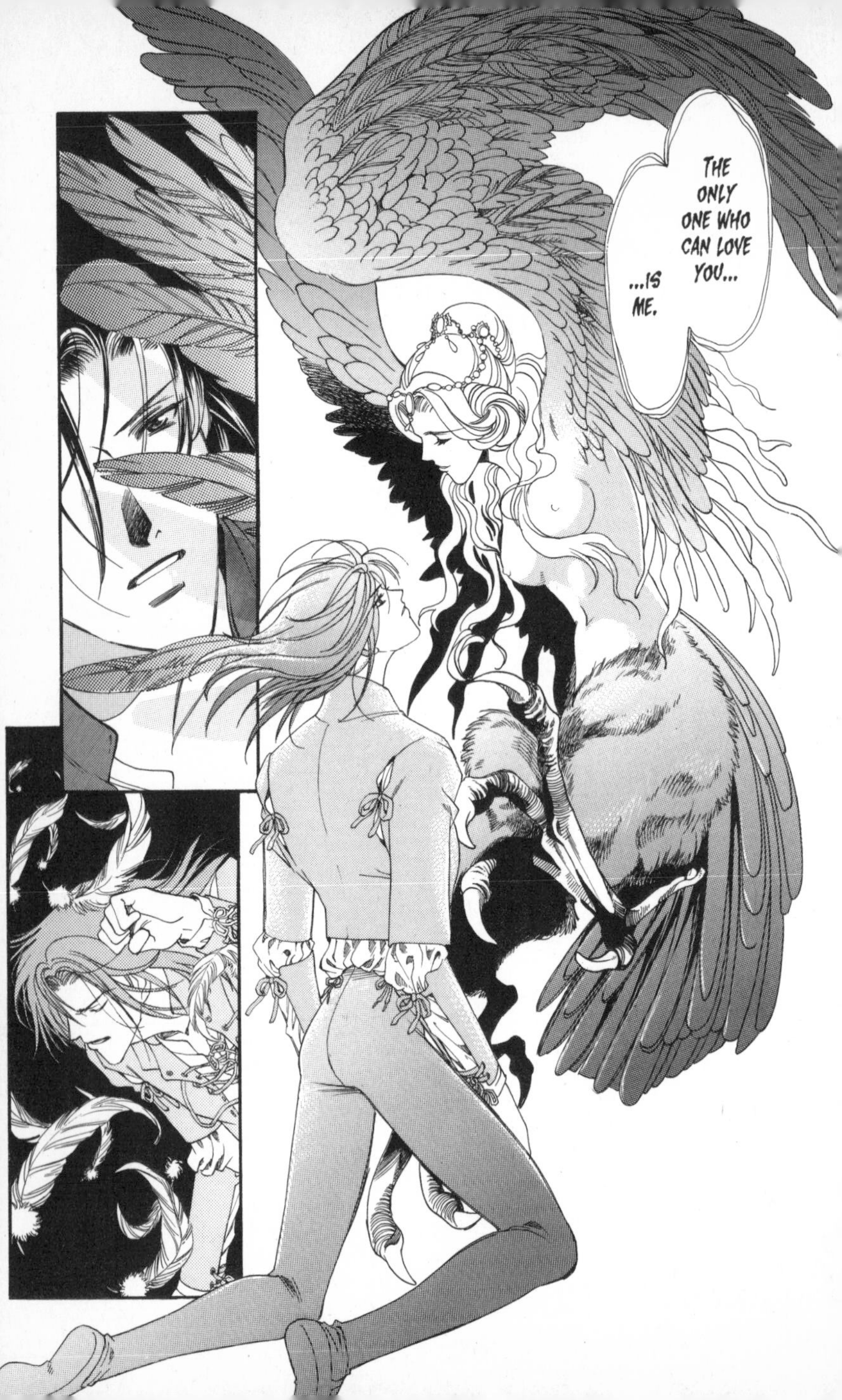
THE ONLY ONE WHO CAN LOVE YOU...
...IS ME.

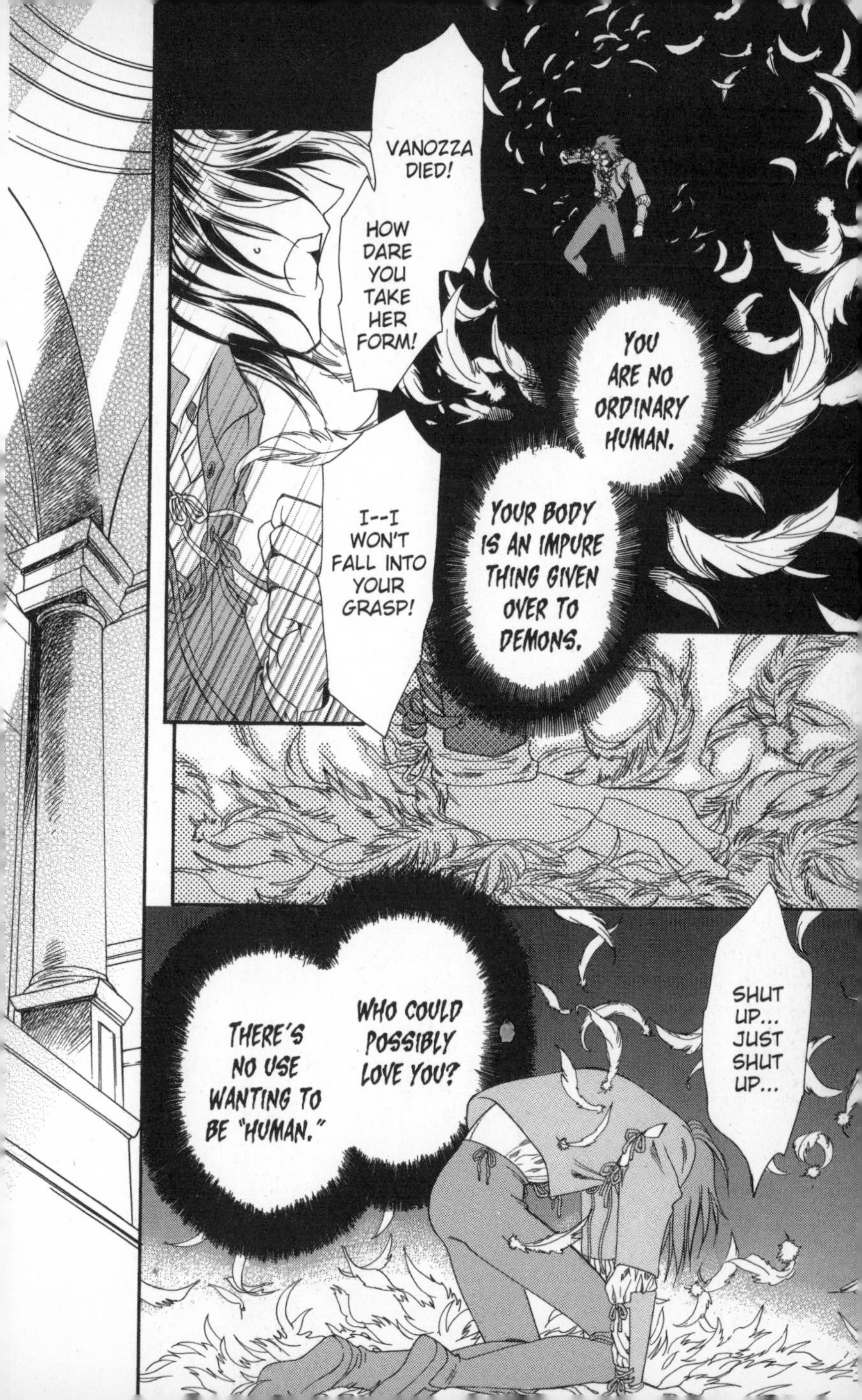
VANOZZA DIED!
HOW DARE YOU TAKE HER FORM!
YOU ARE NO ORDINARY HUMAN.
I--I WON'T FALL INTO YOUR GRASP!
YOUR BODY IS AN IMPURE THING GIVEN OVER TO DEMONS.
WHO COULD POSSIBLY LOVE YOU?
THERE'S NO USE WANTING TO BE "HUMAN."
SHUT UP... JUST SHUT UP...

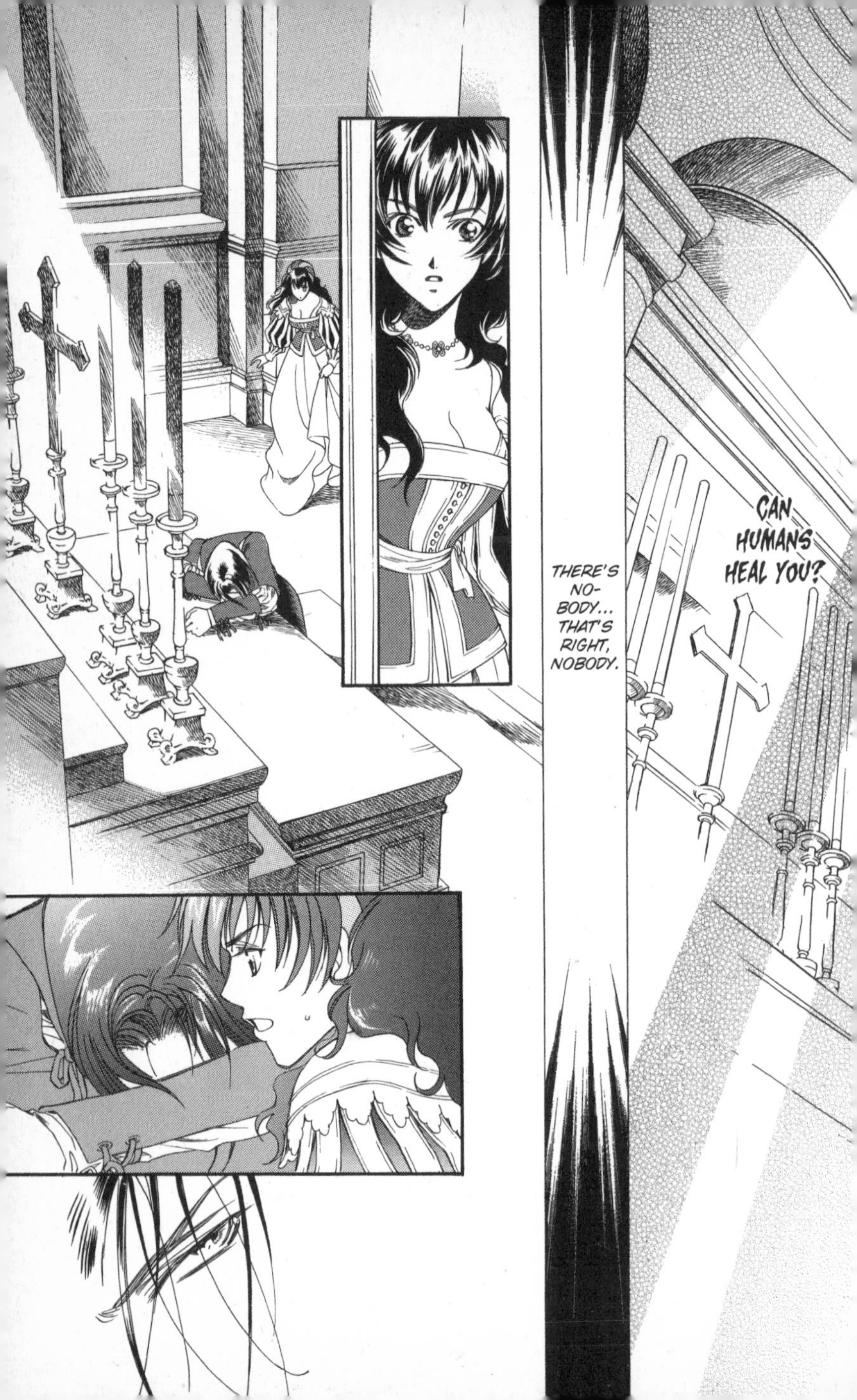
CAN HUMANS HEAL YOU?
THERE'S NO-BODY... THAT'S RIGHT, NOBODY.

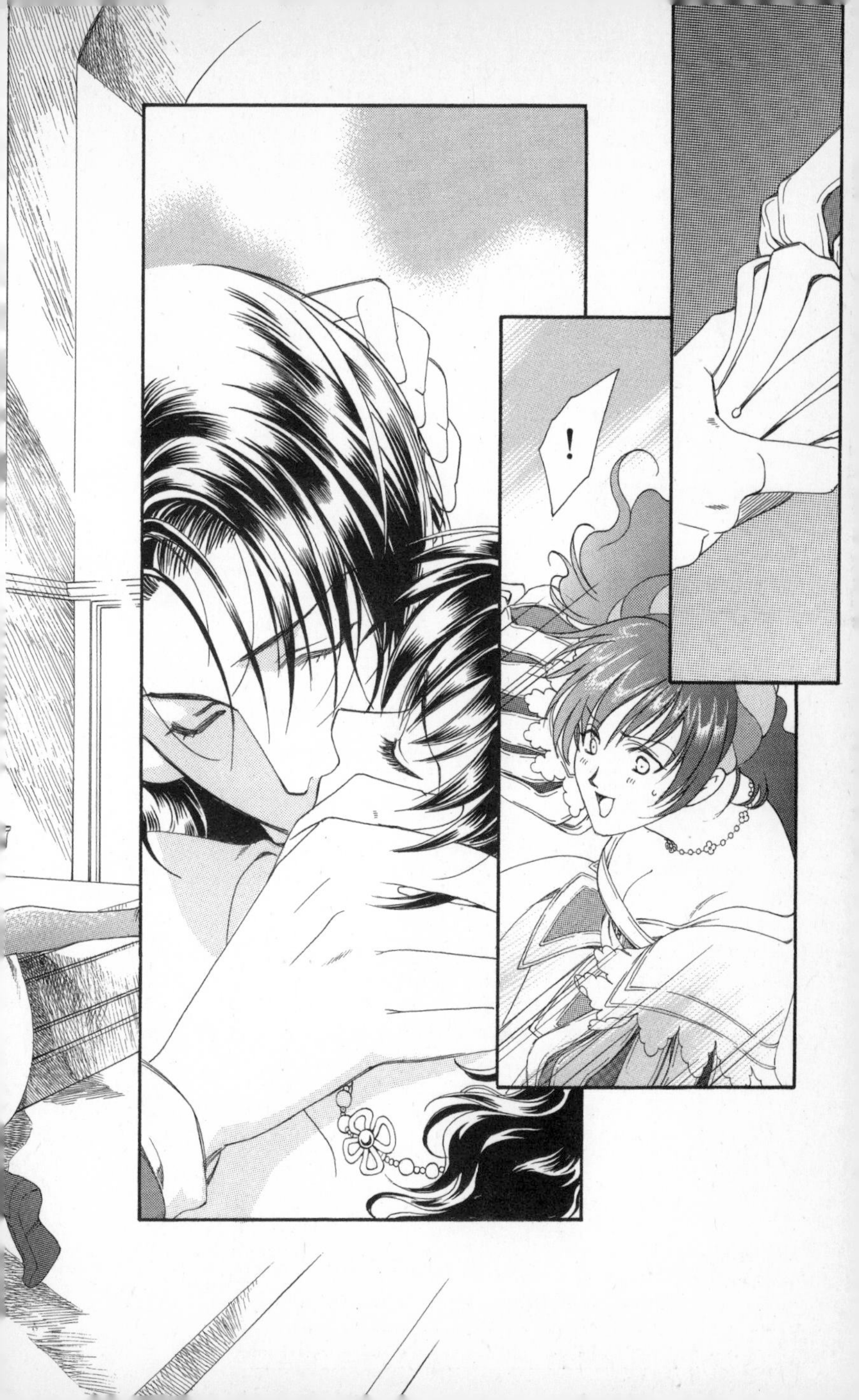
!

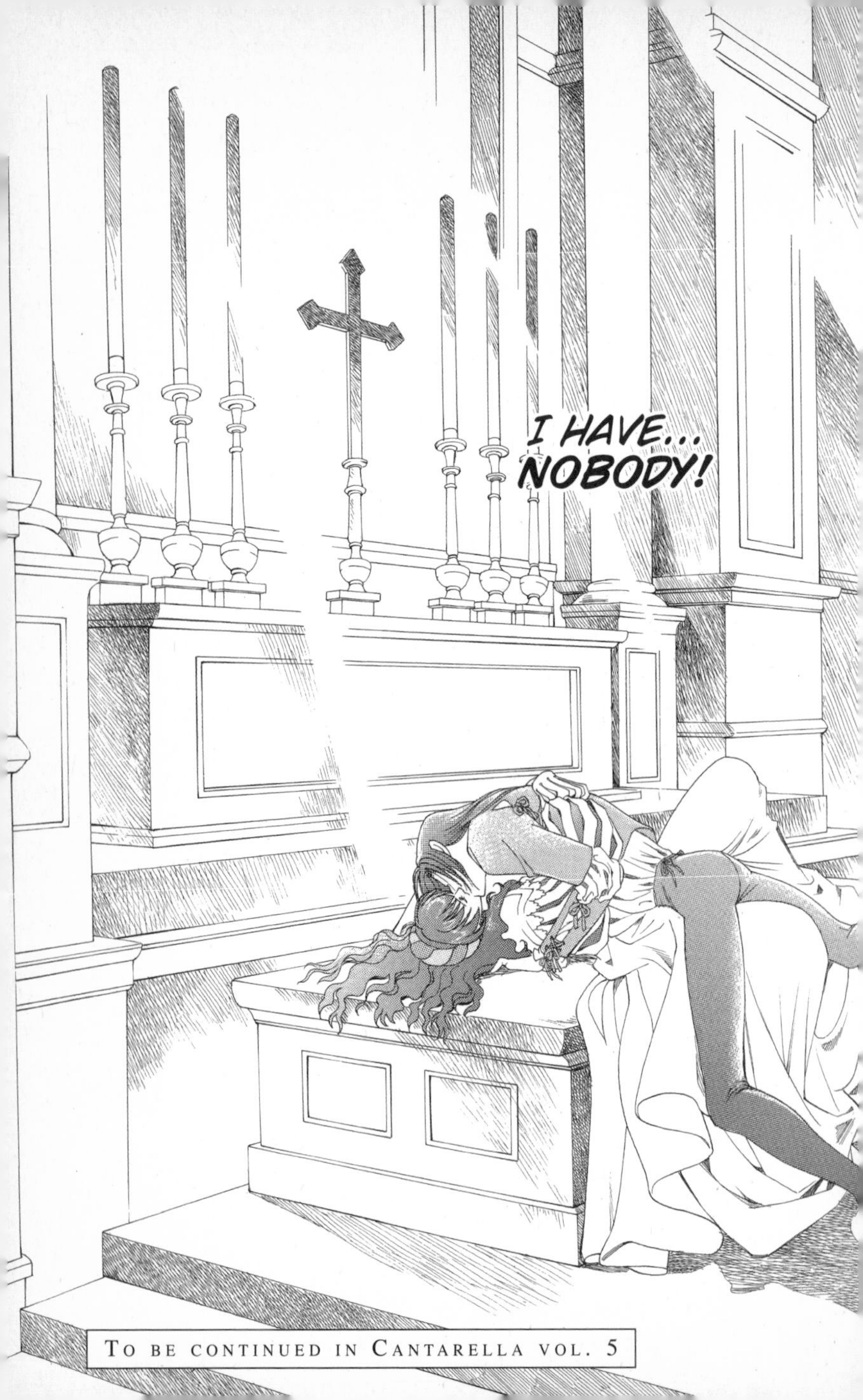
I HAVE...
NOBODY!
TO BE CONTINUED IN CANTARELLA VOL. 5

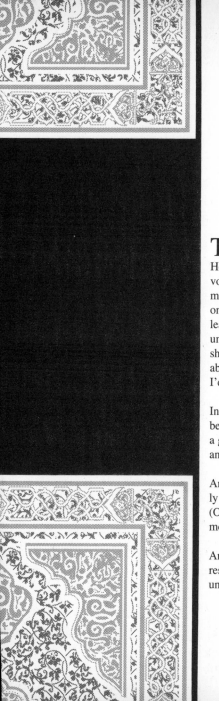

Thank you for picking up this book! How did everybody like Cantarella's fourth volume? Even though I hate studying, making this manga took a lot of research on the Renaissance period. But the more I learned about it, the more it felt like I was untangling a complicated web of relationships and it actually got me to start thinking about things in a way that was deeper than I'd ever thought before.

In fact, even though I've traveled to Europe before, I've only just begun to see how big a gap there was between what I knew then and what I know now.

And the more I've learned, the more acutely I've begun to feel how ignorant I am... (Oh god, I'm starting to sound like that moth sorcerer.)

Anyway, now that I've thoroughly researched the matter, the tale can now unfold Higuri-style.

Since my mind is still running with tons of wild ideas of this nature and that, hold on tight to the railing and try not to fall off as we continue the crazy ride.

Since I'm the type who tries to remain sensitive to the reader's passion while composing my tale, it'd make me so happy if I could receive constructive comments via letters and such.

Also, I'm sorry that this isn't for everyone, but I'll be preparing a small gift for 10 lucky winners so my best regards! (Editor's note: This was for a contest held only in Japan.)

I received a lot of help in the creation of this manga. Nakatsuji Naoko-san, Izumi Hijiri-san, Asakura-san, Miyakoshi Wakusa-san, Kaoru Matsuri-san, Fuyutsuki Mitsuru-san, Takanashi Kenkichi-san, Hondo Mako-san, Chief Assistant Oda Ryoka and to O-call-san who lent me all that material: thank you so very much!

And to all my lovely readers, did you have fun? If so, then there is nothing else in the world that could make me happier.

August, 2002
You Higuri

I'll be waiting for your letters:

YOU HIGURI c/o Audry Taylor
Go! Media Entertainment, LLC
5737 Kanan Rd. #591
Agoura Hills CA 91301

Or visit her official website in English at:
http://www.youhiguri.com

*V*arious cities and territories of Italy during *Cantarella* period

(end of the 15th century)

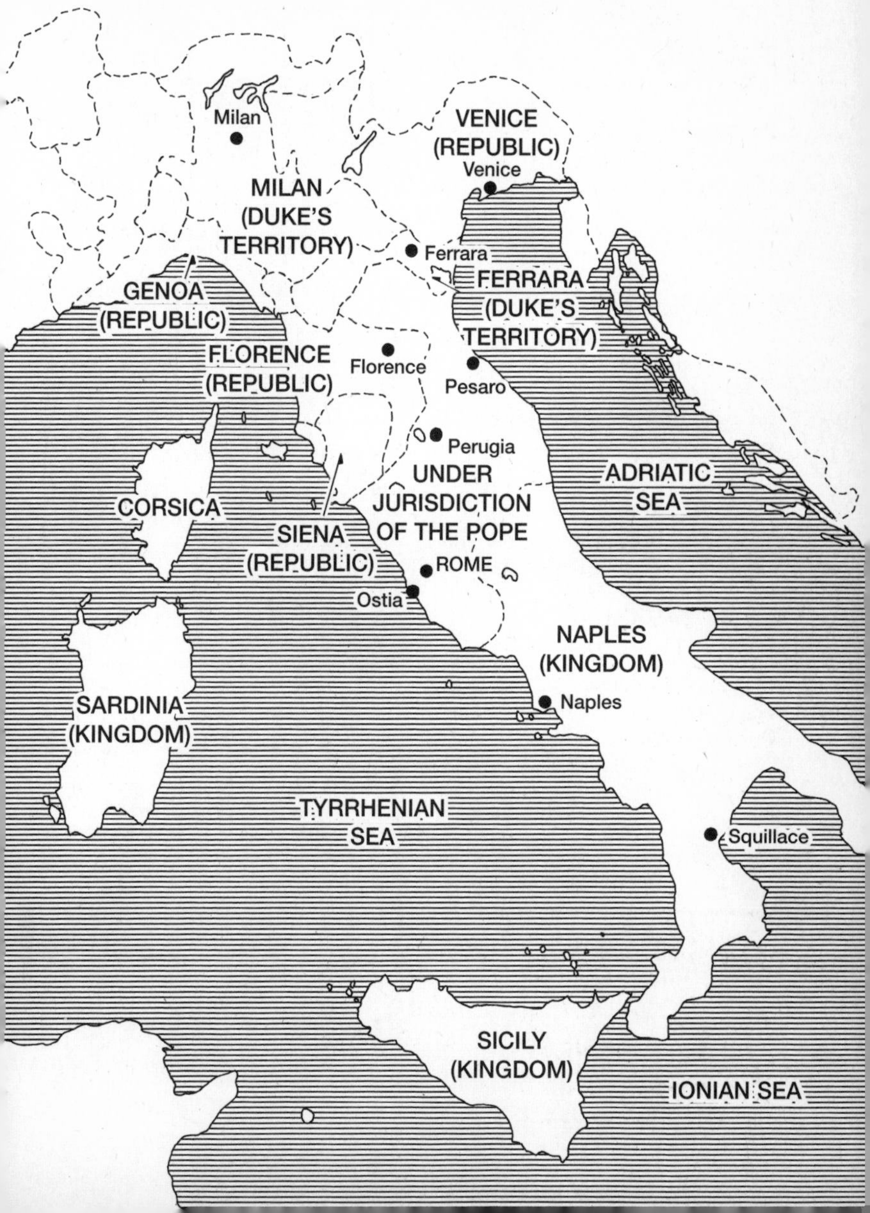
Milan
VENICE (REPUBLIC)
Venice
MILAN (DUKE'S TERRITORY)
Ferrara
FERRARA (DUKE'S TERRITORY)
GENOA (REPUBLIC)
FLORENCE (REPUBLIC)
Florence
Pesaro
Perugia
UNDER JURISDICTION OF THE POPE
ADRIATIC SEA
CORSICA
SIENA (REPUBLIC)
ROME
Ostia
NAPLES (KINGDOM)
Naples
SARDINIA (KINGDOM)
TYRRHENIAN SEA
Squillace
SICILY (KINGDOM)
IONIAN SEA

Family Tree of the Borgia household in *Cantarella*

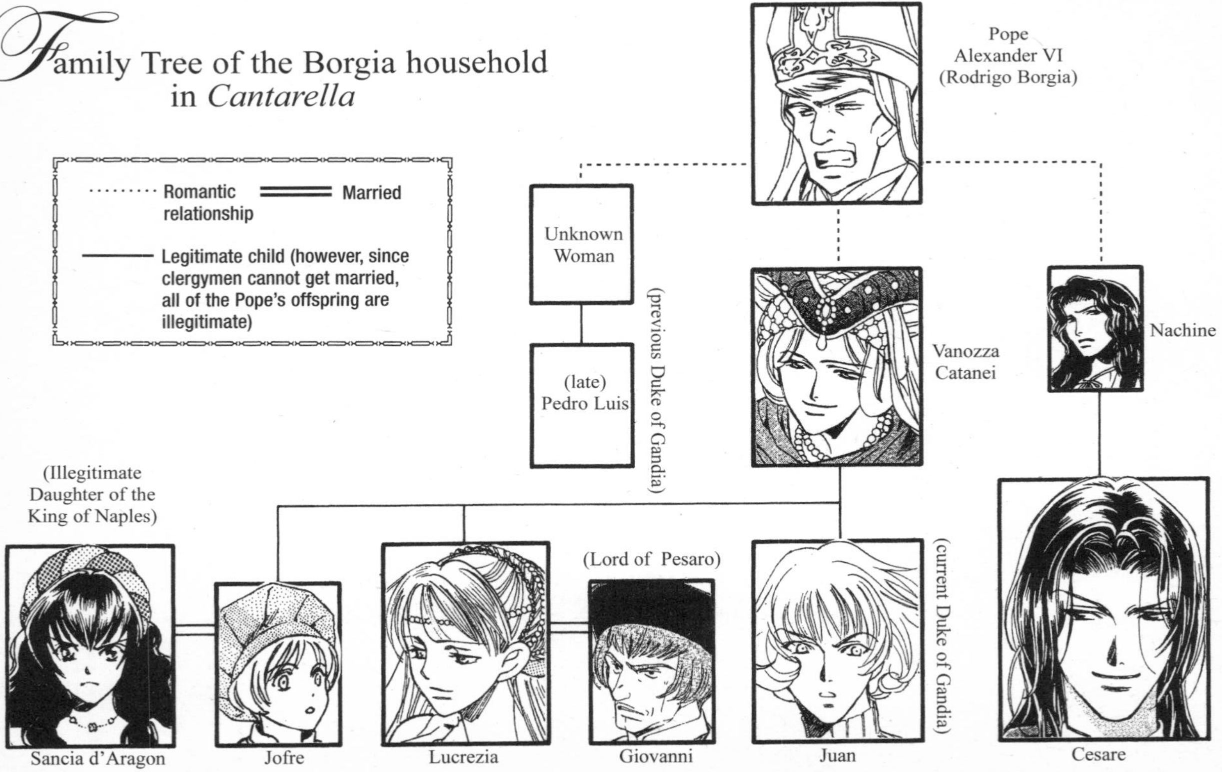

Romantic relationship
Married
Legitimate child (however, since clergymen cannot get married, all of the Pope's offspring are illegitimate)
Pope Alexander VI (Rodrigo Borgia)
Unknown Woman
(late) Pedro Luis
(previous Duke of Gandia)
Vanozza Catanei
Nachine
(Illegitimate Daughter of the King of Naples)
Sancia d'Aragon
Jofre
Lucrezia
(Lord of Pesaro)
Giovanni
Juan
(current Duke of Gandia)
Cesare

New Manga Series From go!comi

AFTER SCHOOL NIGHTMARE

SPECIAL PREVIEW

You have just awakened to find your darkest secret revealed to a group of people who would do anything to destroy you: your classmates!

That's what happens to Mashiro Ichijo, whose elite school education turns into the most horrifying experience of his life when he's enlisted to participate in an after-hours class. The only way for Mashiro to graduate is to enter into a nightmare world where his body and soul will be at the mercy of his worst enemies. Can Mashiro keep the life-long secret that he is not truly a "he" nor entirely a "she" -- or will he finally be "outted" in the most humiliating way possible?

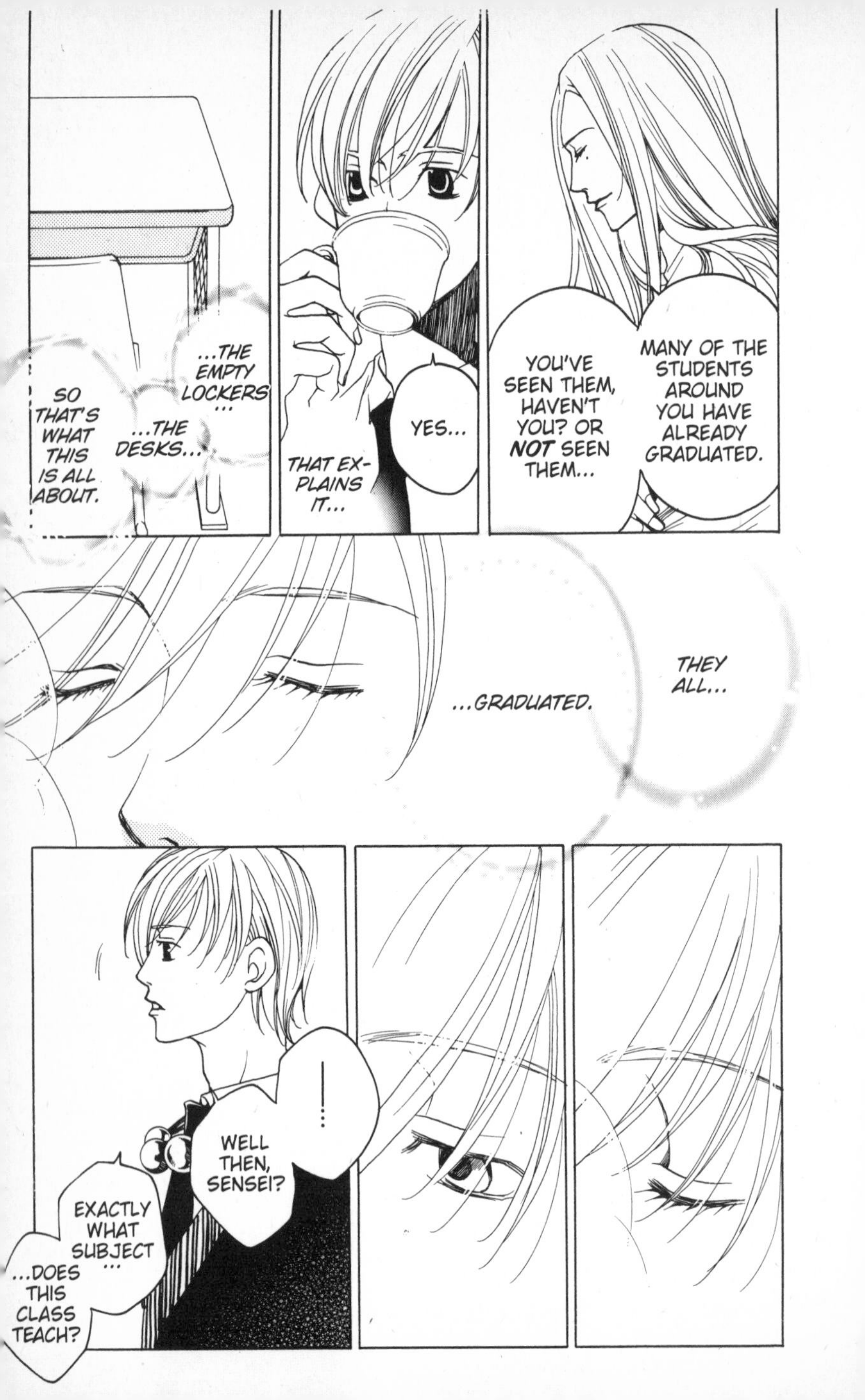

MANY OF THE STUDENTS AROUND YOU HAVE ALREADY GRADUATED.
YOU'VE SEEN THEM, HAVEN'T YOU? OR **NOT** SEEN THEM...
YES...
THAT EX-PLAINS IT...
...THE EMPTY LOCKERS...
...THE DESKS...
SO THAT'S WHAT THIS IS ALL ABOUT.
THEY ALL...
...GRADUATED.
......
WELL THEN, SENSEI?
EXACTLY WHAT SUBJECT...
...DOES THIS CLASS TEACH?

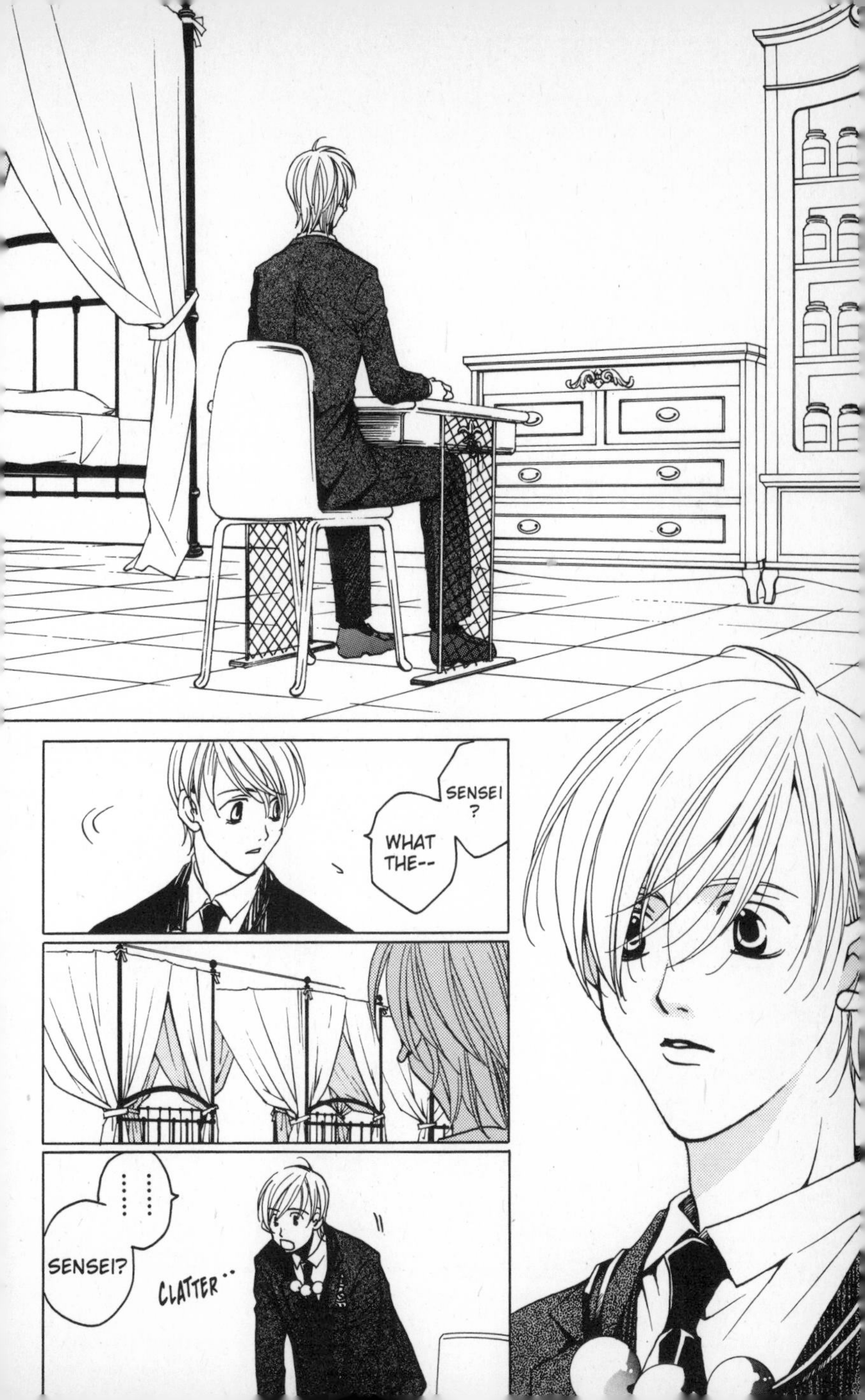
SENSEI ?
WHAT THE--
......
SENSEI?
CLATTER ..

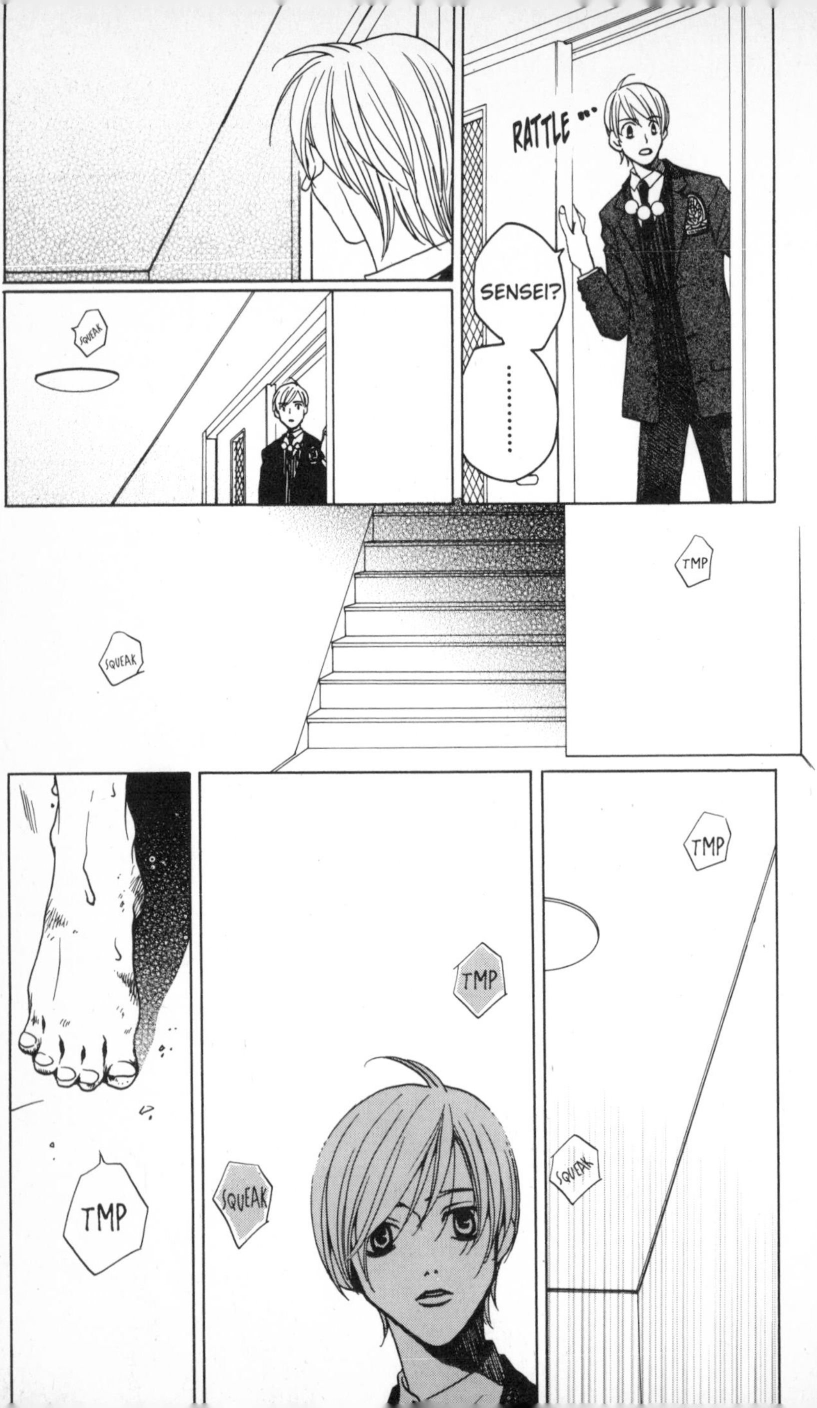
RATTLE...
SENSEI?
......
SQUEAK
TMP
SQUEAK
TMP
SQUEAK
TMP
SQUEAK
TMP

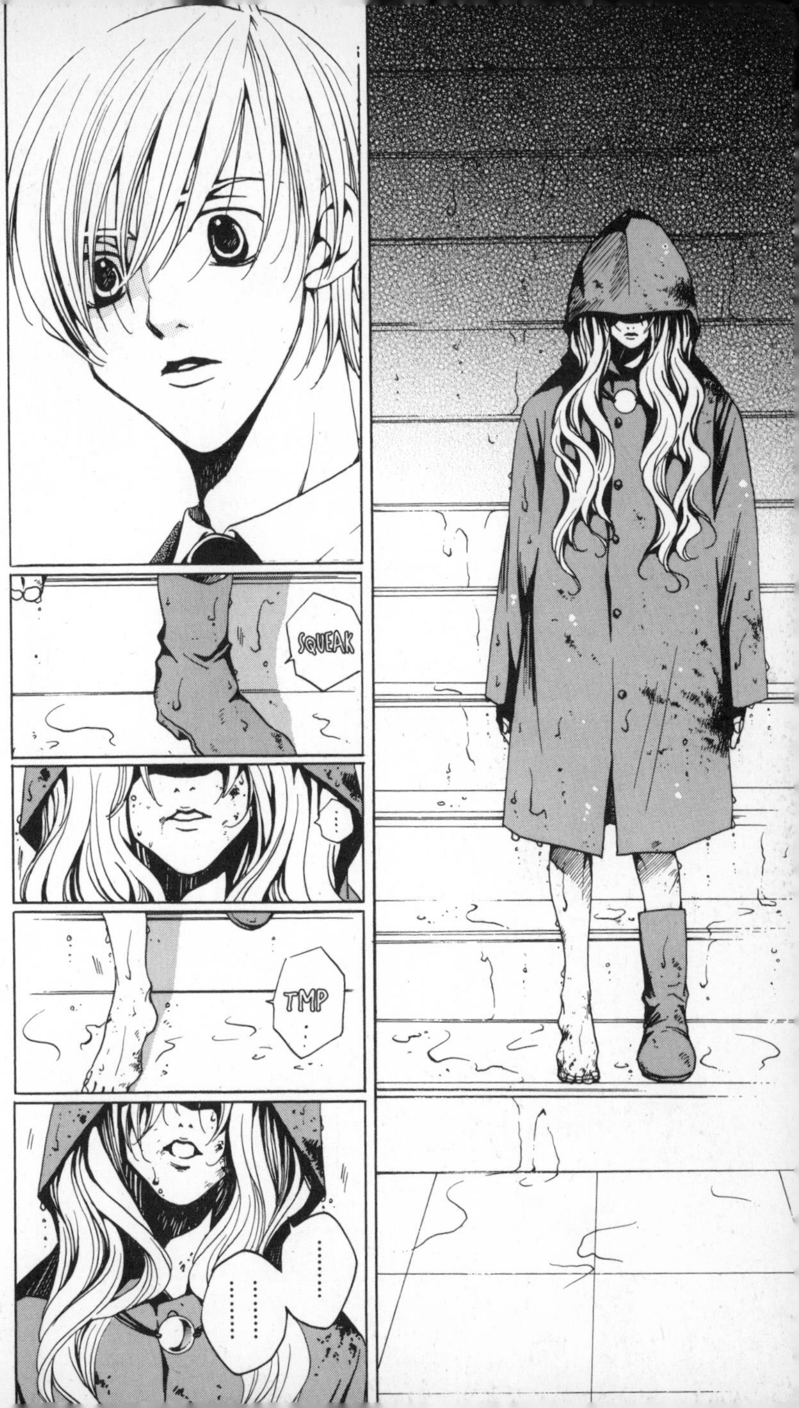
SQUEAK
...
TMP
...
......

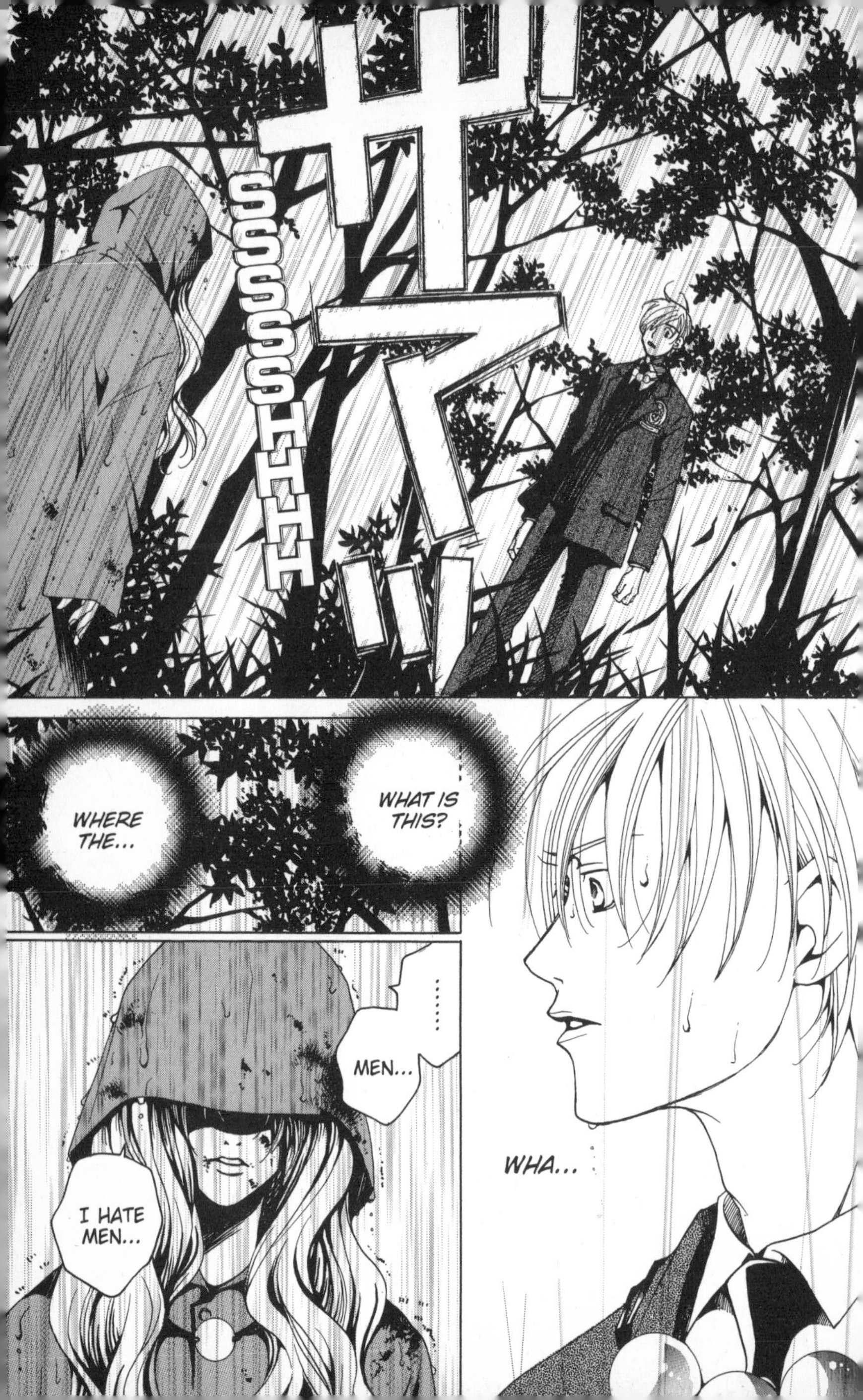
SSSSSSHHHH
WHA...
WHAT IS THIS?
WHERE THE...
......
MEN...
I HATE MEN...

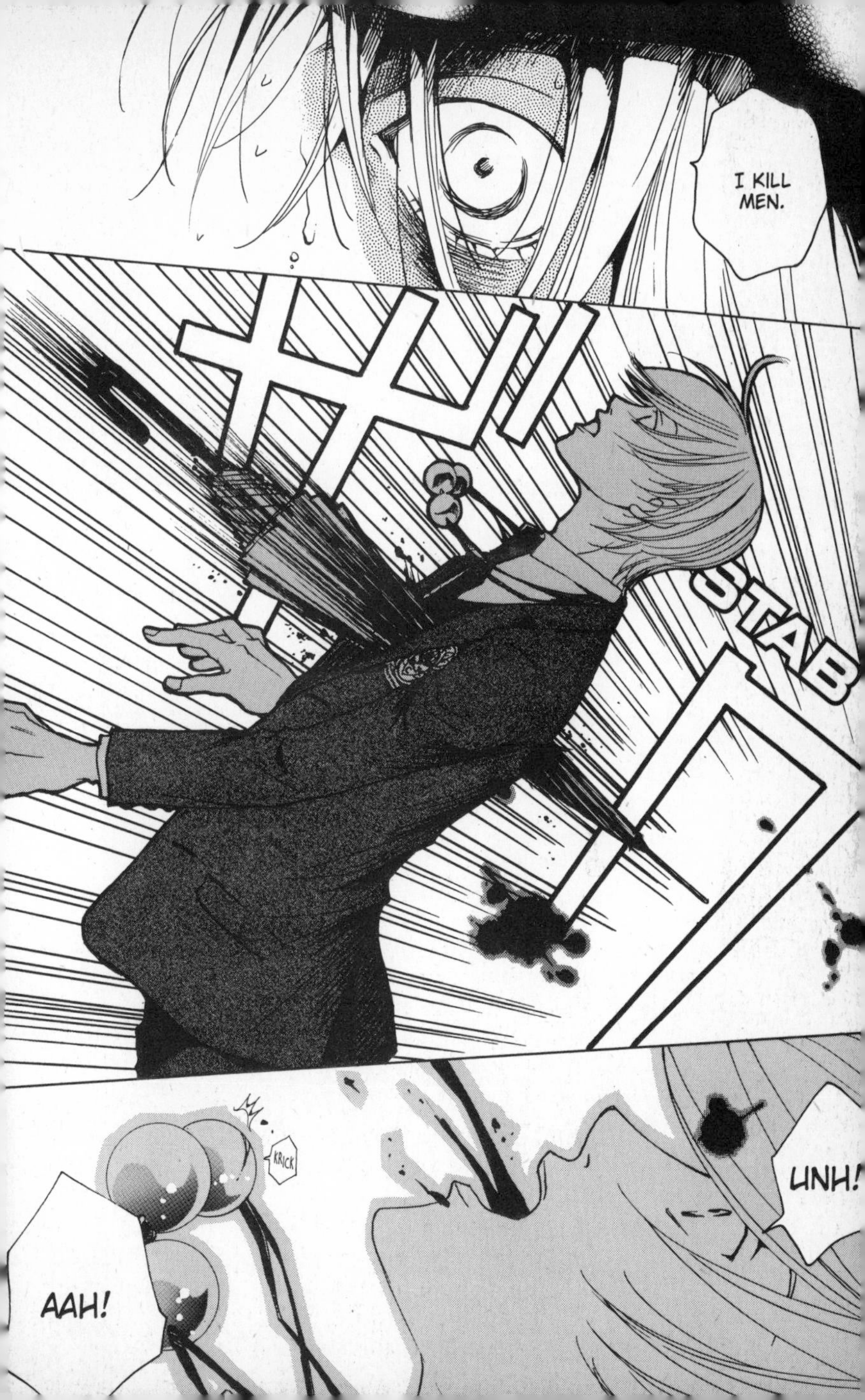
I KILL MEN.
STAB
UNH!
KRICK
AAH!

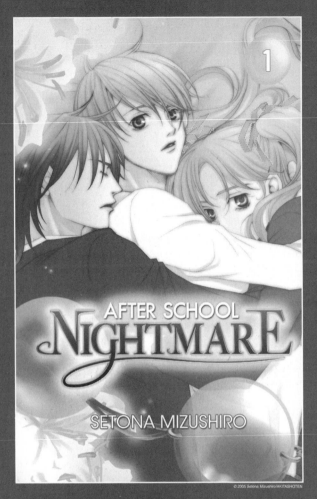

This dream draws blood.

AFTER SCHOOL
NIGHTMARE

In the next volume of Cantarella...

As Cesare struggles against the dark forces that have seized his heart, tensions come to a climax between him and his brother Juan. The temptation to draw swords...and blood...may at last settle their feud, but it may also force Cesare to give up the final shred of his humanity!

FIND OUT IN VOLUME 4
OF CANTARELLA!
AVAILABLE NOVEMBER 2006

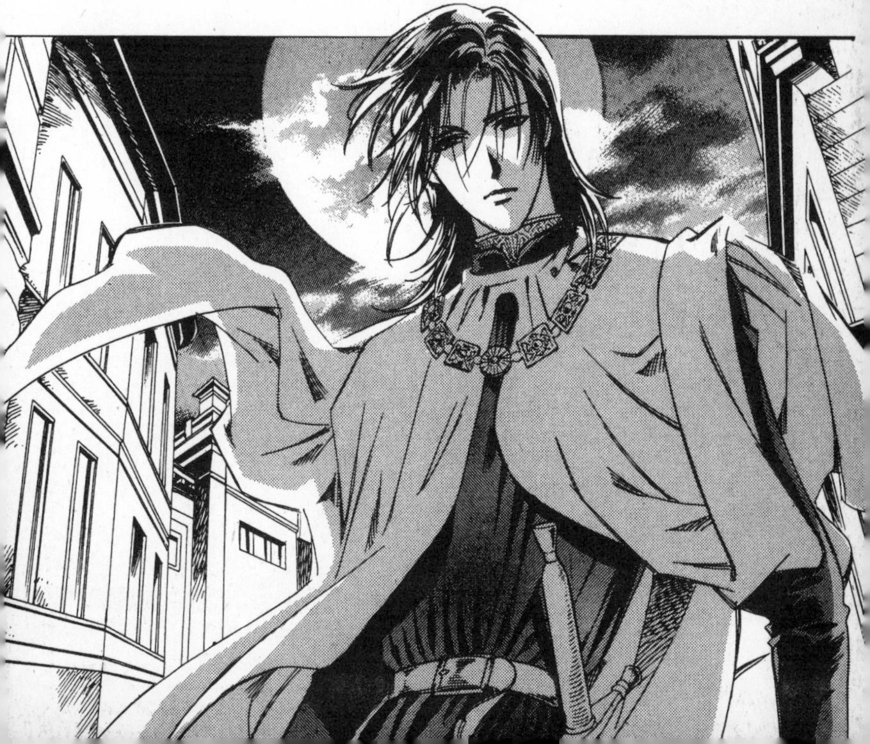

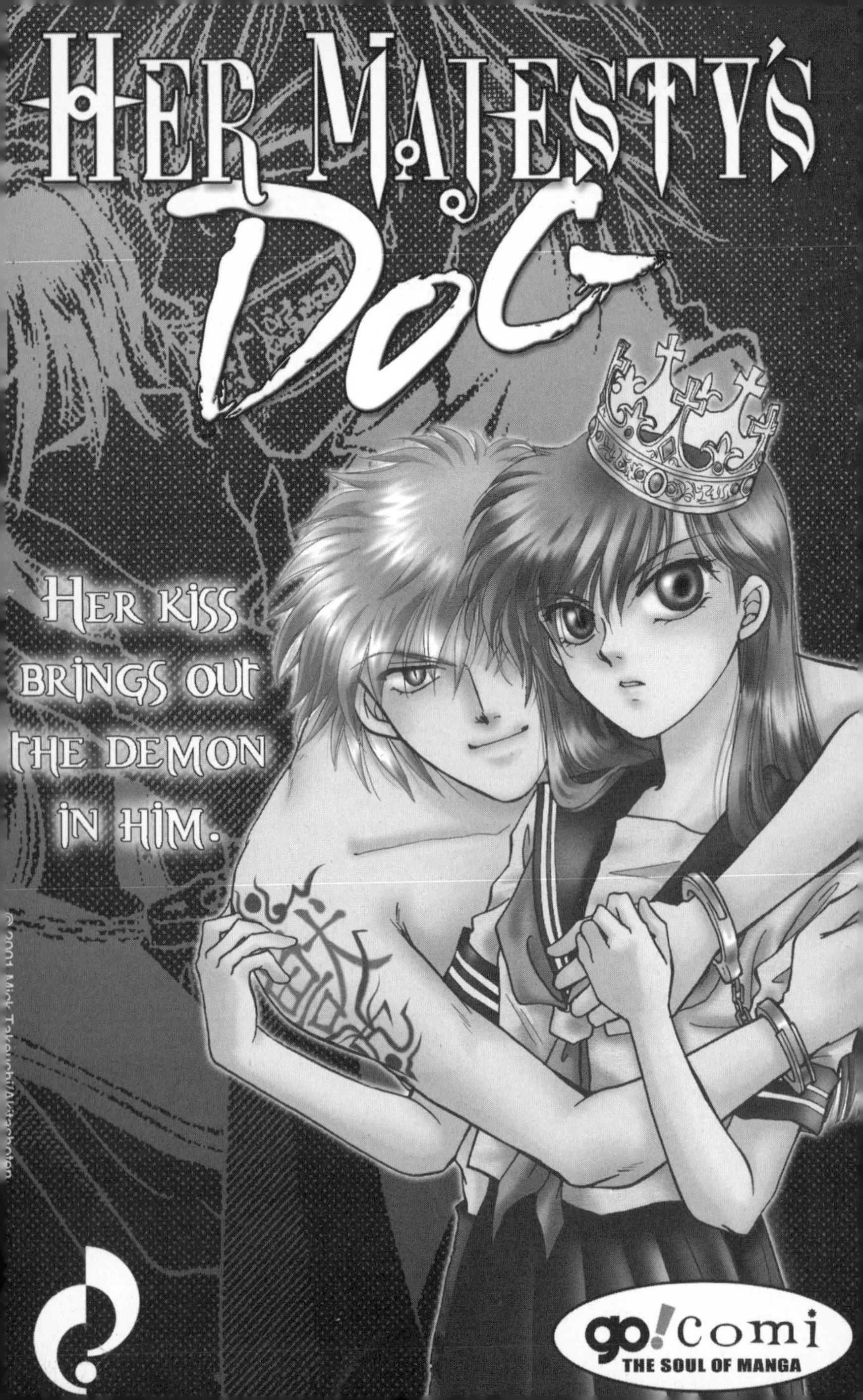
HER MAJESTY'S DOG
HER KISS BRINGS OUT THE DEMON IN HIM.
© 2001 Mick Takeuchi/Akitashoten
go!comi
THE SOUL OF MANGA

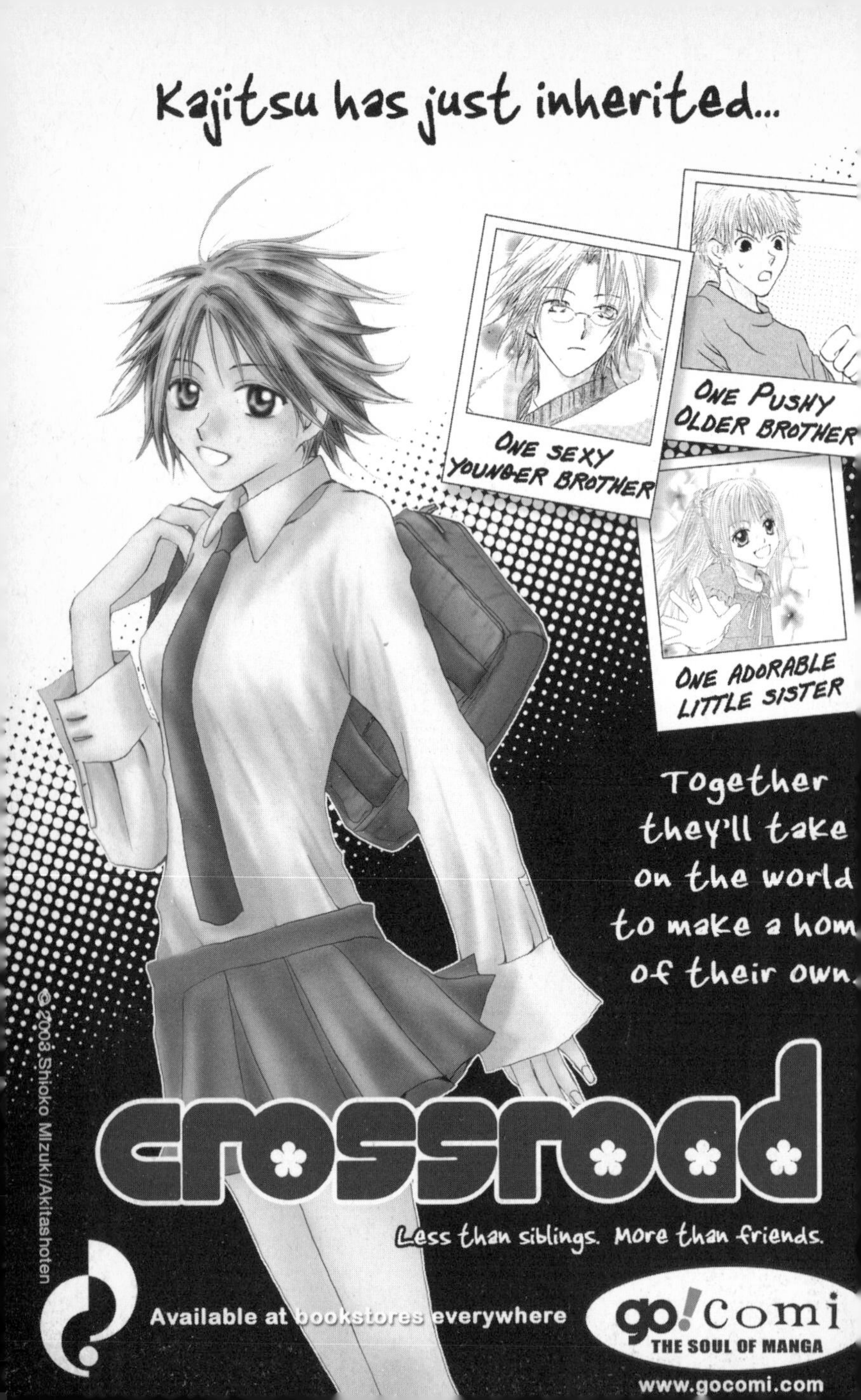